I've heard that when it comes to running, it's easier on your foot to hit the ground with the entire sole rather than heel first. I wonder if that's true… This year, I want to run a half-marathon, and if possible, a full one.

(My current weight…67 kg!! Whooooa!!)

—Mitsutoshi Shimabukuro, 2013

Mitsutoshi Shimabukuro made his debut in **Weekly Shonen Jump** in 1996. He is best known for **Seikimatsu Leader Den Takeshi!** for which he won the 46th Shogakukan Manga Award for children's manga in 2001. His current series, **Toriko**, began serialization in Japan in 2008.

TORIKO VOL. 24
SHONEN JUMP Manga Edition

STORY AND ART BY **MITSUTOSHI SHIMABUKURO**

Translation/Christine Dashiell
Weekly Shonen Jump Lettering/Erika Terriquez
Graphic Novel Touch-Up Art & Lettering/Elena Diaz
Design/Matt Hinrichs
Editor/Hope Donovan

Printed in Canada

Published by VIZ Media, LLC
P.O. Box 77010
San Francisco, CA 94107

10 9 8 7 6 5 4 3 2 1
First printing, October 2014

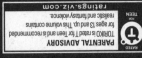

www.viz.com

www.shonenjump.com

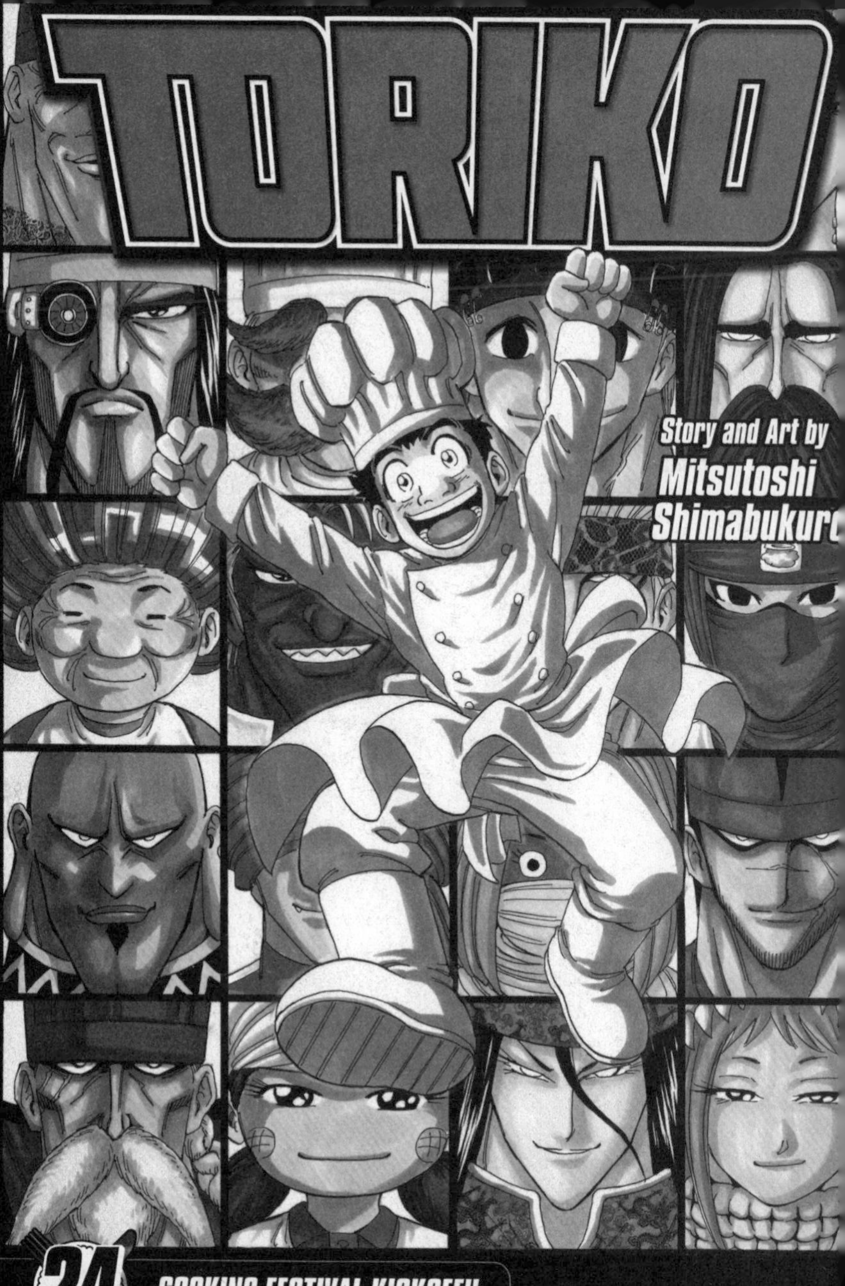
TORIKO
Story and Art by
Mitsutoshi
Shimabukuro
24
COOKING FESTIVAL KICKOFF!!

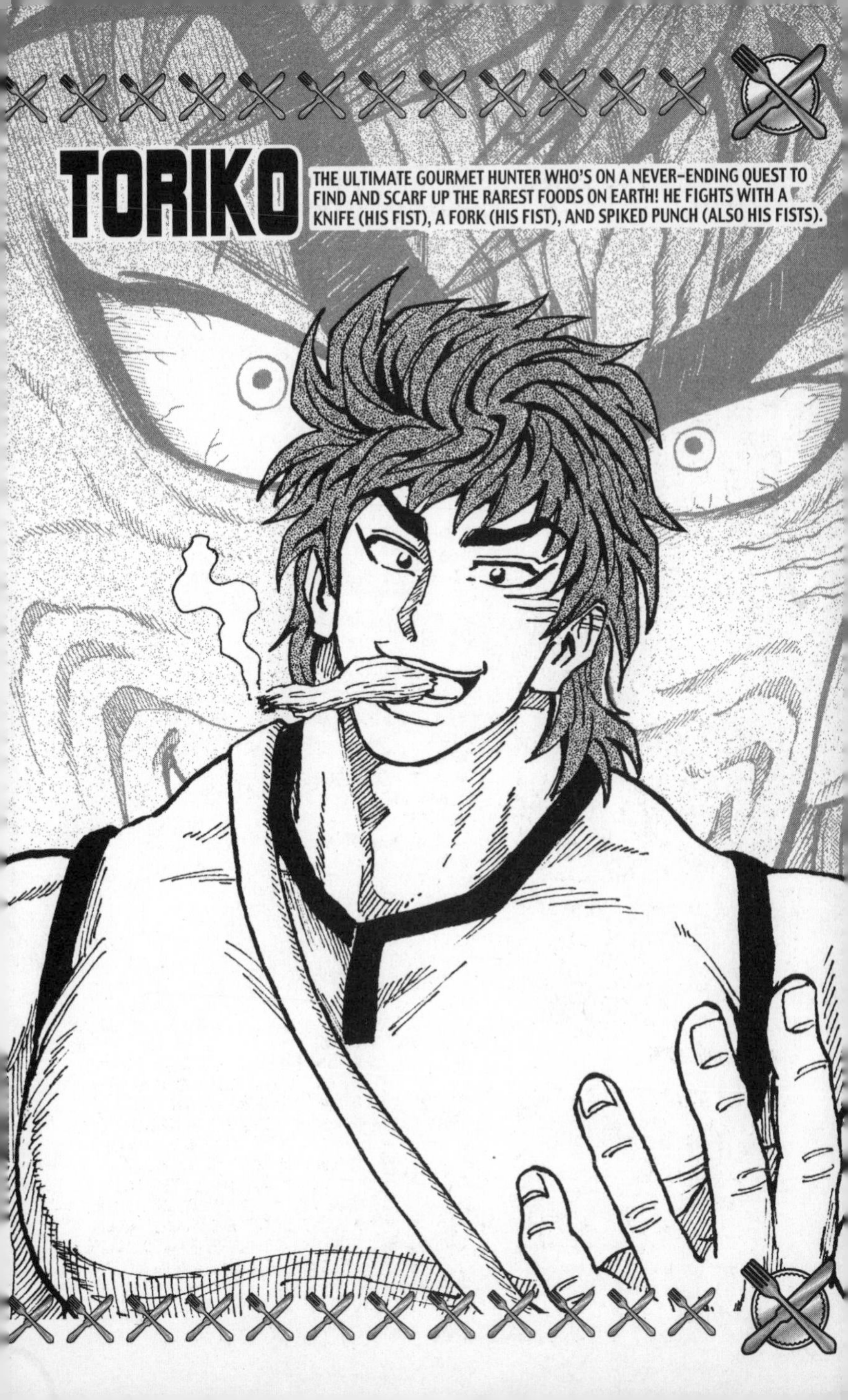
TORIKO
THE ULTIMATE GOURMET HUNTER WHO'S ON A NEVER-ENDING QUEST TO FIND AND SCARF UP THE RAREST FOODS ON EARTH! HE FIGHTS WITH A KNIFE (HIS FIST), A FORK (HIS FIST), AND SPIKED PUNCH (ALSO HIS FISTS).

●KOMATSU

TALENTED IGO HOTEL CHEF AND TORIKO'S #1 FAN.

●ZEBRA

A GOURMET HUNTER AND ONE OF THE FOUR KINGS. A DANGEROUS INDIVIDUAL WITH SUPERHUMAN HEARING AND VOCAL POWERS.

●SUNNY

A GOURMET HUNTER AND ONE OF THE FOUR KINGS. SENSORS IN HIS LONG HAIR ENABLE HIM TO "TASTE" THE WORLD. OBSESSED WITH ALL THAT IS BEAUTIFUL.

●COCO

ONE OF THE FOUR KINGS, THOUGH HE IS ALSO A FORTUNETELLER. SPECIAL ABILITY: POISON FLOWS IN HIS VEINS.

●TEPPEI

A GOURMET REVIVER. PROTECTS RARE FOODS FROM GOURMET HUNTERS.

●SETSUNO

AKA GRANNY SETSU. MASTER CHEF AND GOURMET LIVING LEGEND.

WHAT'S FOR DINNER

IT'S THE AGE OF GOURMET! KOMATSU, THE HEAD CHEF AT THE HOTEL OWNED BY THE IGO (INTERNATIONAL GOURMET ORGANIZATION), BECAME FAST FRIENDS WITH THE LEGENDARY GOURMET HUNTER TORIKO WHILE GATOR HUNTING. NOW KOMATSU ACCOMPANIES TORIKO ON HIS LIFELONG QUEST TO CREATE THE PERFECT FULL-COURSE MEAL. THROUGH THEIR ADVENTURES, THEY FIND THEMSELVES ENTANGLED IN THE IGO'S RIVALRY WITH THE NEFARIOUS GOURMET CORP. WITH TORIKO'S EVERY HUNT, THE INEVITABLE CLASH GROWS CLOSER!

GOURMET CORP. ASIDE, NOW THAT TORIKO AND KOMATSU ARE PARTNERS, THEY HAVE BEGUN TRAINING TO ENTER THE GOURMET WORLD BY COLLECTING FOODS FROM A TRAINING LIST PROVIDED BY IGO PRESIDENT ICHIRYU.

ONE DAY, THE FOUR-BEASTS AWAKENS! TORIKO, COCO, SUNNY AND ZEBRA DEFEAT THE FOUR INDIVIDUAL FOUR-BEASTS, BUT THEN THE FOUR-BEASTS IS REVEALED TO BE A SINGLE GIANT MONSTER THAT CRAVES HUMAN FLESH! TORIKO AND THE FOUR KINGS RUSH TO THE CENTER OF THE HUMAN WORLD TO STOP IT FROM CONSUMING THE HELPLESS POPULACE. BUT AS SOON AS THEY GET THERE, IT UNLEASHES A TOXIC RAIN. WHILE KOMATSU COOKS UP A LIFE-SAVING CURE, THE FOUR KINGS POOL THEIR APPETITE FOR THE ULTIMATE COMBINATION ATTACK!

WHOOOM
YOURS OR OURS!!

MEANWHILE, TEPPEI THE REVIVER TRACKS DOWN A MYSTERIOUS FIGURE WHO SEEMS TO HAVE SOMETHING TO DO WITH THE ATTACK...!!

I'M NO SLOUCH AT TRACKING.
ESPECIALLY WHEN IT COMES TO SUSPICIOUS CHARACTERS.

Contents

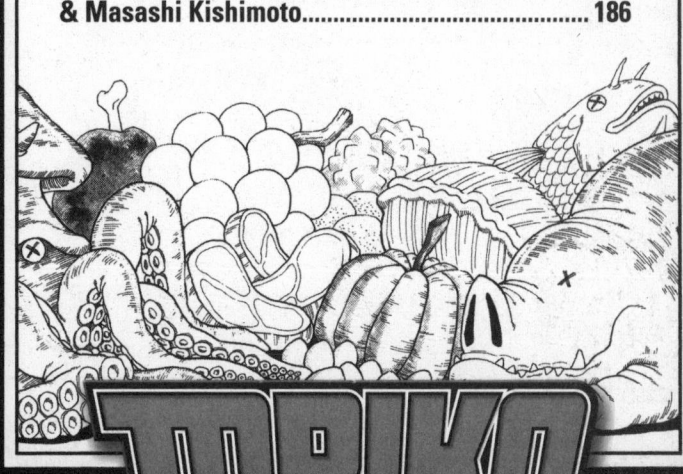

TORIKO

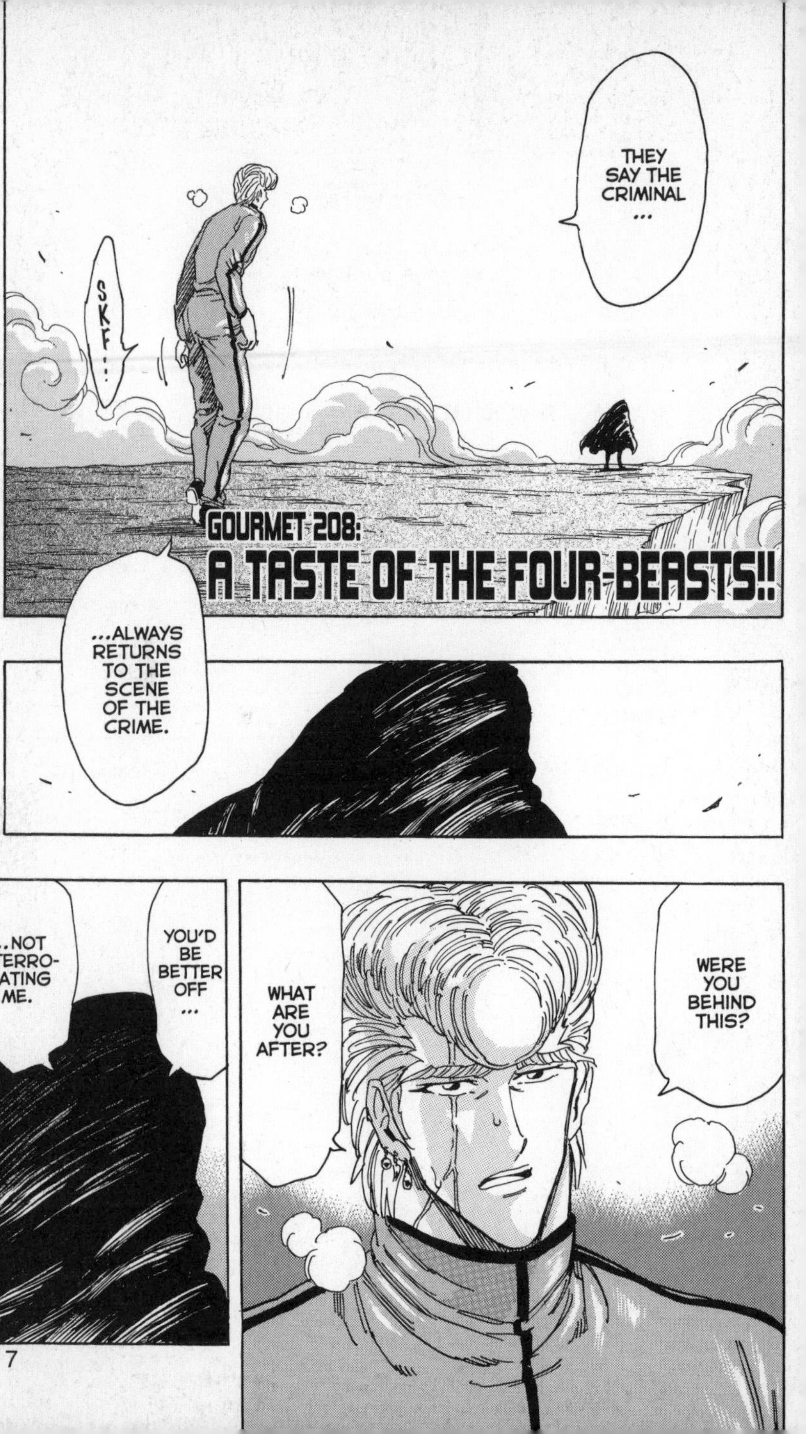
THEY SAY THE CRIMINAL ...
SKF...
GOURMET 208:
A TASTE OF THE FOUR-BEASTS!!
...ALWAYS RETURNS TO THE SCENE OF THE CRIME.
WERE YOU BEHIND THIS?
WHAT ARE YOU AFTER?
YOU'D BE BETTER OFF ...
...NOT INTERROGATING ME.

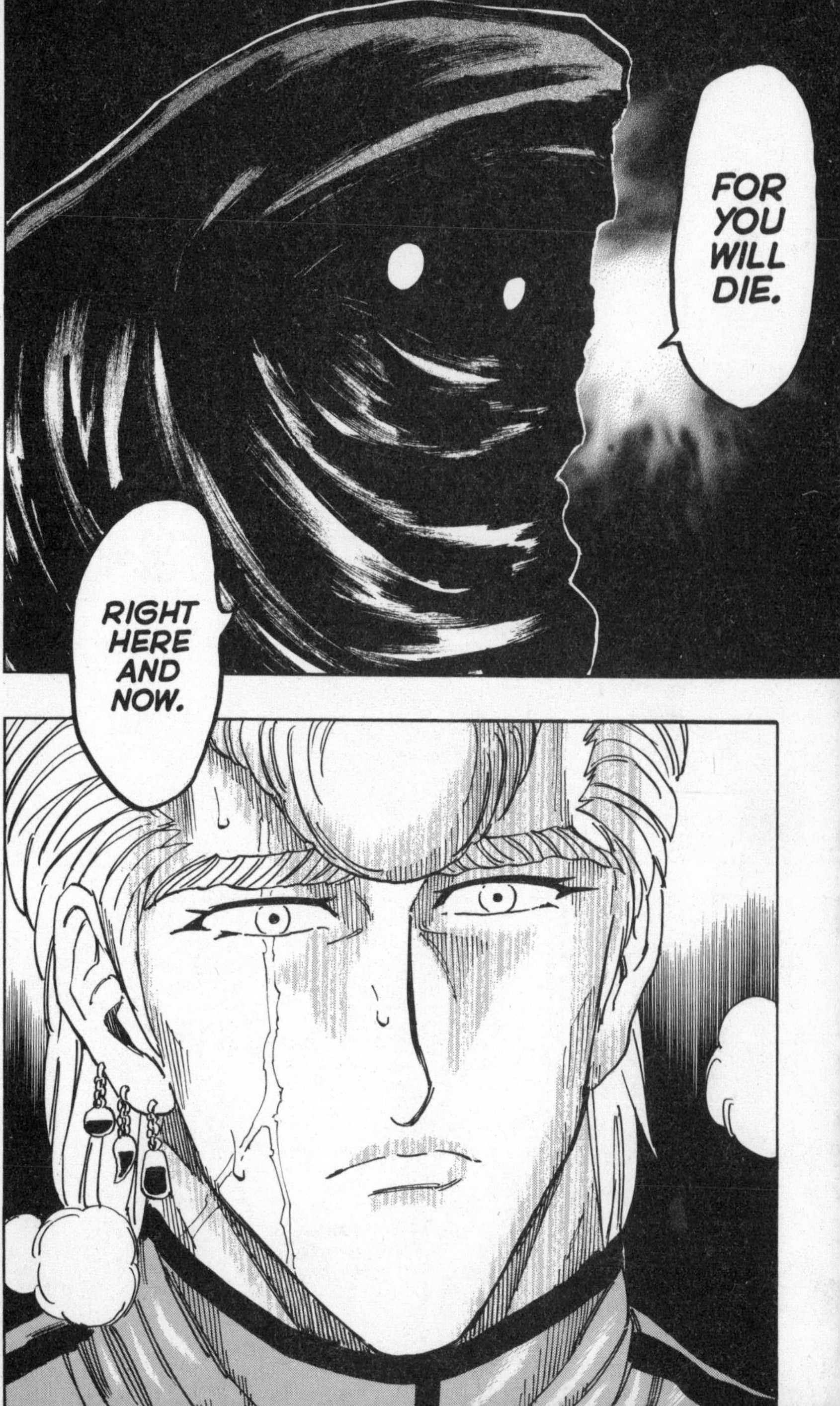
FOR YOU WILL DIE.
RIGHT HERE AND NOW.

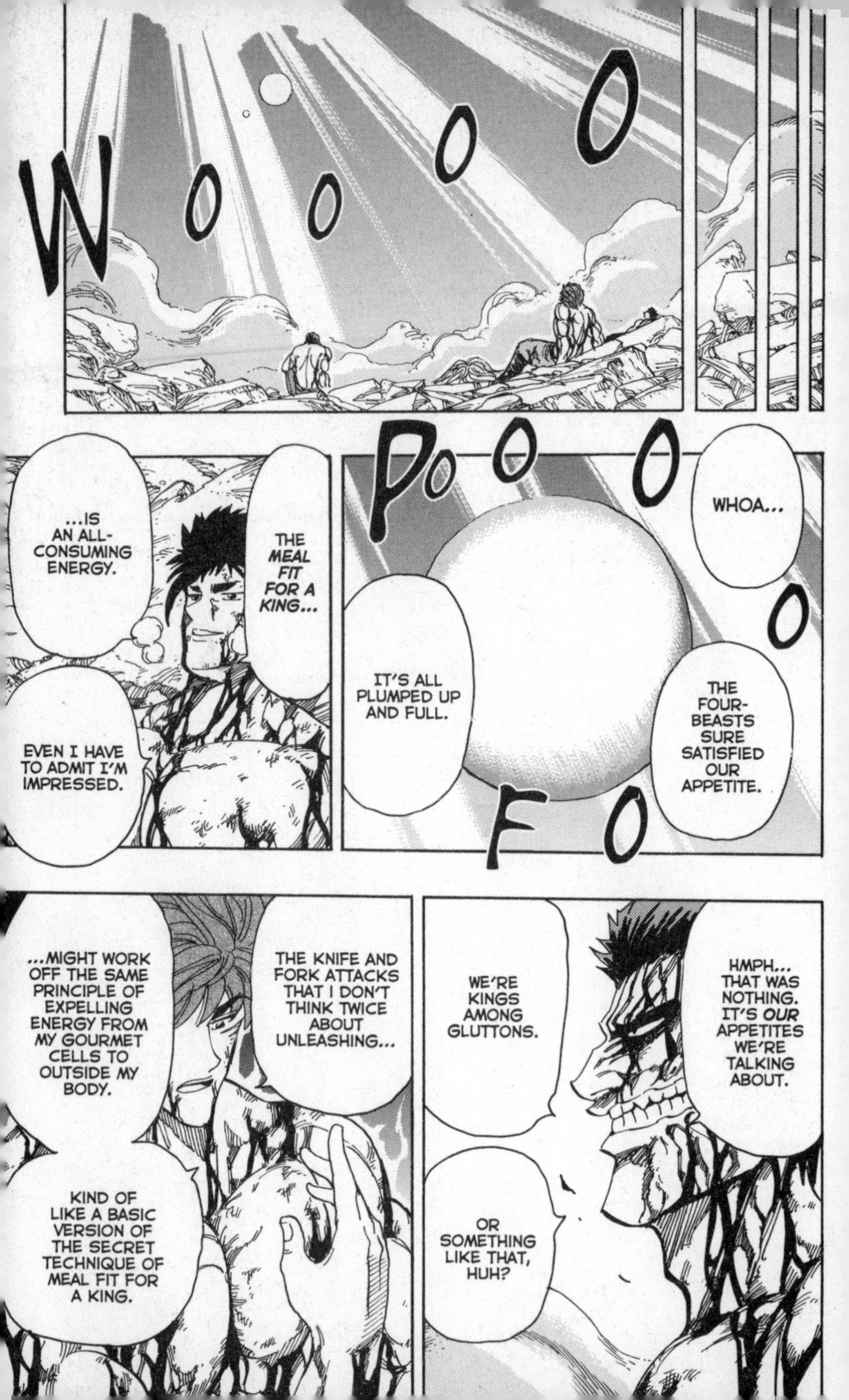
WOOOO
WHOA...
THE FOUR-BEASTS SURE SATISFIED OUR APPETITE.
IT'S ALL PLUMPED UP AND FULL.
POOOO
FO
THE *MEAL FIT FOR A KING*...
...IS AN ALL-CONSUMING ENERGY.
EVEN I HAVE TO ADMIT I'M IMPRESSED.
HMPH... THAT WAS NOTHING. IT'S *OUR* APPETITES WE'RE TALKING ABOUT.
WE'RE KINGS AMONG GLUTTONS.
OR SOMETHING LIKE THAT, HUH?
THE KNIFE AND FORK ATTACKS THAT I DON'T THINK TWICE ABOUT UNLEASHING...
...MIGHT WORK OFF THE SAME PRINCIPLE OF EXPELLING ENERGY FROM MY GOURMET CELLS TO OUTSIDE MY BODY.
KIND OF LIKE A BASIC VERSION OF THE SECRET TECHNIQUE OF MEAL FIT FOR A KING.

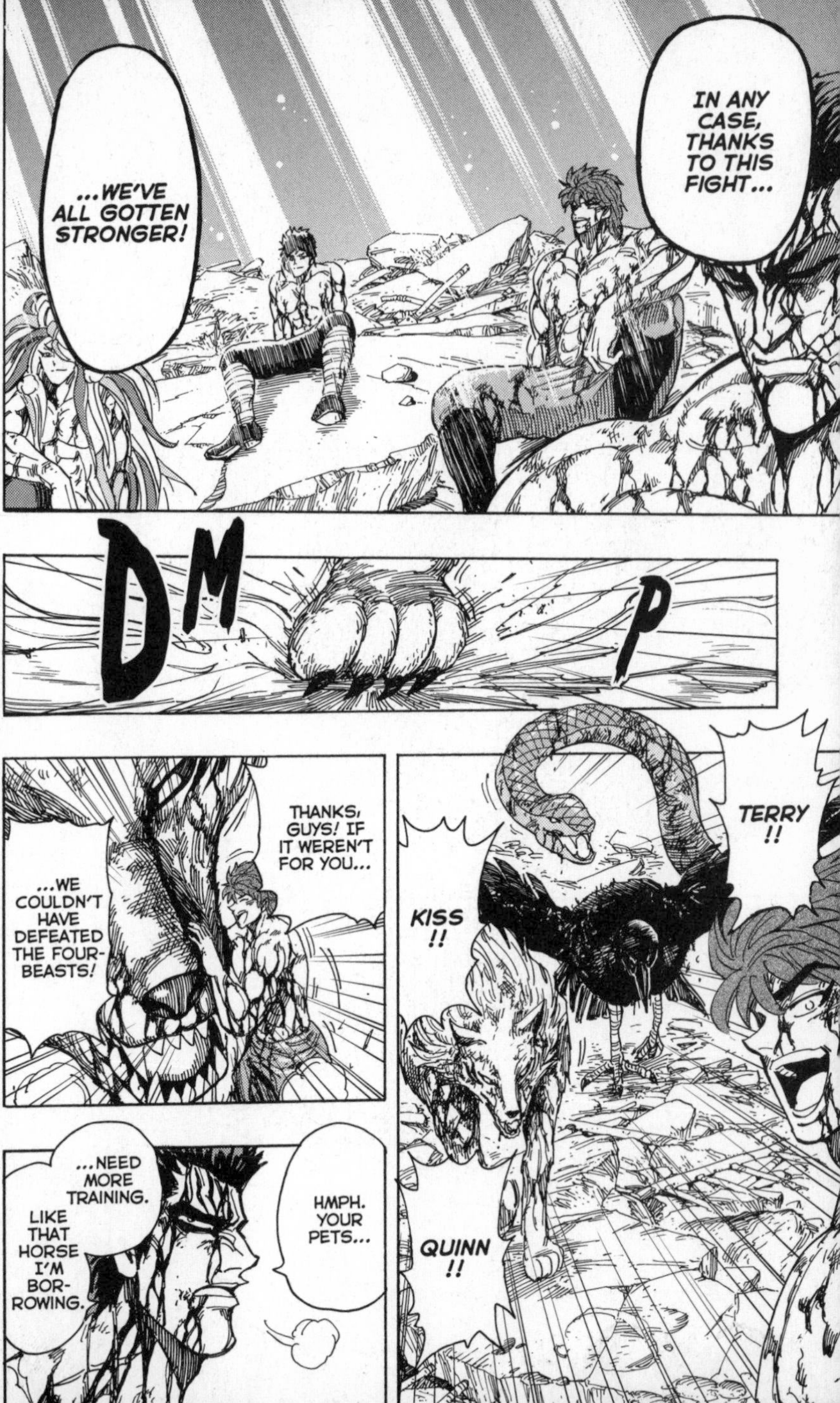
IN ANY CASE, THANKS TO THIS FIGHT...
...WE'VE ALL GOTTEN STRONGER!
DMP
TERRY !!
KISS !!
QUINN !!
THANKS, GUYS! IF IT WEREN'T FOR YOU...
...WE COULDN'T HAVE DEFEATED THE FOUR-BEASTS!
HMPH. YOUR PETS...
...NEED MORE TRAINING.
LIKE THAT HORSE I'M BOR-ROWING.

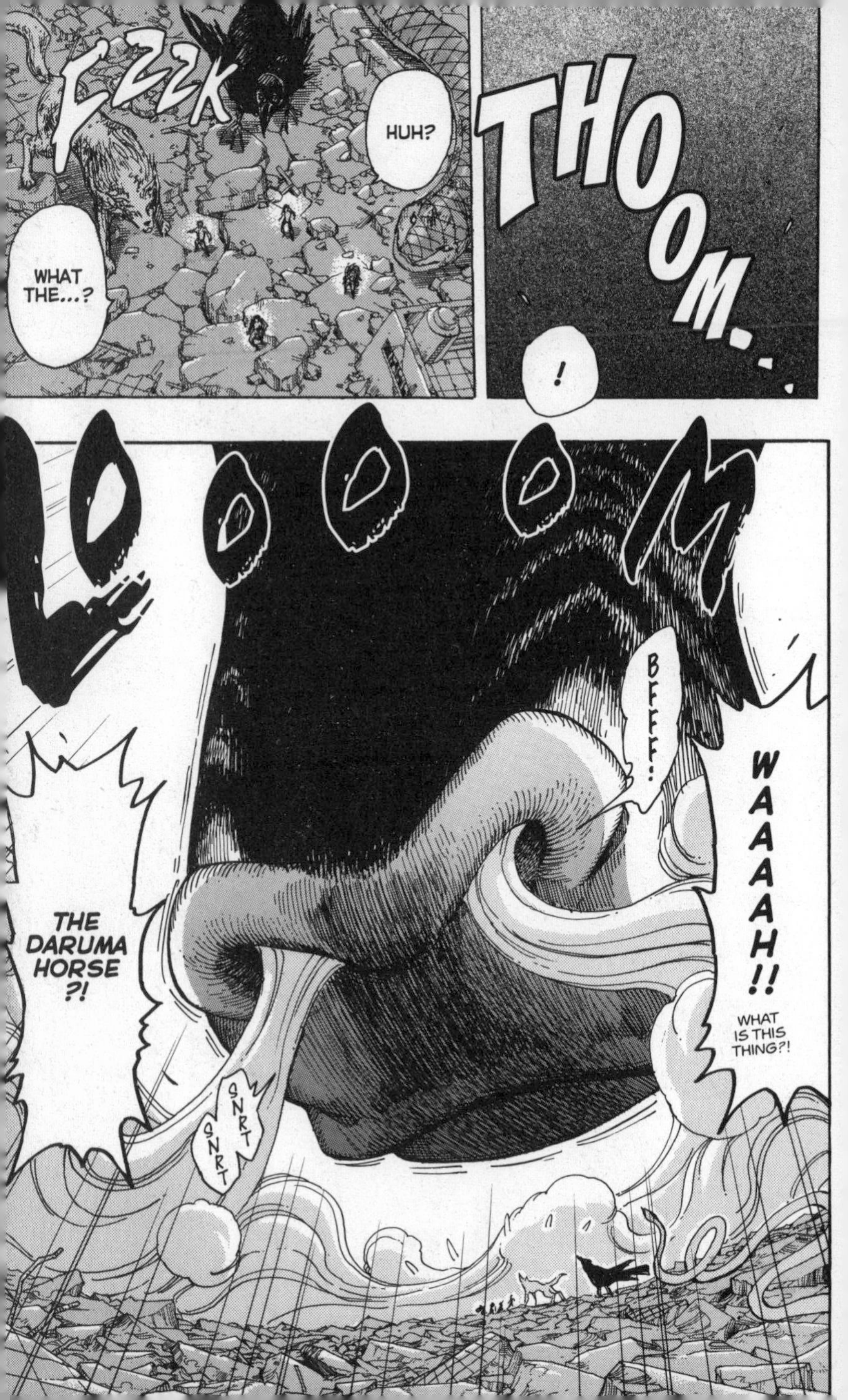
THOOM..
!
HUH?
FZZK
WHAT THE...?
LOOOOM
BFFF..
WAAAAAH!!
WHAT IS THIS THING?!
THE DARUMA HORSE ?!
SNRT SNRT

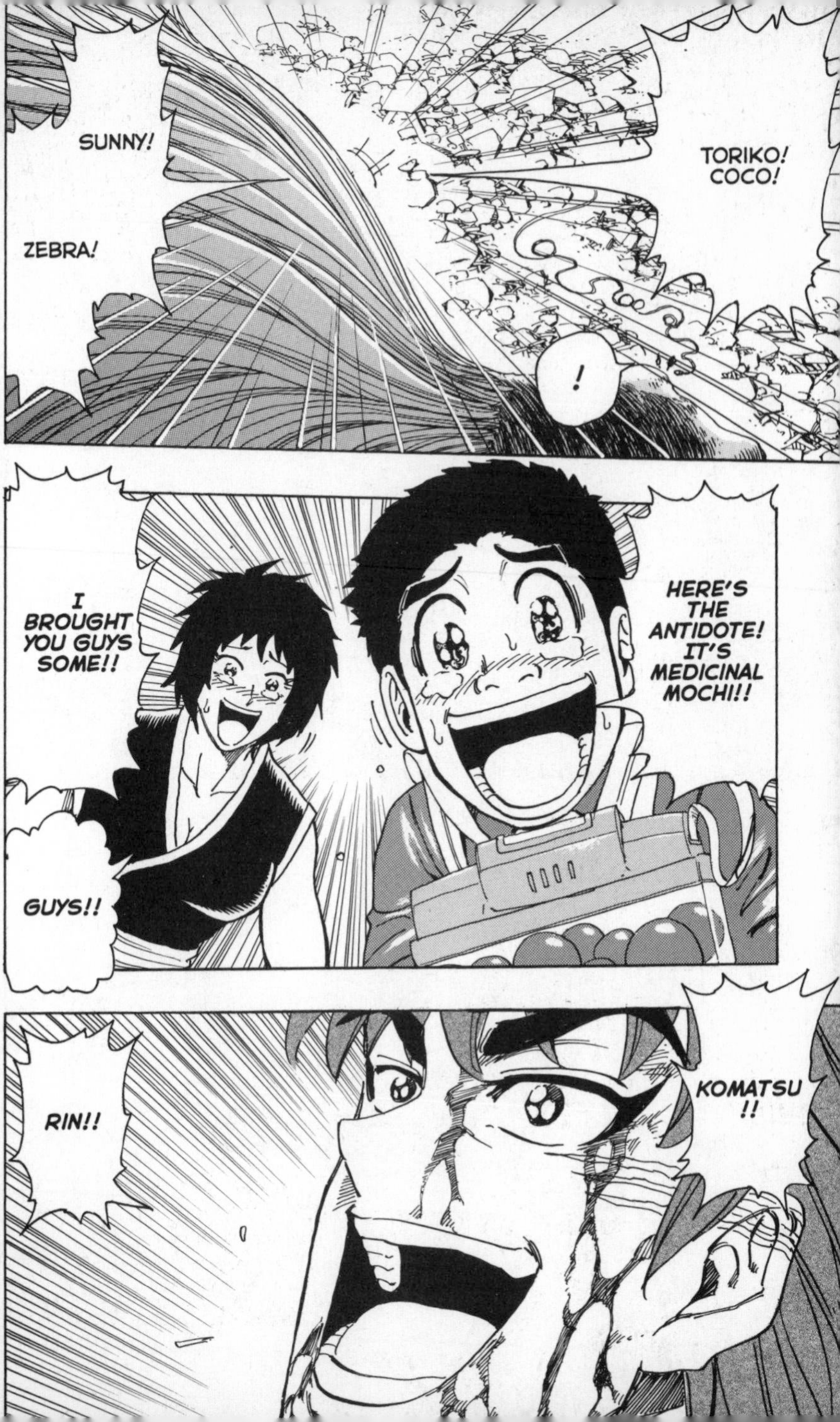
TORIKO! COCO!
SUNNY!
ZEBRA!
!
HERE'S THE ANTIDOTE! IT'S MEDICINAL MOCHI!!
I BROUGHT YOU GUYS SOME!!
GUYS!!
KOMATSU!!
RIN!!

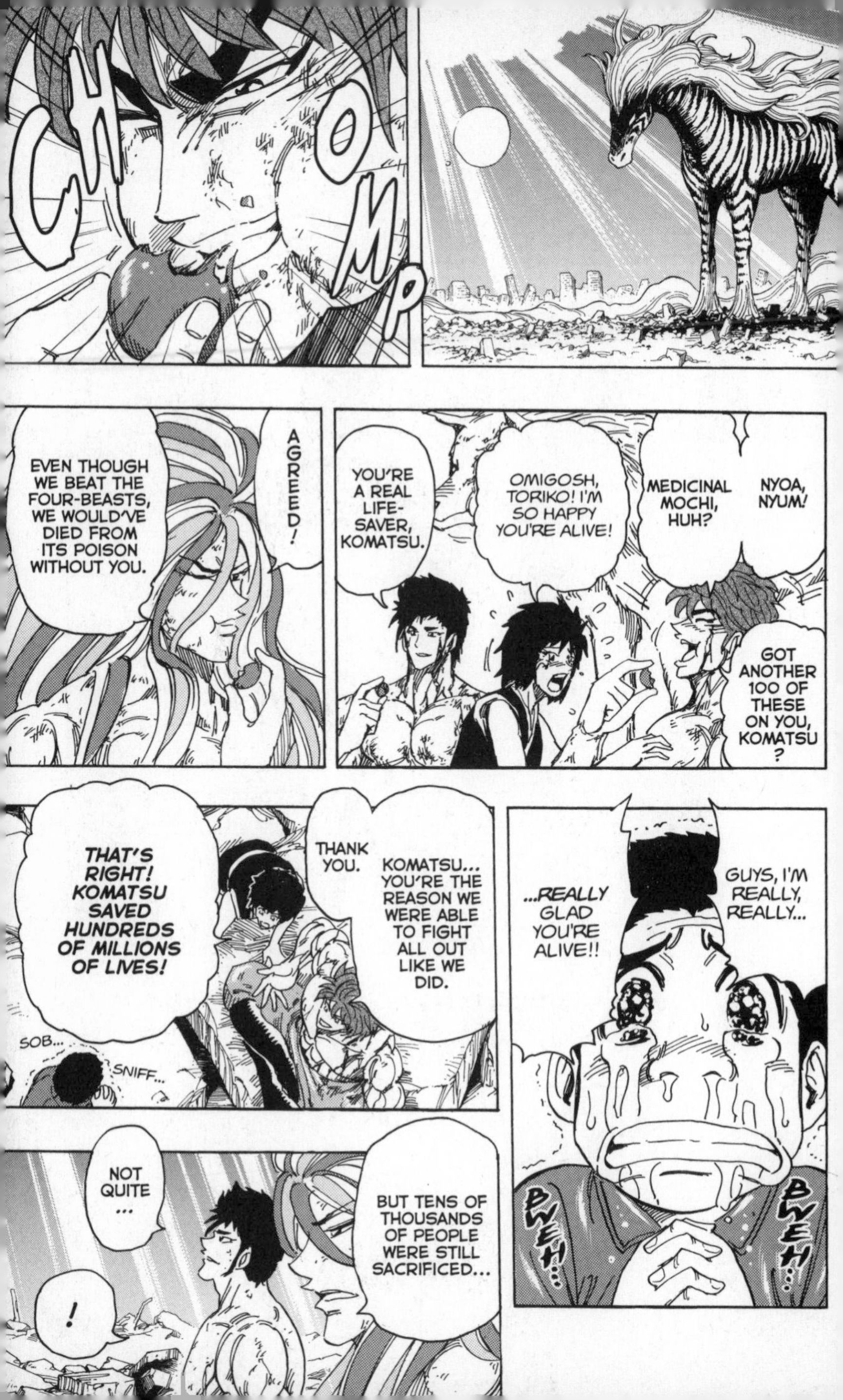
CHOMP
NYOA, NYUM!
MEDICINAL MOCHI, HUH?
OMIGOSH, TORIKO! I'M SO HAPPY YOU'RE ALIVE!
YOU'RE A REAL LIFE-SAVER, KOMATSU.
GOT ANOTHER 100 OF THESE ON YOU, KOMATSU?
AGREED!
EVEN THOUGH WE BEAT THE FOUR-BEASTS, WE WOULD'VE DIED FROM ITS POISON WITHOUT YOU.
GUYS, I'M REALLY, REALLY...
...REALLY GLAD YOU'RE ALIVE!!
BWEH...
BWEH...
THANK YOU.
KOMATSU... YOU'RE THE REASON WE WERE ABLE TO FIGHT ALL OUT LIKE WE DID.
THAT'S RIGHT! KOMATSU SAVED HUNDREDS OF MILLIONS OF LIVES!
SOB...
SNIFF...
BUT TENS OF THOUSANDS OF PEOPLE WERE STILL SACRIFICED...
NOT QUITE ...
!

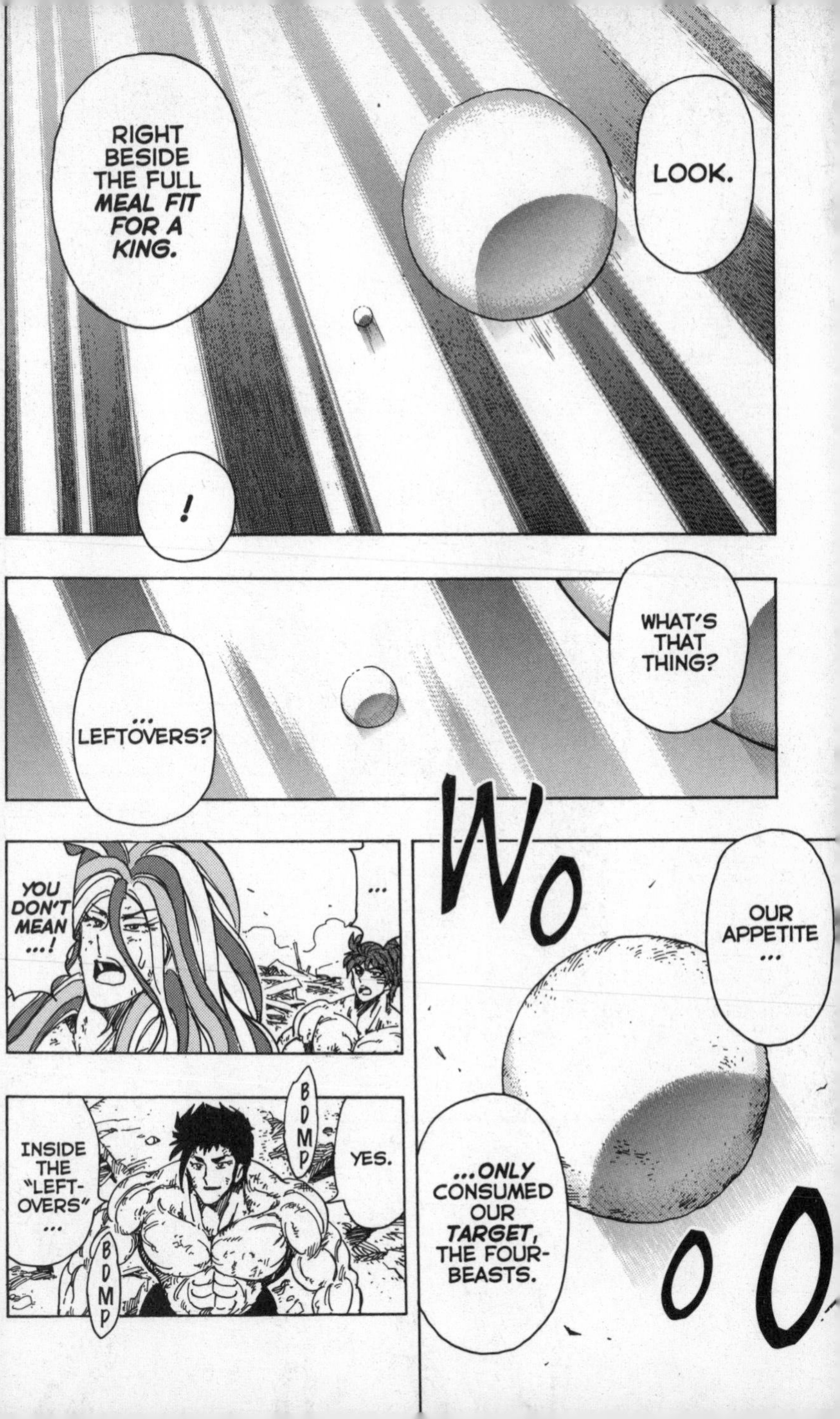
LOOK.
RIGHT BESIDE THE FULL MEAL FIT FOR A KING.
!
WHAT'S THAT THING?
... LEFTOVERS?
OUR APPETITE ...
...ONLY CONSUMED OUR TARGET, THE FOUR-BEASTS.
WOOO
...
YOU DON'T MEAN ...!
YES.
BDMP
INSIDE THE "LEFT-OVERS" ...
BDMP

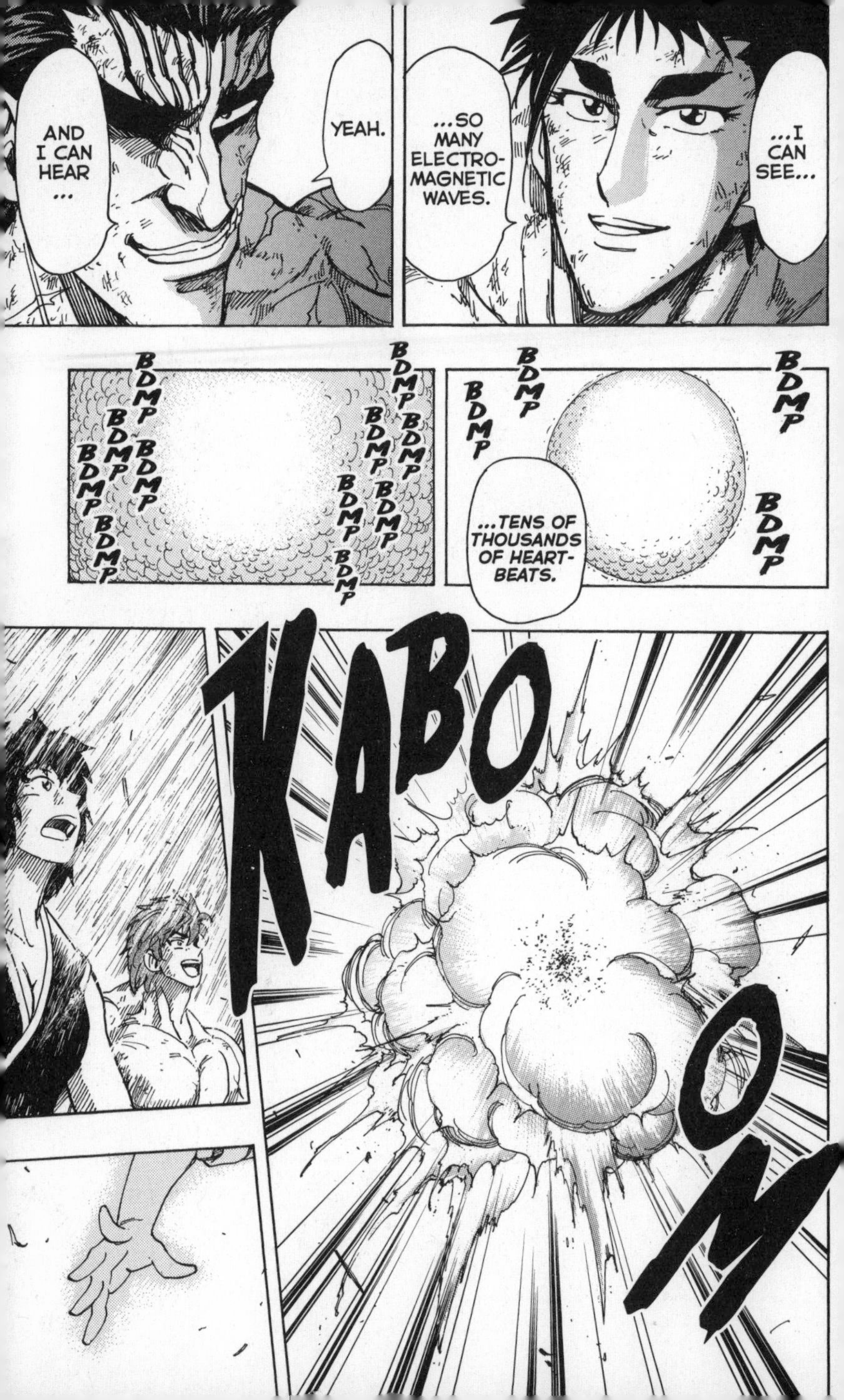
...I CAN SEE...
...SO MANY ELECTRO-MAGNETIC WAVES.
YEAH.
AND I CAN HEAR ...
BDMP
BDMP
BDMP
...TENS OF THOUSANDS OF HEART-BEATS.
BDMP BDMP BDMP BDMP BDMP BDMP BDMP BDMP BDMP BDMP
KABOOM

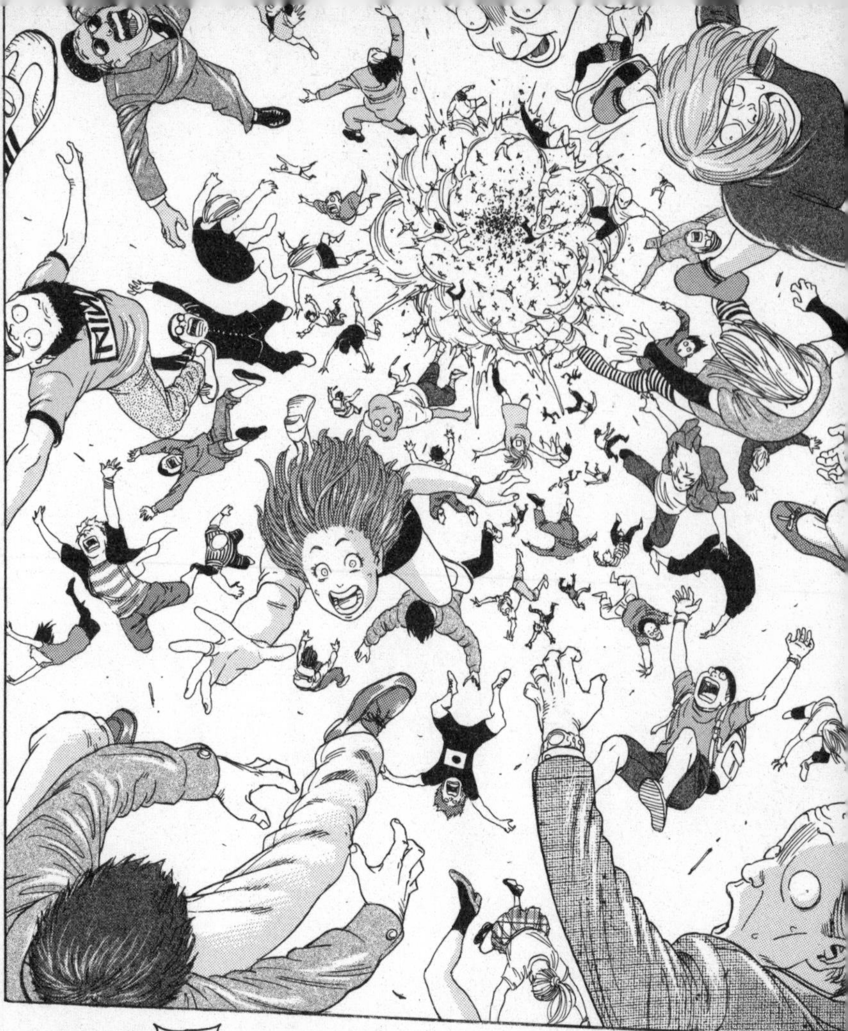
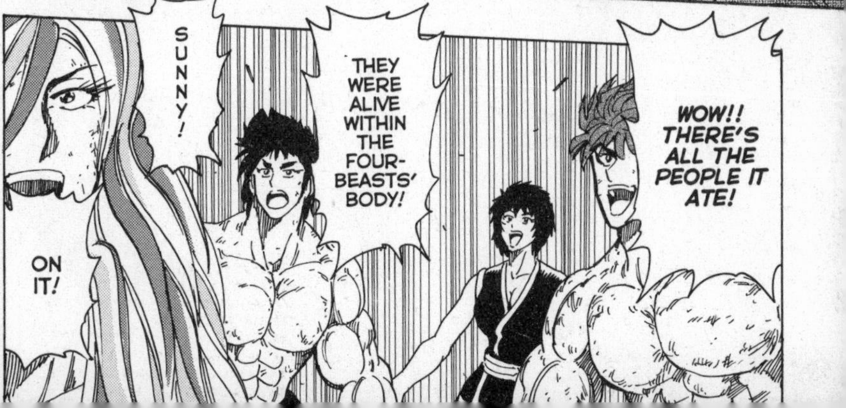
WOW!! THERE'S ALL THE PEOPLE IT ATE!
THEY WERE ALIVE WITHIN THE FOUR-BEASTS' BODY!
SUNNY!
ON IT!

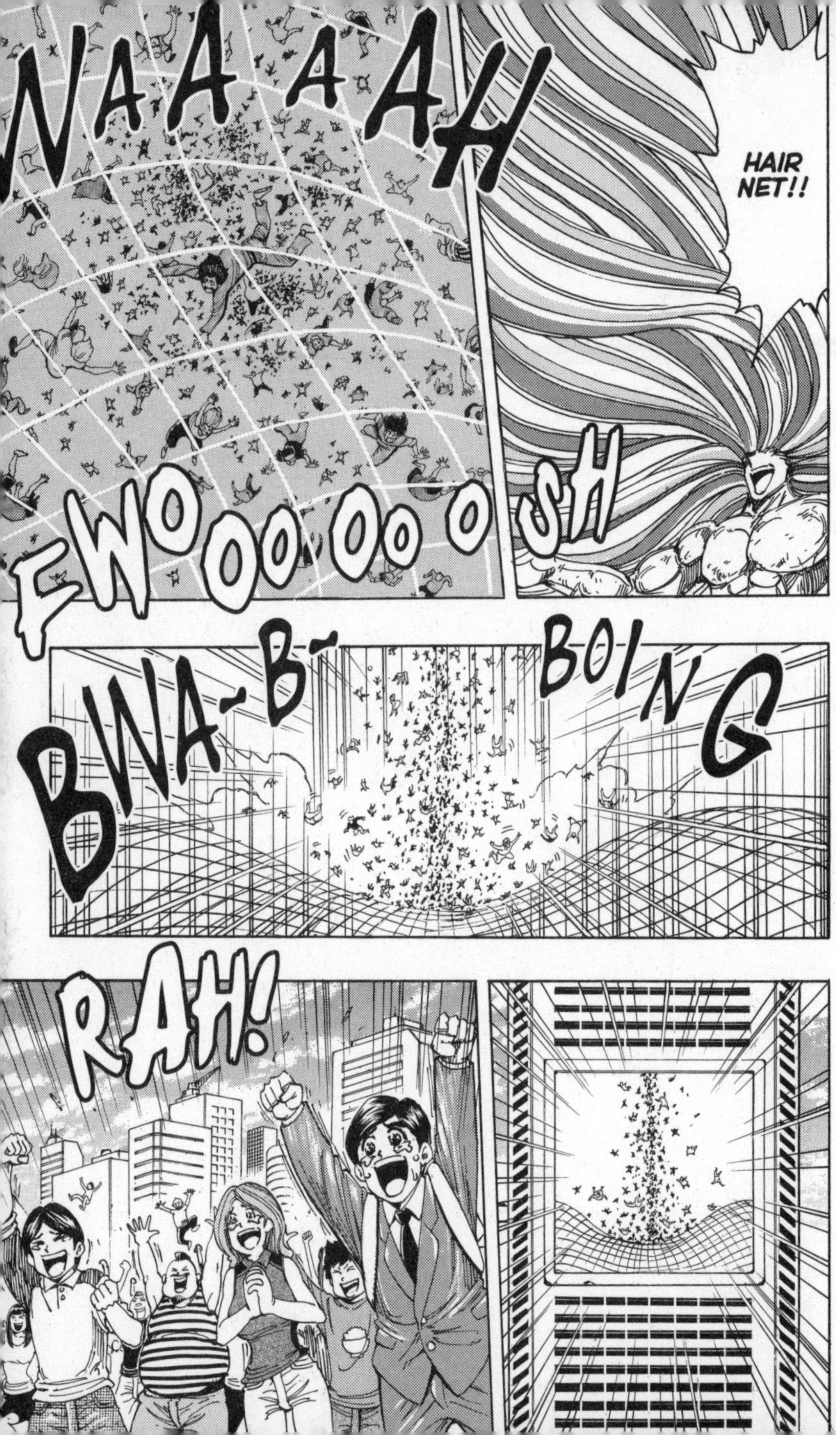
HAIR NET!!
NAA A AH
FWOOOO OO O SH
BWA-B-BOING
RAH!

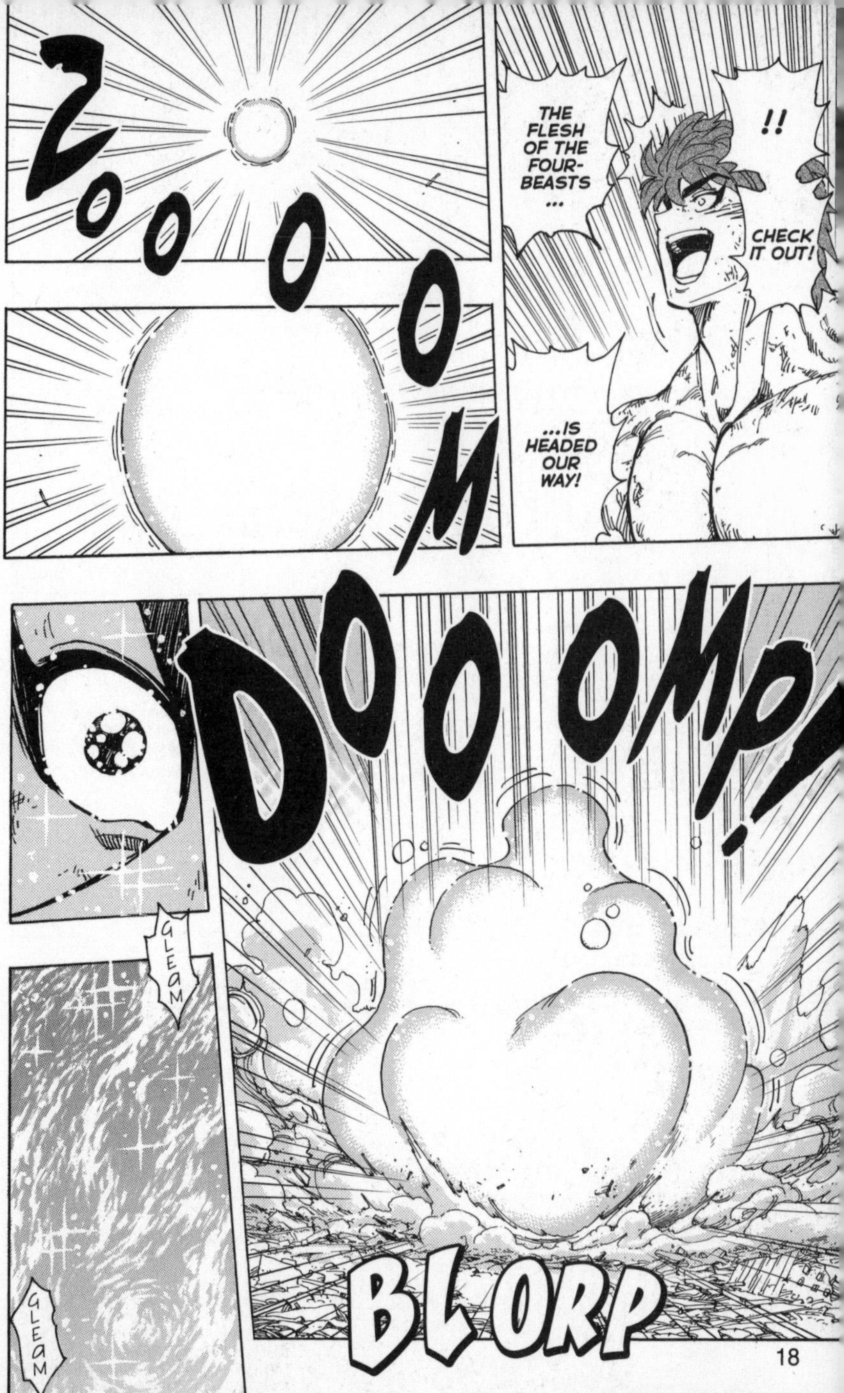
!!
CHECK IT OUT!
THE FLESH OF THE FOUR-BEASTS...
...IS HEADED OUR WAY!
ZOOOOOM
DOOOMP!!
BLORP
GLEAM
GLEAM

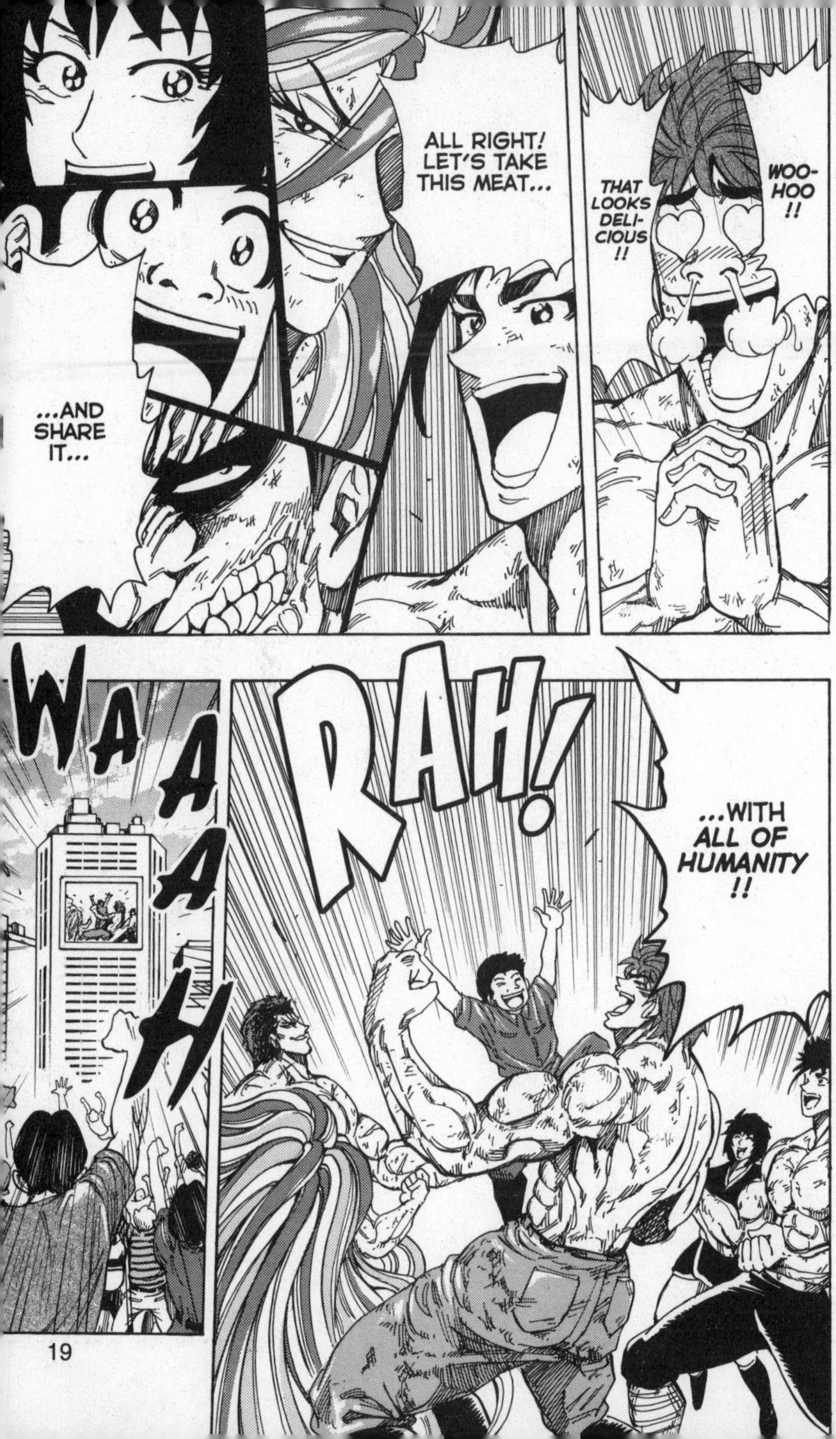
WOO-HOO !!
THAT LOOKS DELI-CIOUS !!
ALL RIGHT! LET'S TAKE THIS MEAT...
...AND SHARE IT...
...WITH ALL OF HUMANITY !!
RAH!
WAAAAH

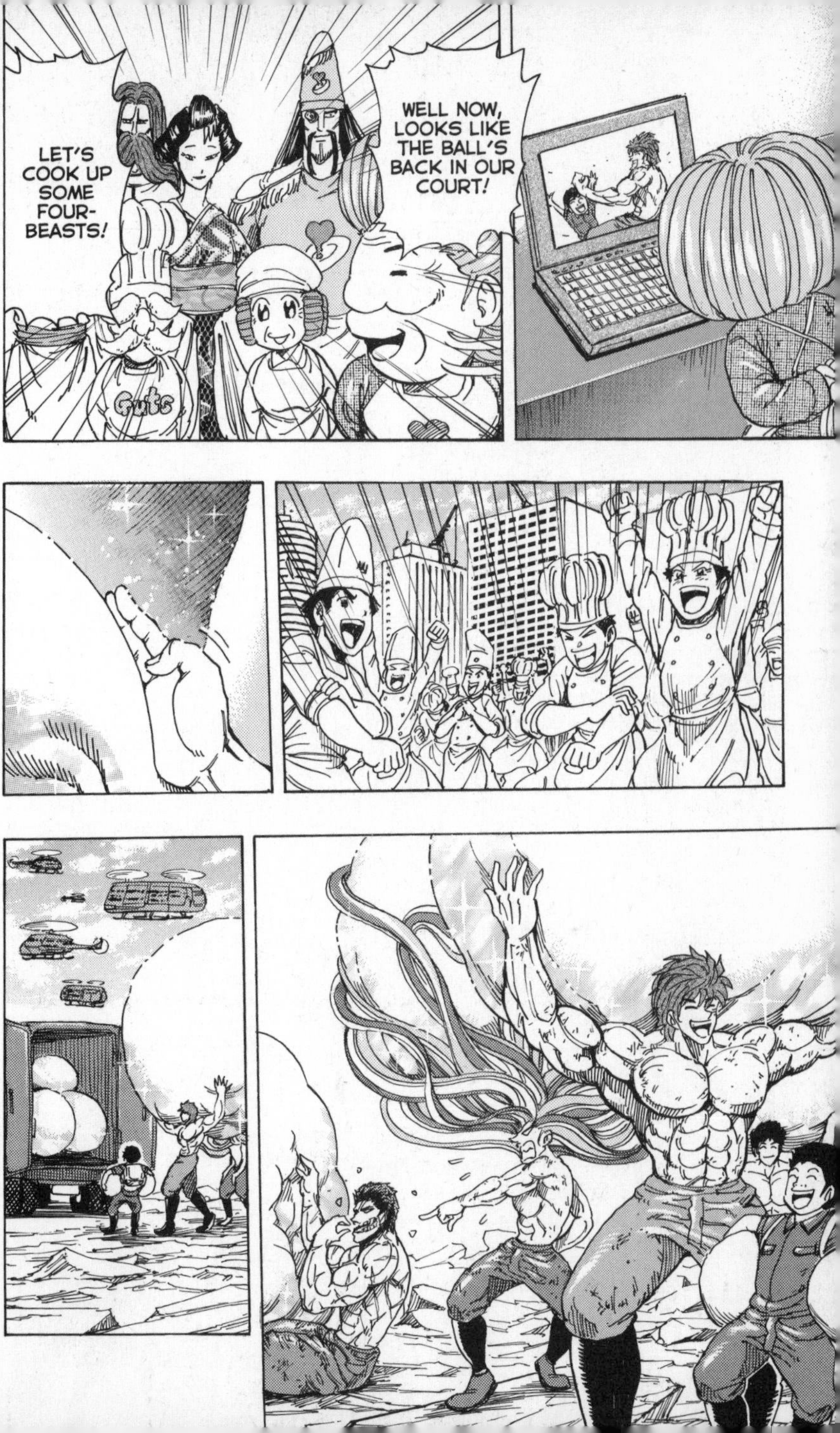
WELL NOW, LOOKS LIKE THE BALL'S BACK IN OUR COURT!
LET'S COOK UP SOME FOUR-BEASTS!

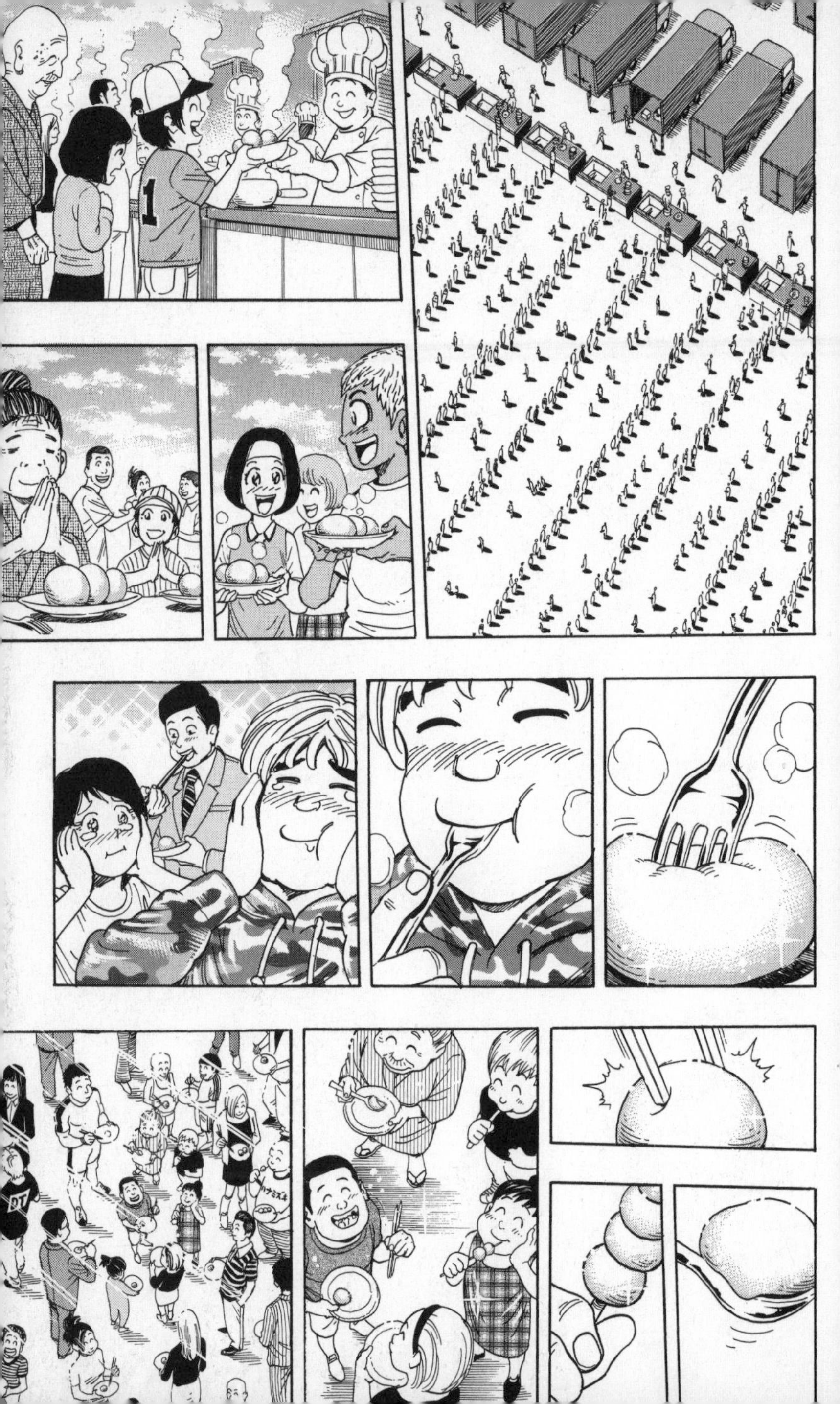

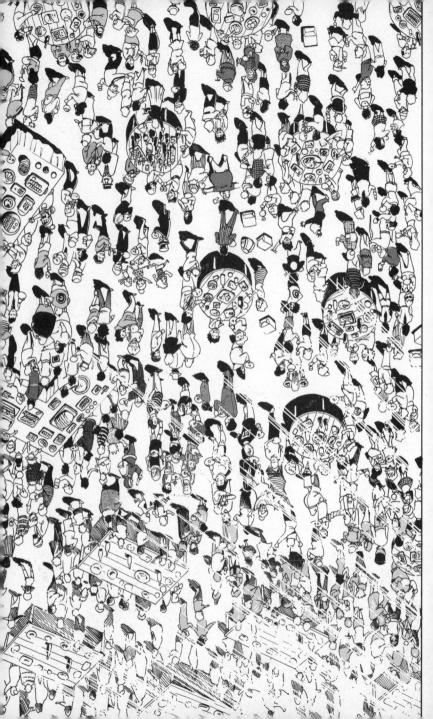

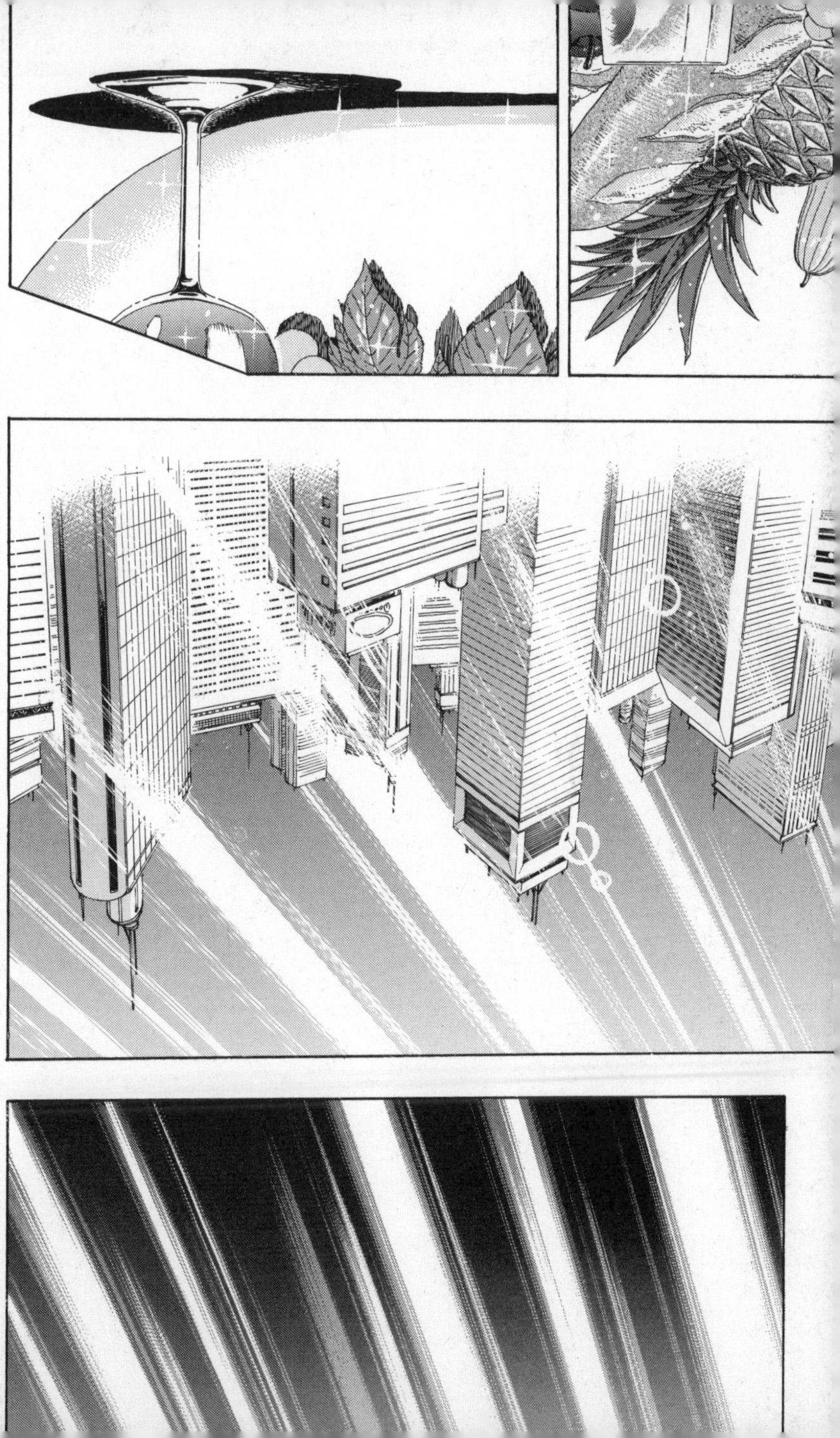

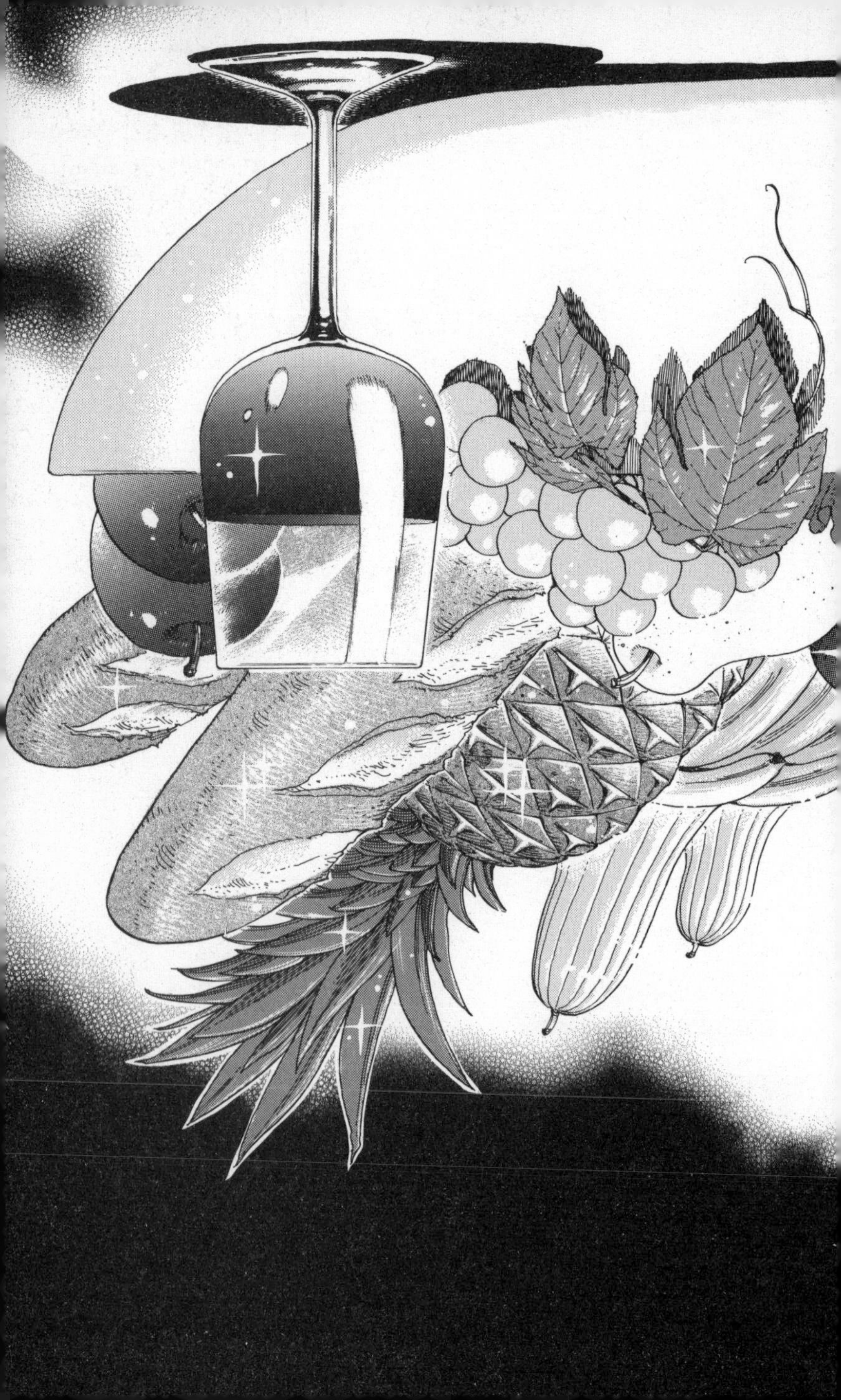

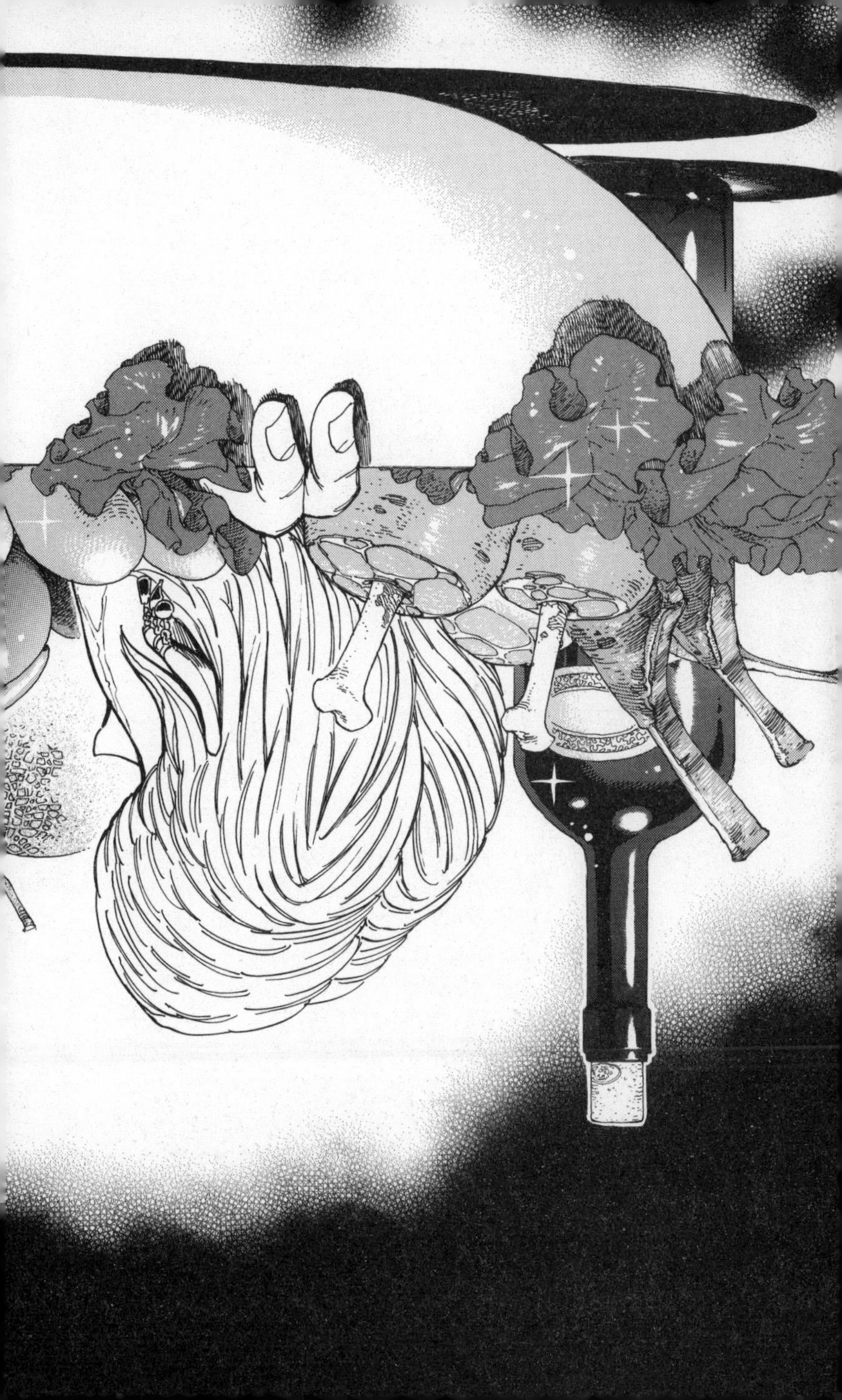

TORIKO

GOURMET CHECKLIST

Vol. 241

SAUSAGE WORM
(ANNELID)

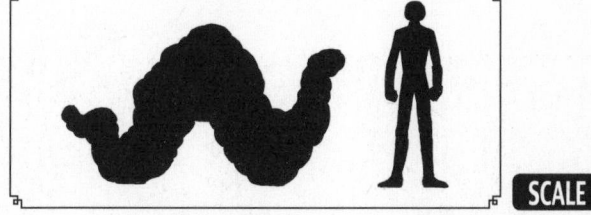

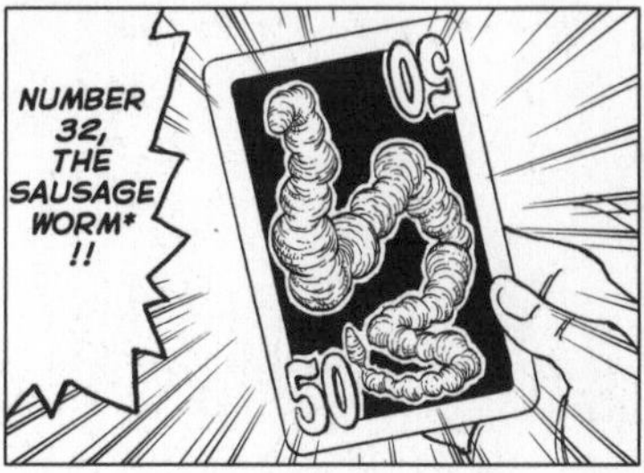
NUMBER 32, THE SAUSAGE WORM* !!
50
50

CAPTURE LEVEL: 10
HABITAT: DEEP JUNGLES
LENGTH: 2.5 METERS
HEIGHT: ---
WEIGHT: 180 KG
PRICE: 100 G / 4,000 YEN

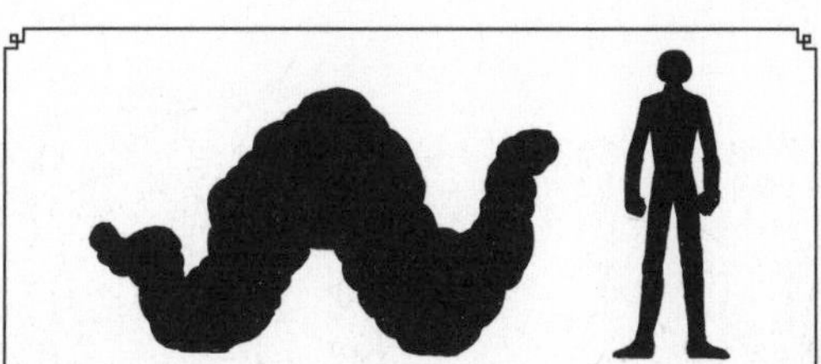

SCALE

A CARNIVOROUS WORM THAT LOOKS LIKE THE MONSTER OF ALL SAUSAGES. IT HAS NO EYES, LIMBS OR SENSE ORGANS AND USUALLY LIVES UNDERGROUND. BUT WHEN IN SEARCH OF PREY, IT WILL CREEP OUT TO THE SURFACE TO HUNT. THE MEAT IT CONSUMES BLENDS WITH INTERNALLY SECRETED SPICES TO MAKE THE WORM'S WHOLE BODY A SAUSAGE. COOKED OR STEAMED PLAIN, IT'S A JUICY TREAT!

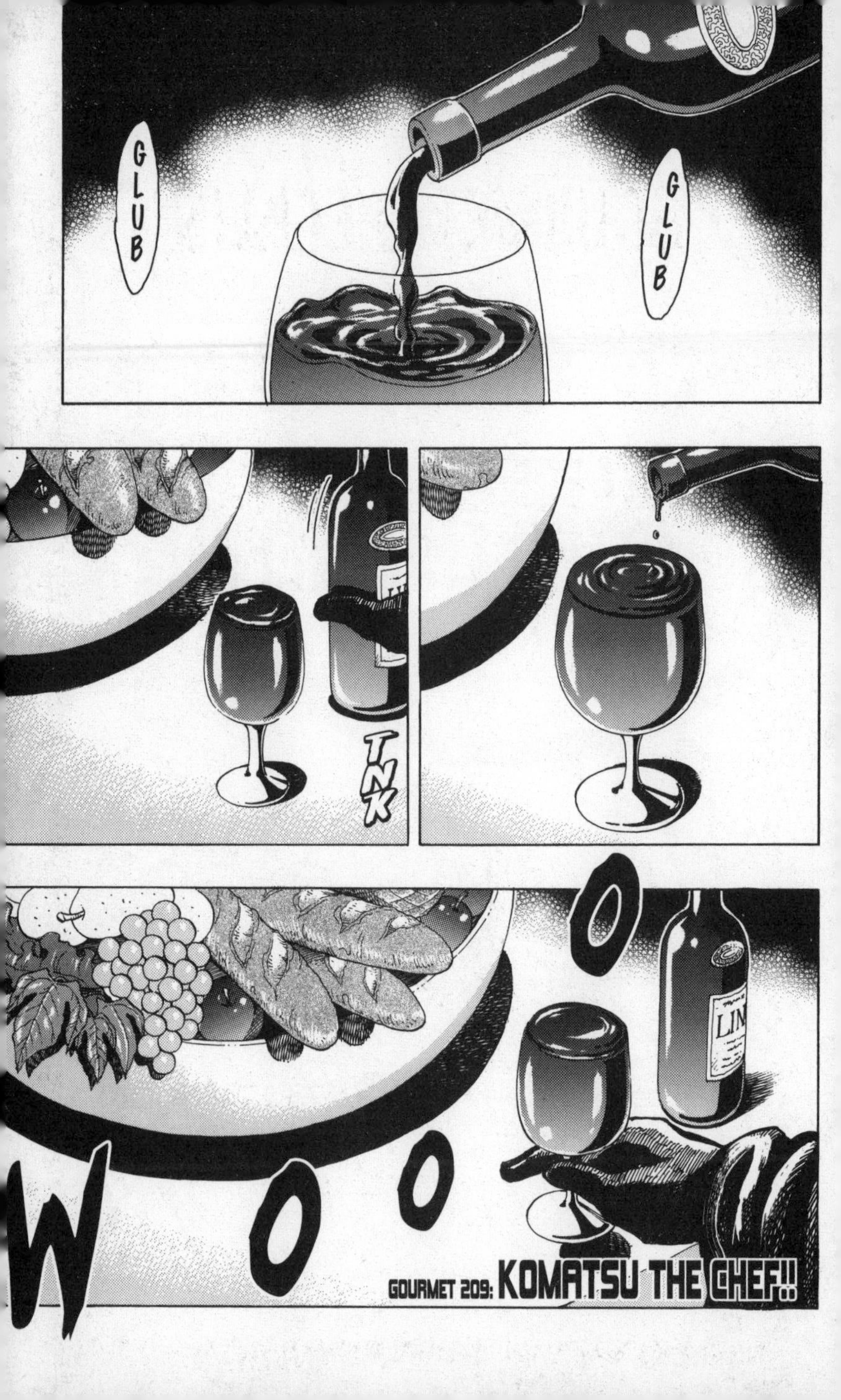
GLUB
GLUB
TNK
WOOOO
GOURMET 209: KOMATSU THE CHEF!!

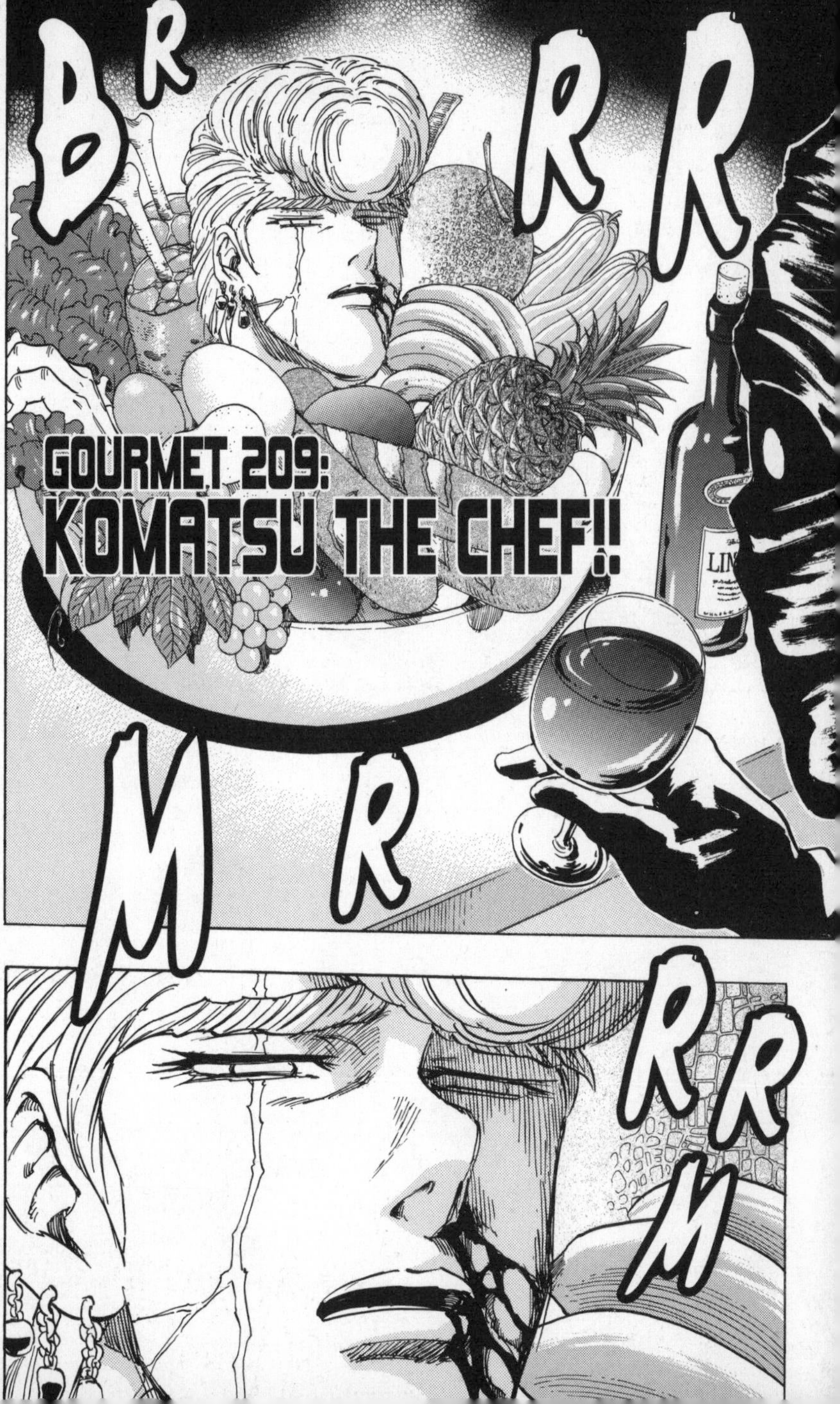
GOURMET 209:
KOMATSU THE CHEF!!
BRRRRMRRRRM

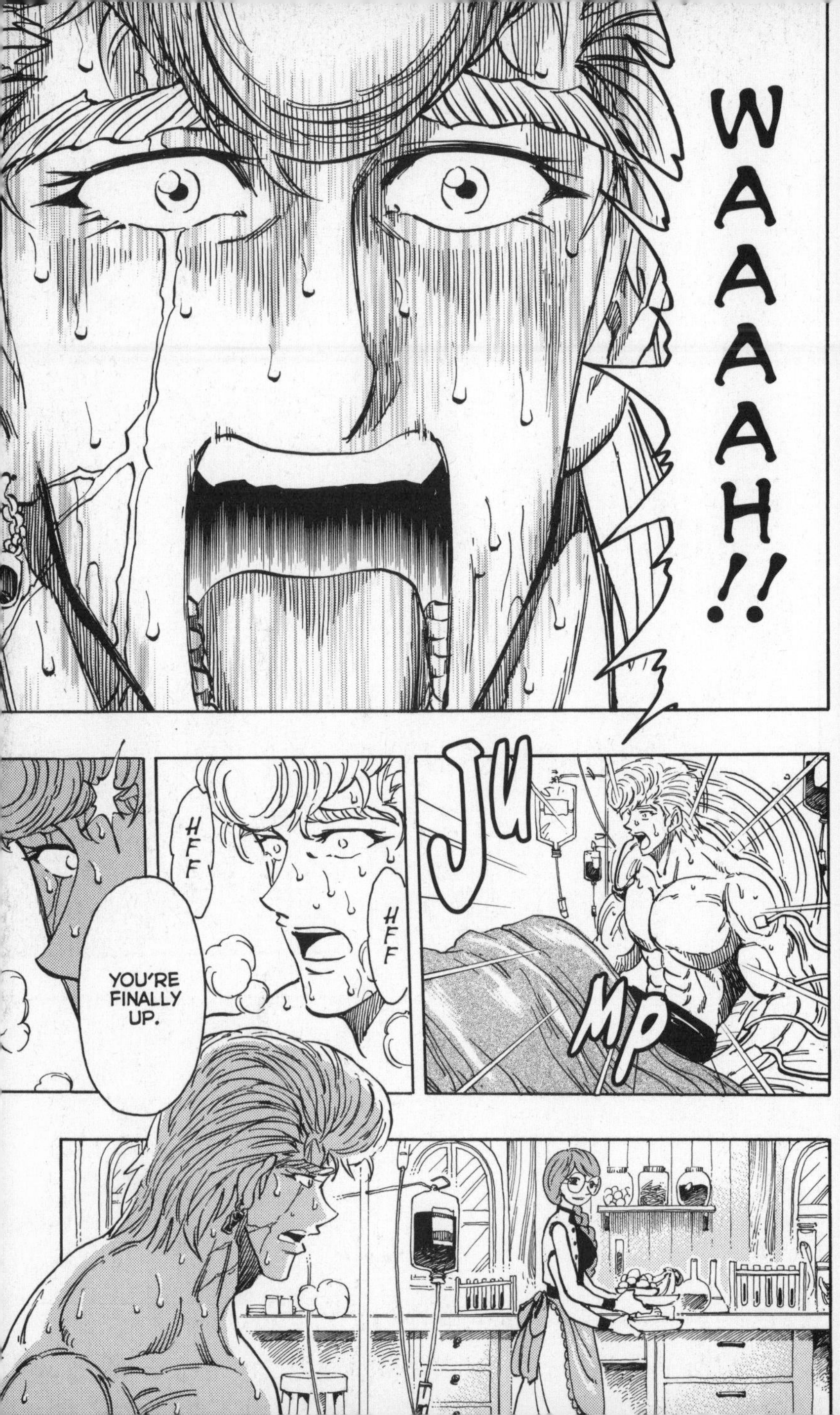
WAAAAH!!
JUMP
HFF
HFF
YOU'RE FINALLY UP.

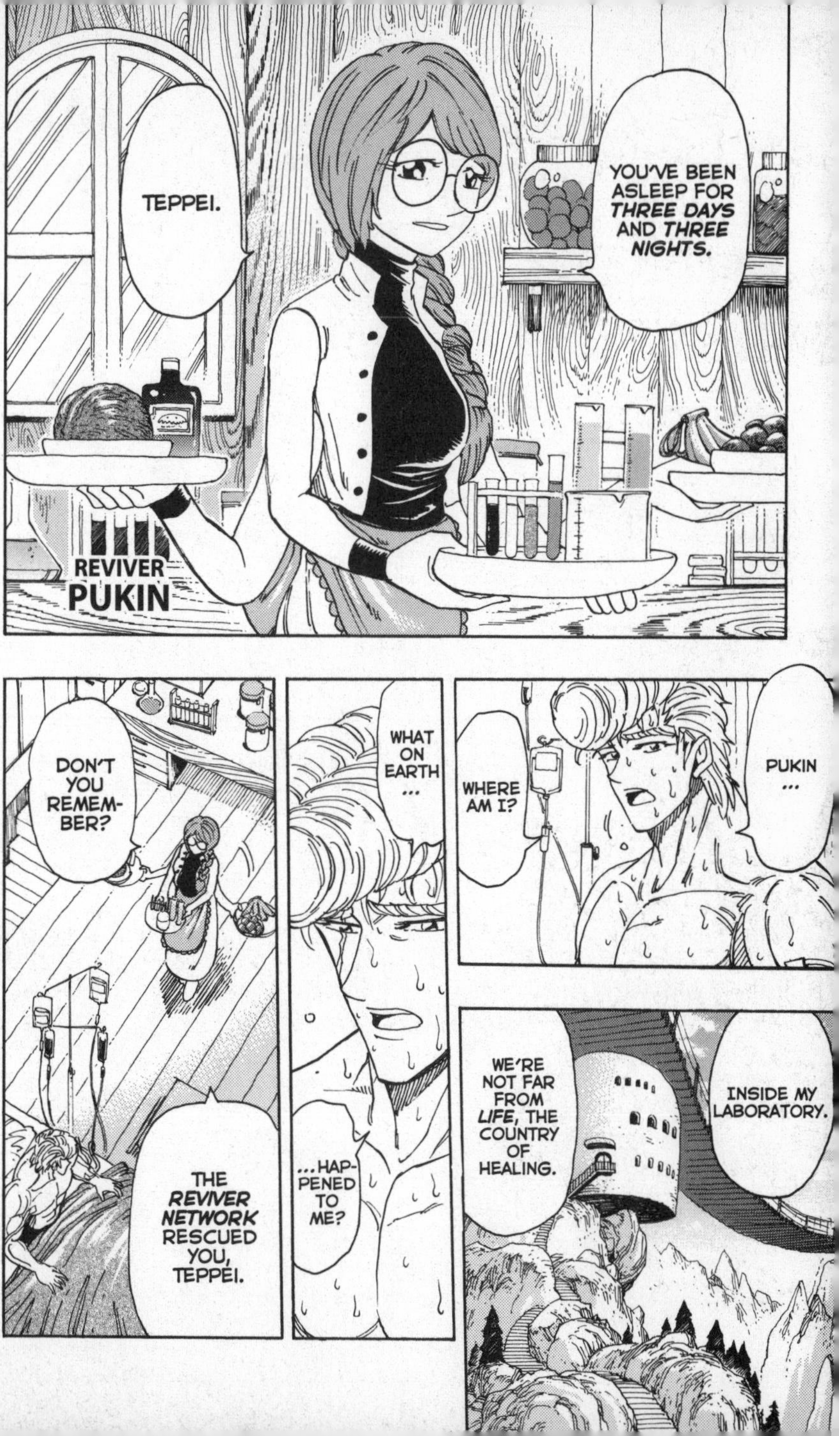
YOU'VE BEEN ASLEEP FOR *THREE DAYS* AND *THREE NIGHTS.*
TEPPEI.
REVIVER PUKIN
PUKIN ...
WHERE AM I?
INSIDE MY LABORATORY.
WE'RE NOT FAR FROM *LIFE*, THE COUNTRY OF HEALING.
WHAT ON EARTH ...
...HAPPENED TO ME?
DON'T YOU REMEMBER?
THE *REVIVER NETWORK* RESCUED YOU, TEPPEI.

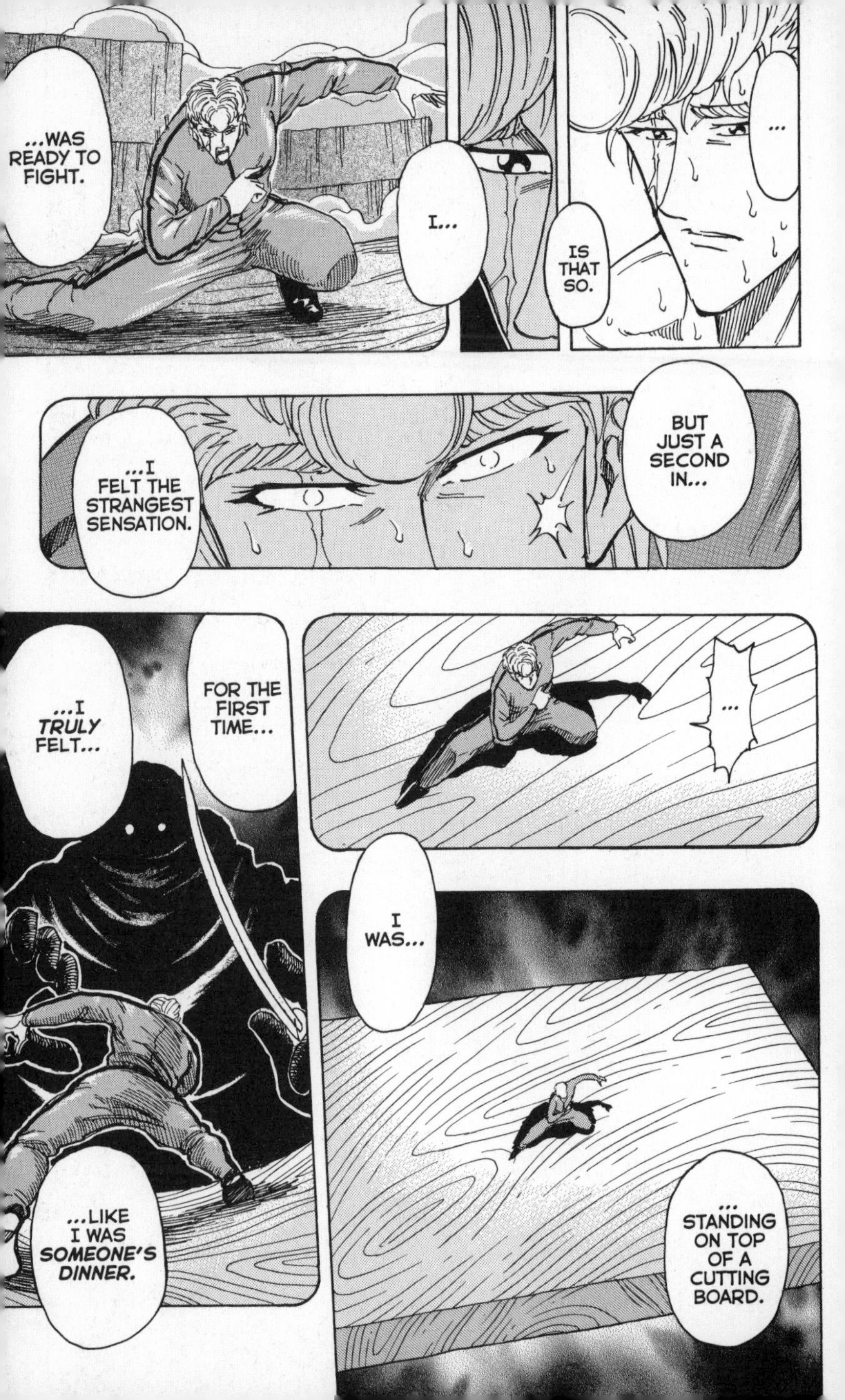
...
IS THAT SO.
I...
...WAS READY TO FIGHT.
BUT JUST A SECOND IN...
...I FELT THE STRANGEST SENSATION.
...
I WAS...
...STANDING ON TOP OF A CUTTING BOARD.
FOR THE FIRST TIME...
...I *TRULY* FELT...
...LIKE I WAS *SOMEONE'S DINNER.*

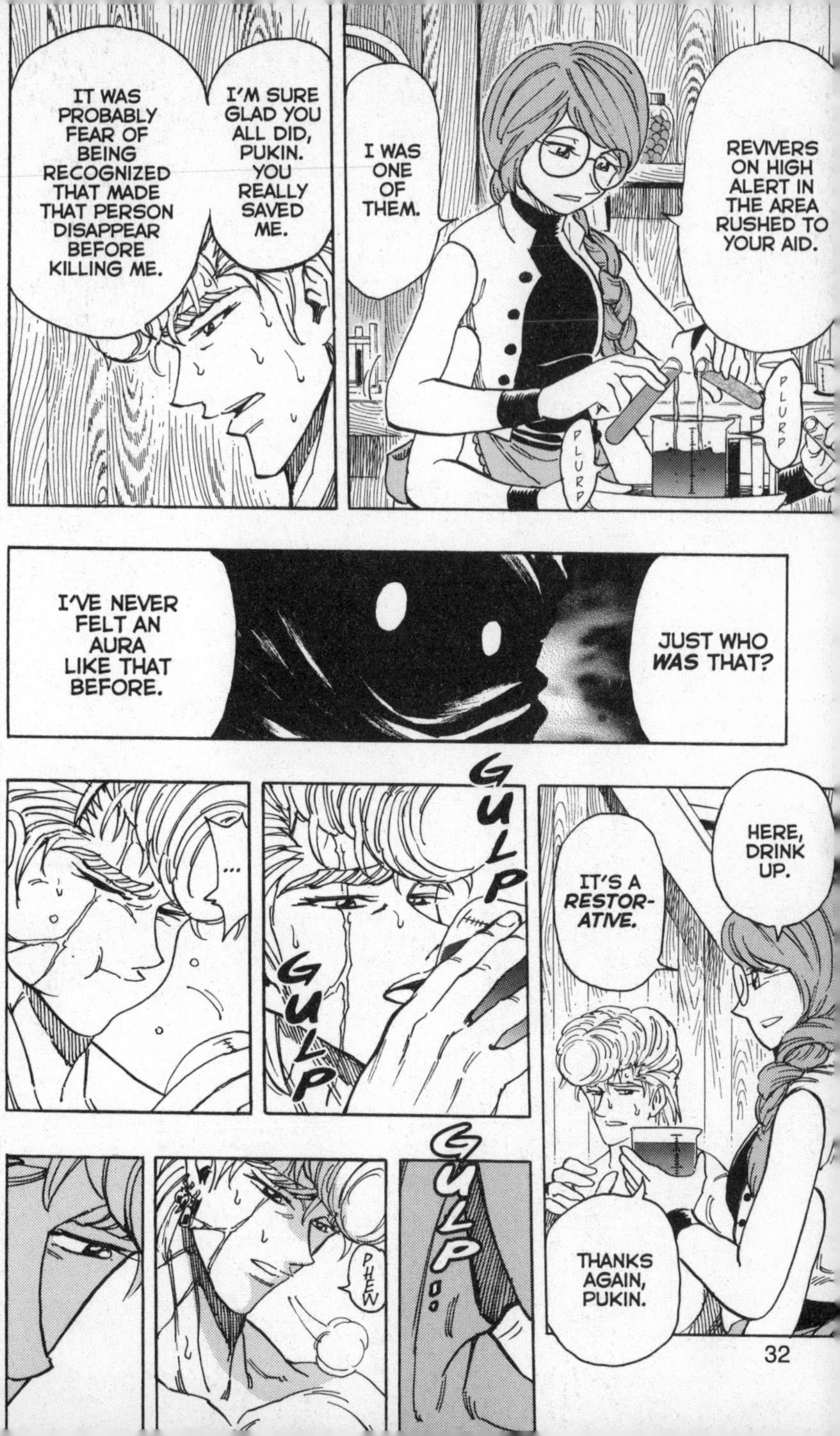
REVIVERS ON HIGH ALERT IN THE AREA RUSHED TO YOUR AID.
PLURP
PLURP
I WAS ONE OF THEM.
I'M SURE GLAD YOU ALL DID, PUKIN. YOU REALLY SAVED ME.
IT WAS PROBABLY FEAR OF BEING RECOGNIZED THAT MADE THAT PERSON DISAPPEAR BEFORE KILLING ME.
JUST WHO *WAS* THAT?
I'VE NEVER FELT AN AURA LIKE THAT BEFORE.
HERE, DRINK UP.
IT'S A *RESTORATIVE.*
GULP
GULP
...
THANKS AGAIN, PUKIN.
GULP
PHEW

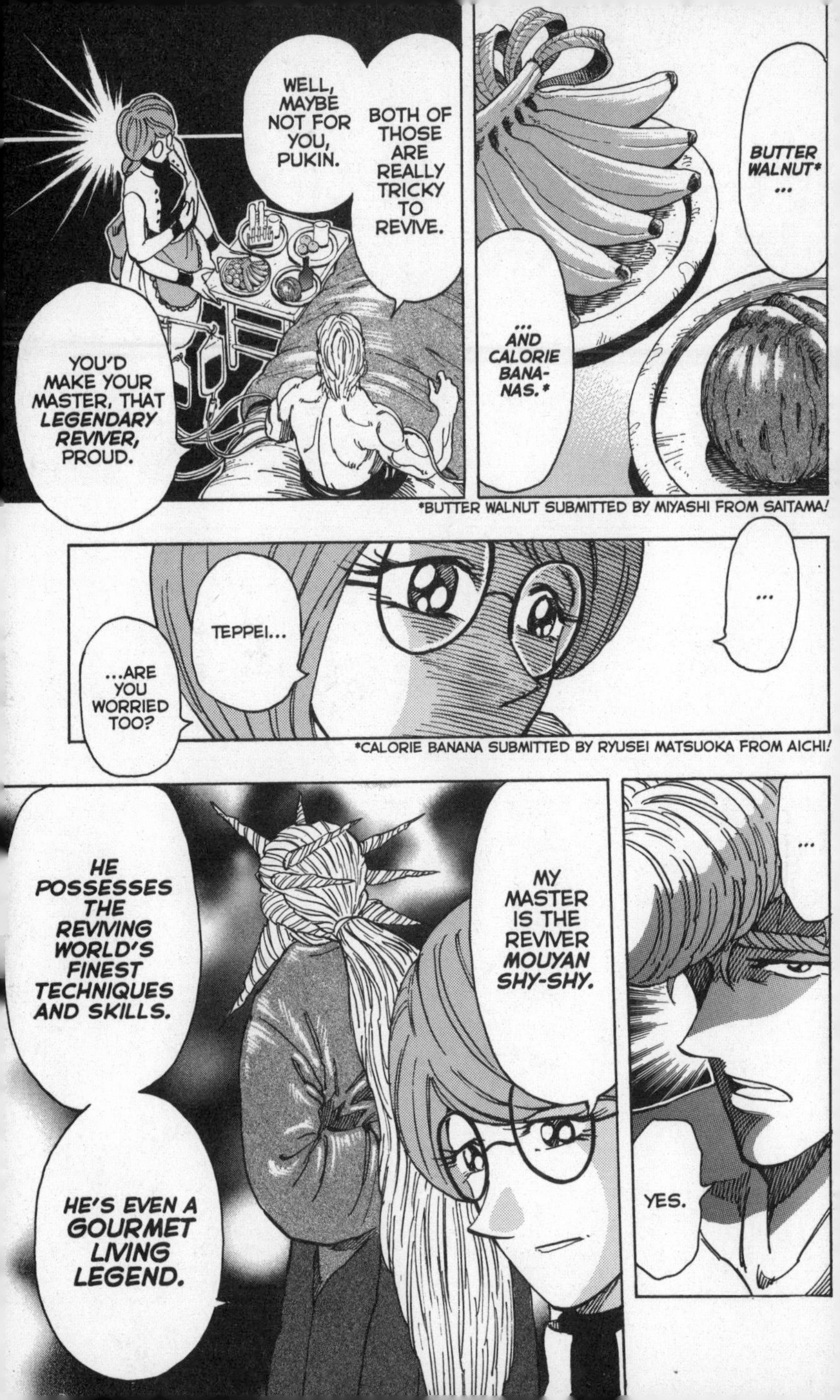
BUTTER WALNUT* ...
...AND CALORIE BANANAS.*
BOTH OF THOSE ARE REALLY TRICKY TO REVIVE.
WELL, MAYBE NOT FOR YOU, PUKIN.
YOU'D MAKE YOUR MASTER, THAT LEGENDARY REVIVER, PROUD.
...
TEPPEI...
...ARE YOU WORRIED TOO?
...
YES.
MY MASTER IS THE REVIVER MOUYAN SHY-SHY.
HE POSSESSES THE REVIVING WORLD'S FINEST TECHNIQUES AND SKILLS.
HE'S EVEN A GOURMET LIVING LEGEND.

*BUTTER WALNUT SUBMITTED BY MIYASHI FROM SAITAMA!

*CALORIE BANANA SUBMITTED BY RYUSEI MATSUOKA FROM AICHI!

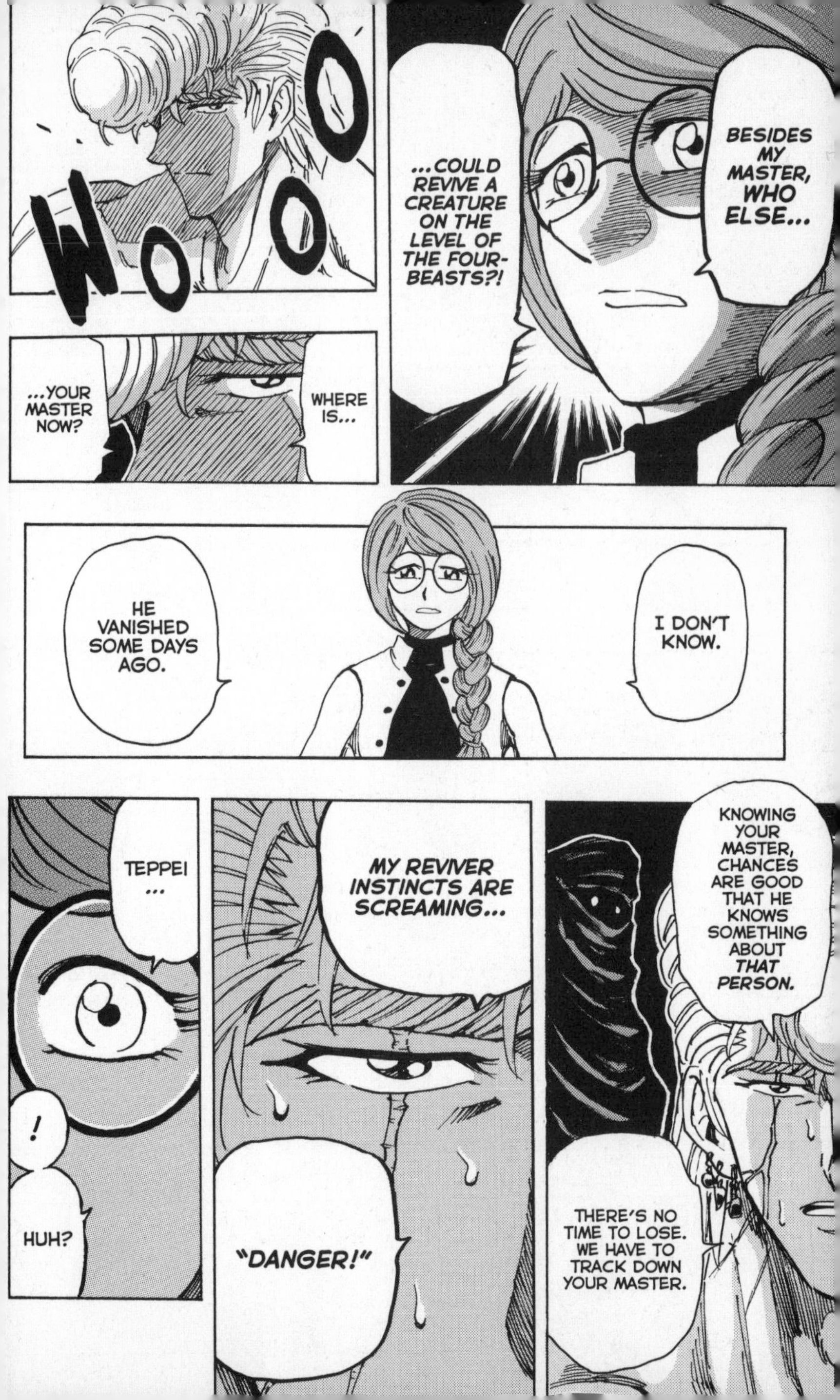
BESIDES MY MASTER, WHO ELSE...
...COULD REVIVE A CREATURE ON THE LEVEL OF THE FOUR-BEASTS?!
WOOOO
WHERE IS...
...YOUR MASTER NOW?
I DON'T KNOW.
HE VANISHED SOME DAYS AGO.
KNOWING YOUR MASTER, CHANCES ARE GOOD THAT HE KNOWS SOMETHING ABOUT *THAT* PERSON.
THERE'S NO TIME TO LOSE. WE HAVE TO TRACK DOWN YOUR MASTER.
MY REVIVER INSTINCTS ARE SCREAMING...
"DANGER!"
TEPPEI...
!
HUH?

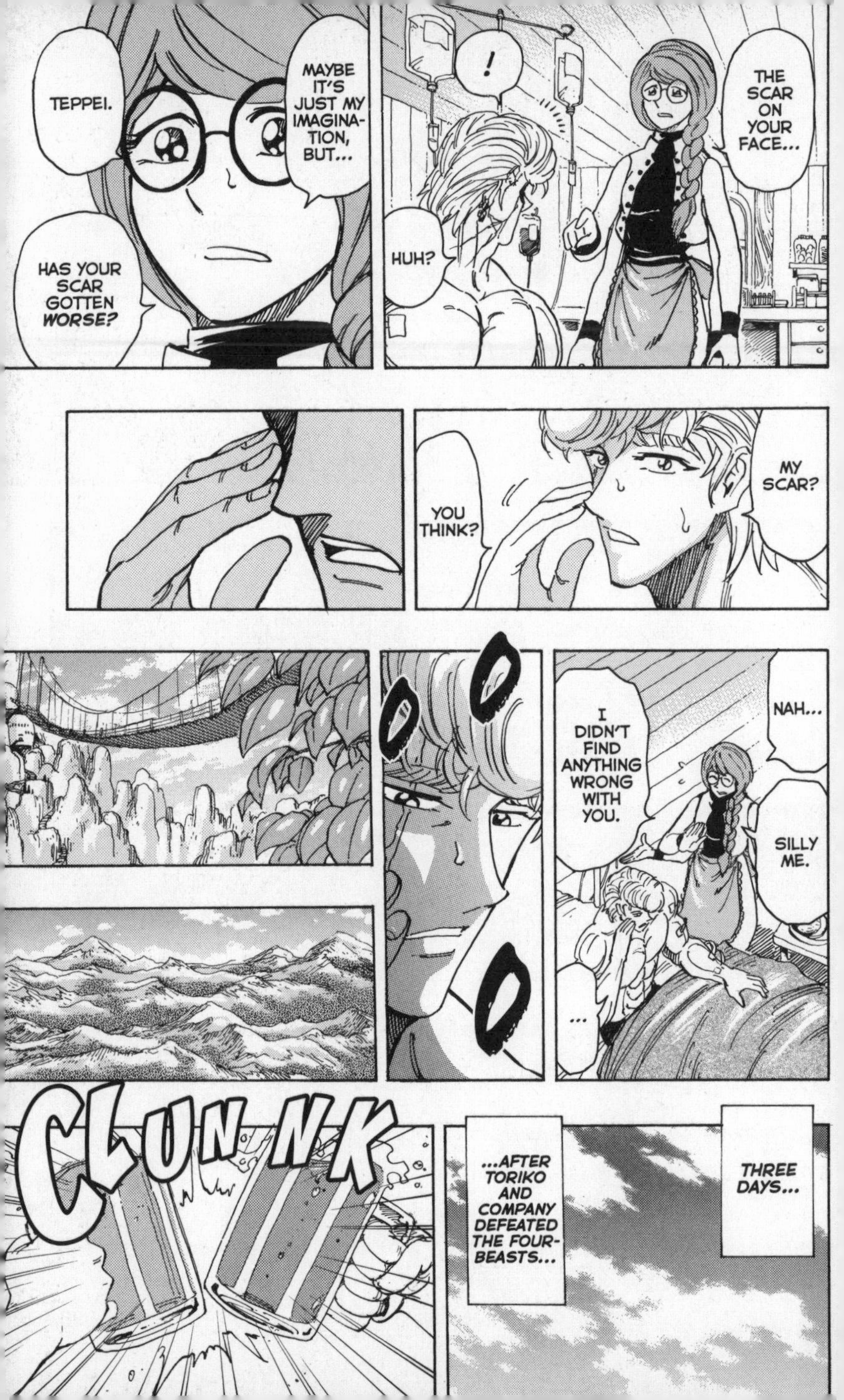
THE SCAR ON YOUR FACE...
!
HUH?
TEPPEI.
MAYBE IT'S JUST MY IMAGINATION, BUT...
HAS YOUR SCAR GOTTEN WORSE?
MY SCAR?
YOU THINK?
NAH...
SILLY ME.
I DIDN'T FIND ANYTHING WRONG WITH YOU.
...
THREE DAYS...
...AFTER TORIKO AND COMPANY DEFEATED THE FOUR-BEASTS...
CLUNNK

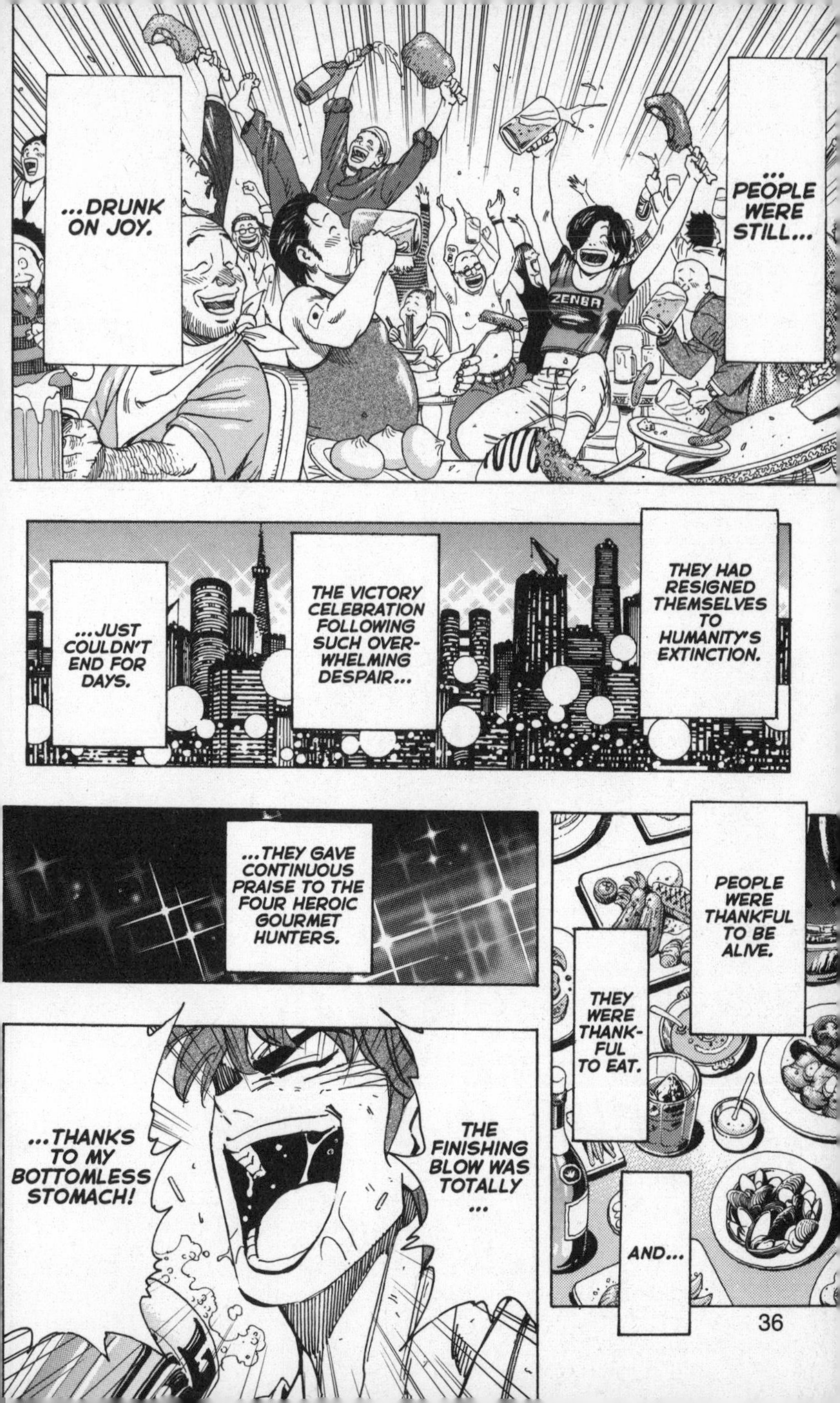
...PEOPLE WERE STILL...
...DRUNK ON JOY.
THEY HAD RESIGNED THEMSELVES TO HUMANITY'S EXTINCTION.
THE VICTORY CELEBRATION FOLLOWING SUCH OVER-WHELMING DESPAIR...
...JUST COULDN'T END FOR DAYS.
PEOPLE WERE THANKFUL TO BE ALIVE.
THEY WERE THANK-FUL TO EAT.
AND...
...THEY GAVE CONTINUOUS PRAISE TO THE FOUR HEROIC GOURMET HUNTERS.
THE FINISHING BLOW WAS TOTALLY ...
...THANKS TO MY BOTTOMLESS STOMACH!
ZENBA

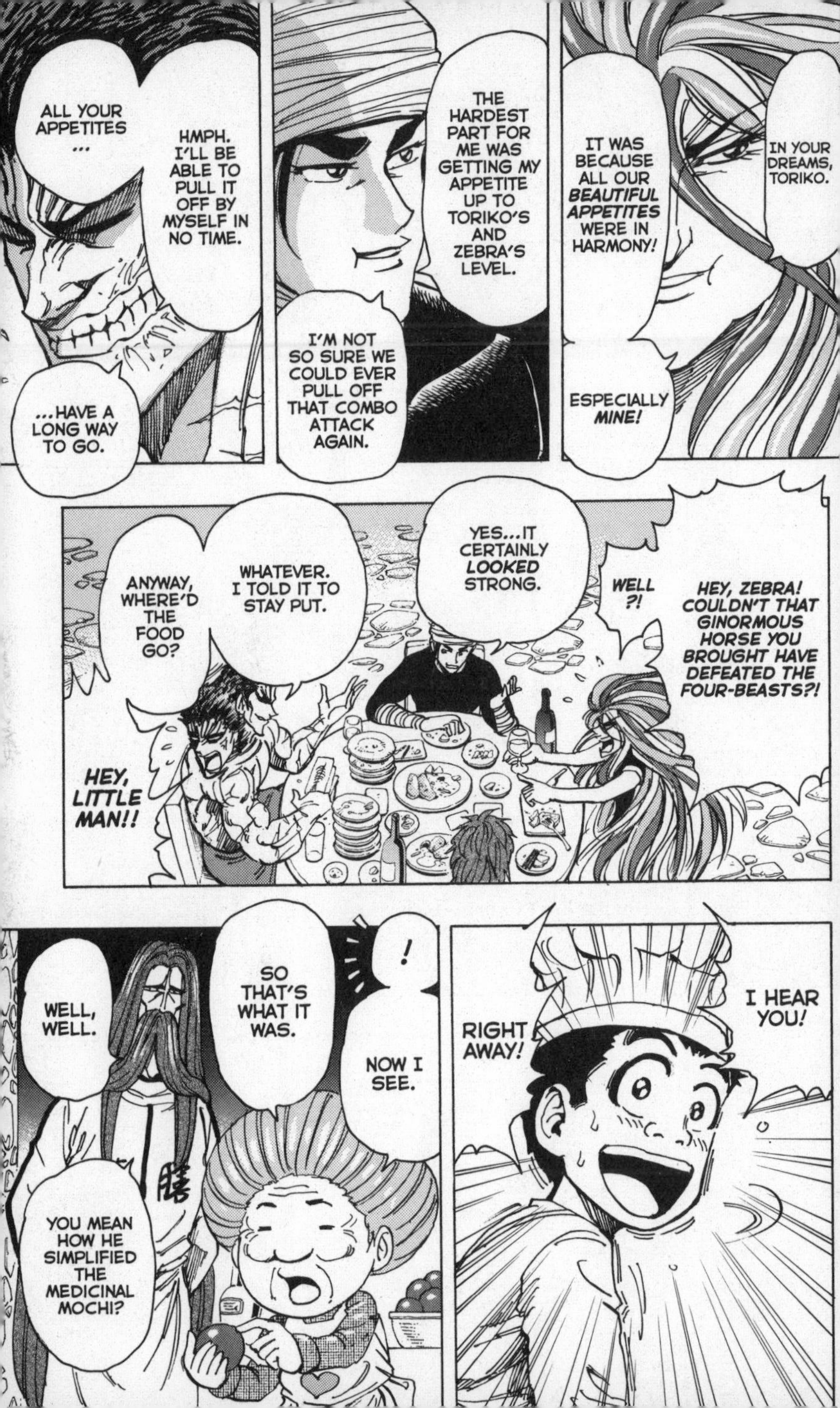
IN YOUR DREAMS, TORIKO.
IT WAS BECAUSE ALL OUR *BEAUTIFUL APPETITES* WERE IN HARMONY!
ESPECIALLY *MINE!*
THE HARDEST PART FOR ME WAS GETTING MY APPETITE UP TO TORIKO'S AND ZEBRA'S LEVEL.
I'M NOT SO SURE WE COULD EVER PULL OFF THAT COMBO ATTACK AGAIN.
HMPH. I'LL BE ABLE TO PULL IT OFF BY MYSELF IN NO TIME.
ALL YOUR APPETITES ...
...HAVE A LONG WAY TO GO.
HEY, ZEBRA! COULDN'T THAT GINORMOUS HORSE YOU BROUGHT HAVE DEFEATED THE FOUR-BEASTS?!
WELL ?!
YES...IT CERTAINLY *LOOKED* STRONG.
WHATEVER. I TOLD IT TO STAY PUT.
ANYWAY, WHERE'D THE FOOD GO?
HEY, LITTLE MAN!!
I HEAR YOU!
RIGHT AWAY!
!
SO THAT'S WHAT IT WAS.
NOW I SEE.
WELL, WELL.
YOU MEAN HOW HE SIMPLIFIED THE MEDICINAL MOCHI?

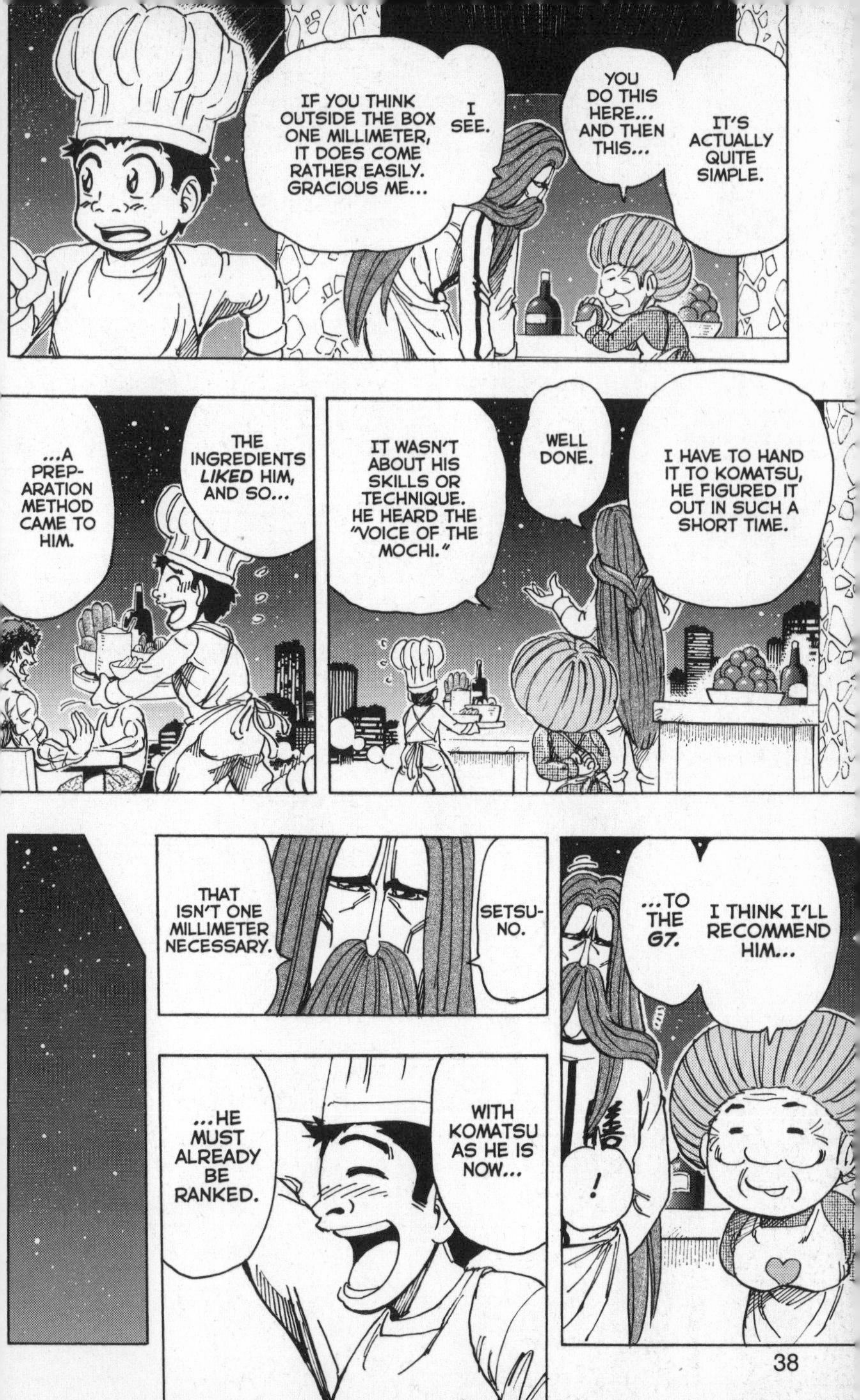
YOU DO THIS HERE... AND THEN THIS...
IT'S ACTUALLY QUITE SIMPLE.
I SEE.
IF YOU THINK OUTSIDE THE BOX ONE MILLIMETER, IT DOES COME RATHER EASILY. GRACIOUS ME...
I HAVE TO HAND IT TO KOMATSU, HE FIGURED IT OUT IN SUCH A SHORT TIME.
WELL DONE.
IT WASN'T ABOUT HIS SKILLS OR TECHNIQUE. HE HEARD THE "VOICE OF THE MOCHI."
THE INGREDIENTS *LIKED* HIM, AND SO...
...A PREPARATION METHOD CAME TO HIM.
I THINK I'LL RECOMMEND HIM...
...TO THE G7.
!
SETSUNO.
THAT ISN'T ONE MILLIMETER NECESSARY.
WITH KOMATSU AS HE IS NOW...
...HE MUST ALREADY BE RANKED.

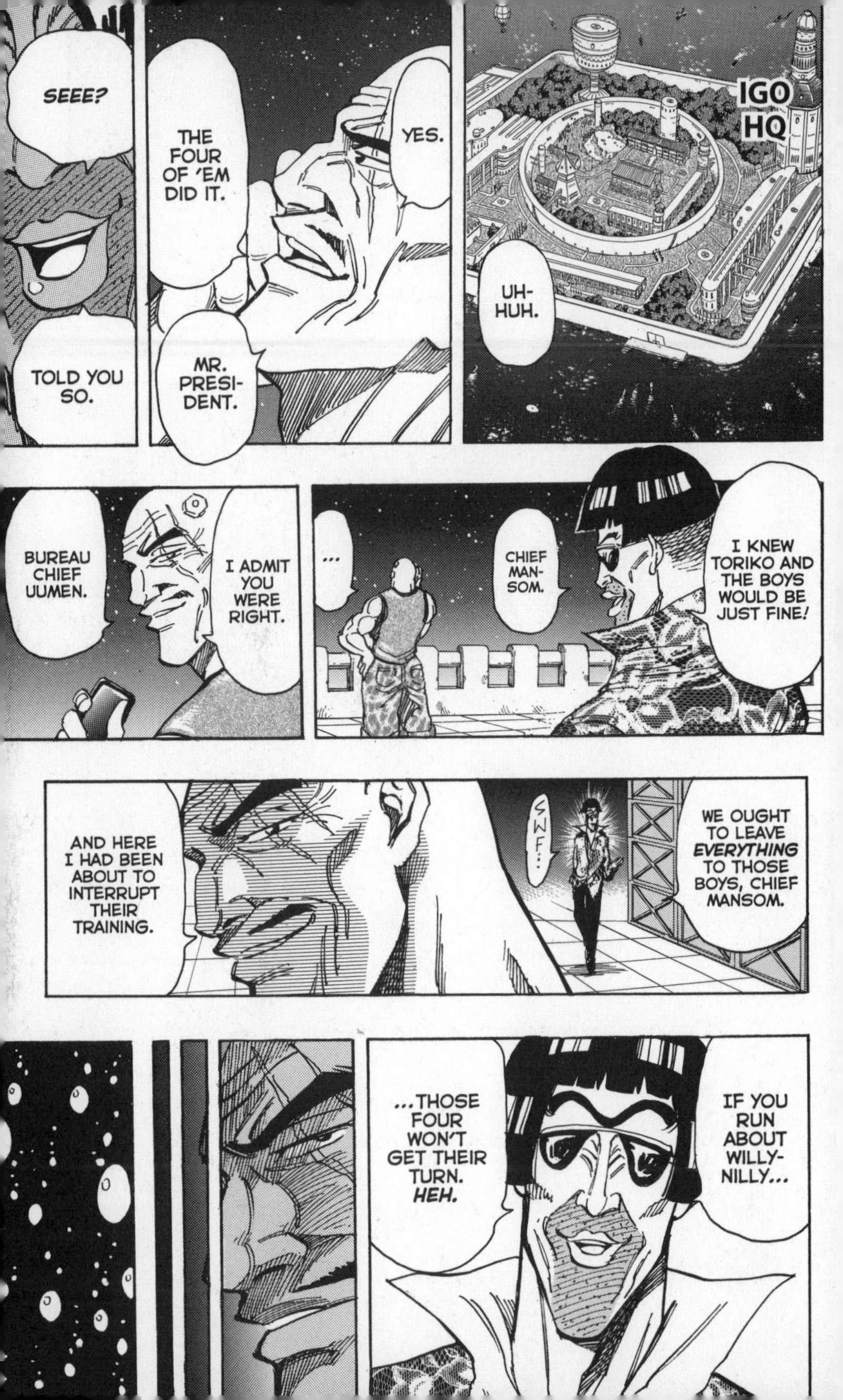
IGO HQ
UH-HUH.
YES.
THE FOUR OF 'EM DID IT.
MR. PRESIDENT.
SEEE?
TOLD YOU SO.
I KNEW TORIKO AND THE BOYS WOULD BE JUST FINE!
CHIEF MANSOM.
...
I ADMIT YOU WERE RIGHT.
BUREAU CHIEF UUMEN.
WE OUGHT TO LEAVE *EVERYTHING* TO THOSE BOYS, CHIEF MANSOM.
SWF...
AND HERE I HAD BEEN ABOUT TO INTERRUPT THEIR TRAINING.
IF YOU RUN ABOUT WILLY-NILLY...
...THOSE FOUR WON'T GET THEIR TURN. *HEH.*

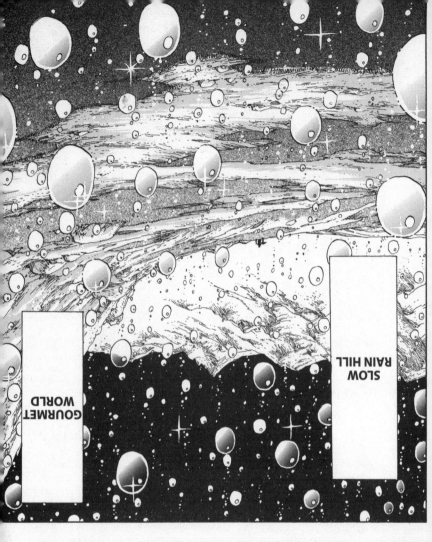

GOURMET WORLD

SLOW RAIN HILL

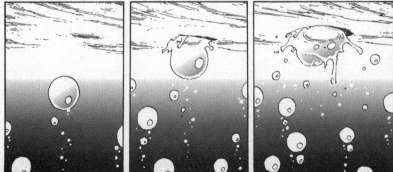

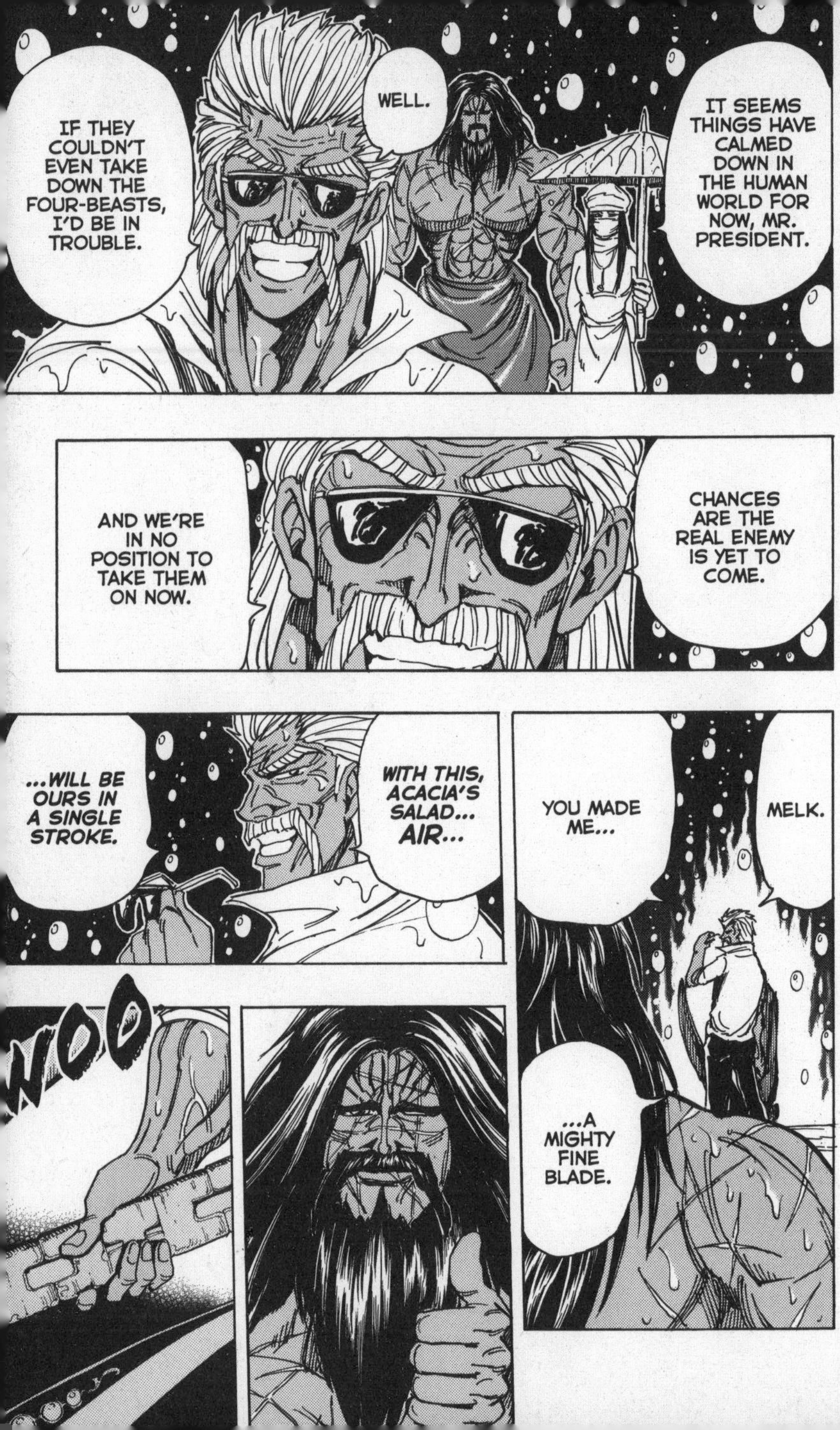
IT SEEMS THINGS HAVE CALMED DOWN IN THE HUMAN WORLD FOR NOW, MR. PRESIDENT.
WELL.
IF THEY COULDN'T EVEN TAKE DOWN THE FOUR-BEASTS, I'D BE IN TROUBLE.
CHANCES ARE THE REAL ENEMY IS YET TO COME.
AND WE'RE IN NO POSITION TO TAKE THEM ON NOW.
WITH THIS, ACACIA'S SALAD... AIR...
...WILL BE OURS IN A SINGLE STROKE.
MELK.
YOU MADE ME...
...A MIGHTY FINE BLADE.
WOO

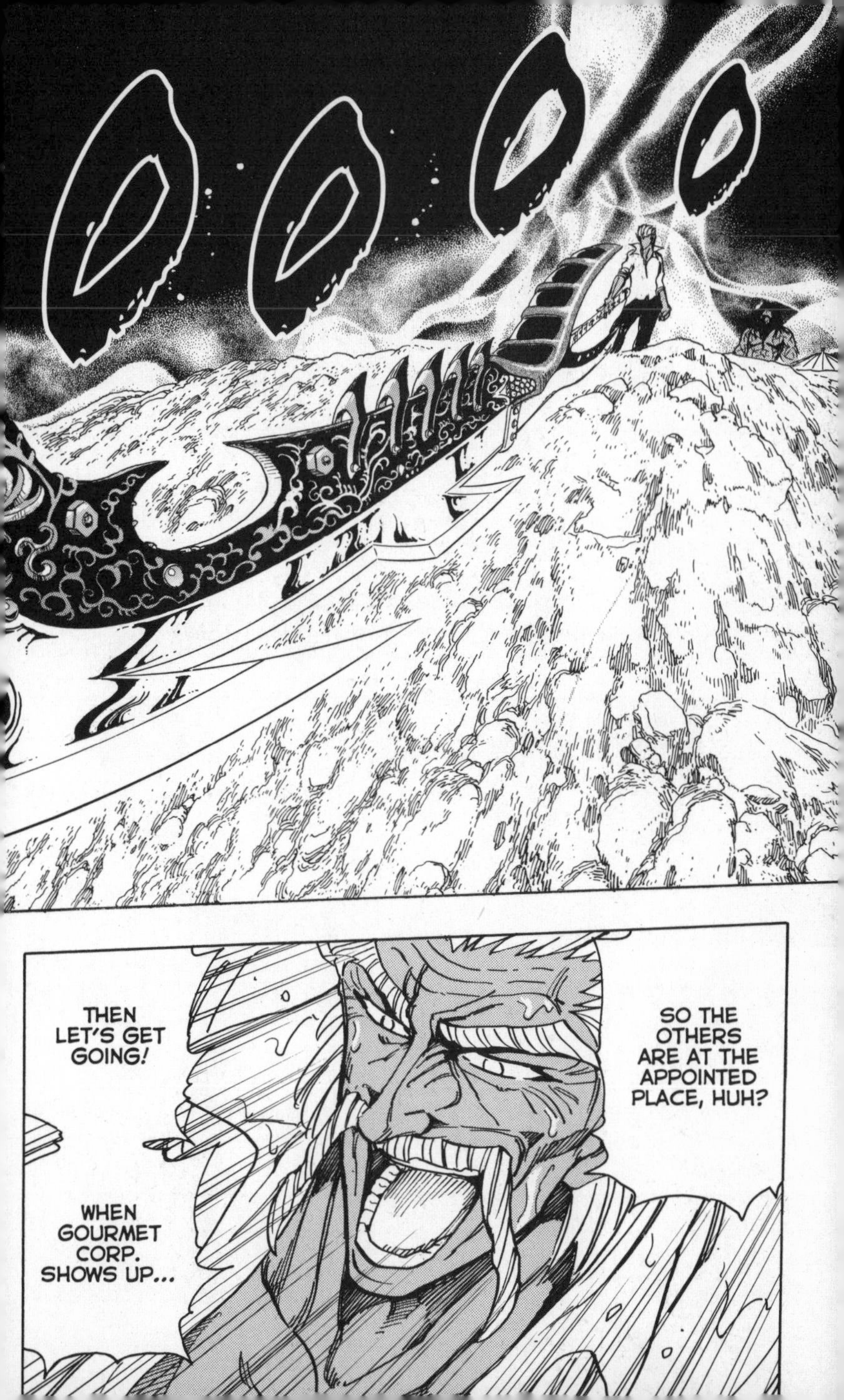
SO THE OTHERS ARE AT THE APPOINTED PLACE, HUH?
THEN LET'S GET GOING!
WHEN GOURMET CORP. SHOWS UP...

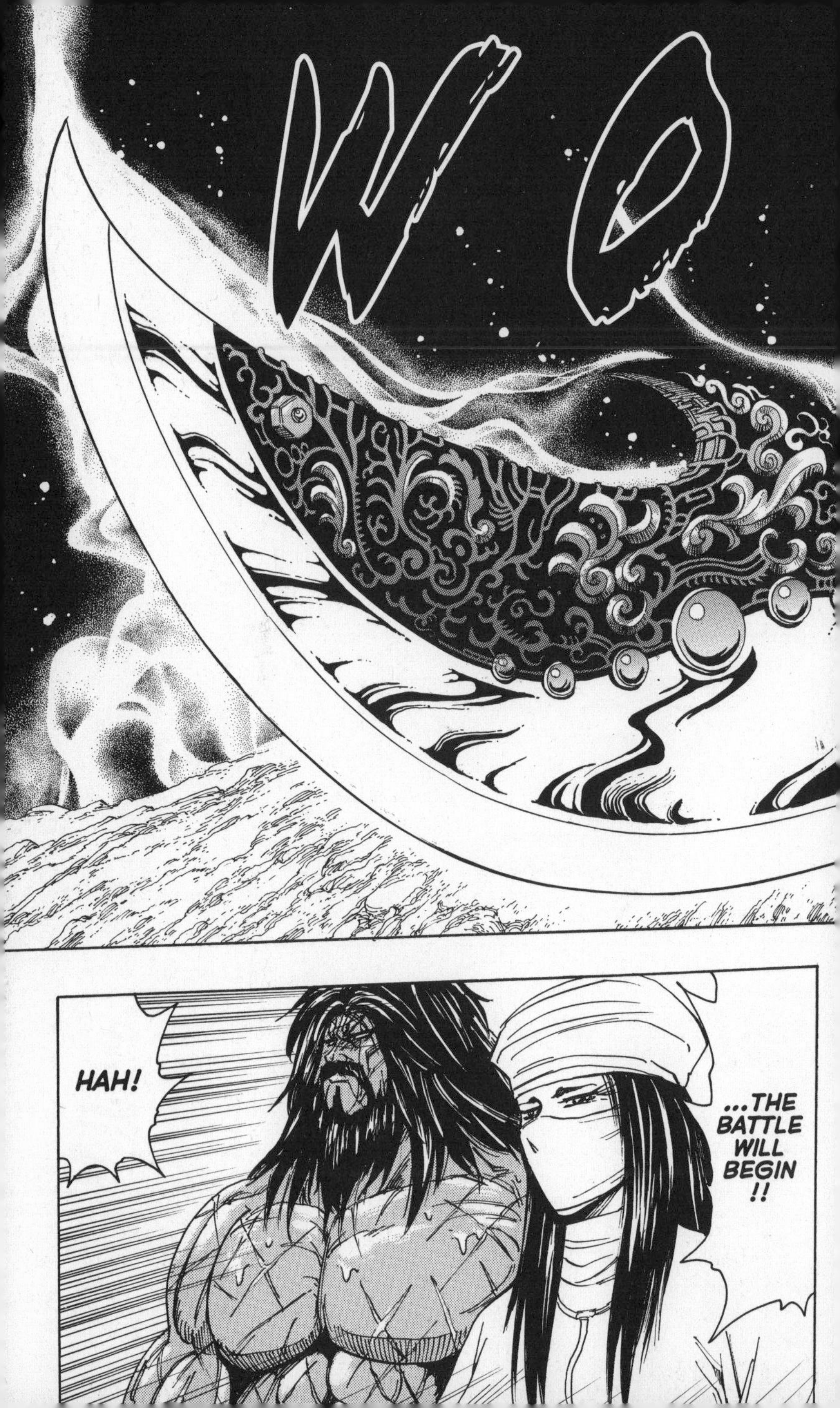
WO
...THE BATTLE WILL BEGIN!!
HAH!

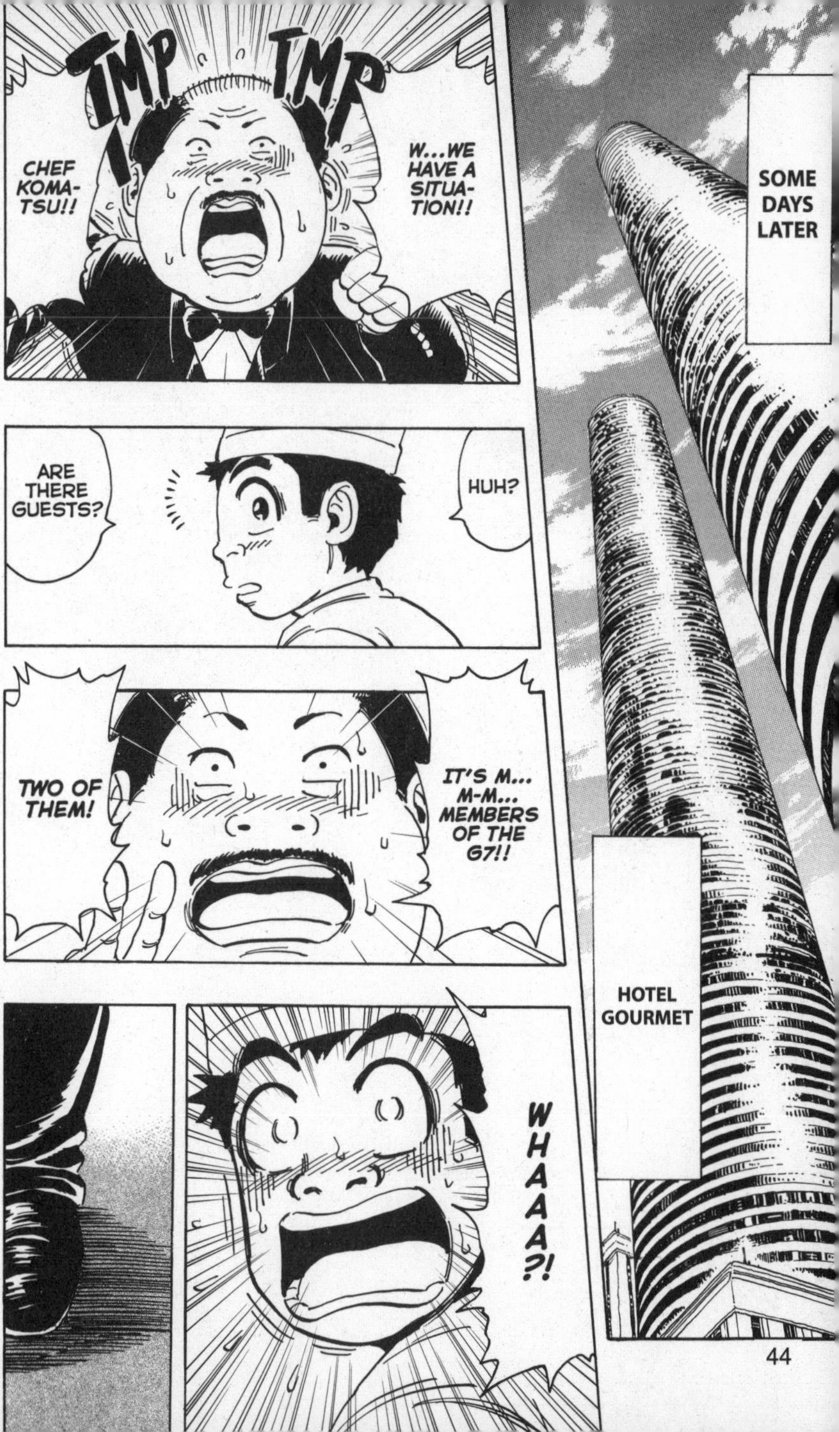
SOME DAYS LATER
HOTEL GOURMET
TMP TMP
W...WE HAVE A SITUA-TION!!
CHEF KOMA-TSU!!
HUH?
ARE THERE GUESTS?
IT'S M... M-M... MEMBERS OF THE G7!!
TWO OF THEM!
WHAAAA?!

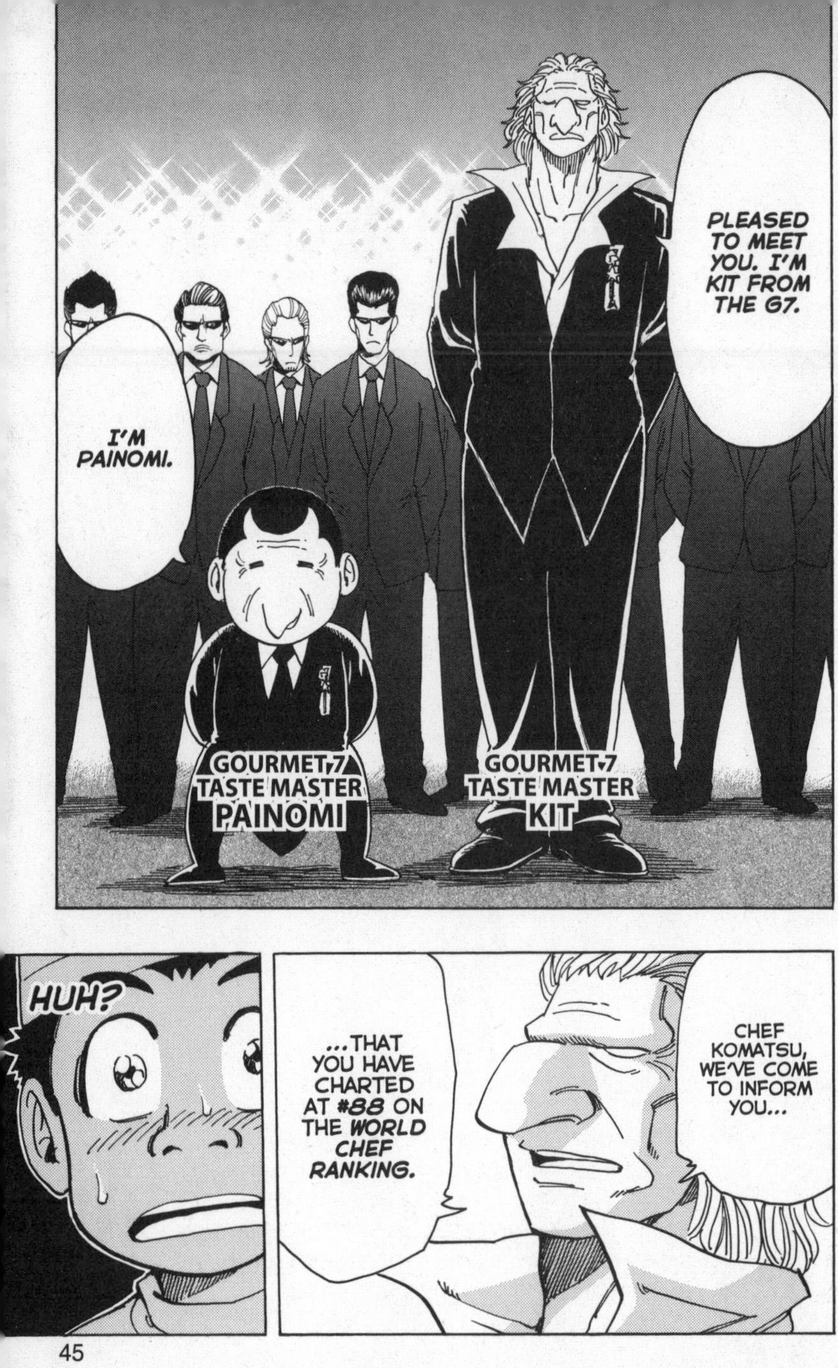
PLEASED TO MEET YOU. I'M KIT FROM THE G7.
GOURMET 7 TASTE MASTER KIT
I'M PAINOMI.
GOURMET 7 TASTE MASTER PAINOMI
CHEF KOMATSU, WE'VE COME TO INFORM YOU...
...THAT YOU HAVE CHARTED AT #88 ON THE WORLD CHEF RANKING.
HUH?

TORIKO

GOURMET CHECKLIST
Vol. 242

⦗ MAN-FACED MUSHROOM ⦘
(FUNGUS)

CAPTURE LEVEL: 14
HABITAT: CURSED FOREST
LENGTH: 12 CM
HEIGHT: ---
WEIGHT: 100 G
PRICE: 8,000 YEN PER STALK

THERE IS A TIME LIMIT FOR FINISHING OFF THE

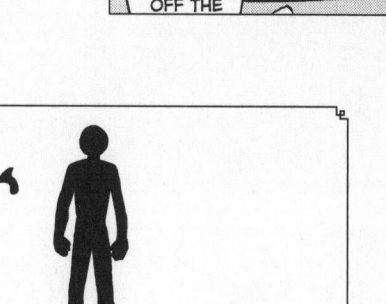

SCALE

A MUSHROOM WHOSE CAP BEARS A STRIKING RESEMBLANCE TO A HUMAN FACE! THEY GROW IN DARK, MOIST PLACES LIKE UNDER THE FLOORBOARDS OF ABANDONED BUILDINGS--IN OTHER WORDS, CREEPY PLACES! IF YOU MAKE EYE CONTACT WITH ONE OF THEM, YOU'LL FEEL LIKE A SPIRIT OF THE DEAD IS POSSESSING YOU. BECAUSE THEY CAN SCAR YOUR PSYCHE, CAUTION IS REQUIRED WHILE PREPARING THEM. THAT'S WHY THIS FOOD HAD A HIGH DIFFICULTY LEVEL IN THE GOURMET TASTING GAME.

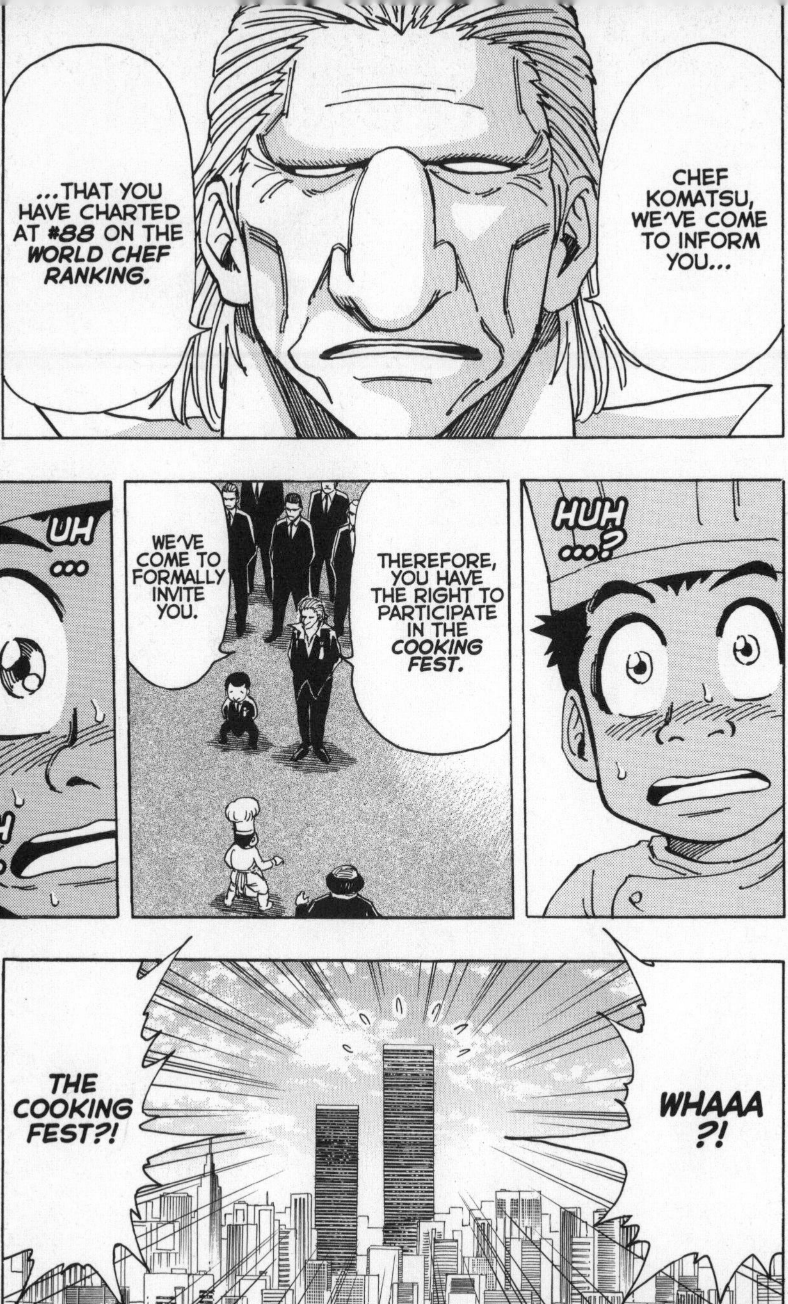
CHEF KOMATSU, WE'VE COME TO INFORM YOU...
...THAT YOU HAVE CHARTED AT #88 ON THE WORLD CHEF RANKING.
HUH ...?
THEREFORE, YOU HAVE THE RIGHT TO PARTICIPATE IN THE COOKING FEST.
WE'VE COME TO FORMALLY INVITE YOU.
UH ...
UH ...
WHAAA ?!
THE COOKING FEST?!

GOURMET 210: NAIL GUN!!

GOURMET 210: NAIL GUN!!

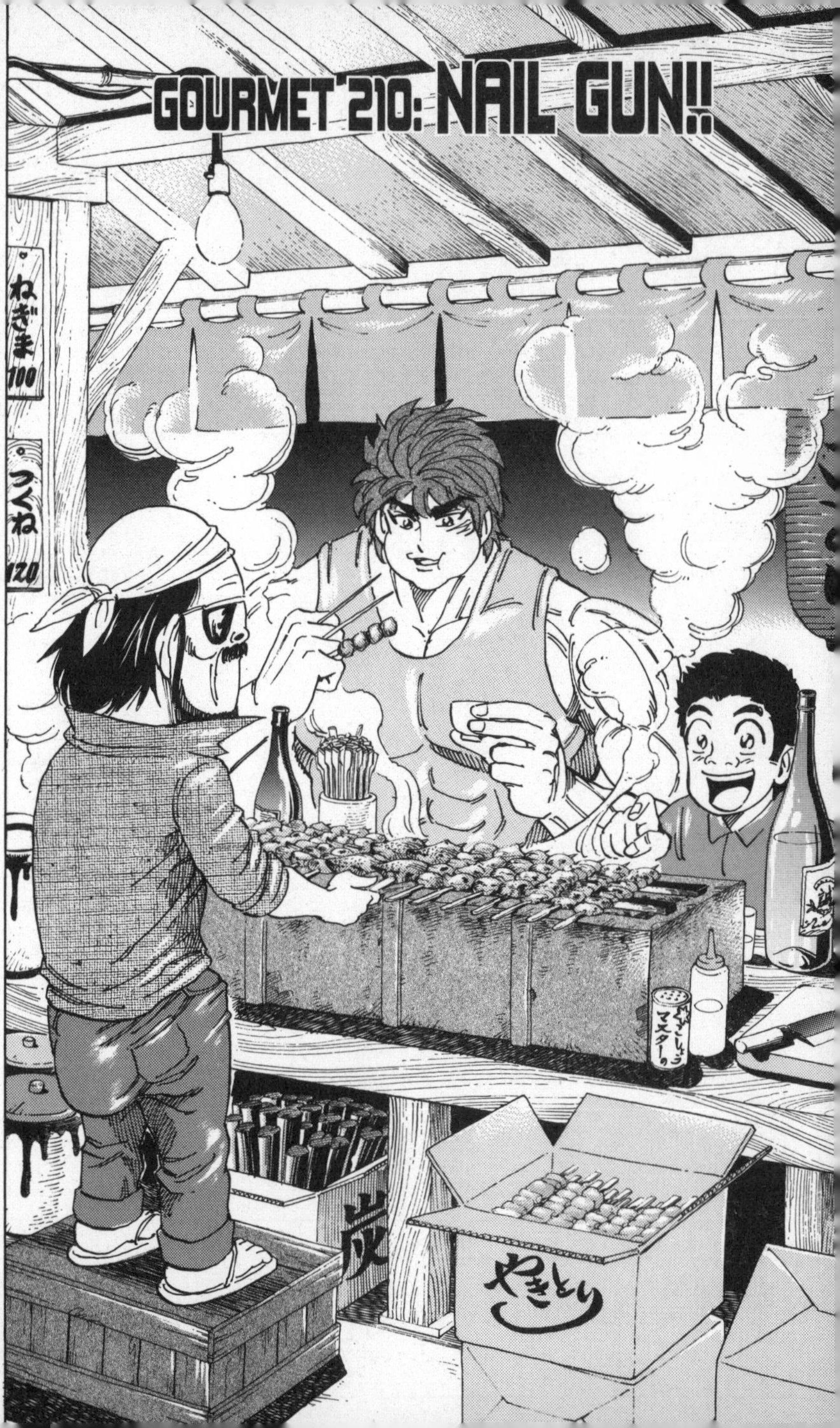

ねぎま
100
つくね
120
炭
やきとり

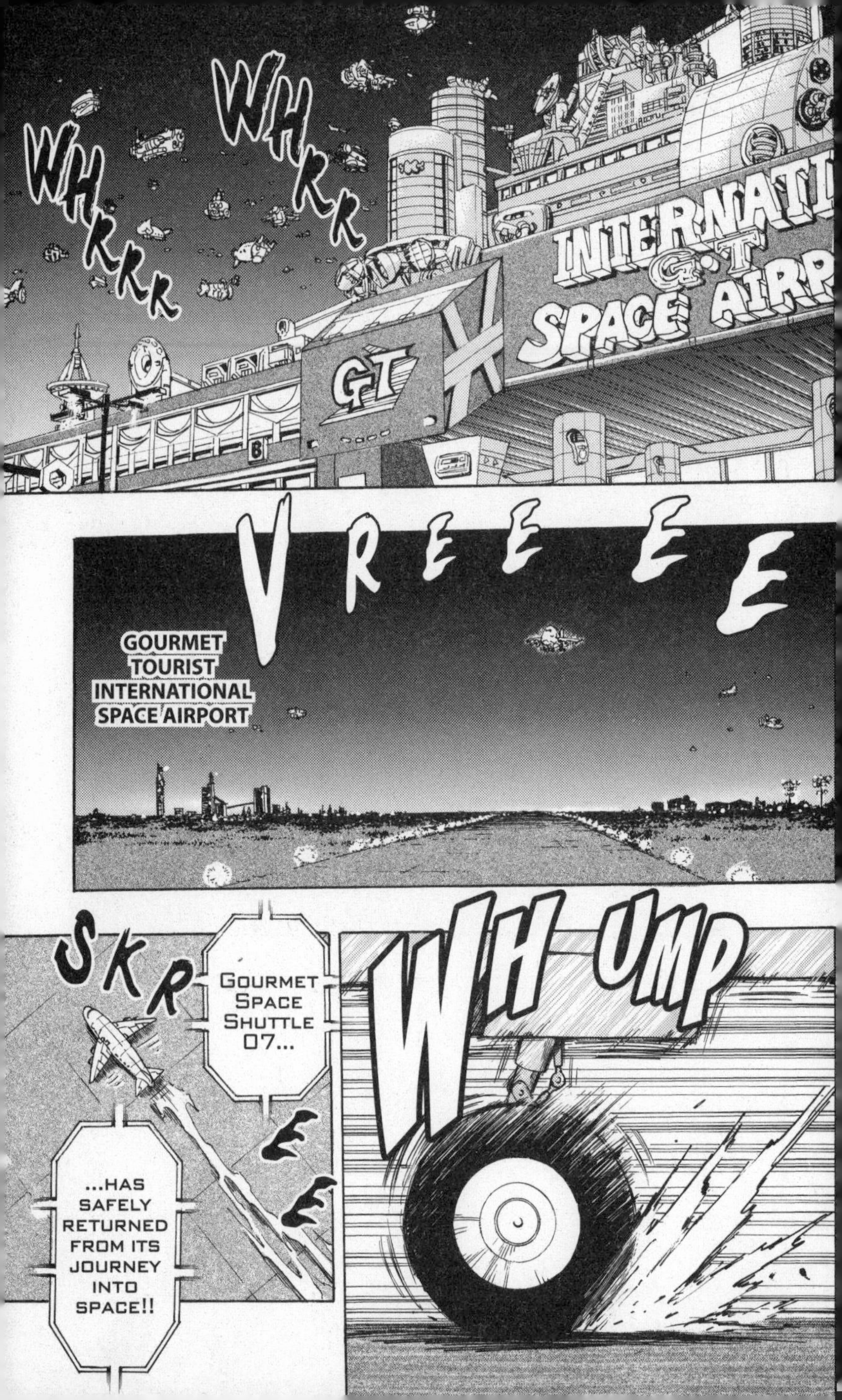
WHRRR
WHRRRR
GT
VREEEE
GOURMET TOURIST INTERNATIONAL SPACE AIRPORT
WHUMP
SKREE
Gourmet Space Shuttle 07...
...HAS SAFELY RETURNED FROM ITS JOURNEY INTO SPACE!!

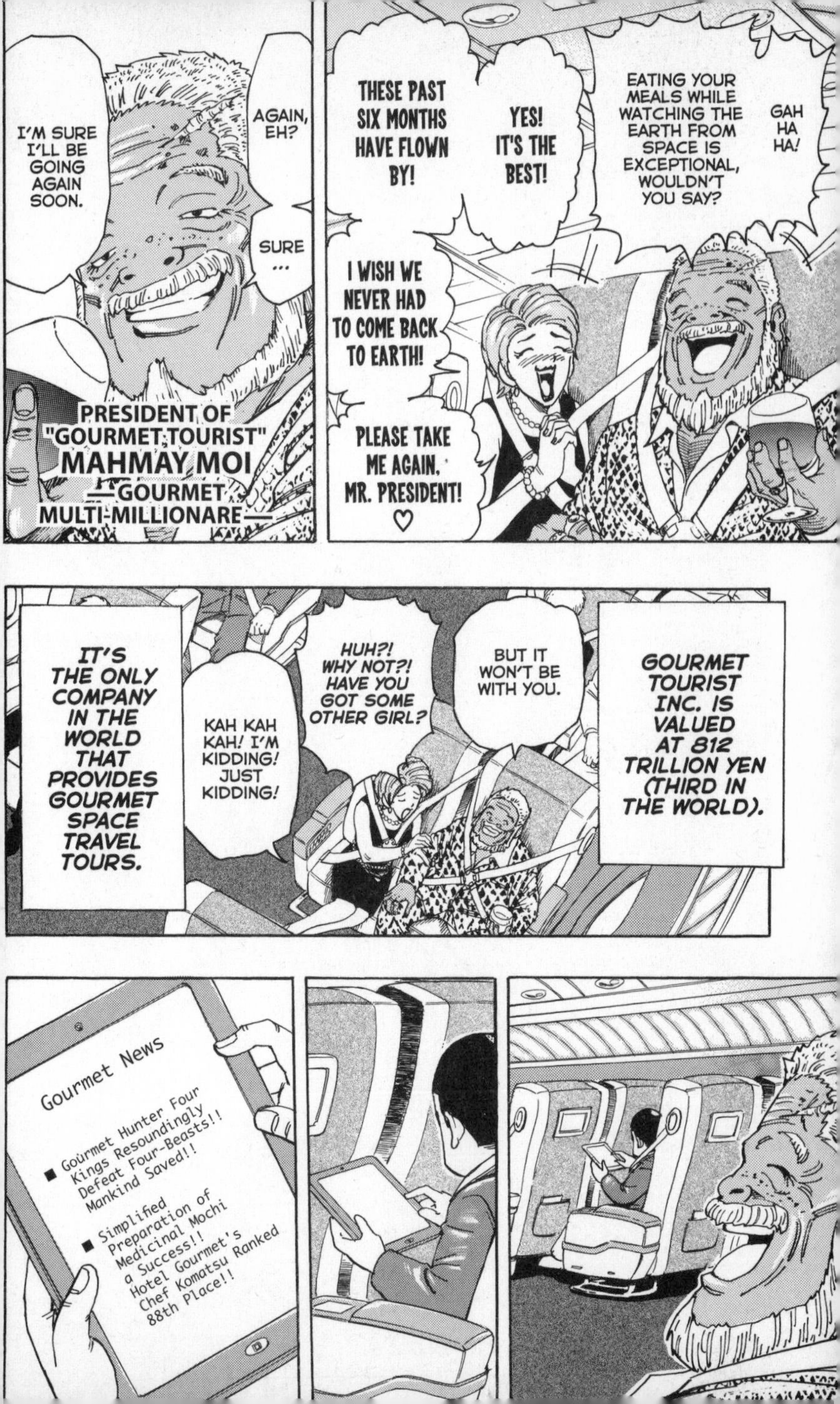
GAH HA HA!
EATING YOUR MEALS WHILE WATCHING THE EARTH FROM SPACE IS EXCEPTIONAL, WOULDN'T YOU SAY?
YES! IT'S THE BEST!
THESE PAST SIX MONTHS HAVE FLOWN BY!
I WISH WE NEVER HAD TO COME BACK TO EARTH!
PLEASE TAKE ME AGAIN, MR. PRESIDENT! ♡
AGAIN, EH?
I'M SURE I'LL BE GOING AGAIN SOON.
SURE...
PRESIDENT OF "GOURMET TOURIST" MAHMAY MOI —GOURMET MULTI-MILLIONARE—
GOURMET TOURIST INC. IS VALUED AT 812 TRILLION YEN (THIRD IN THE WORLD).
BUT IT WON'T BE WITH YOU.
HUH?! WHY NOT?! HAVE YOU GOT SOME OTHER GIRL?
KAH KAH KAH! I'M KIDDING! JUST KIDDING!
IT'S THE ONLY COMPANY IN THE WORLD THAT PROVIDES GOURMET SPACE TRAVEL TOURS.
Gourmet News
■ Gourmet Hunter Four Kings Resoundingly Defeat Four-Beasts!! Mankind Saved!!
■ Simplified Preparation of Medicinal Mochi a Success!! Hotel Gourmet's Chef Komatsu Ranked 88th Place!!

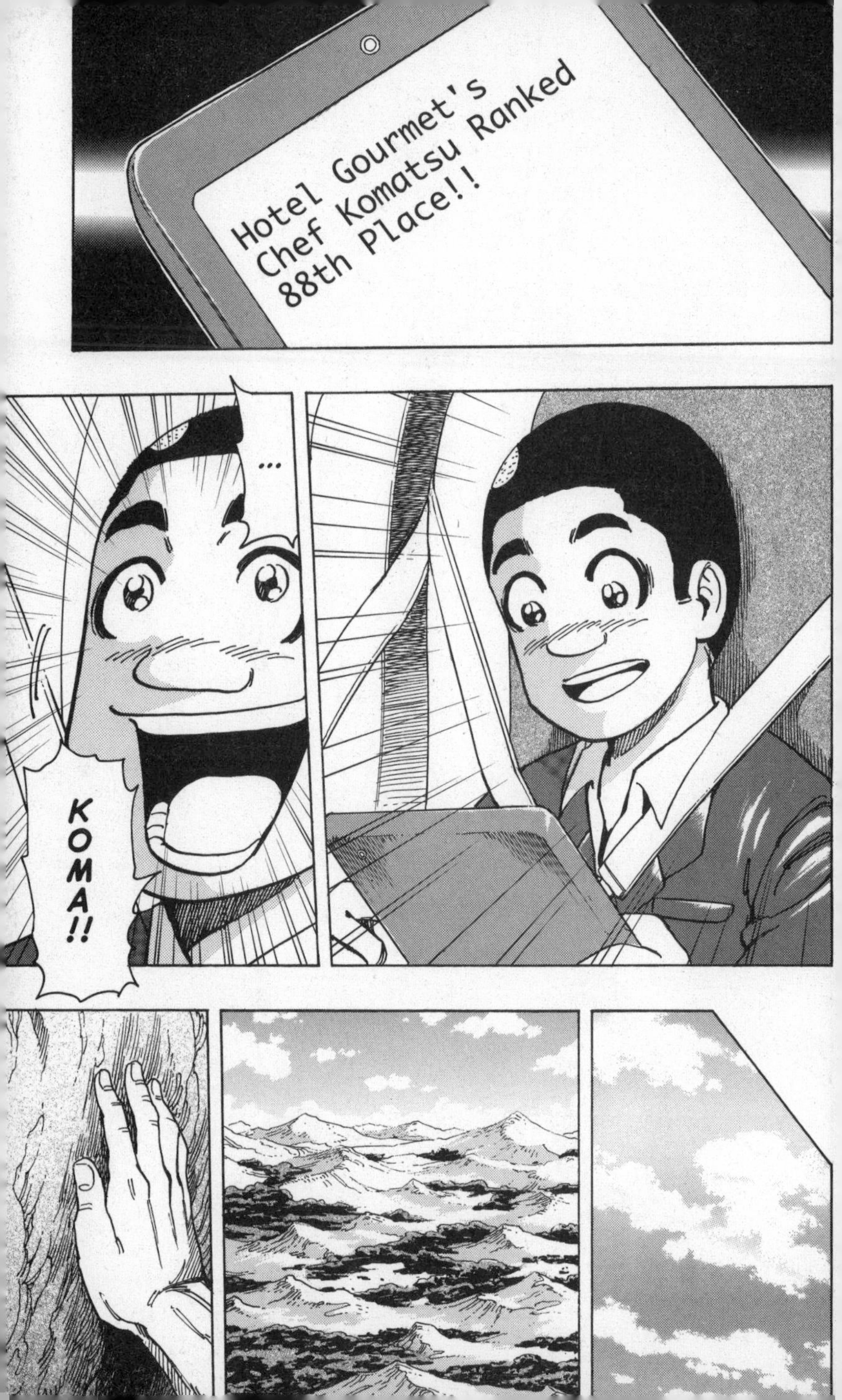
Hotel Gourmet's Chef Komatsu Ranked 88th Place!!
...
KOMA!!

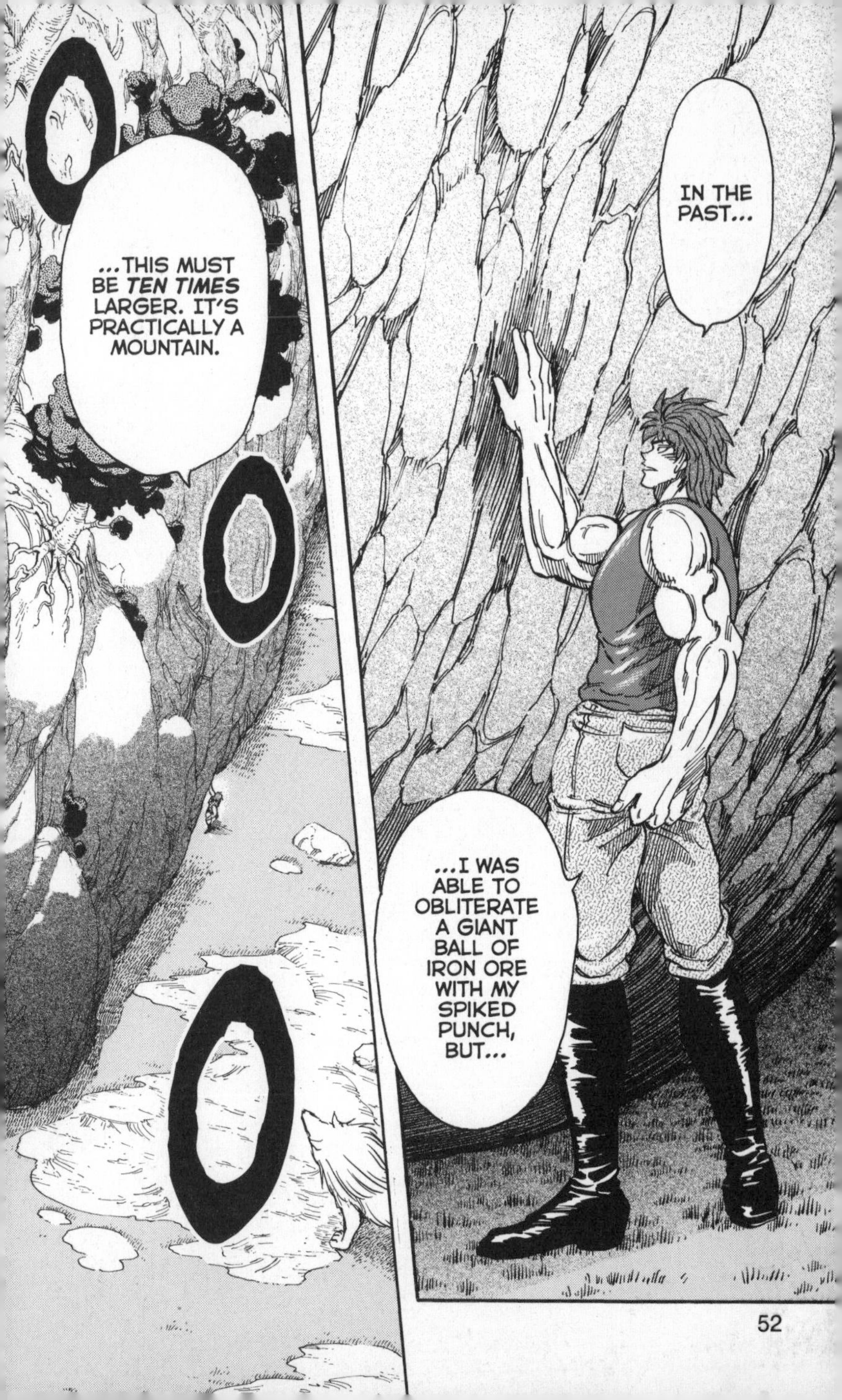
IN THE PAST...
...I WAS ABLE TO OBLITERATE A GIANT BALL OF IRON ORE WITH MY SPIKED PUNCH, BUT...
...THIS MUST BE *TEN TIMES* LARGER. IT'S PRACTICALLY A MOUNTAIN.

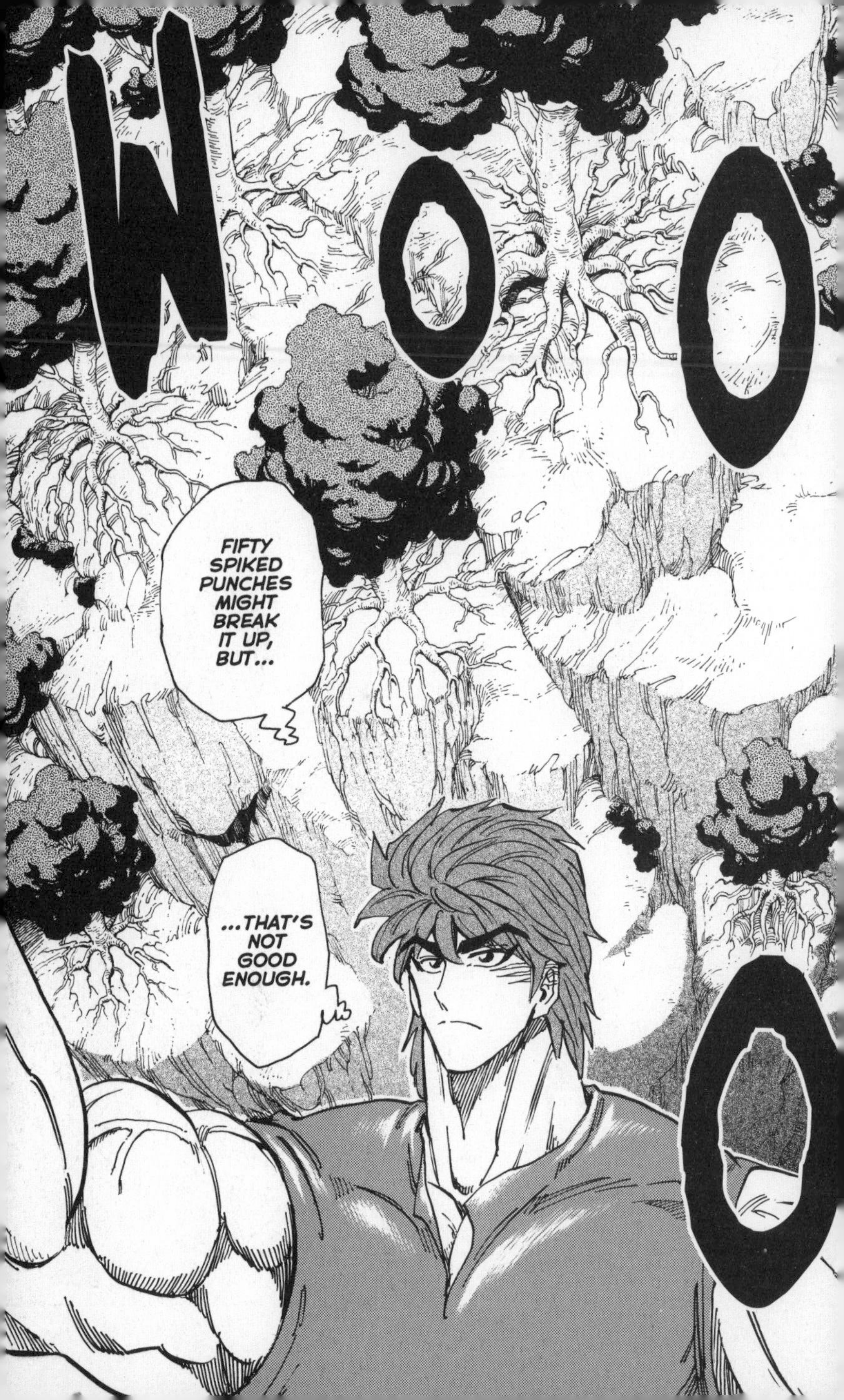
WOOO
FIFTY SPIKED PUNCHES MIGHT BREAK IT UP, BUT...
...THAT'S NOT GOOD ENOUGH.

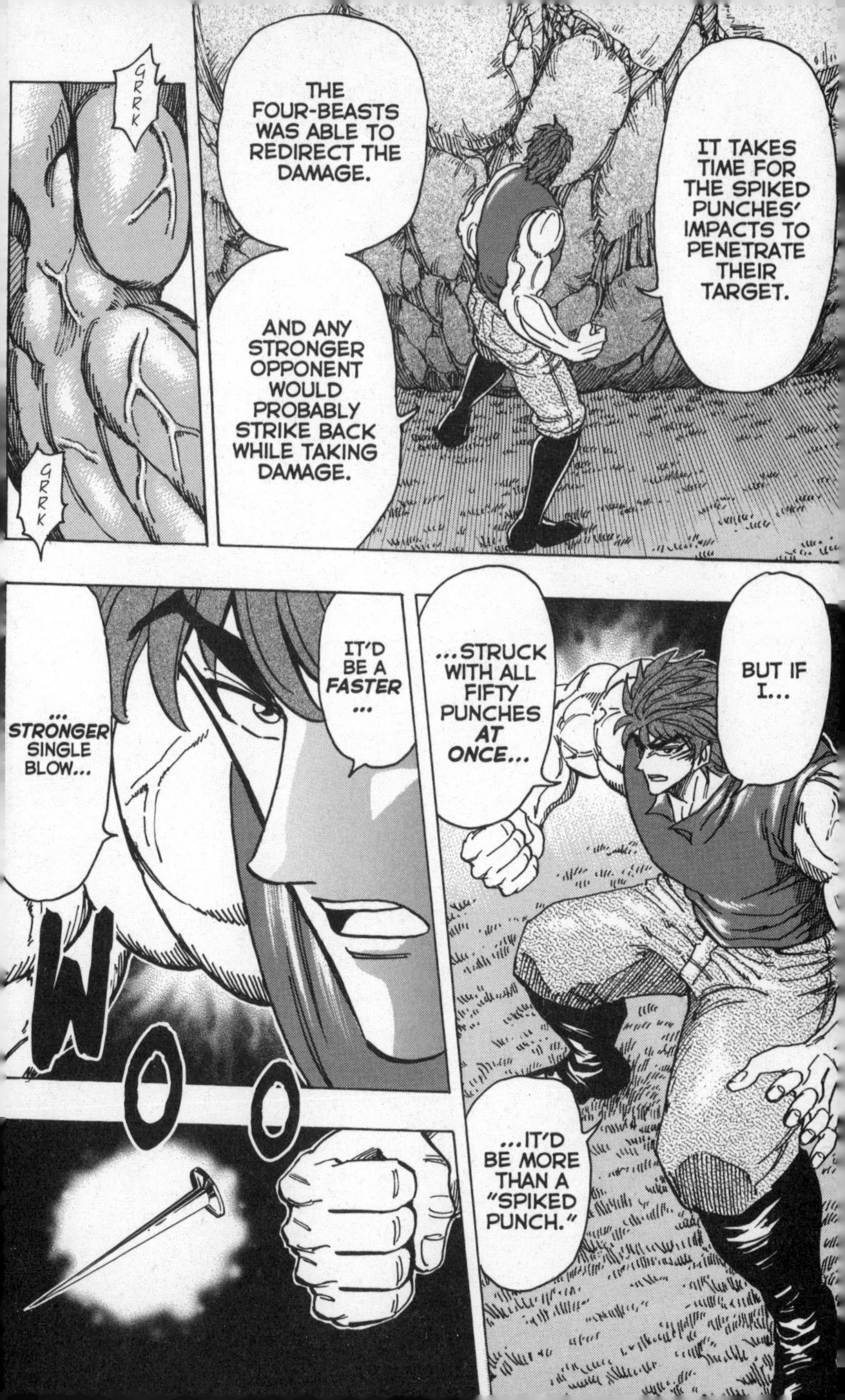
IT TAKES TIME FOR THE SPIKED PUNCHES' IMPACTS TO PENETRATE THEIR TARGET.
THE FOUR-BEASTS WAS ABLE TO REDIRECT THE DAMAGE.
AND ANY STRONGER OPPONENT WOULD PROBABLY STRIKE BACK WHILE TAKING DAMAGE.
GRRK
GRRK
BUT IF I...
...STRUCK WITH ALL FIFTY PUNCHES AT ONCE...
...IT'D BE MORE THAN A "SPIKED PUNCH."
IT'D BE A FASTER...
...STRONGER SINGLE BLOW...
WOOO

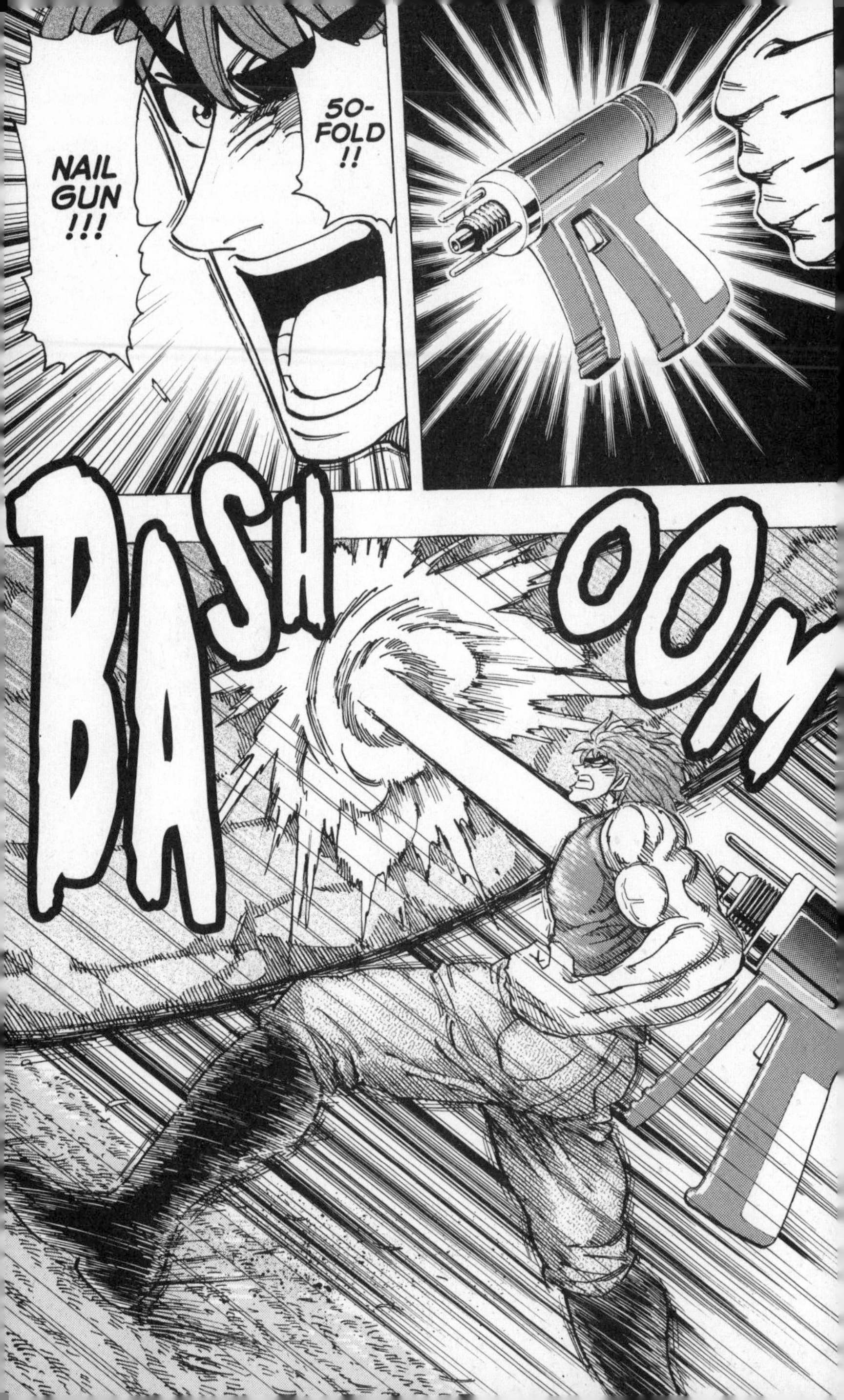
50-FOLD!!
NAIL GUN!!!
BASHOOM

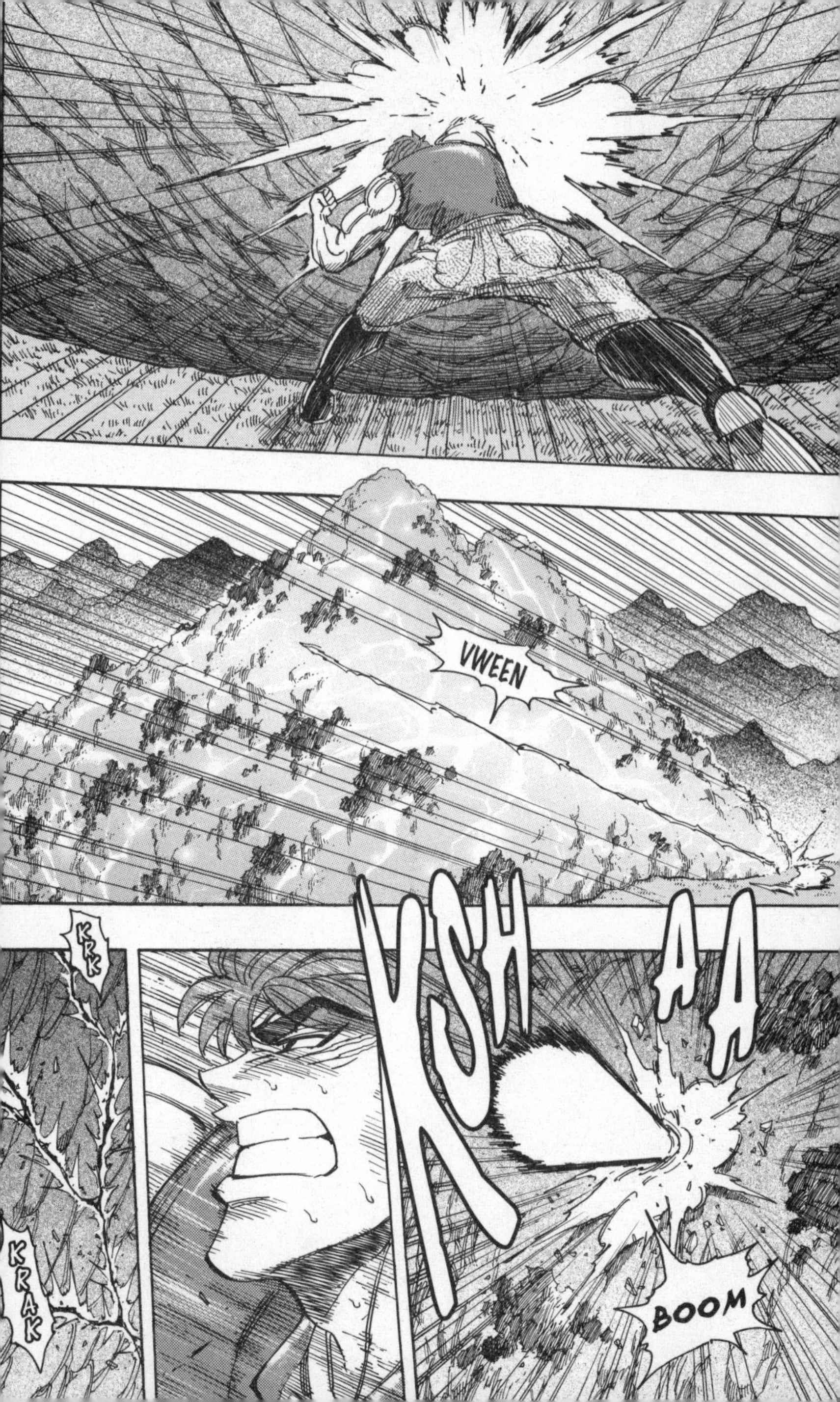
VWEEN
KSH
AA
BOOM
KRK
KRAK

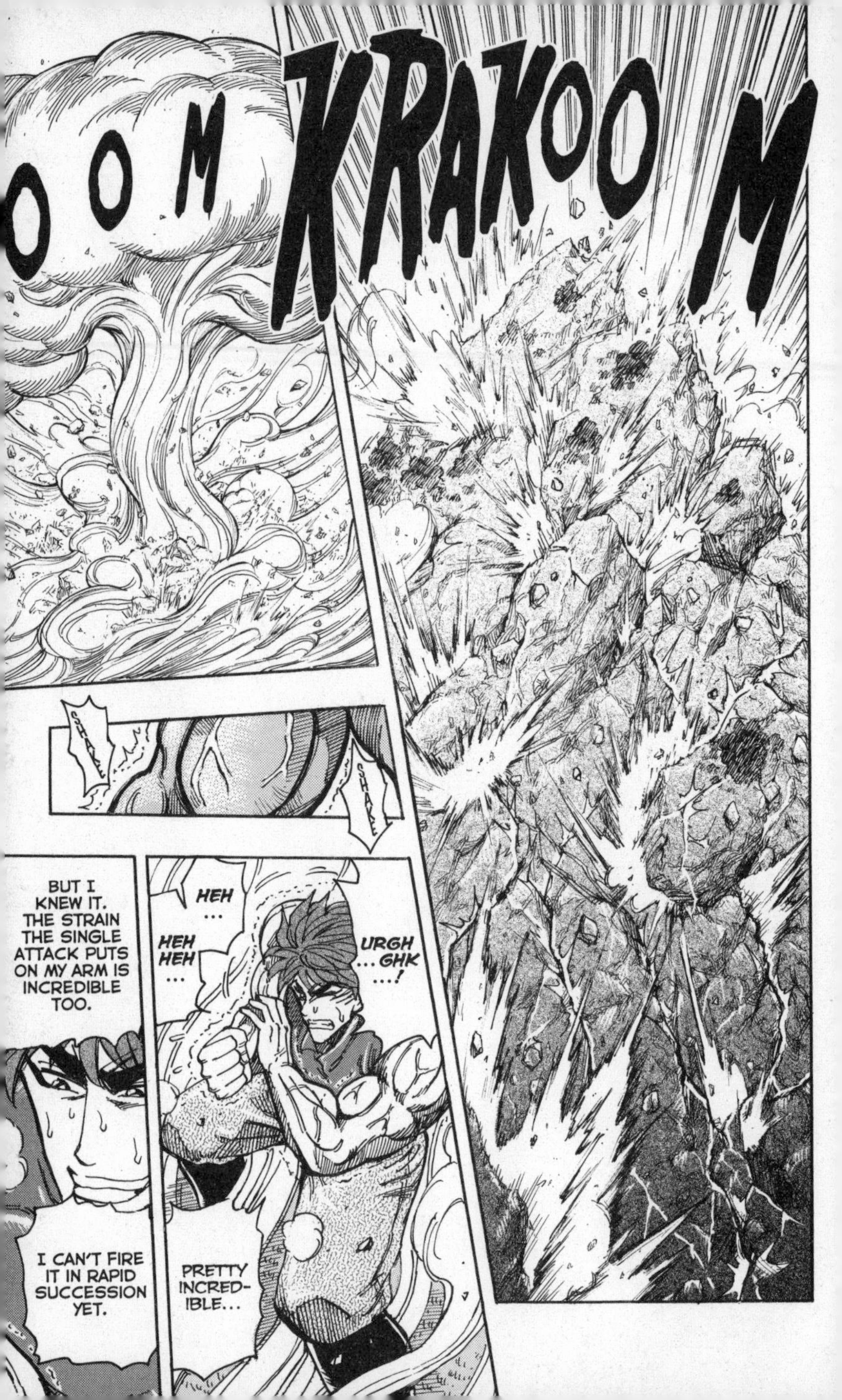
KRAKOOM
OOM
SHAKE
SHAKE
URGH ...GHK ...!
HEH ...
HEH HEH ...
PRETTY INCRED-IBLE...
BUT I KNEW IT. THE STRAIN THE SINGLE ATTACK PUTS ON MY ARM IS INCREDIBLE TOO.
I CAN'T FIRE IT IN RAPID SUCCESSION YET.

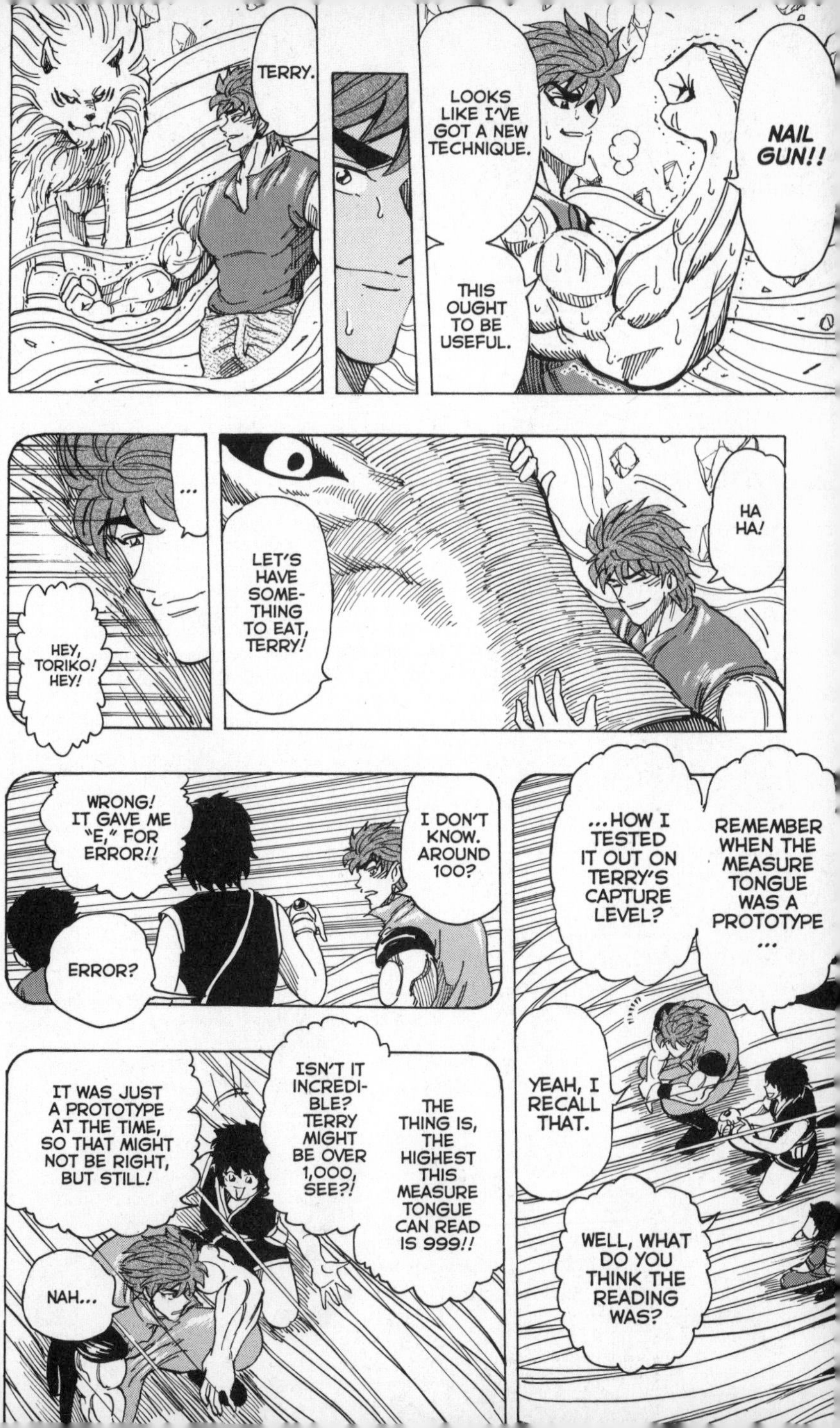
NAIL GUN!!
LOOKS LIKE I'VE GOT A NEW TECHNIQUE.
THIS OUGHT TO BE USEFUL.
TERRY.
HA HA!
LET'S HAVE SOME-THING TO EAT, TERRY!
...
HEY, TORIKO! HEY!
REMEMBER WHEN THE MEASURE TONGUE WAS A PROTOTYPE ...
...HOW I TESTED IT OUT ON TERRY'S CAPTURE LEVEL?
YEAH, I RECALL THAT.
WELL, WHAT DO YOU THINK THE READING WAS?
I DON'T KNOW. AROUND 100?
WRONG! IT GAVE ME "E," FOR ERROR!!
ERROR?
ISN'T IT INCREDI-BLE? TERRY MIGHT BE OVER 1,000, SEE?!
THE THING IS, THE HIGHEST THIS MEASURE TONGUE CAN READ IS 999!!
IT WAS JUST A PROTOTYPE AT THE TIME, SO THAT MIGHT NOT BE RIGHT, BUT STILL!
NAH...

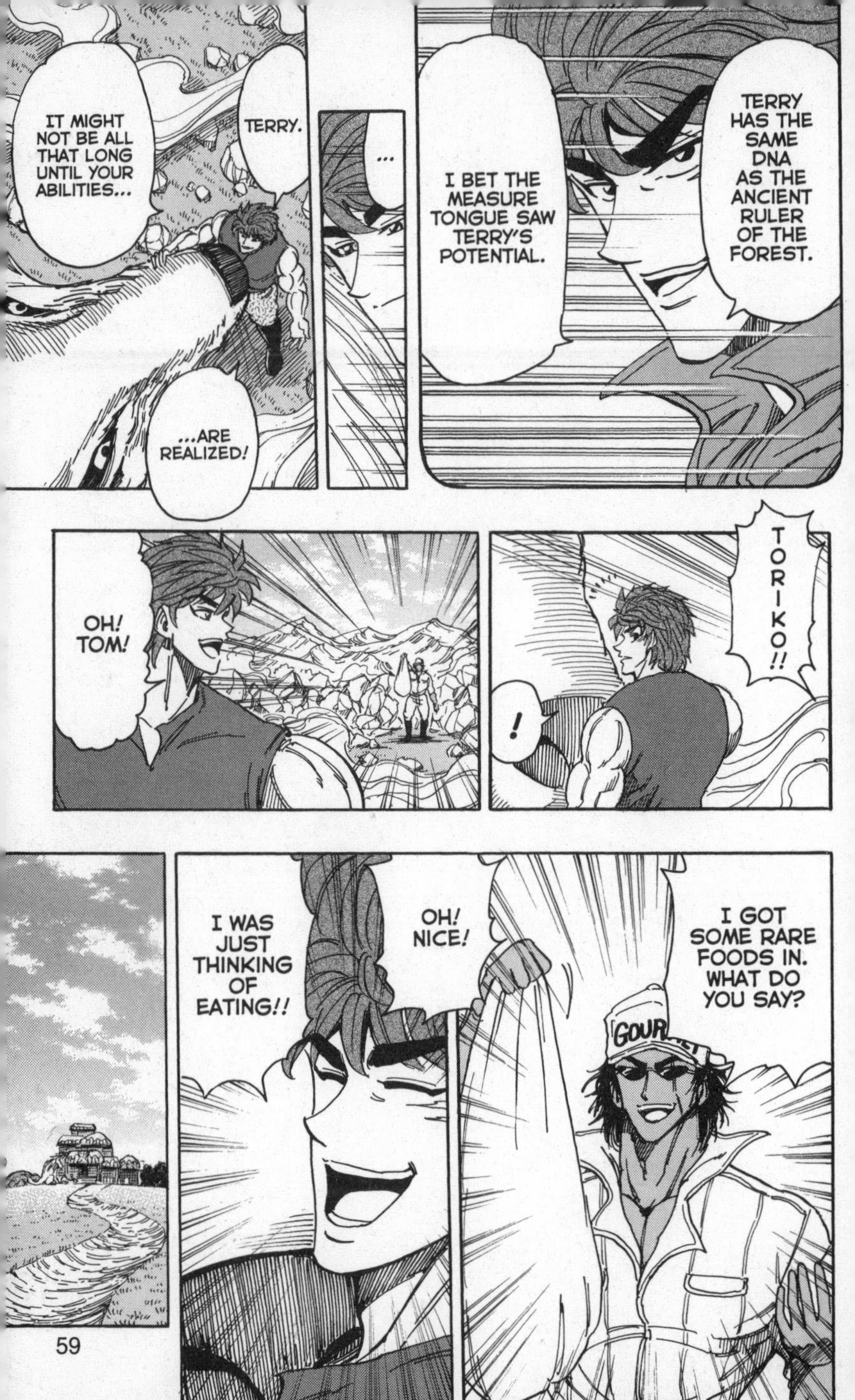
TERRY HAS THE SAME DNA AS THE ANCIENT RULER OF THE FOREST.
I BET THE MEASURE TONGUE SAW TERRY'S POTENTIAL.
...
TERRY.
IT MIGHT NOT BE ALL THAT LONG UNTIL YOUR ABILITIES...
...ARE REALIZED!
TORIKO!!
!
OH! TOM!
I GOT SOME RARE FOODS IN. WHAT DO YOU SAY?
GOUR
OH! NICE!
I WAS JUST THINKING OF EATING!!

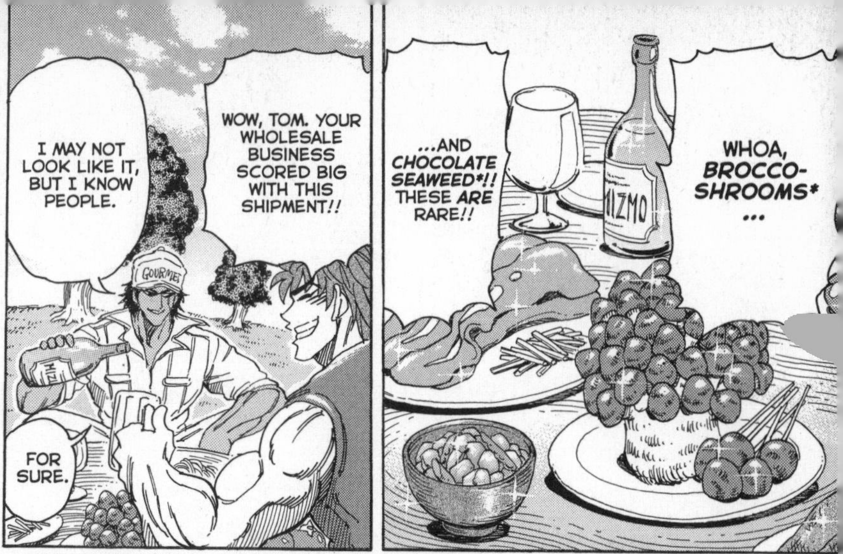
WHOA, BROCCO-SHROOMS* ...
...AND CHOCOLATE SEAWEED*!! THESE ARE RARE!!
MIZMO
WOW, TOM. YOUR WHOLESALE BUSINESS SCORED BIG WITH THIS SHIPMENT!!
I MAY NOT LOOK LIKE IT, BUT I KNOW PEOPLE.
GOURMET
FOR SURE.

*BROCCO-SHROOMS SUBMITTED BY IKKO SAKAKIBARA FROM MIE!

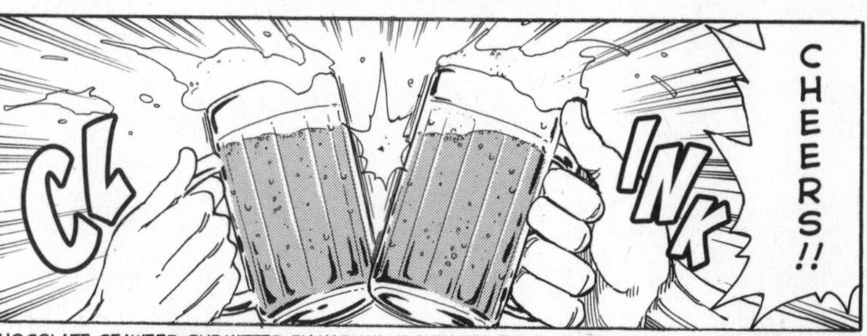
CHEERS!!
CL
INK

*CHOCOLATE SEAWEED SUBMITTED BY HARUMI YOSHIMOTO FROM HIROSHIMA!

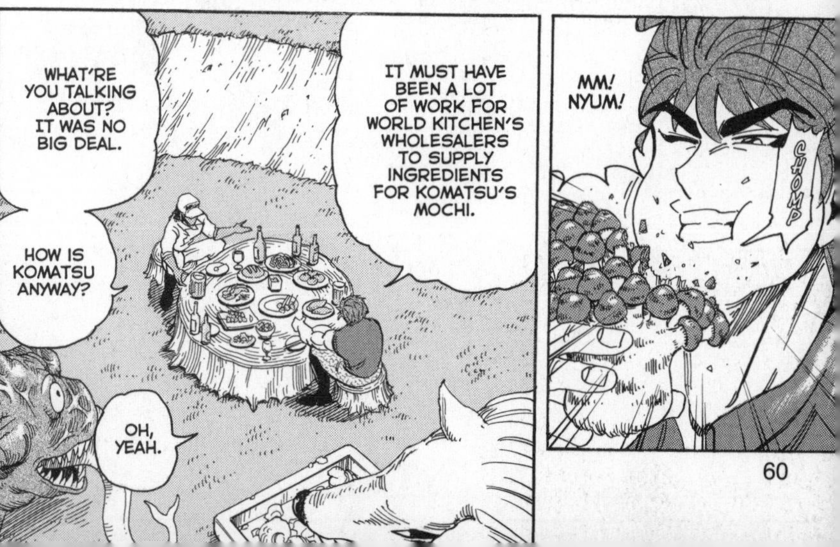
MM! NYUM!
CHOMP
IT MUST HAVE BEEN A LOT OF WORK FOR WORLD KITCHEN'S WHOLESALERS TO SUPPLY INGREDIENTS FOR KOMATSU'S MOCHI.
WHAT'RE YOU TALKING ABOUT? IT WAS NO BIG DEAL.
HOW IS KOMATSU ANYWAY?
OH, YEAH.

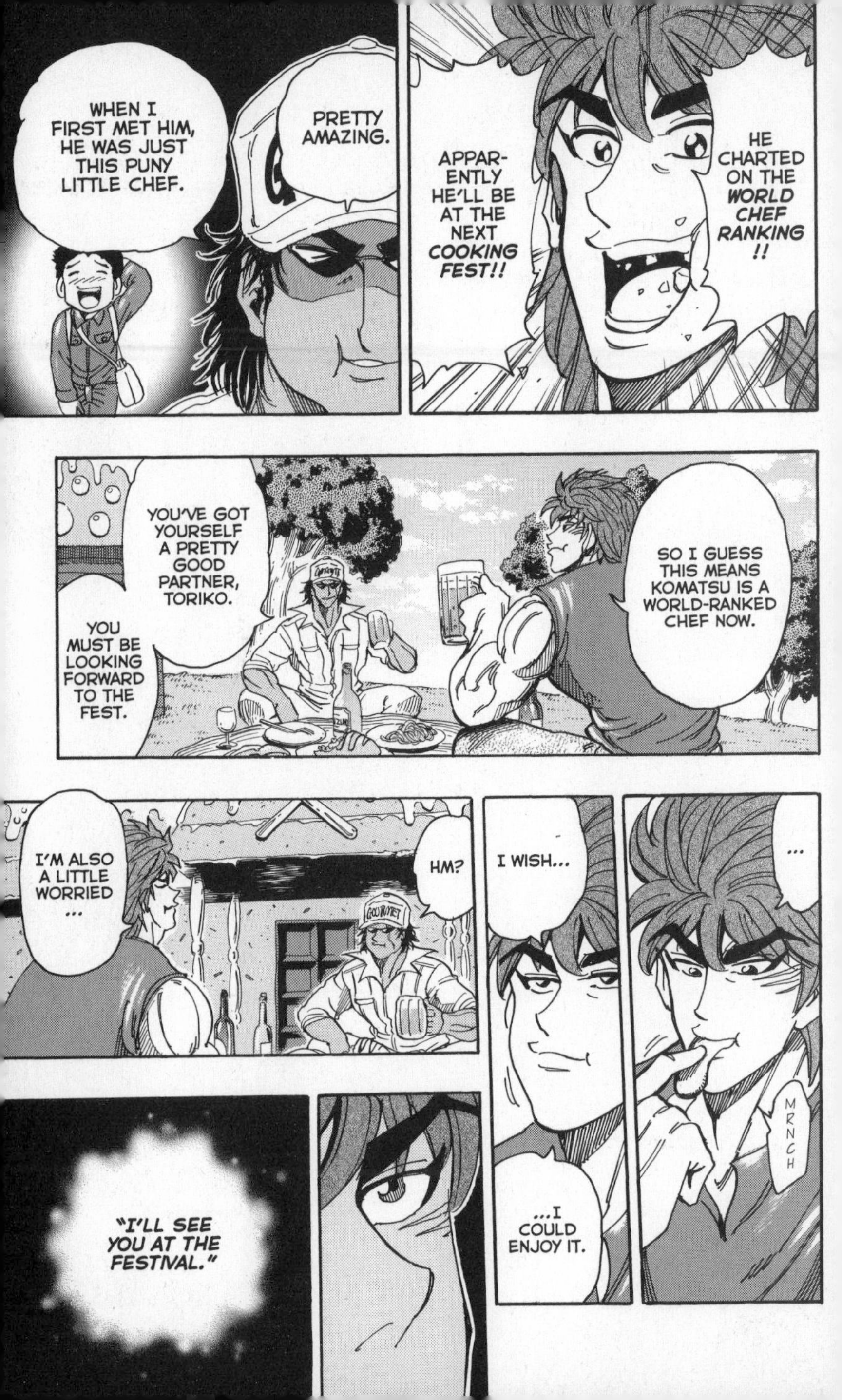
HE CHARTED ON THE WORLD CHEF RANKING !!
APPARENTLY HE'LL BE AT THE NEXT COOKING FEST!!
PRETTY AMAZING.
WHEN I FIRST MET HIM, HE WAS JUST THIS PUNY LITTLE CHEF.
SO I GUESS THIS MEANS KOMATSU IS A WORLD-RANKED CHEF NOW.
YOU'VE GOT YOURSELF A PRETTY GOOD PARTNER, TORIKO.
YOU MUST BE LOOKING FORWARD TO THE FEST.
...
MRNCH
I WISH...
...I COULD ENJOY IT.
I'M ALSO A LITTLE WORRIED ...
HM?
"I'LL SEE YOU AT THE FESTIVAL."

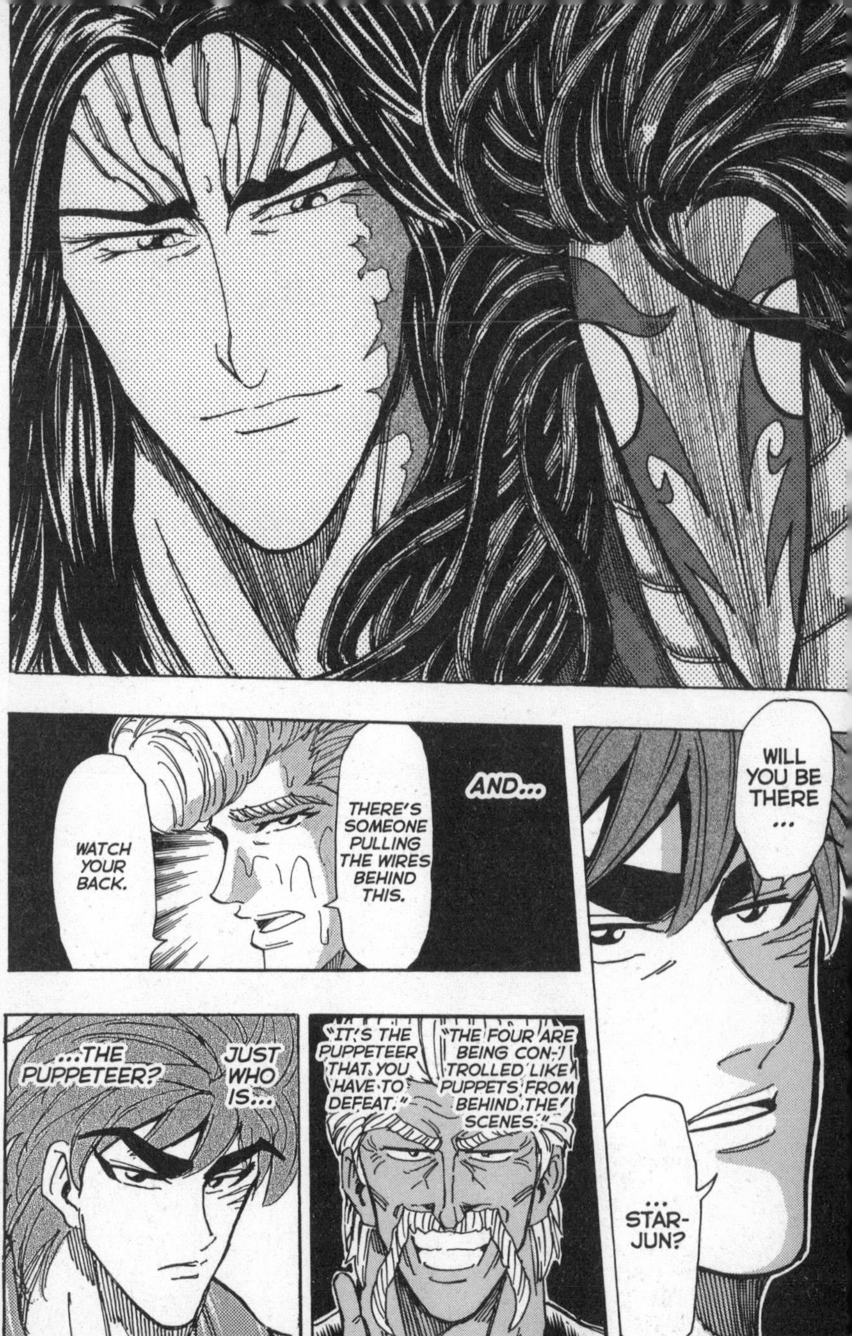
WILL YOU BE THERE ...
... STAR-JUN?
WATCH YOUR BACK.
THERE'S SOMEONE PULLING THE WIRES BEHIND THIS.
AND...
"THE FOUR ARE BEING CON-TROLLED LIKE PUPPETS FROM BEHIND THE SCENES."
"IT'S THE PUPPETEER THAT YOU HAVE TO DEFEAT."
JUST WHO IS...
...THE PUPPETEER?

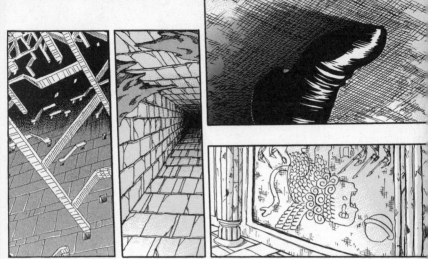

GOURMET PYRAMID

OOOM

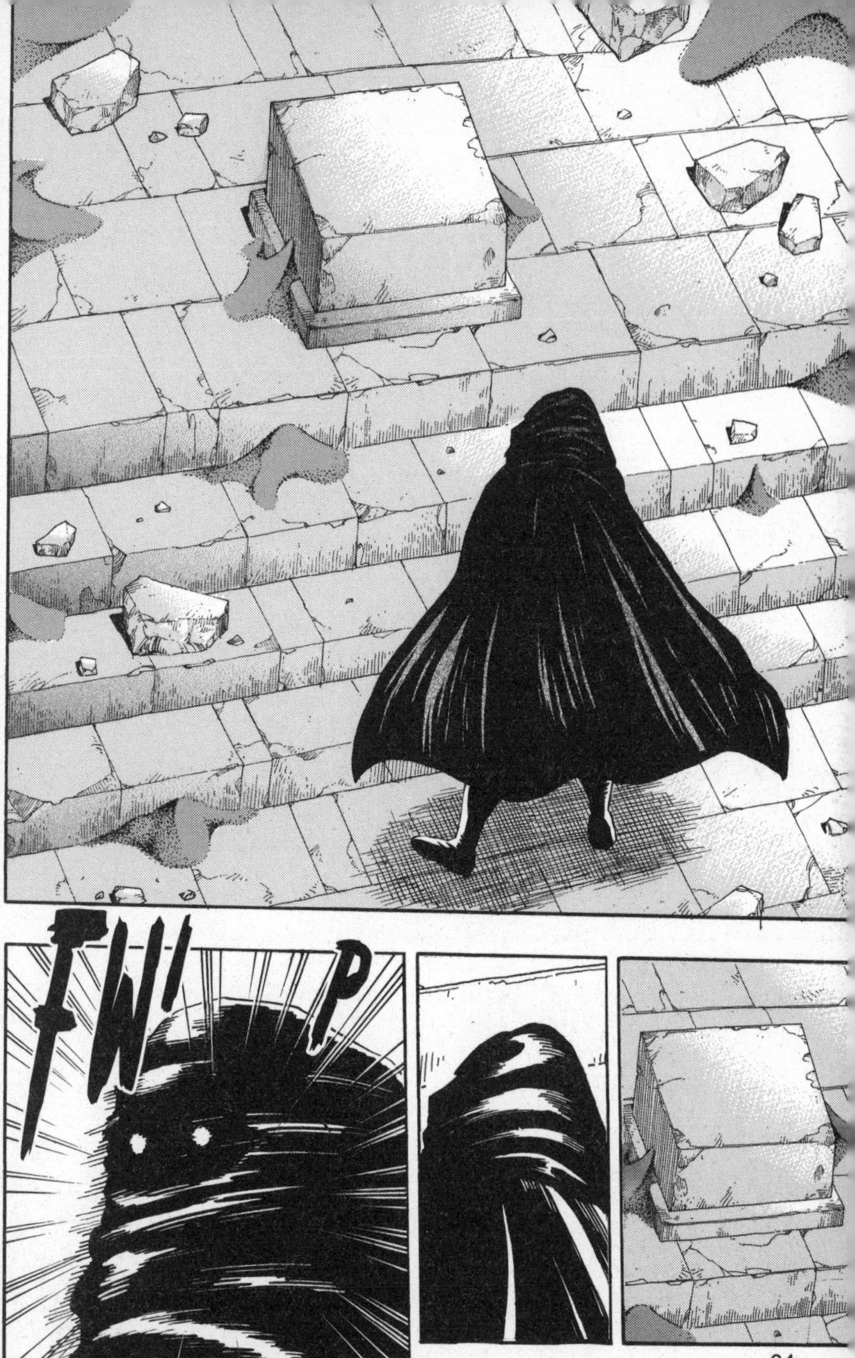
FWIP

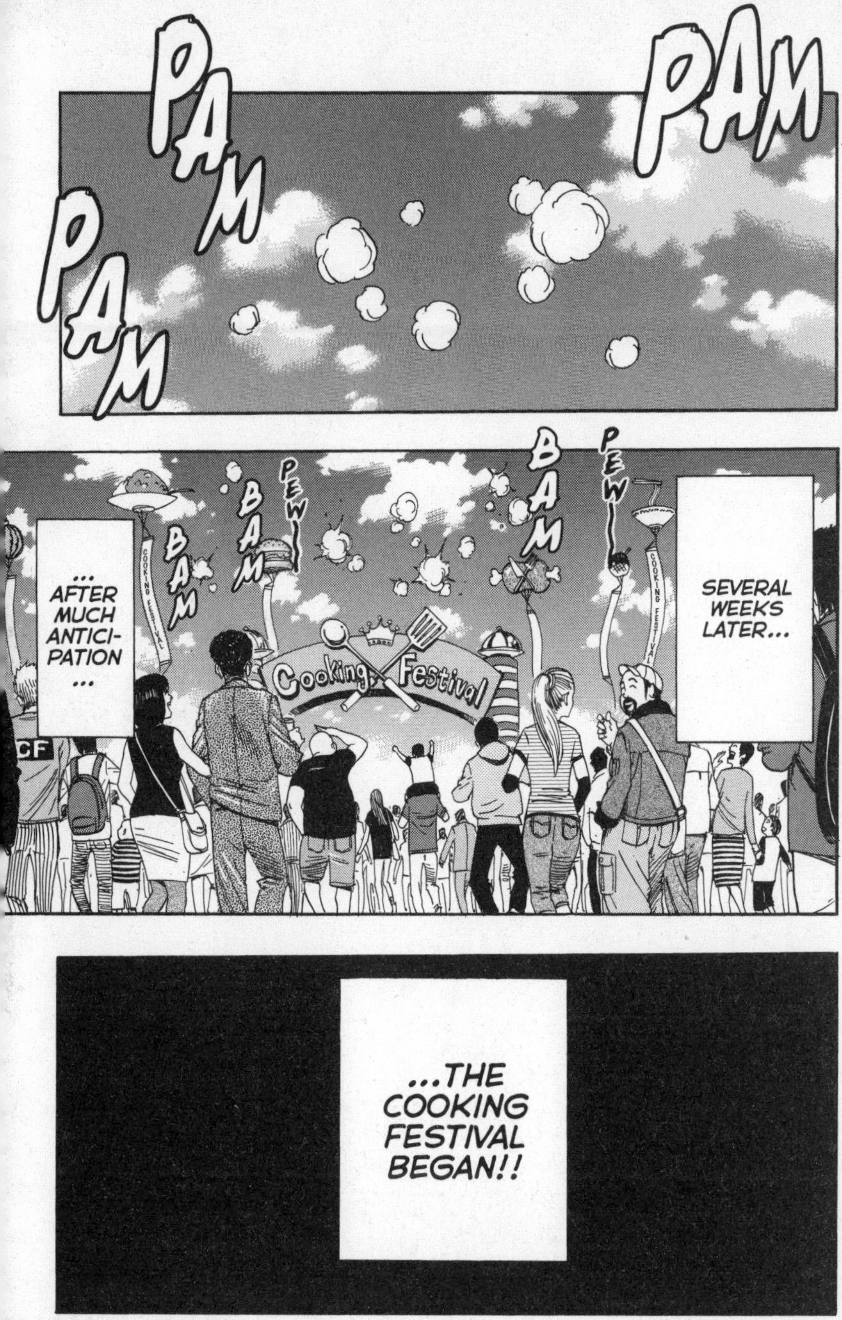
PAM
PAM
PAM
SEVERAL WEEKS LATER...
PEW!
BAM
PEW!
BAM
BAM
COOKING FESTIVAL
COOKING FESTIVAL
Cooking Festival
... AFTER MUCH ANTICI-PATION ...
CF
...THE COOKING FESTIVAL BEGAN!!

TORIKO

GOURMET CHECKLIST

Vol. 243

MELON EGG
(EGG)

CAPTURE LEVEL: 12
HABITAT: TREACHEROUS MOUNTAIN RANGES
LENGTH: 15 CM
HEIGHT: ---
WEIGHT: 200 G
PRICE: 350,000 YEN

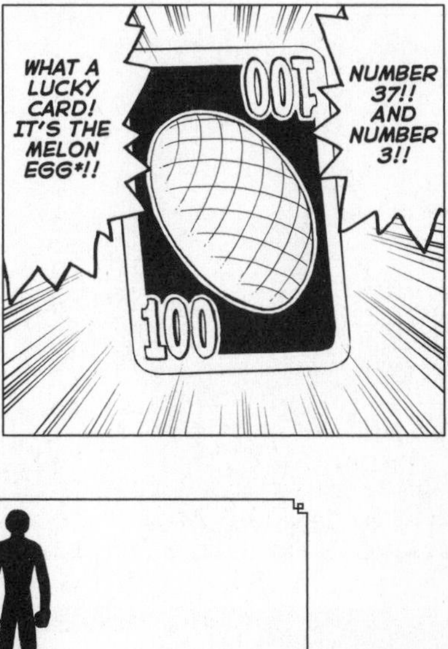

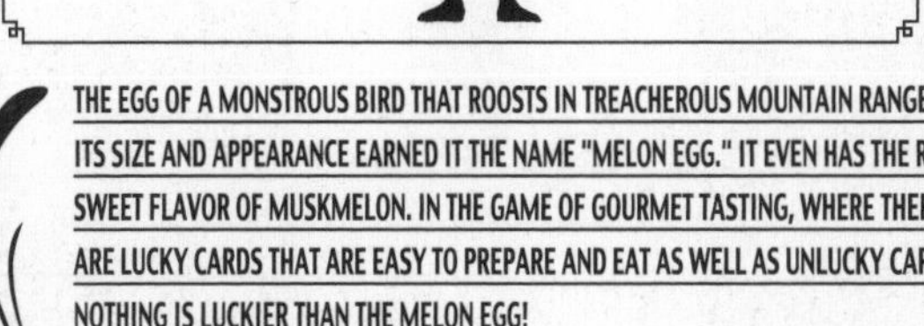

NUMBER 37!! AND NUMBER 3!!
WHAT A LUCKY CARD! IT'S THE MELON EGG*!!
100
100

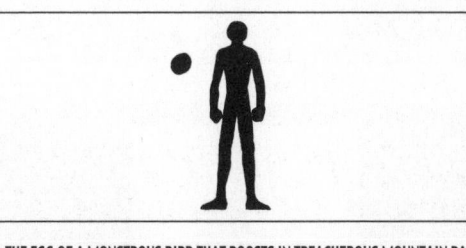

SCALE

THE EGG OF A MONSTROUS BIRD THAT ROOSTS IN TREACHEROUS MOUNTAIN RANGES. ITS SIZE AND APPEARANCE EARNED IT THE NAME "MELON EGG." IT EVEN HAS THE REFINED SWEET FLAVOR OF MUSKMELON. IN THE GAME OF GOURMET TASTING, WHERE THERE ARE LUCKY CARDS THAT ARE EASY TO PREPARE AND EAT AS WELL AS UNLUCKY CARDS, NOTHING IS LUCKIER THAN THE MELON EGG!

GOURMET 211: COOKING FESTIVAL KICKOFF!!

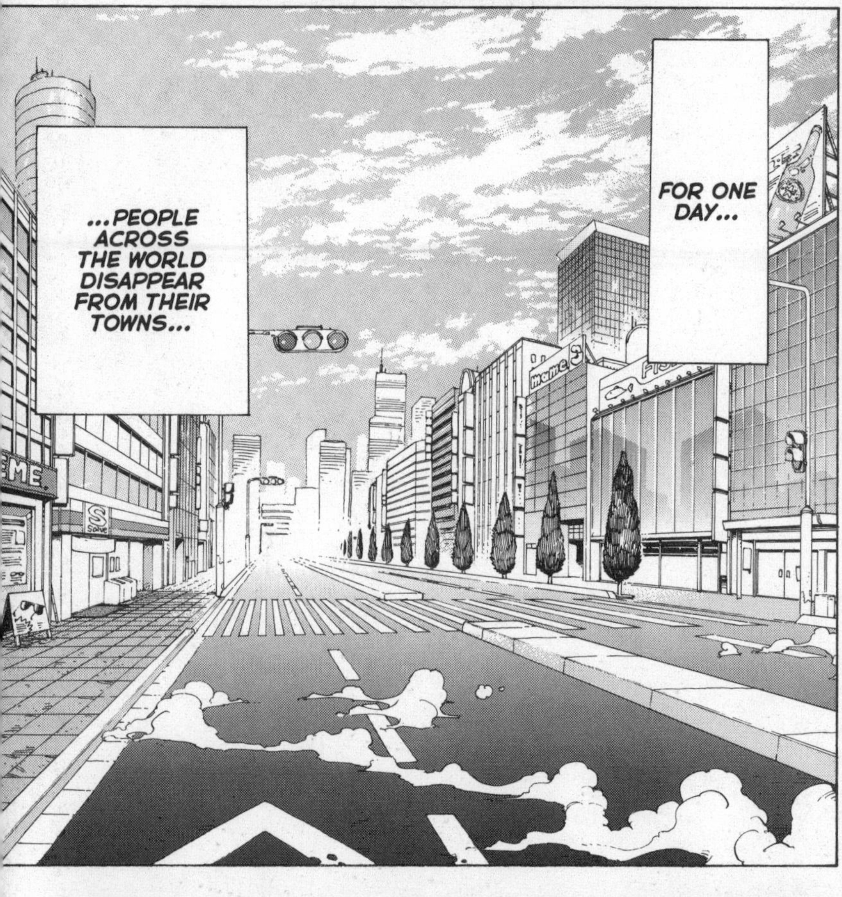
FOR ONE DAY...
...PEOPLE ACROSS THE WORLD DISAPPEAR FROM THEIR TOWNS...
SOLVE
ME

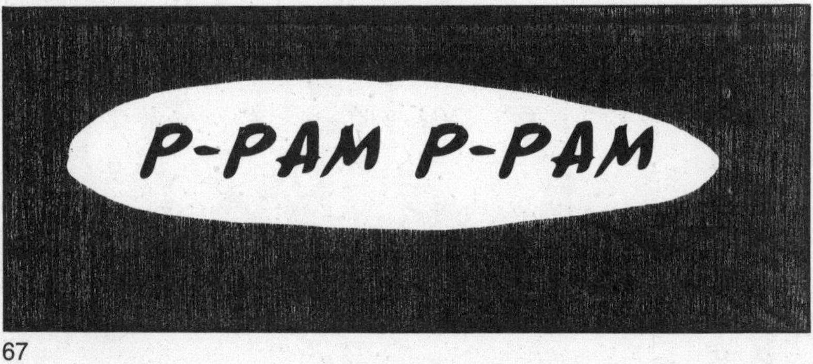
P-PAM P-PAM

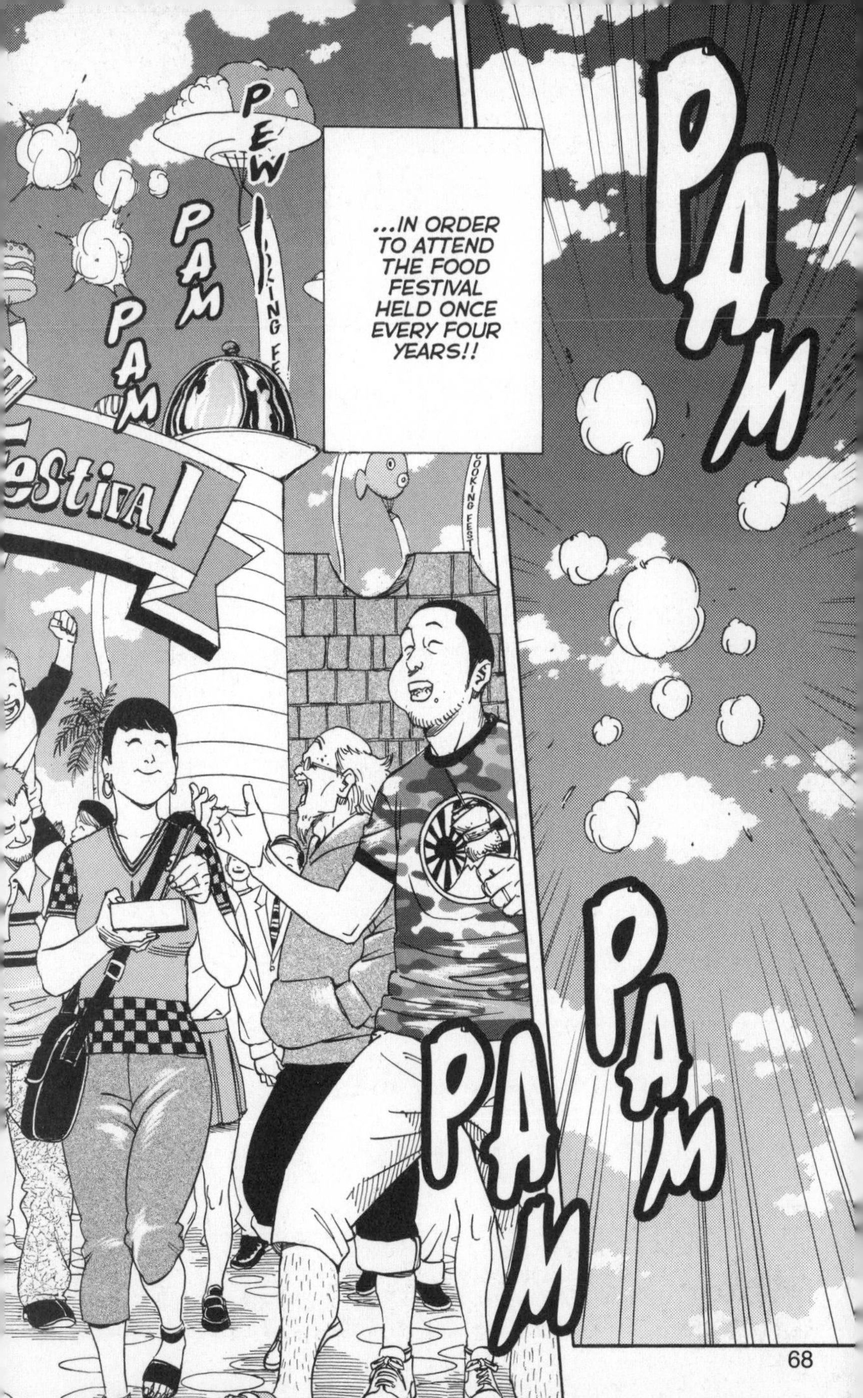
PAM
PAM
PAM
...IN ORDER TO ATTEND THE FOOD FESTIVAL HELD ONCE EVERY FOUR YEARS!!
PEW
PAM
PAM
COOKING FESTI
Festival

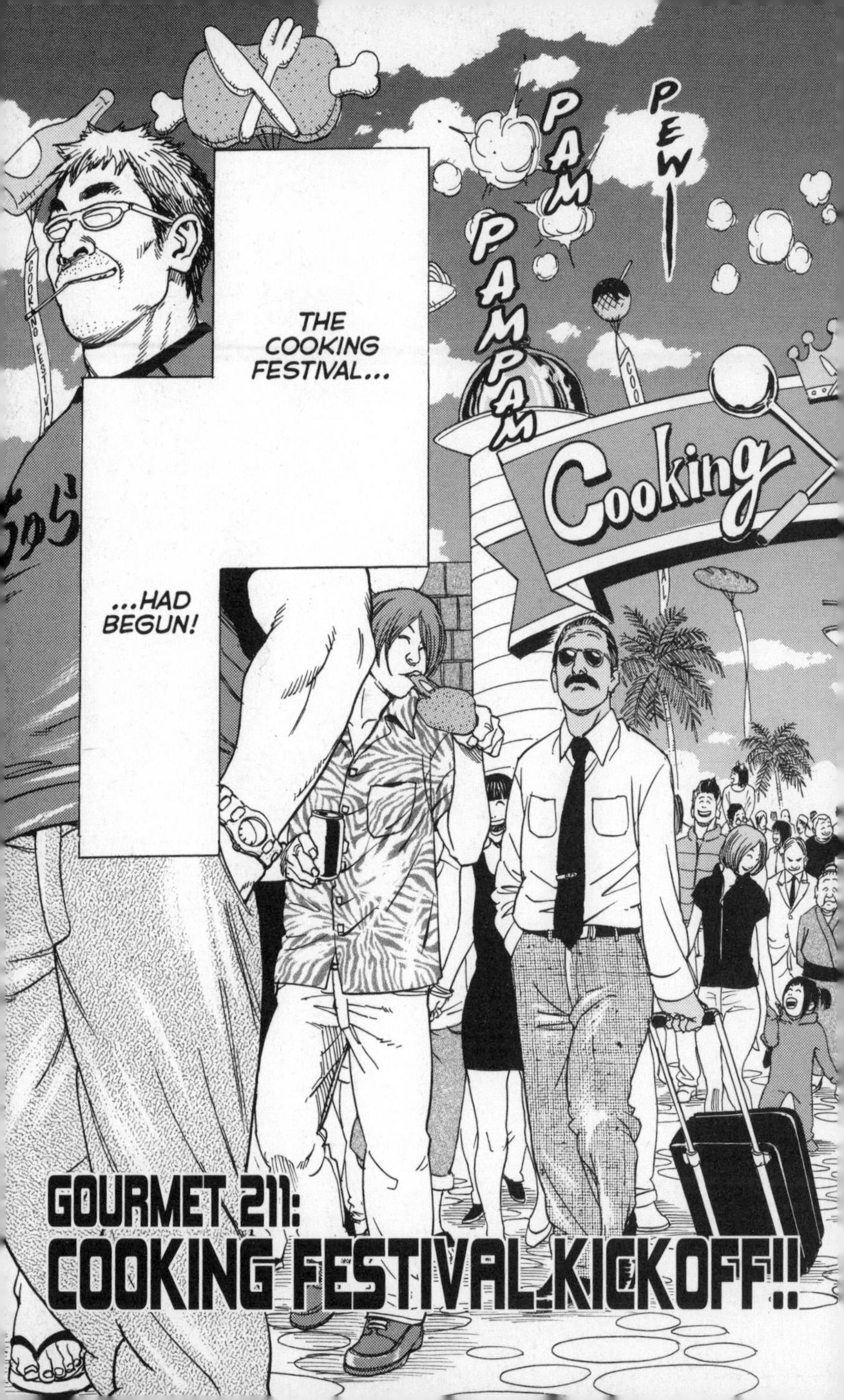
PEW
PAM
PAMPAM
Cooking
THE COOKING FESTIVAL...
...HAD BEGUN!
GOURMET 211:
COOKING FESTIVAL KICKOFF!!

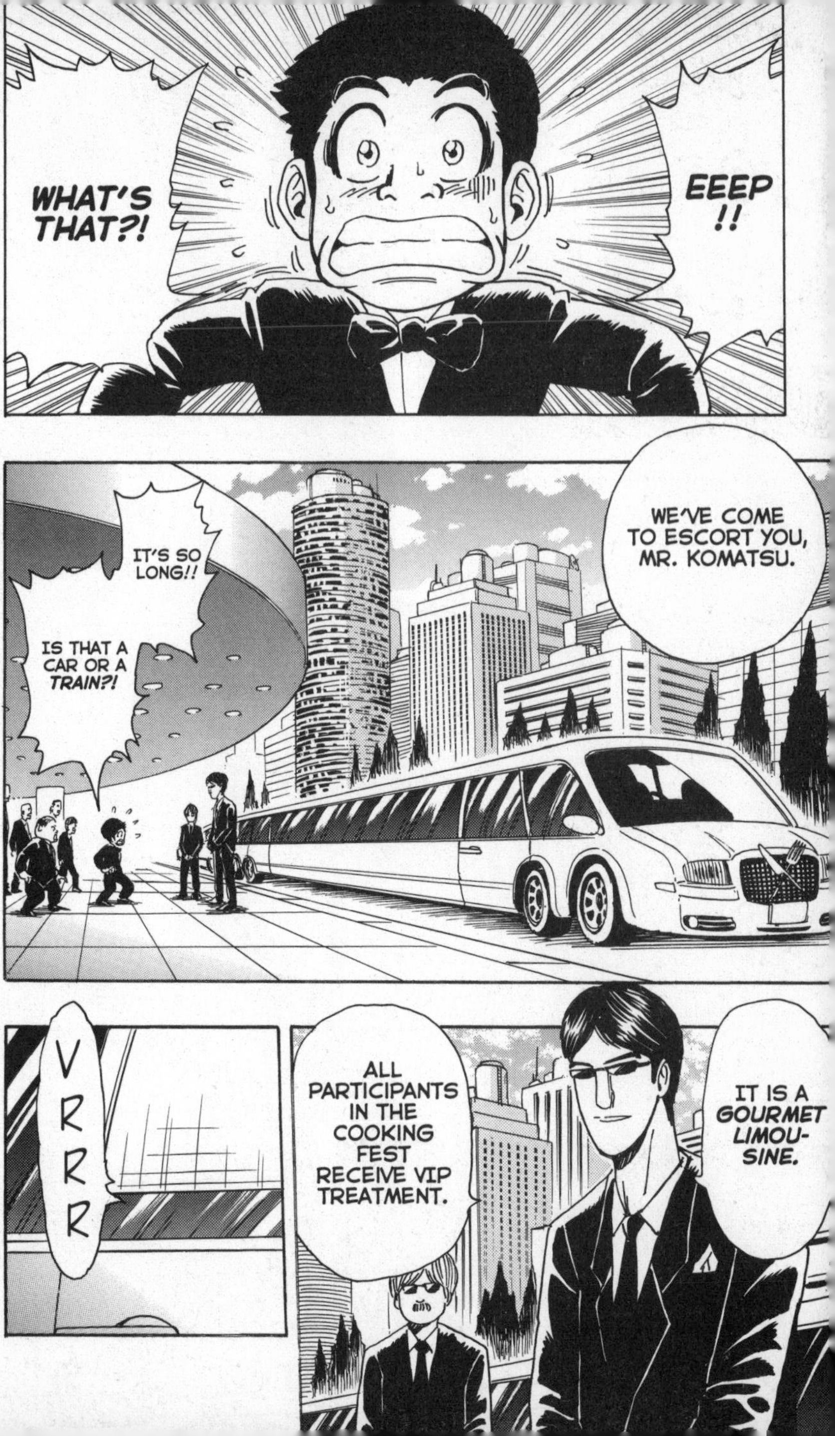
EEEP !!
WHAT'S THAT?!
WE'VE COME TO ESCORT YOU, MR. KOMATSU.
IT'S SO LONG!!
IS THAT A CAR OR A TRAIN?!
IT IS A GOURMET LIMOU-SINE.
ALL PARTICIPANTS IN THE COOKING FEST RECEIVE VIP TREATMENT.
VRRR

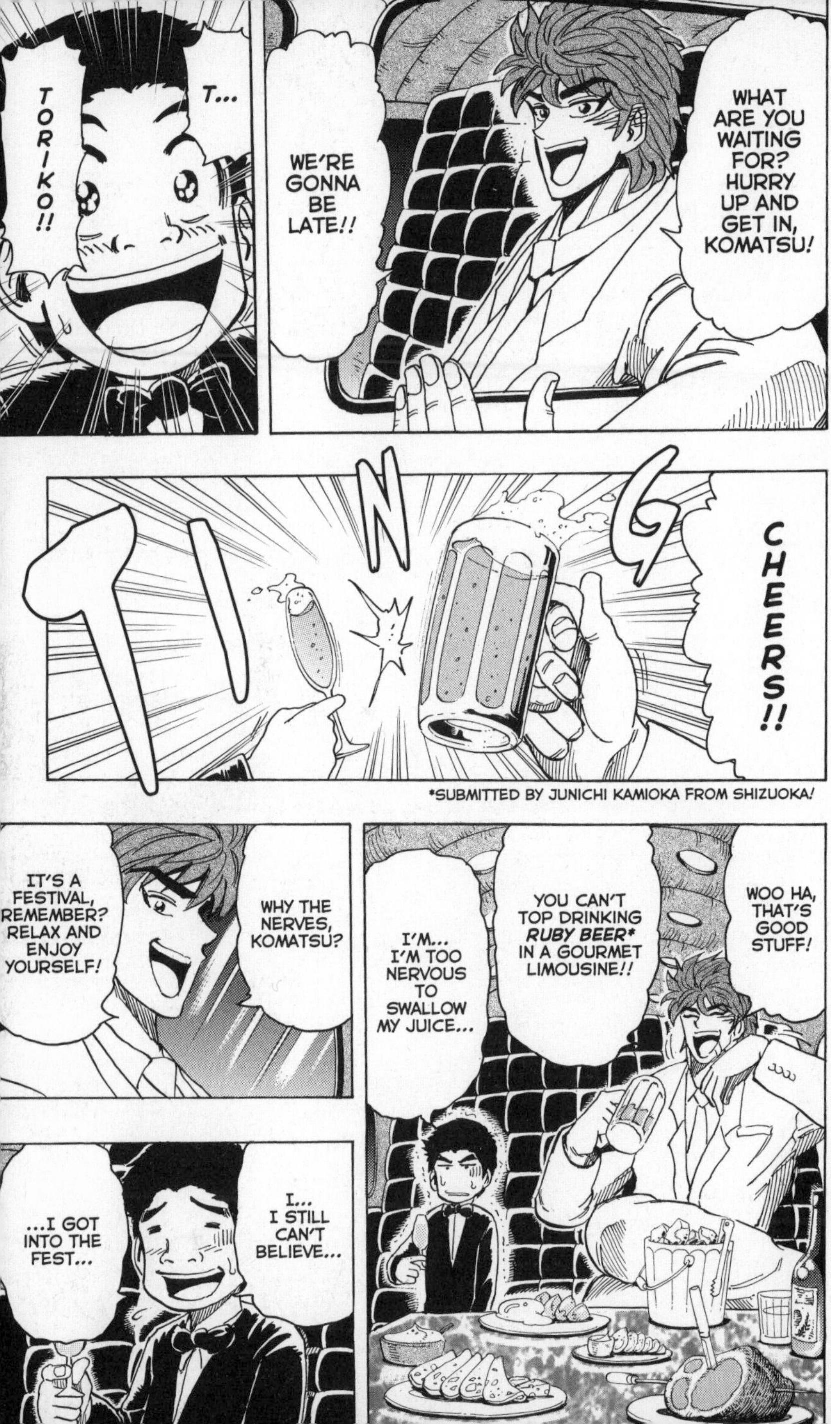
WHAT ARE YOU WAITING FOR? HURRY UP AND GET IN, KOMATSU!
WE'RE GONNA BE LATE!!
T...
TORIKO!!
CHEERS!!
TING
WOO HA, THAT'S GOOD STUFF!
YOU CAN'T TOP DRINKING *RUBY BEER** IN A GOURMET LIMOUSINE!!
I'M... I'M TOO NERVOUS TO SWALLOW MY JUICE...
WHY THE NERVES, KOMATSU?
IT'S A FESTIVAL, REMEMBER? RELAX AND ENJOY YOURSELF!
I... I STILL CAN'T BELIEVE...
...I GOT INTO THE FEST...
*SUBMITTED BY JUNICHI KAMIOKA FROM SHIZUOKA!

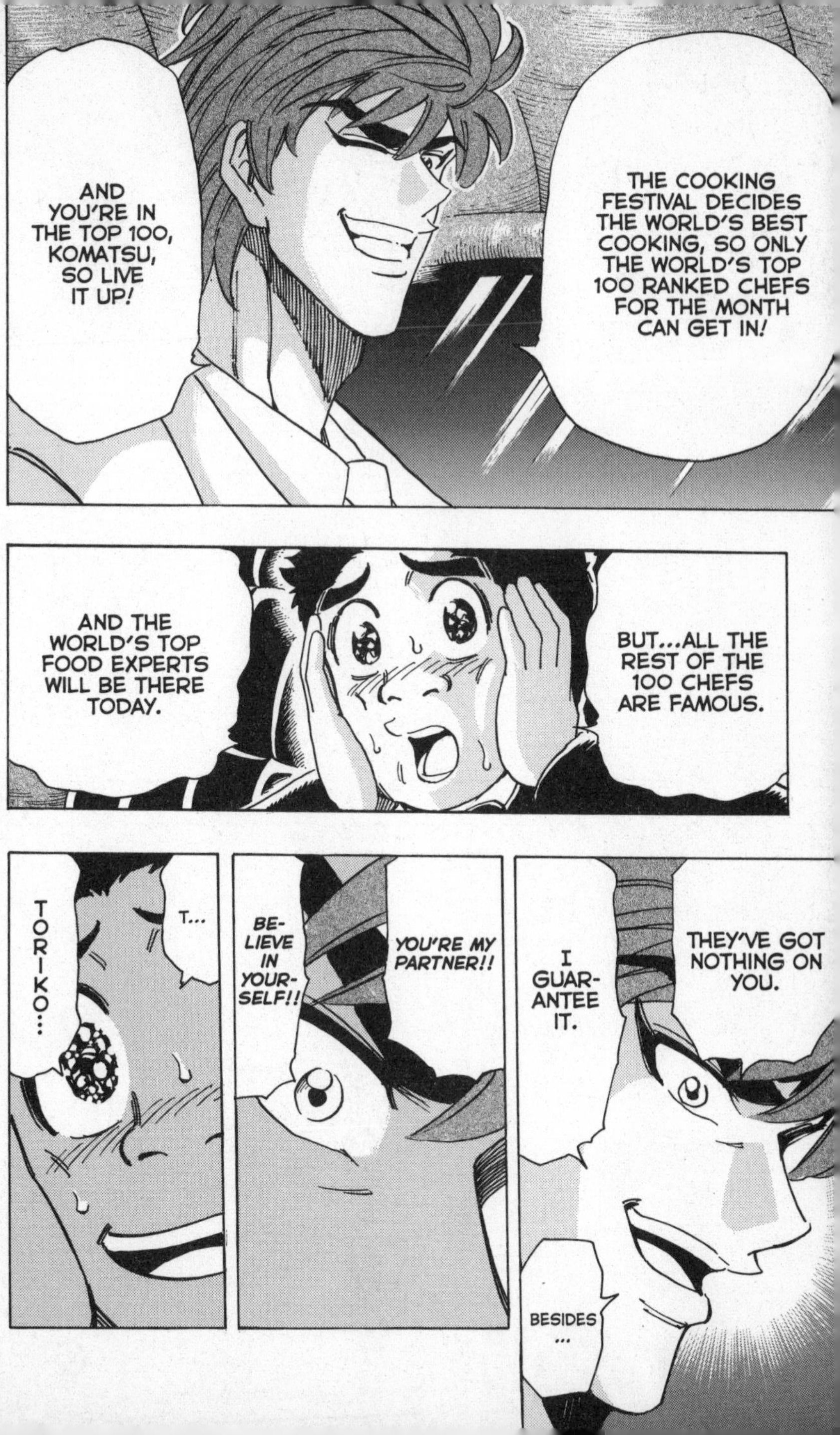
THE COOKING FESTIVAL DECIDES THE WORLD'S BEST COOKING, SO ONLY THE WORLD'S TOP 100 RANKED CHEFS FOR THE MONTH CAN GET IN!
AND YOU'RE IN THE TOP 100, KOMATSU, SO LIVE IT UP!
BUT...ALL THE REST OF THE 100 CHEFS ARE FAMOUS.
AND THE WORLD'S TOP FOOD EXPERTS WILL BE THERE TODAY.
THEY'VE GOT NOTHING ON YOU.
I GUAR-ANTEE IT.
BESIDES...
YOU'RE MY PARTNER!!
BE-LIEVE IN YOUR-SELF!!
T...
TORIKO...

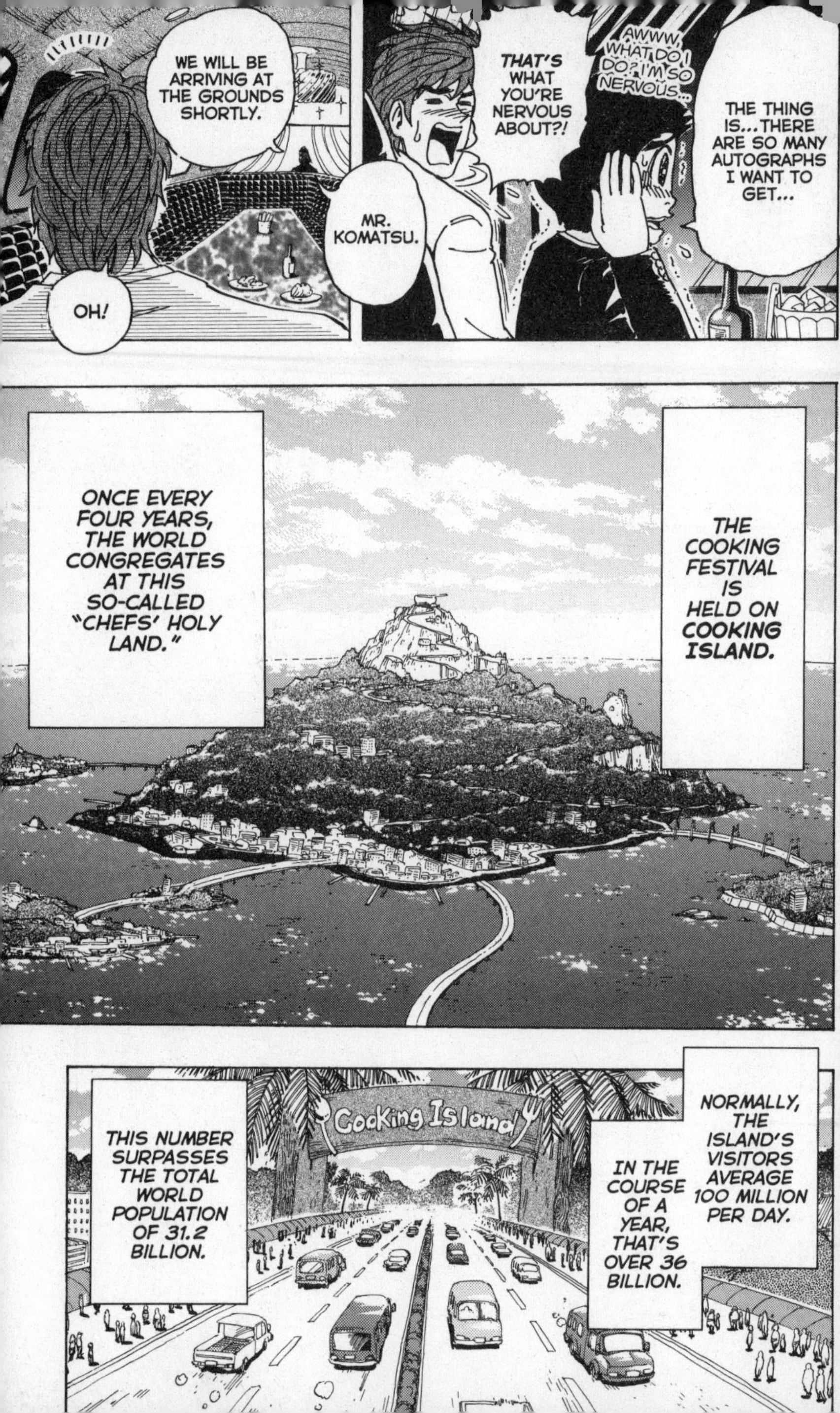
THE THING IS...THERE ARE SO MANY AUTOGRAPHS I WANT TO GET...
AWWW, WHAT DO I DO?! I'M SO NERVOUS...
THAT'S WHAT YOU'RE NERVOUS ABOUT?!
MR. KOMATSU.
WE WILL BE ARRIVING AT THE GROUNDS SHORTLY.
OH!
THE COOKING FESTIVAL IS HELD ON COOKING ISLAND.
ONCE EVERY FOUR YEARS, THE WORLD CONGREGATES AT THIS SO-CALLED "CHEFS' HOLY LAND."
NORMALLY, THE ISLAND'S VISITORS AVERAGE 100 MILLION PER DAY.
IN THE COURSE OF A YEAR, THAT'S OVER 36 BILLION.
Cooking Island
THIS NUMBER SURPASSES THE TOTAL WORLD POPULATION OF 31.2 BILLION.

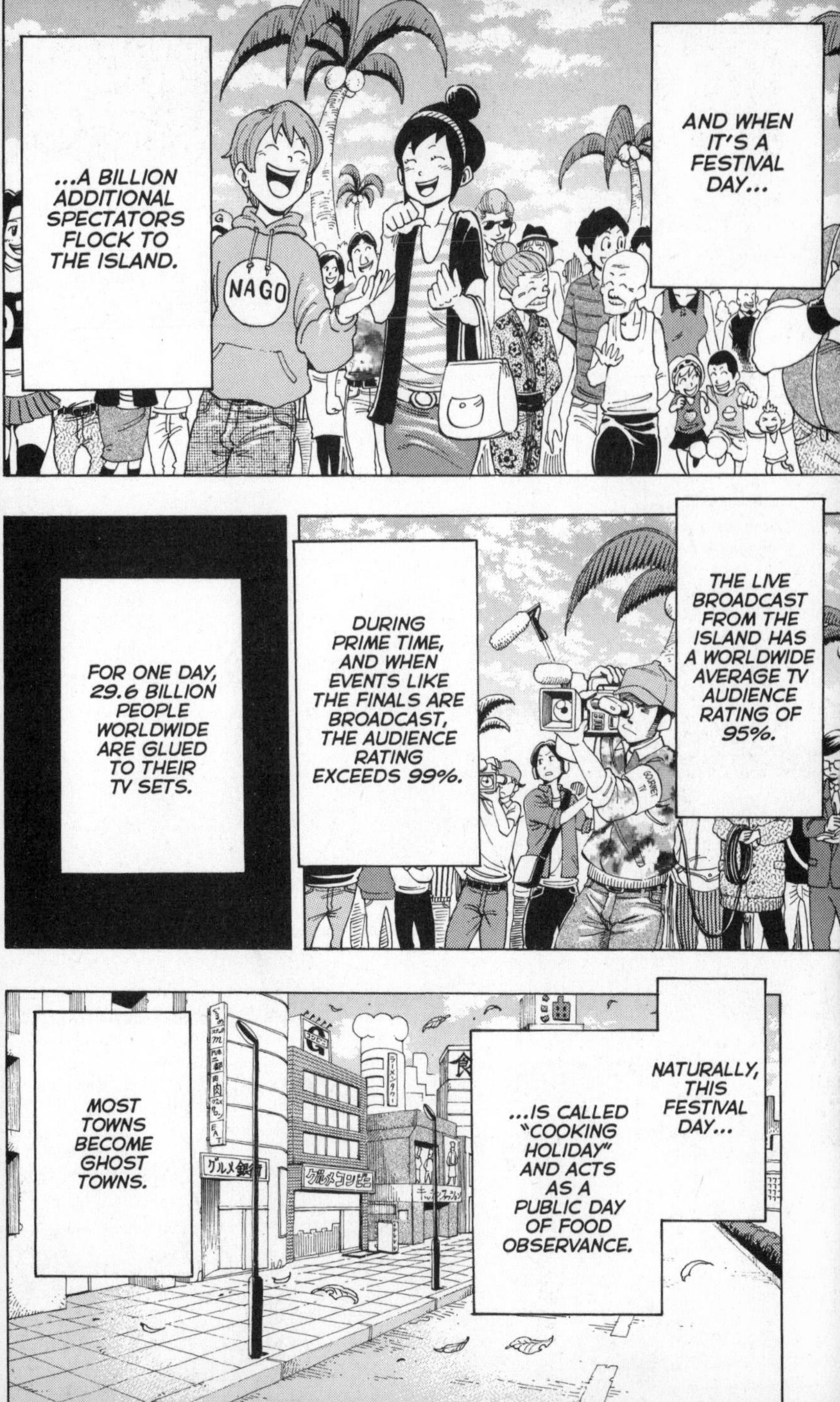
AND WHEN IT'S A FESTIVAL DAY...
...A BILLION ADDITIONAL SPECTATORS FLOCK TO THE ISLAND.
NAGO
THE LIVE BROADCAST FROM THE ISLAND HAS A WORLDWIDE AVERAGE TV AUDIENCE RATING OF 95%.
DURING PRIME TIME, AND WHEN EVENTS LIKE THE FINALS ARE BROADCAST, THE AUDIENCE RATING EXCEEDS 99%.
FOR ONE DAY, 29.6 BILLION PEOPLE WORLDWIDE ARE GLUED TO THEIR TV SETS.
NATURALLY, THIS FESTIVAL DAY...
...IS CALLED "COOKING HOLIDAY" AND ACTS AS A PUBLIC DAY OF FOOD OBSERVANCE.
MOST TOWNS BECOME GHOST TOWNS.
グルメ銀行
グルメコンビニ

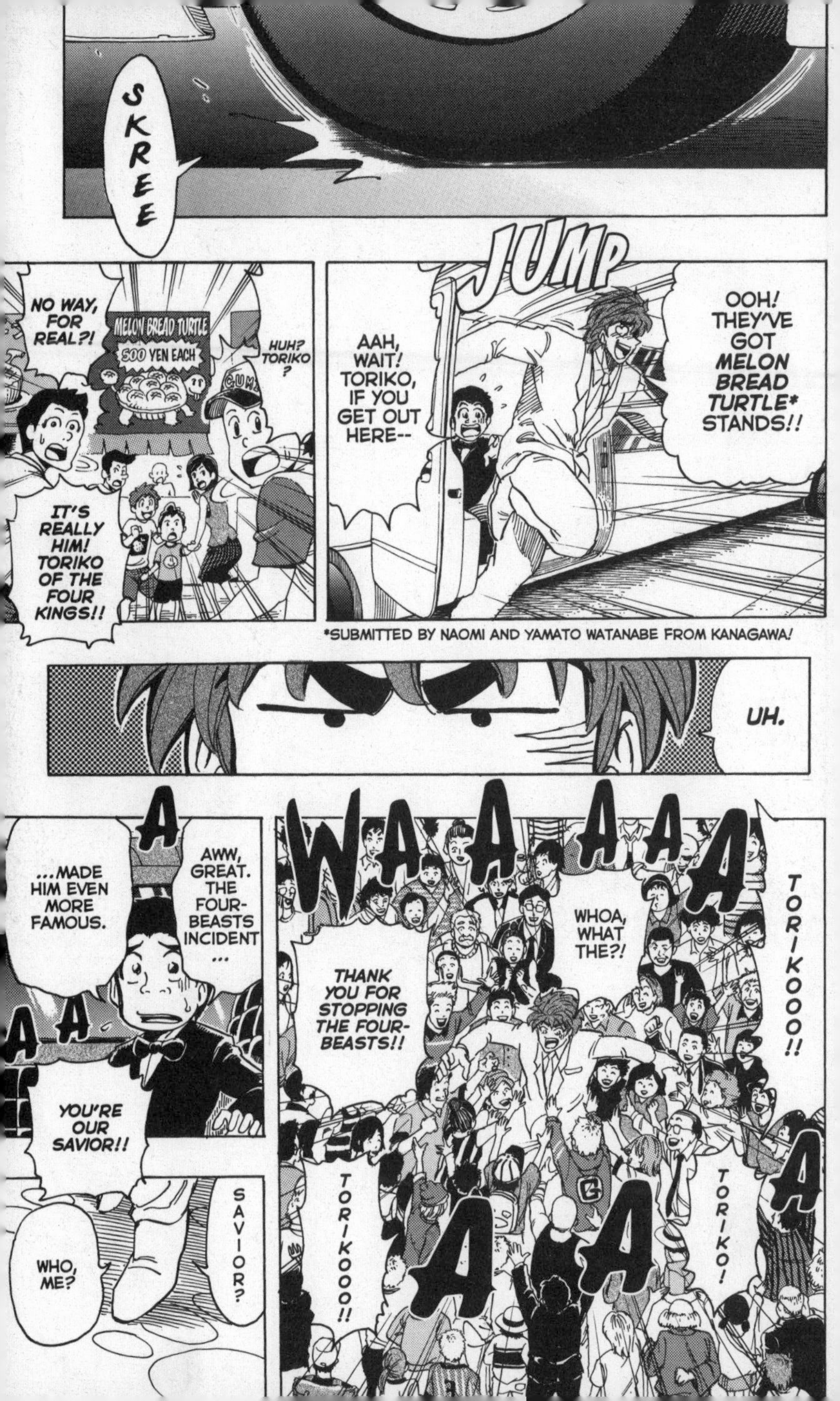
SKREE
JUMP
OOH! THEY'VE GOT MELON BREAD TURTLE* STANDS!!
AAH, WAIT! TORIKO, IF YOU GET OUT HERE--
HUH? TORIKO?
MELON BREAD TURTLE
500 YEN EACH
NO WAY, FOR REAL?!
IT'S REALLY HIM! TORIKO OF THE FOUR KINGS!!
*SUBMITTED BY NAOMI AND YAMATO WATANABE FROM KANAGAWA!
UH.
WAAAAAA
TORIKOOOO!!
WHOA, WHAT THE?!
THANK YOU FOR STOPPING THE FOUR-BEASTS!!
TORIKO!
TORIKOOO!!
AWW, GREAT. THE FOUR-BEASTS INCIDENT...
...MADE HIM EVEN MORE FAMOUS.
YOU'RE OUR SAVIOR!!
SAVIOR?
WHO, ME?

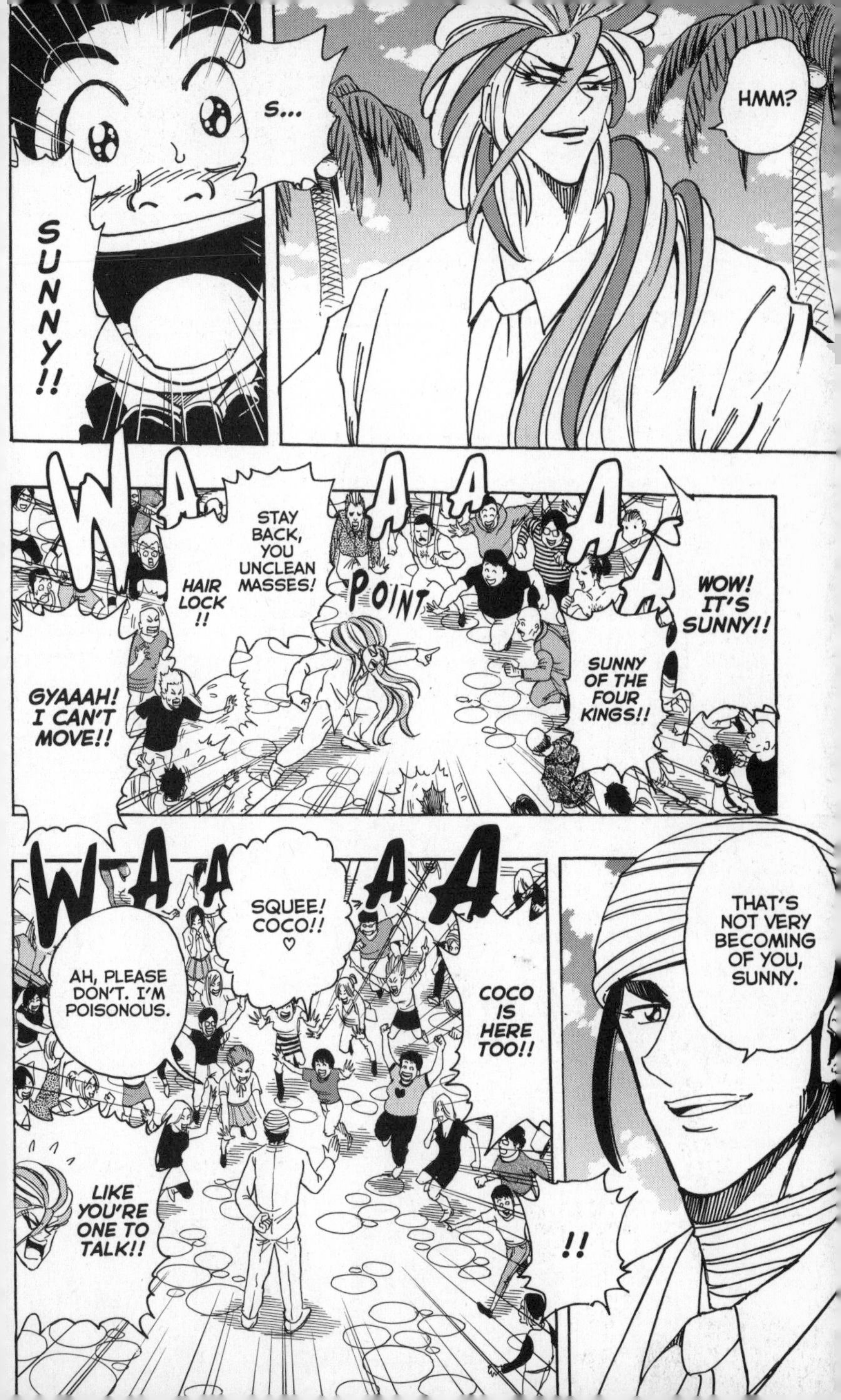
HMM?
S...
SUNNY!!
WAAAAA
WOW! IT'S SUNNY!!
SUNNY OF THE FOUR KINGS!!
POINT
STAY BACK, YOU UNCLEAN MASSES!
HAIR LOCK!!
GYAAAH! I CAN'T MOVE!!
THAT'S NOT VERY BECOMING OF YOU, SUNNY.
!!
WAAAA
COCO IS HERE TOO!!
SQUEE! COCO!! ♡
AH, PLEASE DON'T. I'M POISONOUS.
LIKE YOU'RE ONE TO TALK!!

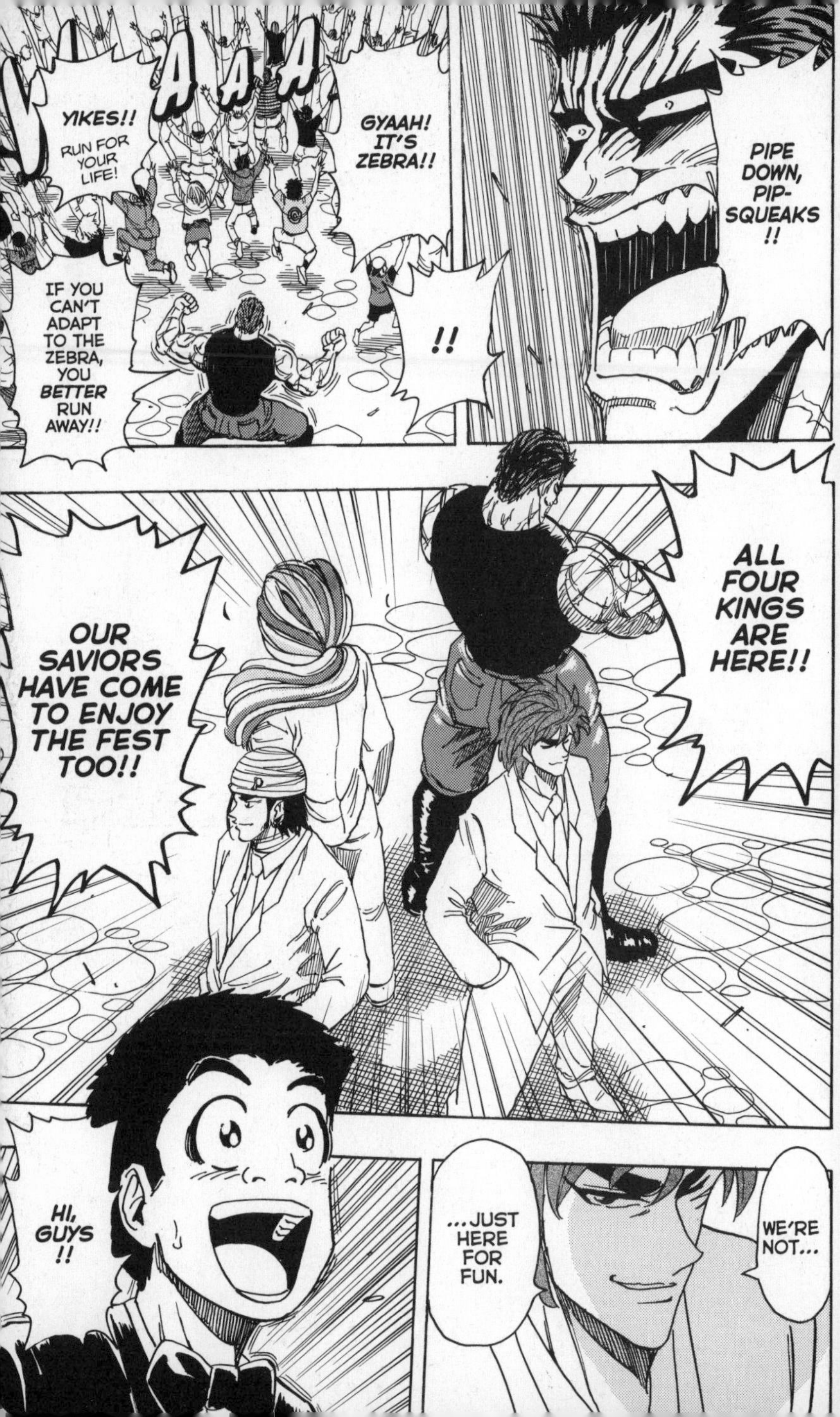
PIPE DOWN, PIP-SQUEAKS !!
A A A
GYAAH! IT'S ZEBRA!!
!!
YIKES!!
RUN FOR YOUR LIFE!
IF YOU CAN'T ADAPT TO THE ZEBRA, YOU BETTER RUN AWAY!!
ALL FOUR KINGS ARE HERE!!
OUR SAVIORS HAVE COME TO ENJOY THE FEST TOO!!
WE'RE NOT...
...JUST HERE FOR FUN.
HI, GUYS !!

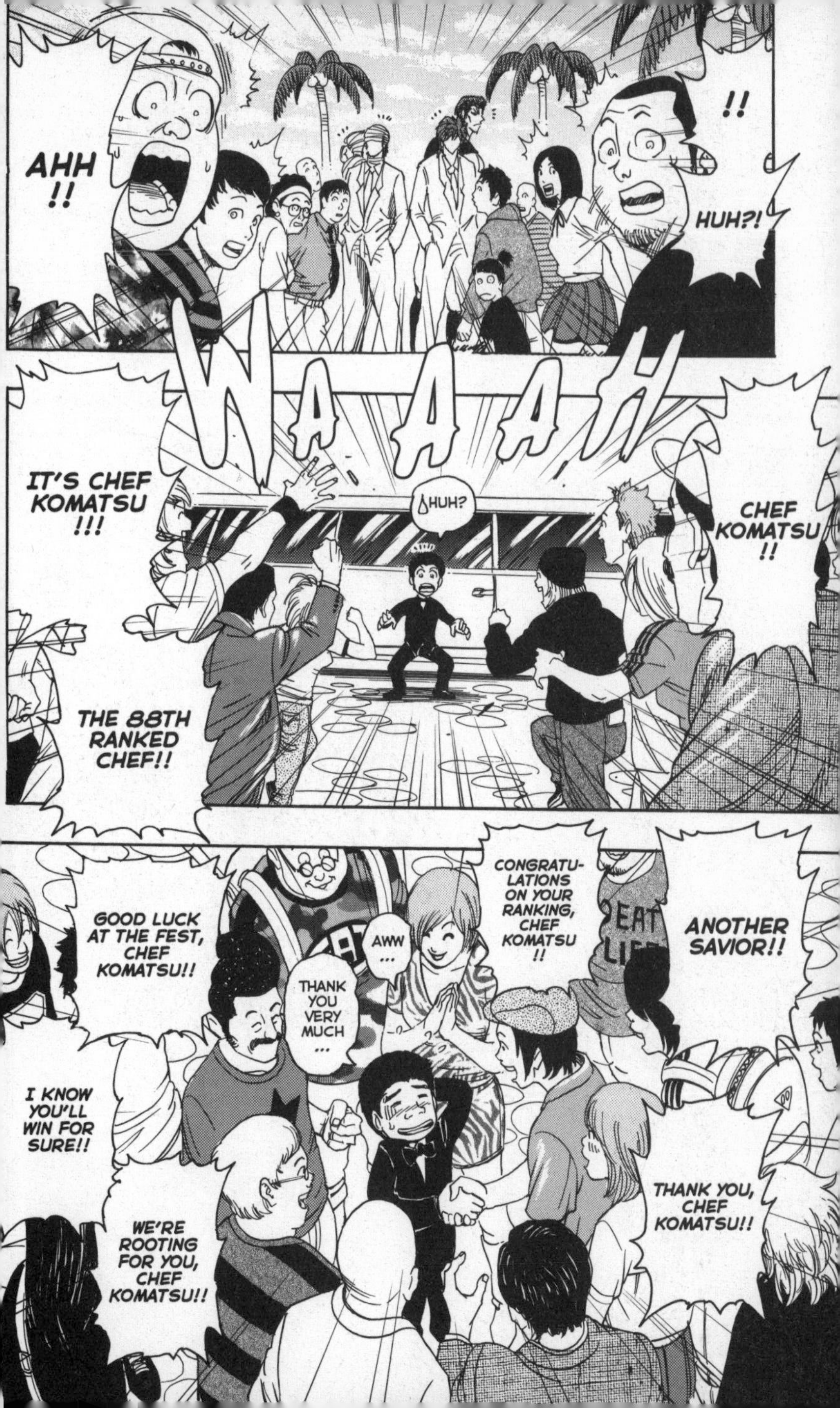
!!
HUH?!
AHH !!
WAAAH
CHEF KOMATSU !!
HUH?
IT'S CHEF KOMATSU !!!
THE 88TH RANKED CHEF!!
ANOTHER SAVIOR!!
CONGRATULATIONS ON YOUR RANKING, CHEF KOMATSU !!
AWW ...
THANK YOU VERY MUCH ...
GOOD LUCK AT THE FEST, CHEF KOMATSU!!
THANK YOU, CHEF KOMATSU!!
WE'RE ROOTING FOR YOU, CHEF KOMATSU!!
I KNOW YOU'LL WIN FOR SURE!!

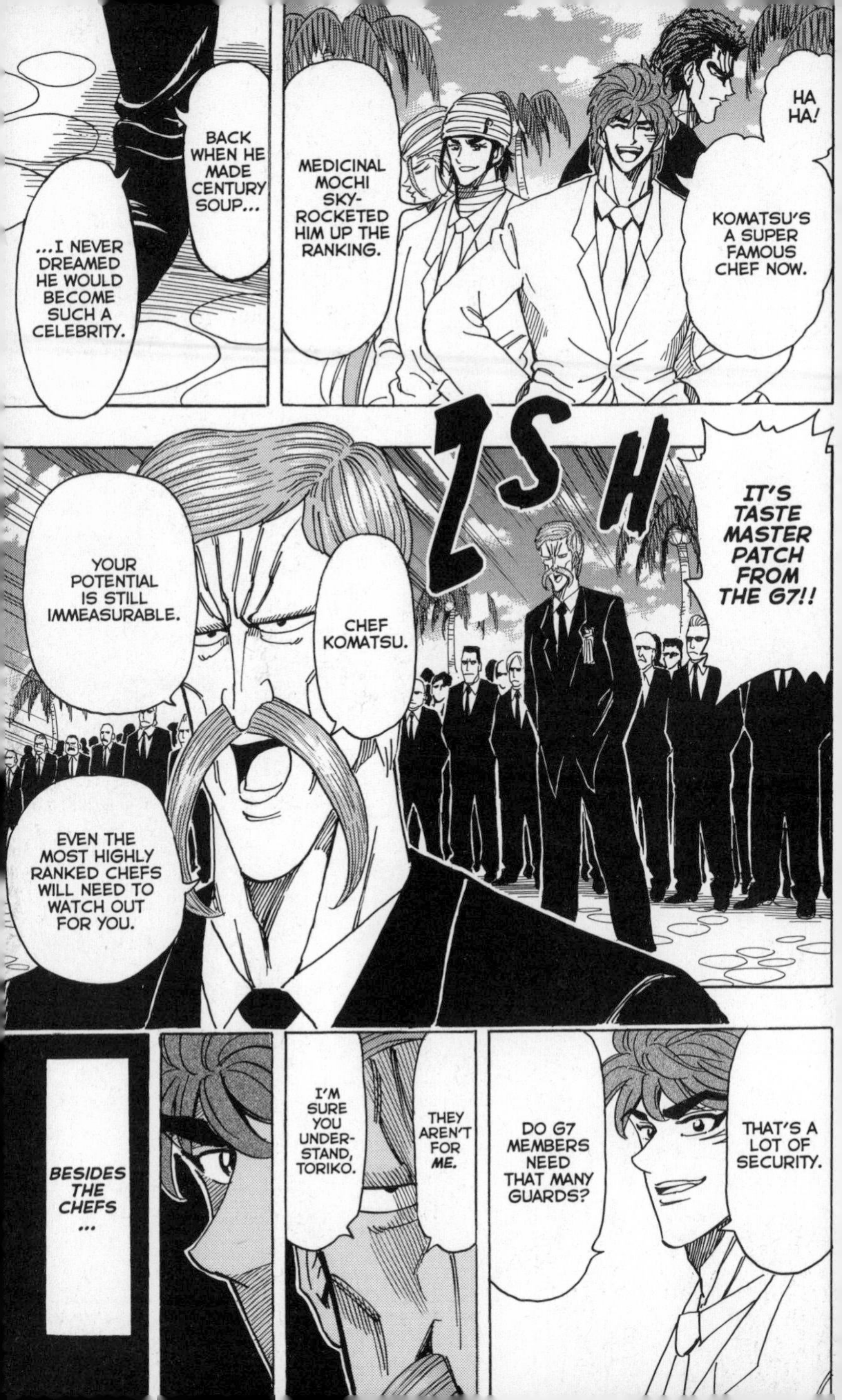
HA HA!
KOMATSU'S A SUPER FAMOUS CHEF NOW.
MEDICINAL MOCHI SKY-ROCKETED HIM UP THE RANKING.
BACK WHEN HE MADE CENTURY SOUP...
...I NEVER DREAMED HE WOULD BECOME SUCH A CELEBRITY.
IT'S TASTE MASTER PATCH FROM THE G7!!
ZSH
CHEF KOMATSU.
YOUR POTENTIAL IS STILL IMMEASURABLE.
EVEN THE MOST HIGHLY RANKED CHEFS WILL NEED TO WATCH OUT FOR YOU.
THAT'S A LOT OF SECURITY.
DO G7 MEMBERS NEED THAT MANY GUARDS?
THEY AREN'T FOR ME.
I'M SURE YOU UNDER-STAND, TORIKO.
BESIDES THE CHEFS ...

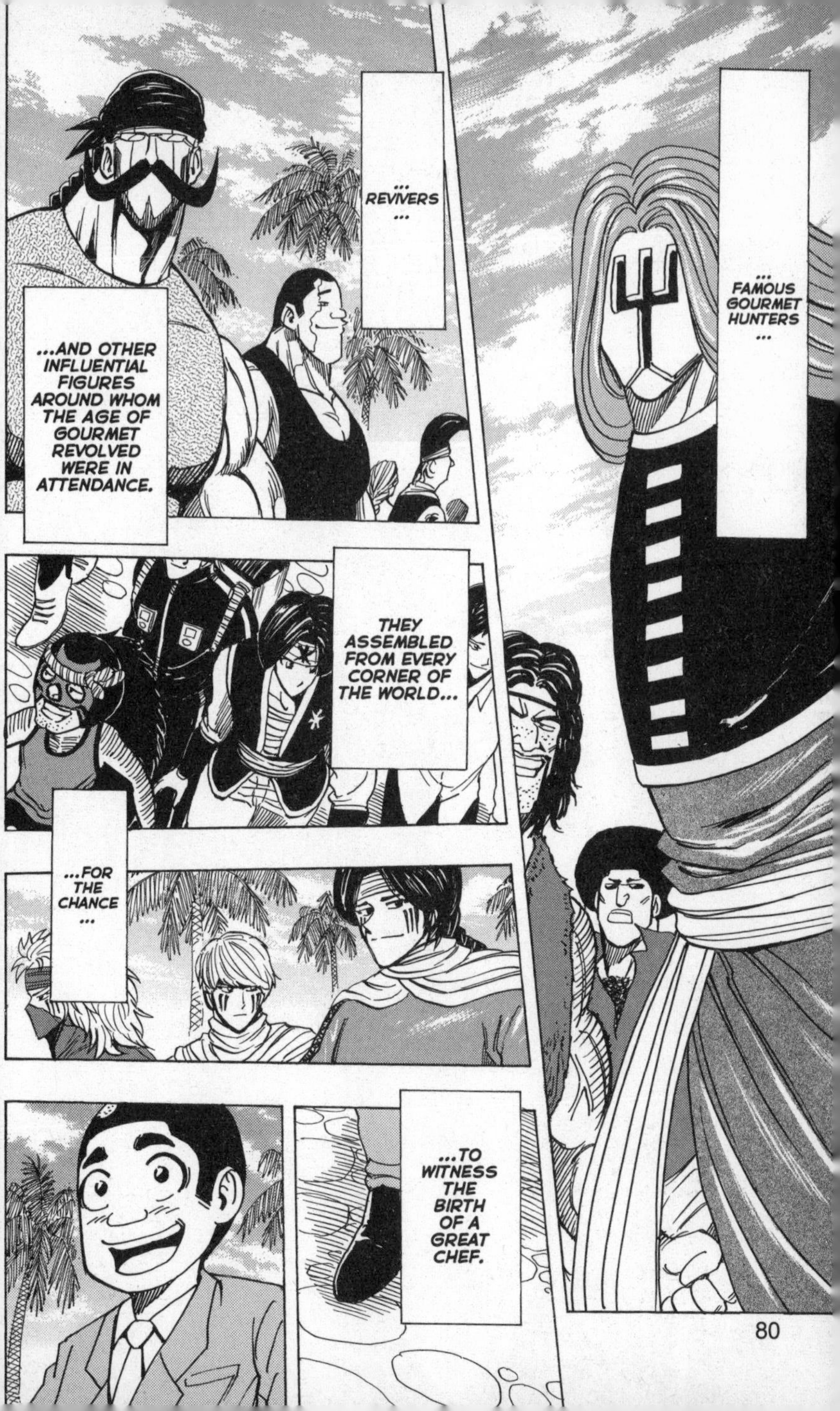
...FAMOUS GOURMET HUNTERS...
...REVIVERS...
...AND OTHER INFLUENTIAL FIGURES AROUND WHOM THE AGE OF GOURMET REVOLVED WERE IN ATTENDANCE.
THEY ASSEMBLED FROM EVERY CORNER OF THE WORLD...
...FOR THE CHANCE...
...TO WITNESS THE BIRTH OF A GREAT CHEF.

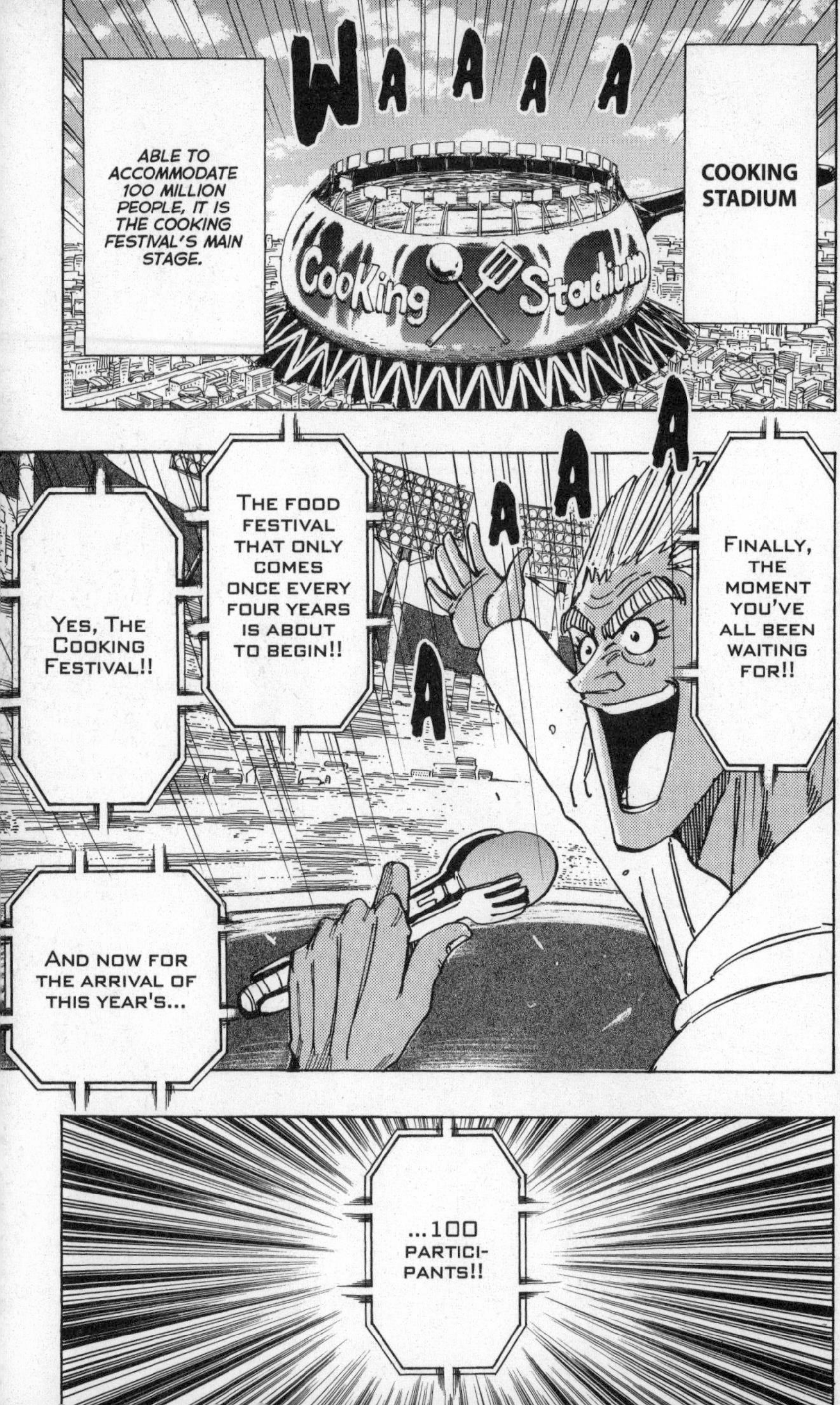
COOKING STADIUM
WAAAA
Cooking Stadium
ABLE TO ACCOMMODATE 100 MILLION PEOPLE, IT IS THE COOKING FESTIVAL'S MAIN STAGE.
FINALLY, THE MOMENT YOU'VE ALL BEEN WAITING FOR!!
AAAA
THE FOOD FESTIVAL THAT ONLY COMES ONCE EVERY FOUR YEARS IS ABOUT TO BEGIN!!
YES, THE COOKING FESTIVAL!!
AND NOW FOR THE ARRIVAL OF THIS YEAR'S...
...100 PARTICI-PANTS!!

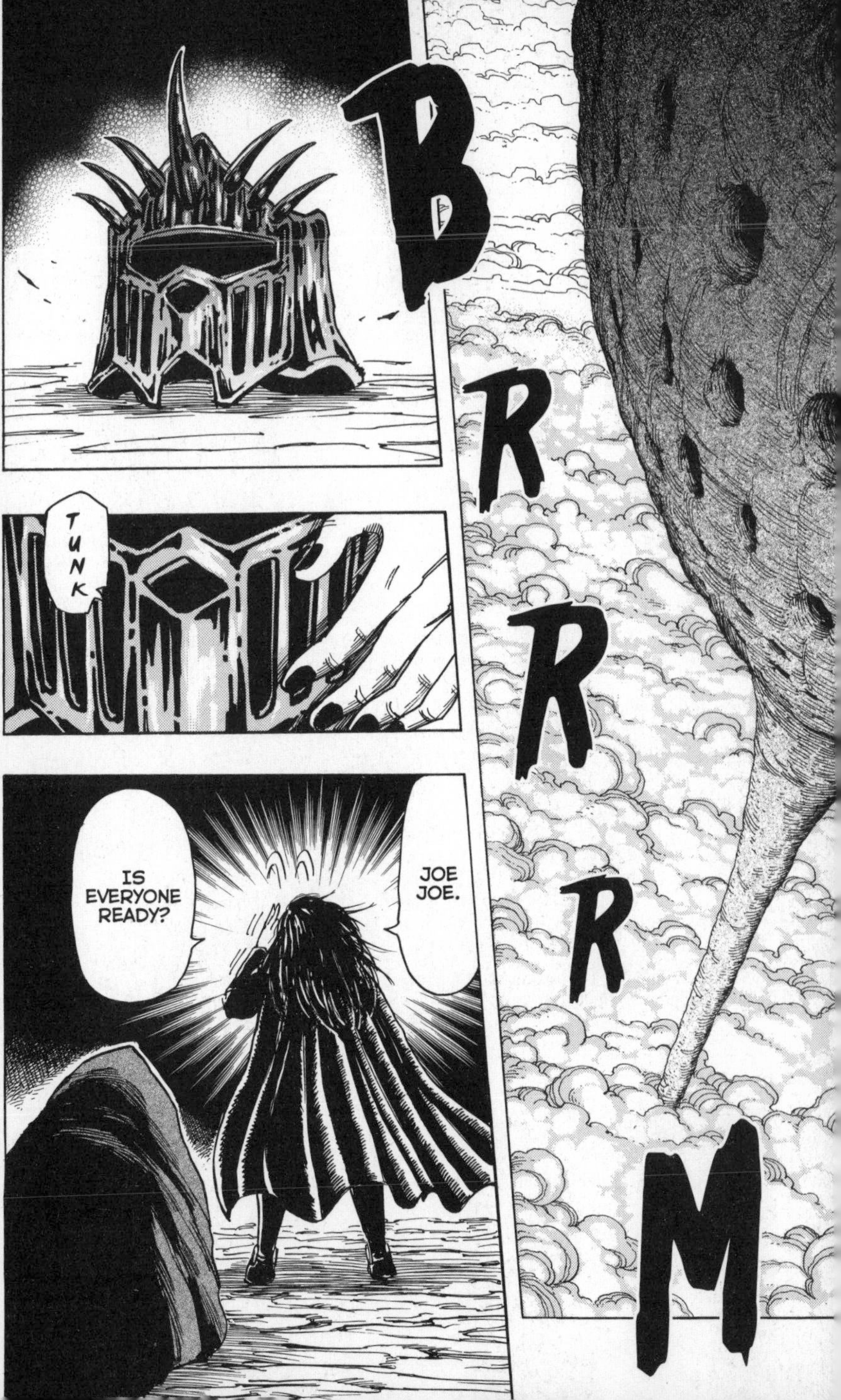
BRRRRM
TUNK
JOE JOE.
IS EVERYONE READY?

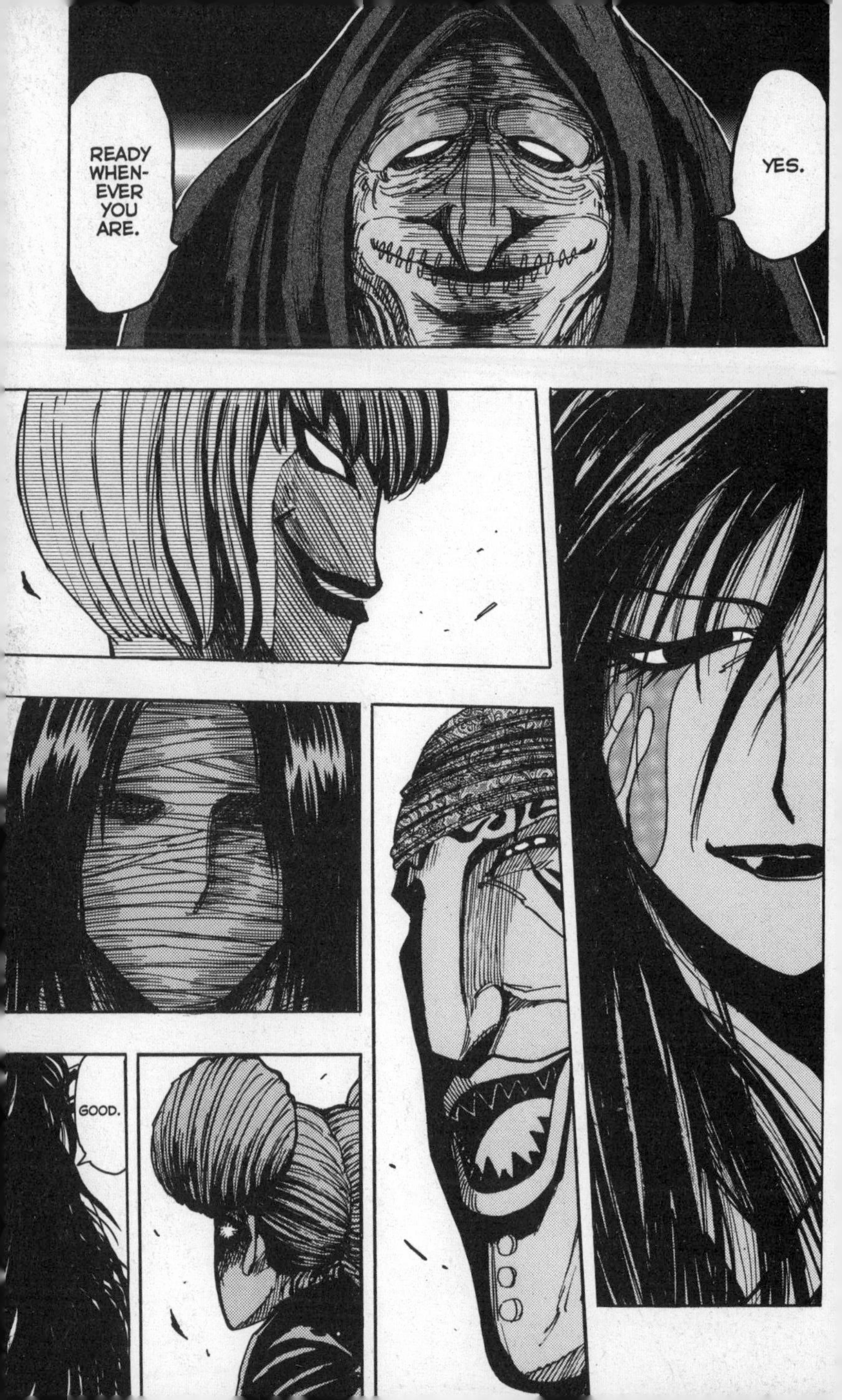
YES.
READY WHEN-EVER YOU ARE.
GOOD.

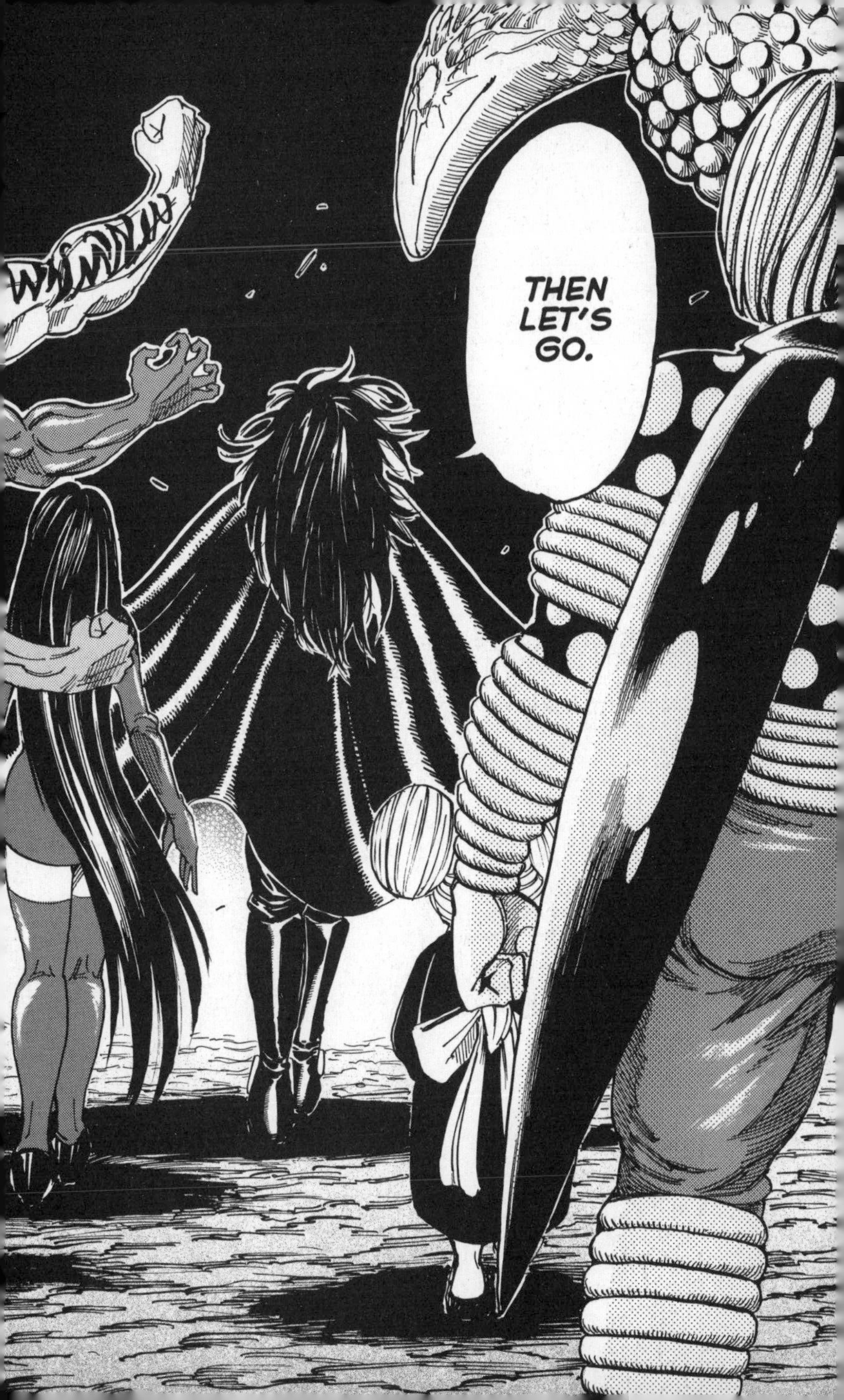
THEN LET'S GO.

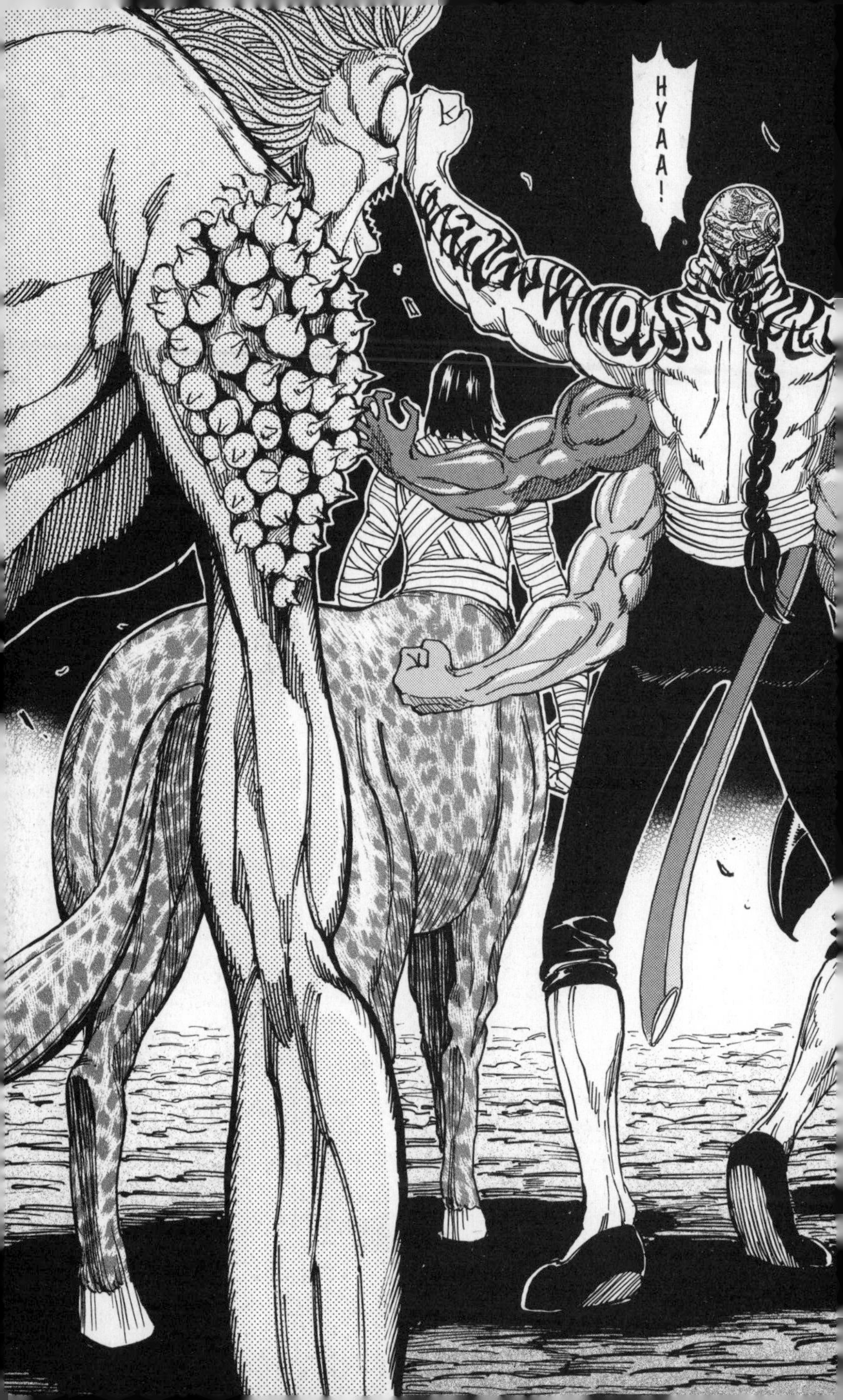
HYAAA!

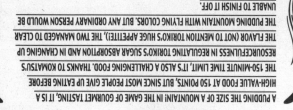

TORIKO

GOURMET CHECKLIST

Vol. 244

PUDDING MOUNTAIN
(DESSERT)

CAPTURE LEVEL: 20
HABITAT: SWEETS LAND
LENGTH: ---
HEIGHT: 5,000 METERS
(THE ONE TORIKO ATE
WAS 150 METERS)
WEIGHT: 1.5 BILLION TONS
PRICE: 1 CUP (150 G) / 2,000 YEN

GARMPH !!
ARF
ARF
YUM! AWW YEAH!
NOMF NOMF
SLURP
SLURP

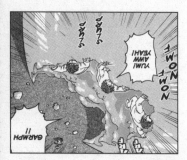

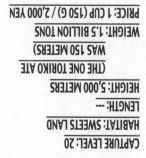

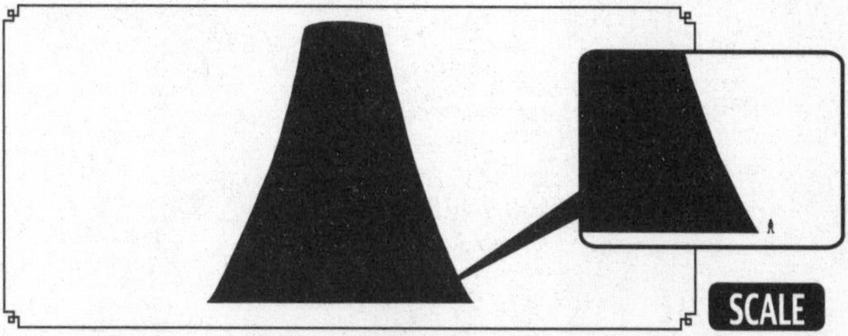

SCALE

A PUDDING THE SIZE OF A MOUNTAIN! IN THE GAME OF GOURMET TASTING, IT IS A HIGH-VALUE FOOD AT 150 POINTS, BUT SINCE MOST PEOPLE GIVE UP EATING BEFORE THE 150-MINUTE TIME LIMIT, IT'S ALSO A CHALLENGING FOOD. THANKS TO KOMATSU'S RESOURCEFULNESS IN REGULATING TORIKO'S SUGAR ABSORPTION AND IN CHANGING UP THE FLAVOR (NOT TO MENTION TORIKO'S HUGE APPETITE!), THE TWO MANAGED TO CLEAR THE PUDDING MOUNTAIN WITH FLYING COLORS. BUT ANY ORDINARY PERSON WOULD BE UNABLE TO FINISH IT OFF.

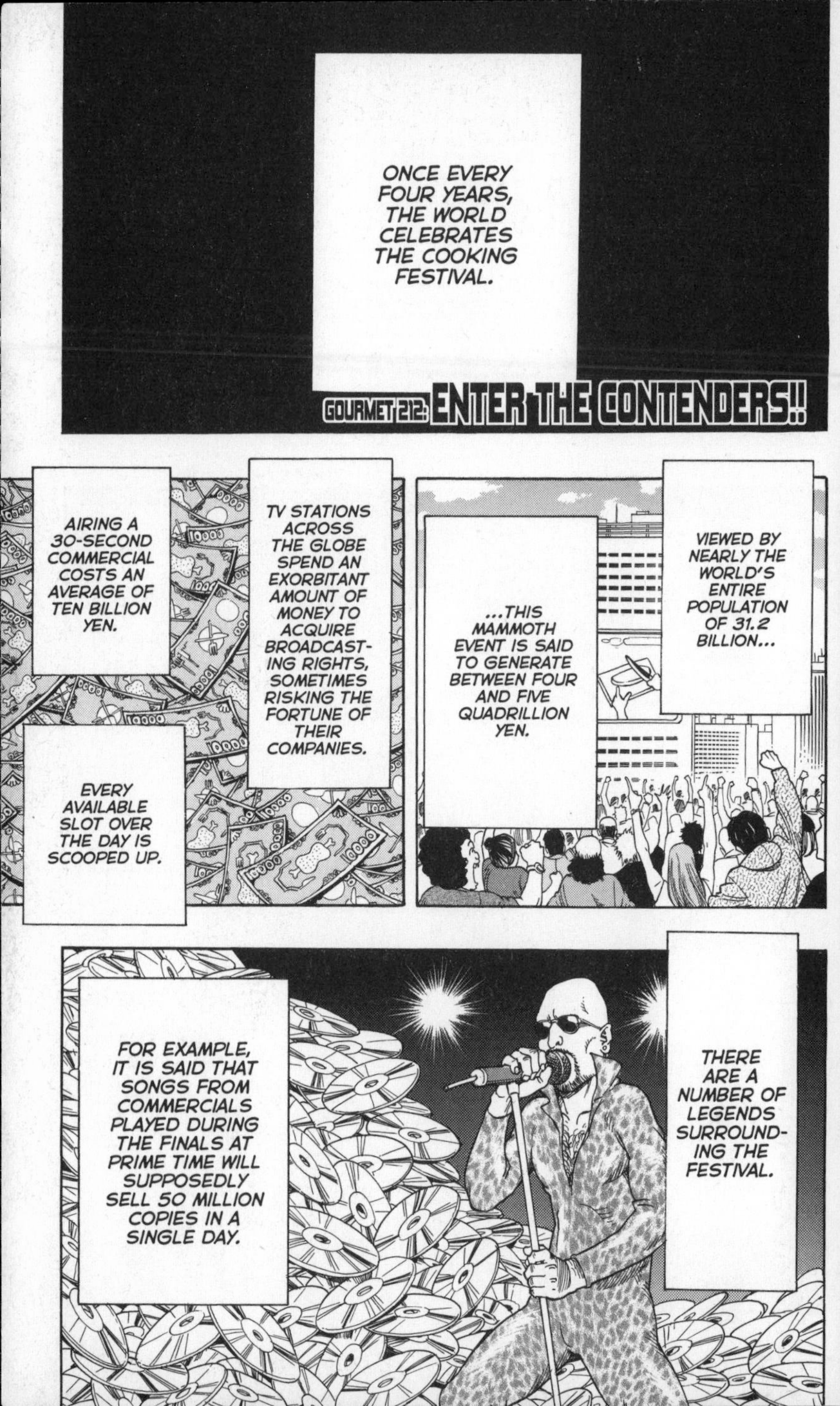
ONCE EVERY FOUR YEARS, THE WORLD CELEBRATES THE COOKING FESTIVAL.
GOURMET 212: ENTER THE CONTENDERS!!
VIEWED BY NEARLY THE WORLD'S ENTIRE POPULATION OF 31.2 BILLION...
...THIS MAMMOTH EVENT IS SAID TO GENERATE BETWEEN FOUR AND FIVE QUADRILLION YEN.
TV STATIONS ACROSS THE GLOBE SPEND AN EXORBITANT AMOUNT OF MONEY TO ACQUIRE BROADCAST-ING RIGHTS, SOMETIMES RISKING THE FORTUNE OF THEIR COMPANIES.
AIRING A 30-SECOND COMMERCIAL COSTS AN AVERAGE OF TEN BILLION YEN.
EVERY AVAILABLE SLOT OVER THE DAY IS SCOOPED UP.
THERE ARE A NUMBER OF LEGENDS SURROUND-ING THE FESTIVAL.
FOR EXAMPLE, IT IS SAID THAT SONGS FROM COMMERCIALS PLAYED DURING THE FINALS AT PRIME TIME WILL SUPPOSEDLY SELL 50 MILLION COPIES IN A SINGLE DAY.

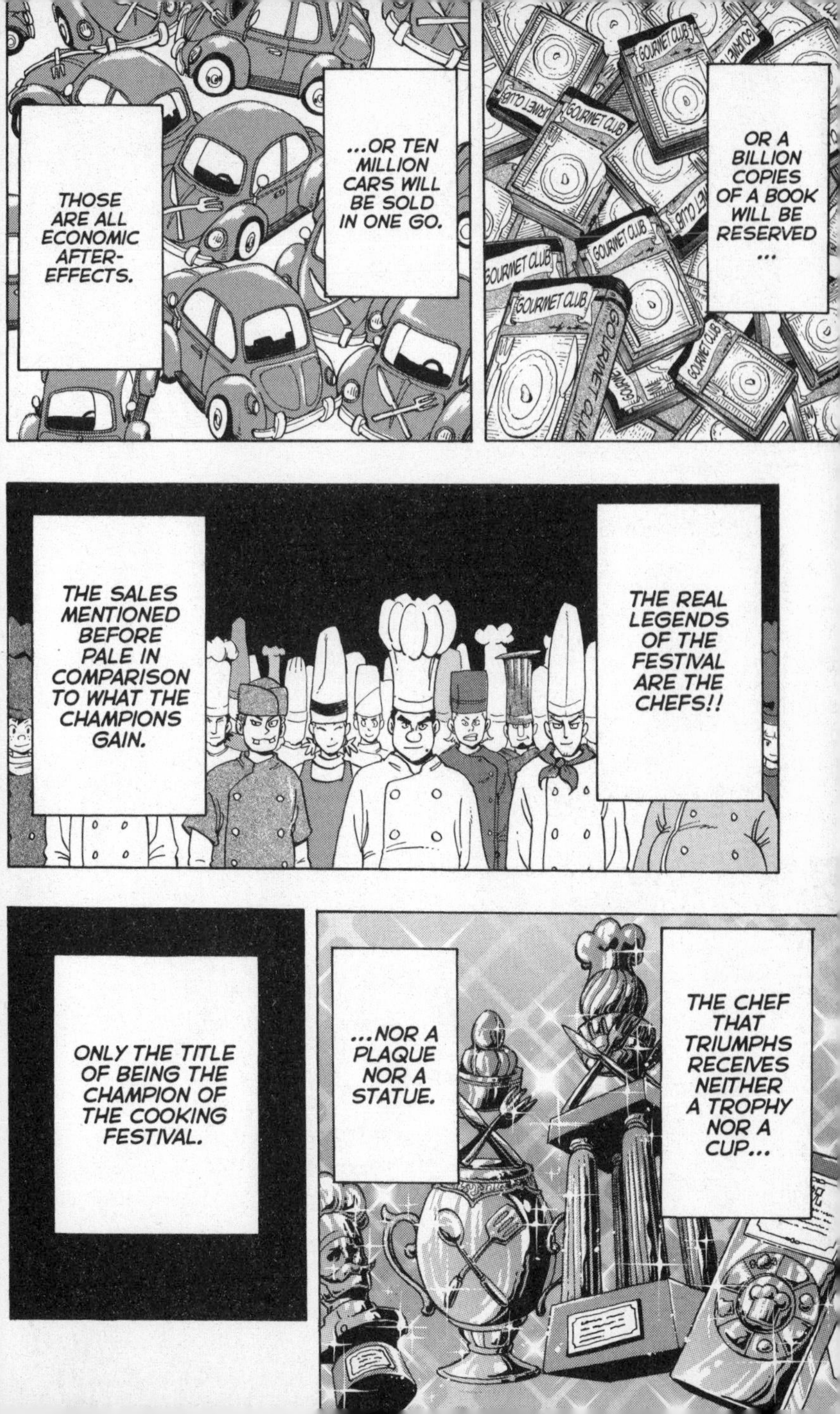
OR A BILLION COPIES OF A BOOK WILL BE RESERVED ...
GOURMET CLUB
...OR TEN MILLION CARS WILL BE SOLD IN ONE GO.
THOSE ARE ALL ECONOMIC AFTER-EFFECTS.
THE REAL LEGENDS OF THE FESTIVAL ARE THE CHEFS!!
THE SALES MENTIONED BEFORE PALE IN COMPARISON TO WHAT THE CHAMPIONS GAIN.
THE CHEF THAT TRIUMPHS RECEIVES NEITHER A TROPHY NOR A CUP...
...NOR A PLAQUE NOR A STATUE.
ONLY THE TITLE OF BEING THE CHAMPION OF THE COOKING FESTIVAL.

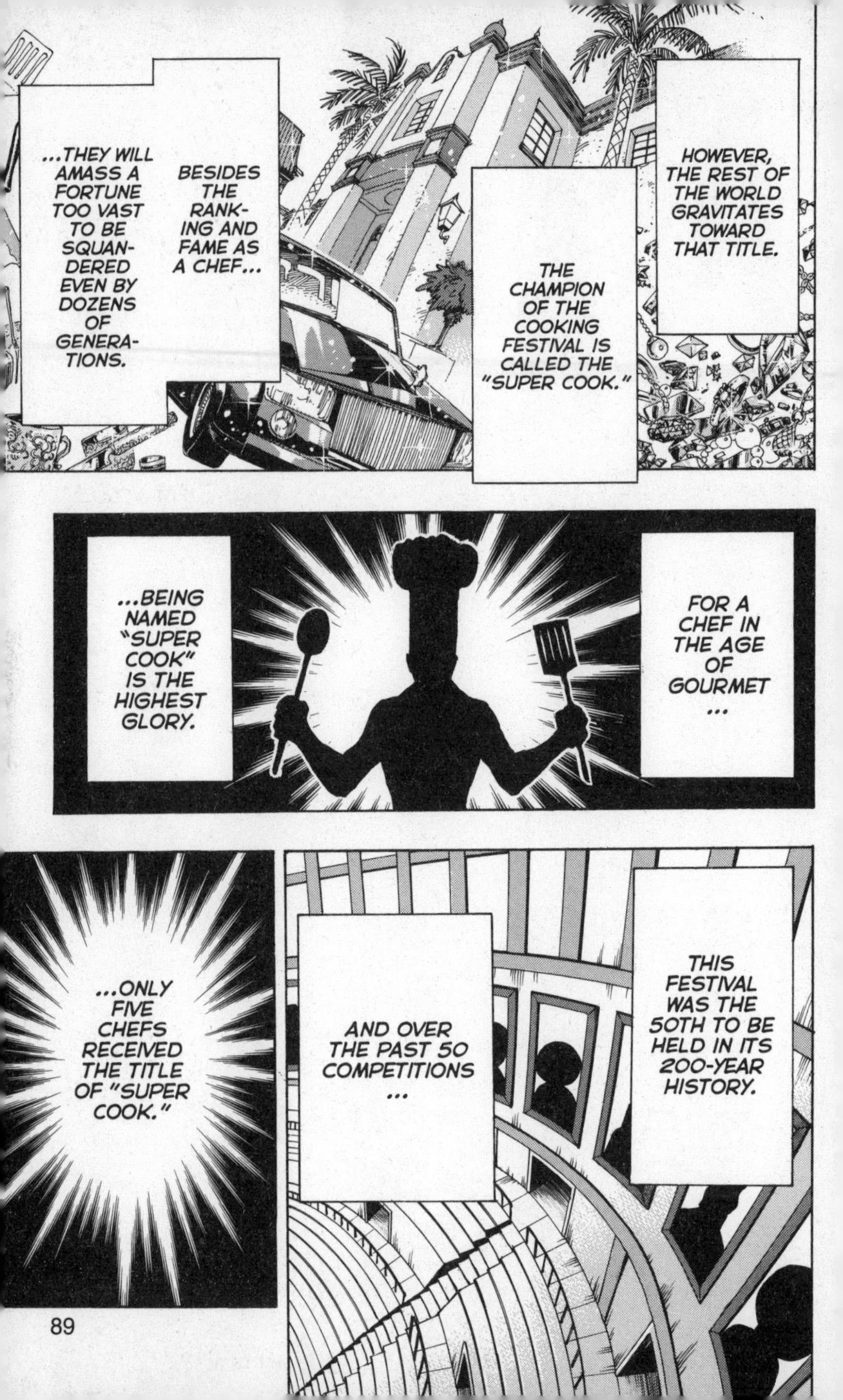
HOWEVER, THE REST OF THE WORLD GRAVITATES TOWARD THAT TITLE.
THE CHAMPION OF THE COOKING FESTIVAL IS CALLED THE "SUPER COOK."
BESIDES THE RANK-ING AND FAME AS A CHEF...
...THEY WILL AMASS A FORTUNE TOO VAST TO BE SQUAN-DERED EVEN BY DOZENS OF GENERA-TIONS.
FOR A CHEF IN THE AGE OF GOURMET ...
...BEING NAMED "SUPER COOK" IS THE HIGHEST GLORY.
THIS FESTIVAL WAS THE 50TH TO BE HELD IN ITS 200-YEAR HISTORY.
AND OVER THE PAST 50 COMPETITIONS ...
...ONLY FIVE CHEFS RECEIVED THE TITLE OF "SUPER COOK."

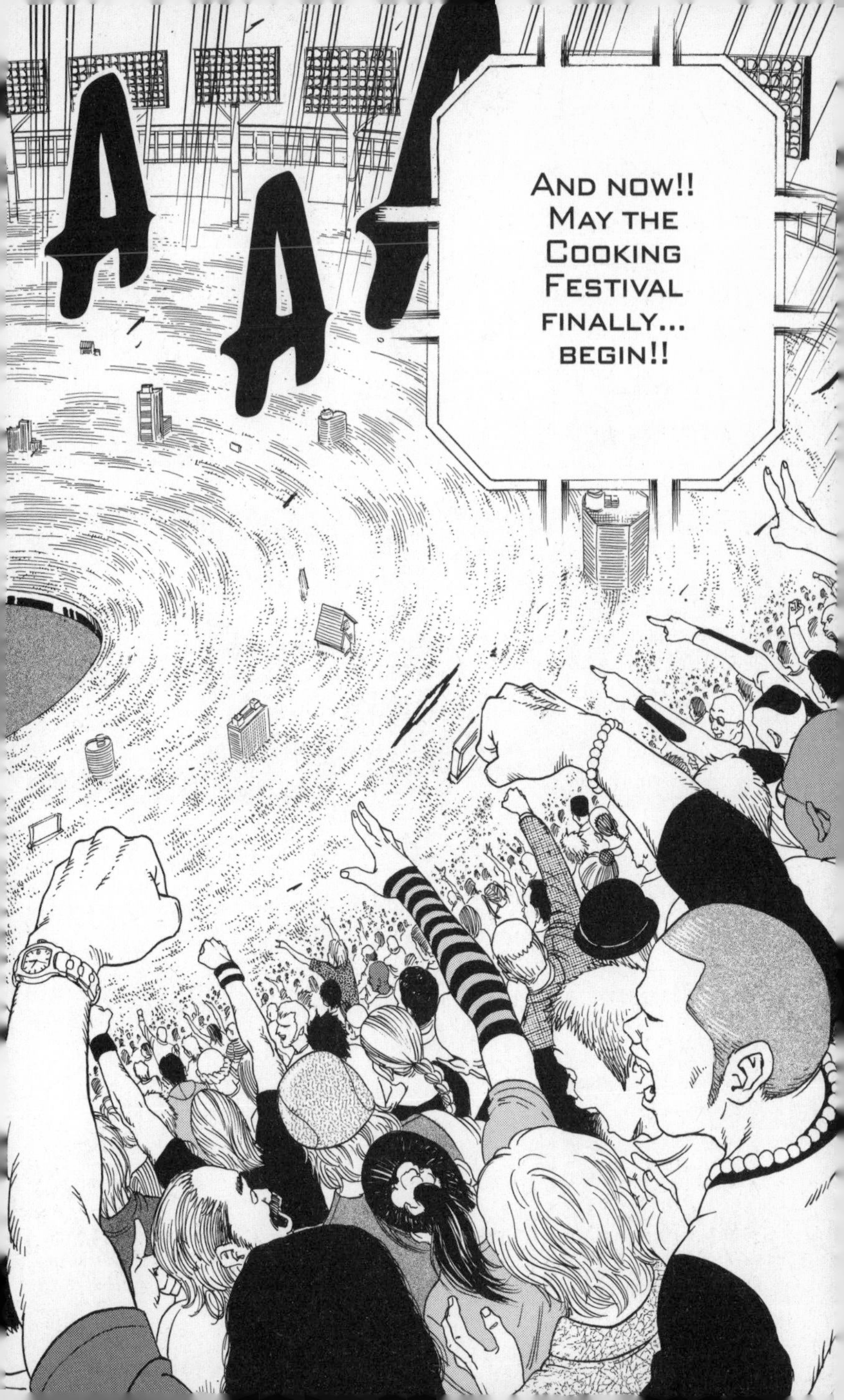
AND NOW!! MAY THE COOKING FESTIVAL FINALLY... BEGIN!!
AAA

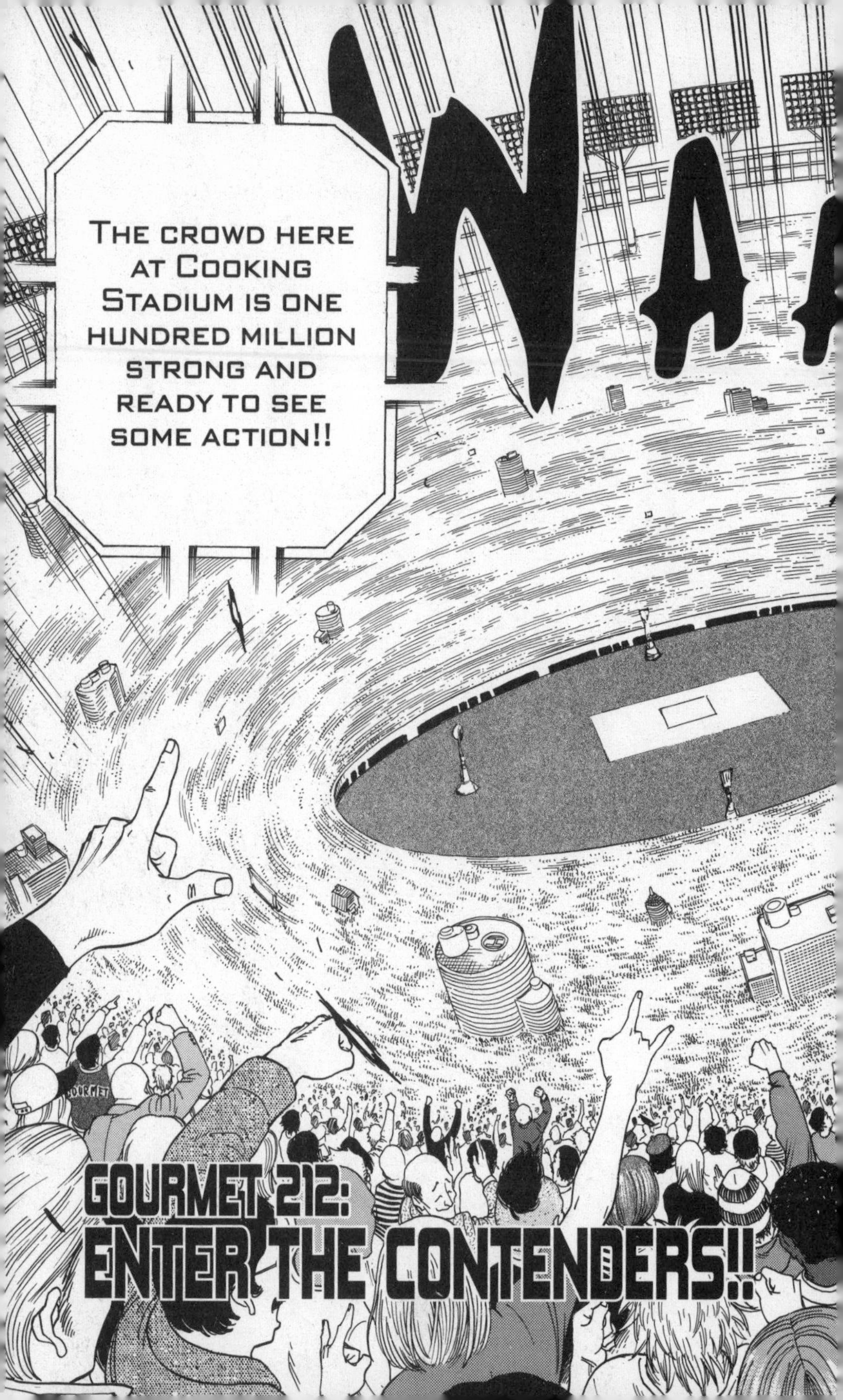
WAA
THE CROWD HERE AT COOKING STADIUM IS ONE HUNDRED MILLION STRONG AND READY TO SEE SOME ACTION!!
GOURMET
GOURMET 212:
ENTER THE CONTENDERS!!

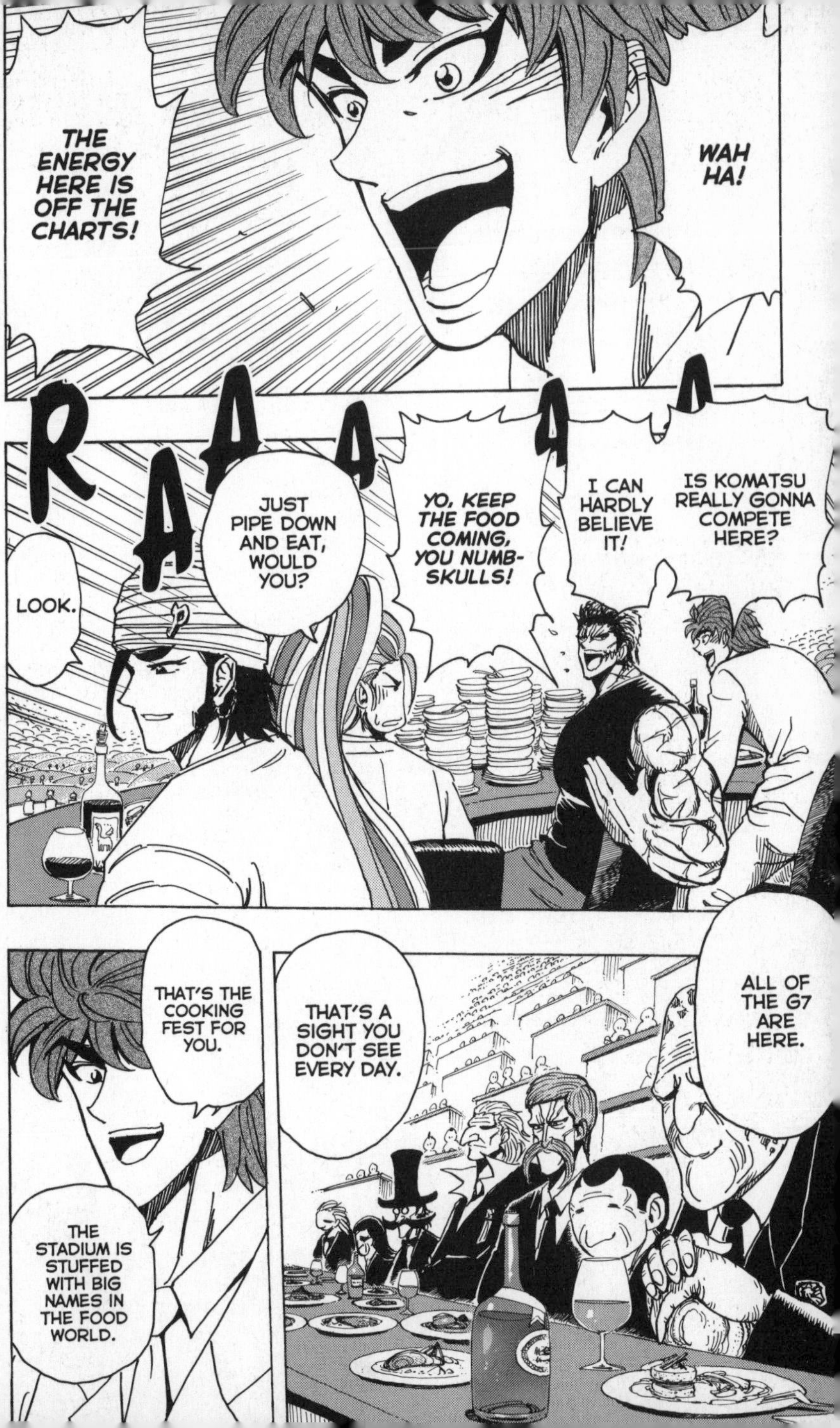
WAH HA!
THE ENERGY HERE IS OFF THE CHARTS!
RAAAAAA
IS KOMATSU REALLY GONNA COMPETE HERE?
I CAN HARDLY BELIEVE IT!
YO, KEEP THE FOOD COMING, YOU NUMB-SKULLS!
JUST PIPE DOWN AND EAT, WOULD YOU?
LOOK.
ALL OF THE G7 ARE HERE.
THAT'S A SIGHT YOU DON'T SEE EVERY DAY.
THAT'S THE COOKING FEST FOR YOU.
THE STADIUM IS STUFFED WITH BIG NAMES IN THE FOOD WORLD.

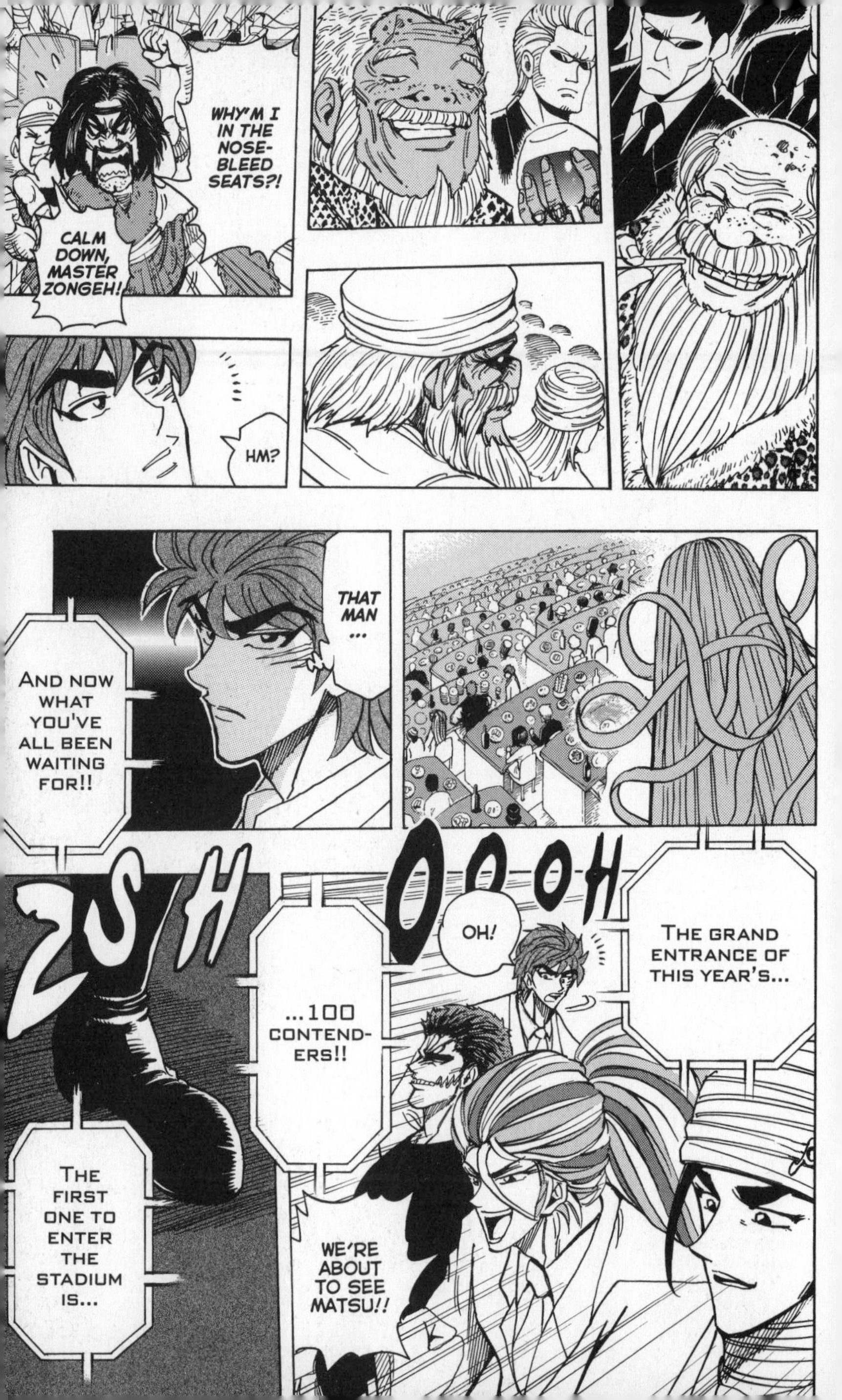
WHY'M I IN THE NOSE-BLEED SEATS?!
CALM DOWN, MASTER ZONGEH!
HM?
THAT MAN...
AND NOW WHAT YOU'VE ALL BEEN WAITING FOR!!
THE GRAND ENTRANCE OF THIS YEAR'S...
OOOH
OH!
...100 CONTENDERS!!
ZSH
WE'RE ABOUT TO SEE MATSU!!
THE FIRST ONE TO ENTER THE STADIUM IS...

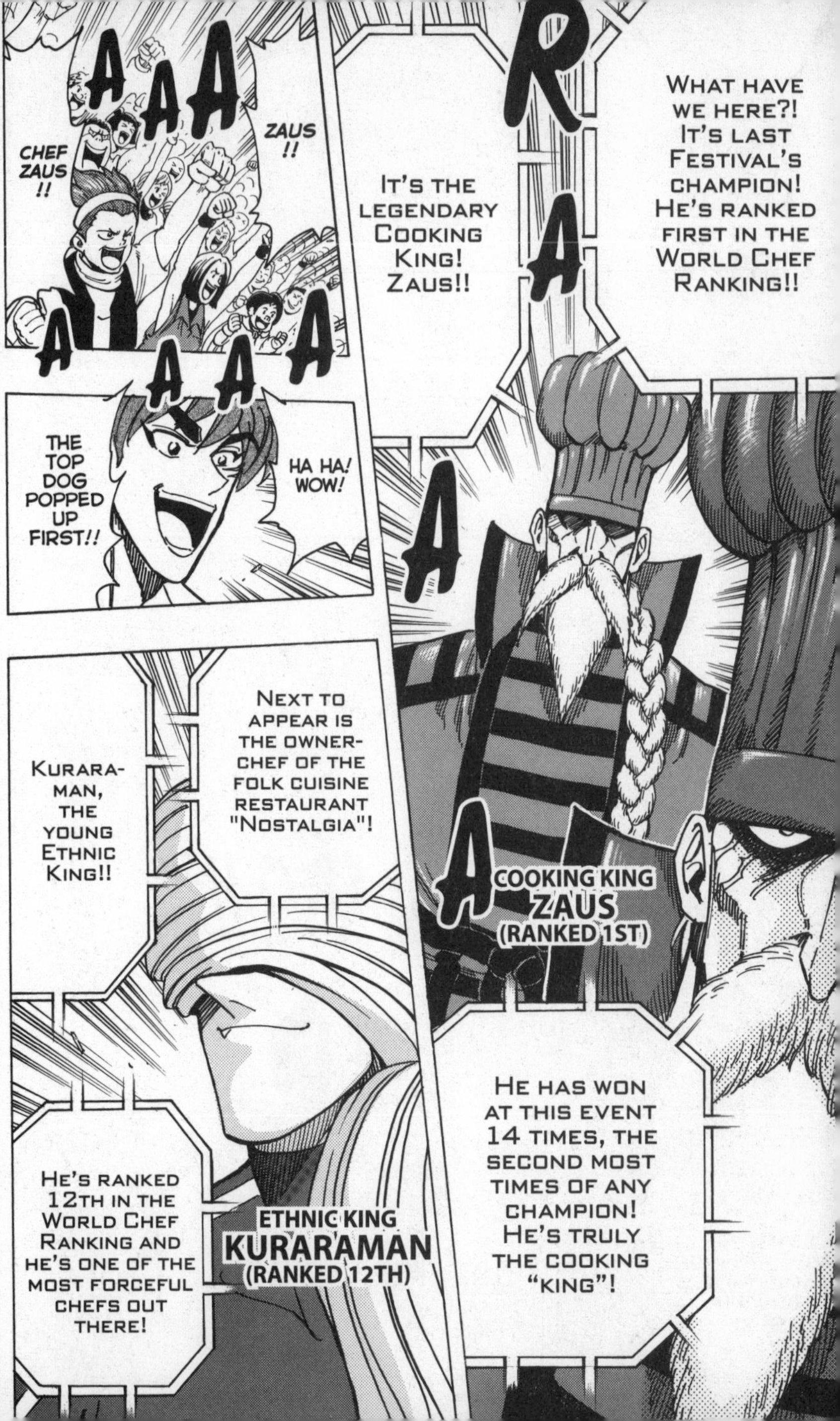
R
What have we here?! It's last Festival's champion! He's ranked first in the World Chef Ranking!!
It's the legendary Cooking King! Zaus!!
A
A
A
A
COOKING KING ZAUS (RANKED 1ST)
He has won at this event 14 times, the second most times of any champion! He's truly the cooking "king"!
AAA
ZAUS !!
CHEF ZAUS !!
AAAA
HA HA! WOW!
THE TOP DOG POPPED UP FIRST!!
Next to appear is the owner-chef of the folk cuisine restaurant "Nostalgia"!
Kurara-man, the young Ethnic King!!
ETHNIC KING KURARAMAN (RANKED 12TH)
He's ranked 12th in the World Chef Ranking and he's one of the most forceful chefs out there!

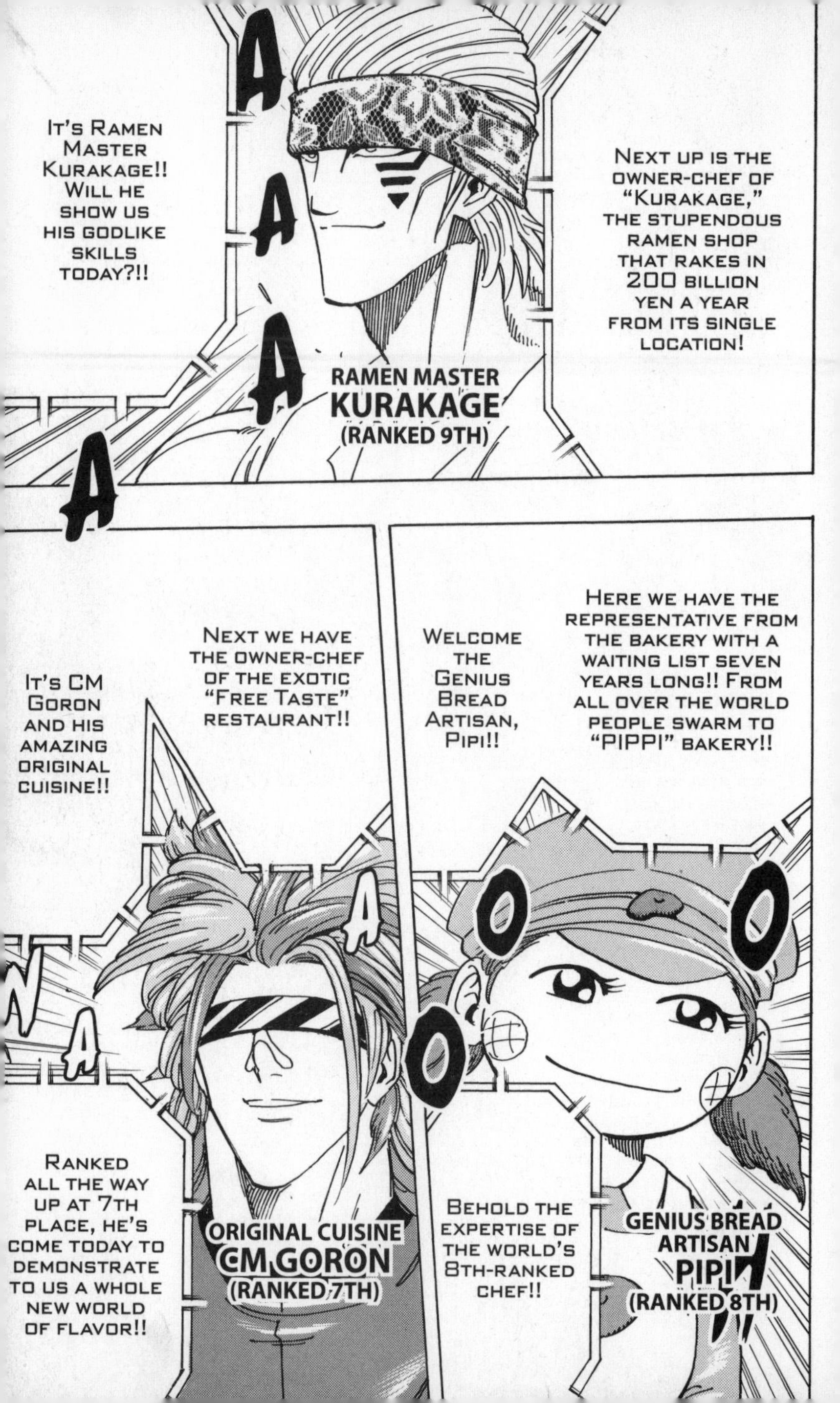
Next up is the owner-chef of "Kurakage," the stupendous ramen shop that rakes in 200 billion yen a year from its single location!
It's Ramen Master Kurakage!! Will he show us his godlike skills today?!!
RAMEN MASTER KURAKAGE (RANKED 9TH)
AAAAA
Here we have the representative from the bakery with a waiting list seven years long!! From all over the world people swarm to "PIPPI" bakery!!
Welcome the Genius Bread Artisan, Pipi!!
Behold the expertise of the world's 8th-ranked chef!!
GENIUS BREAD ARTISAN PIPI (RANKED 8TH)
OOOO
Next we have the owner-chef of the exotic "Free Taste" restaurant!!
It's CM Goron and his amazing original cuisine!!
Ranked all the way up at 7th place, he's come today to demonstrate to us a whole new world of flavor!!
ORIGINAL CUISINE CM GORON (RANKED 7TH)

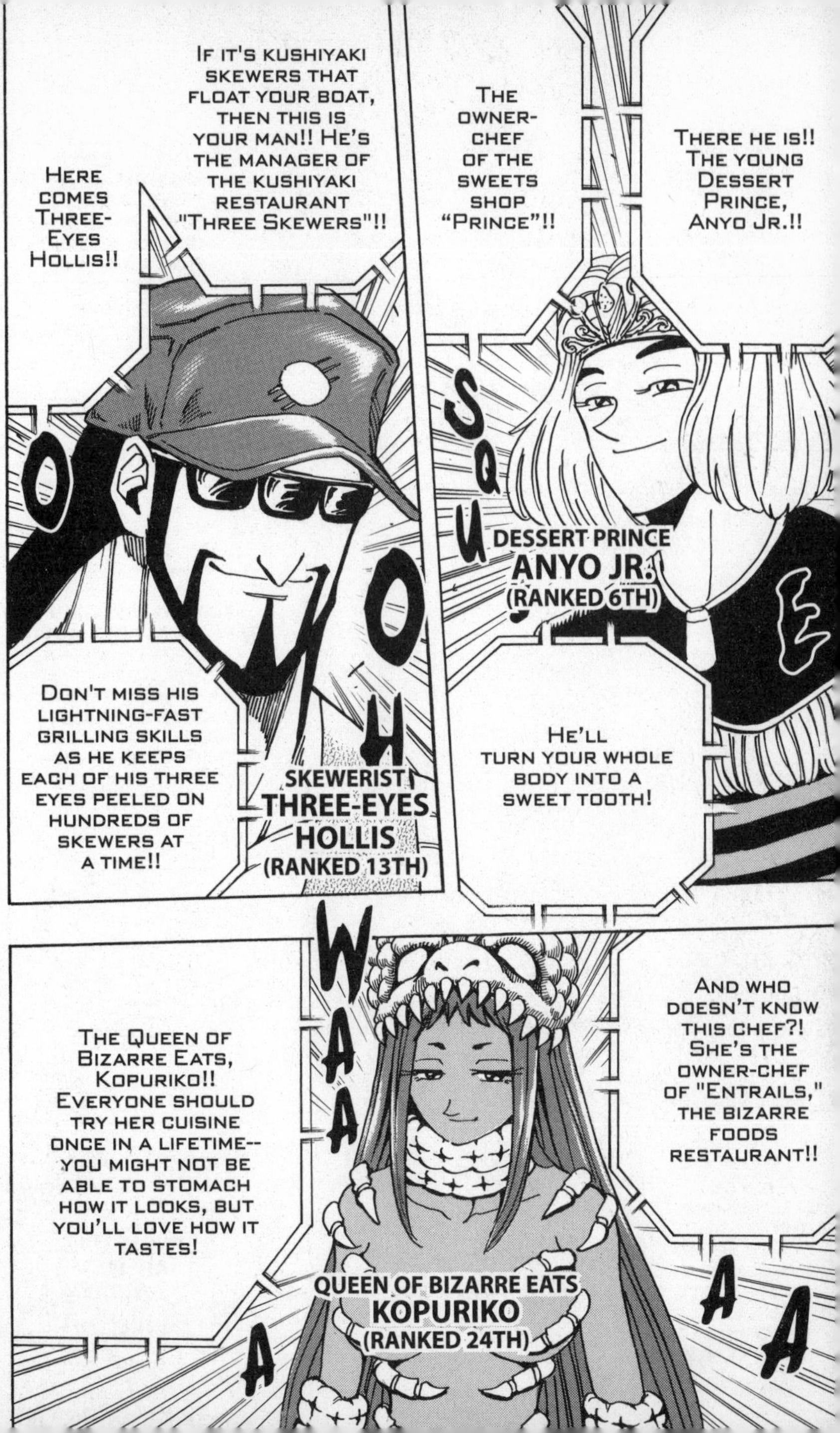
There he is!! The young Dessert Prince, Anyo Jr.!!
The owner-chef of the sweets shop "Prince"!!
SQU
DESSERT PRINCE ANYO JR. (RANKED 6TH)
He'll turn your whole body into a sweet tooth!
Here comes Three-Eyes Hollis!!
If it's kushiyaki skewers that float your boat, then this is your man!! He's the manager of the kushiyaki restaurant "Three Skewers"!!
OOWOOH
Don't miss his lightning-fast grilling skills as he keeps each of his three eyes peeled on hundreds of skewers at a time!!
SKEWERIST THREE-EYES HOLLIS (RANKED 13TH)
WAAAA
And who doesn't know this chef?! She's the owner-chef of "Entrails," the bizarre foods restaurant!!
The Queen of Bizarre Eats, Kopuriko!! Everyone should try her cuisine once in a lifetime-- you might not be able to stomach how it looks, but you'll love how it tastes!
QUEEN OF BIZARRE EATS KOPURIKO (RANKED 24TH)
AAA

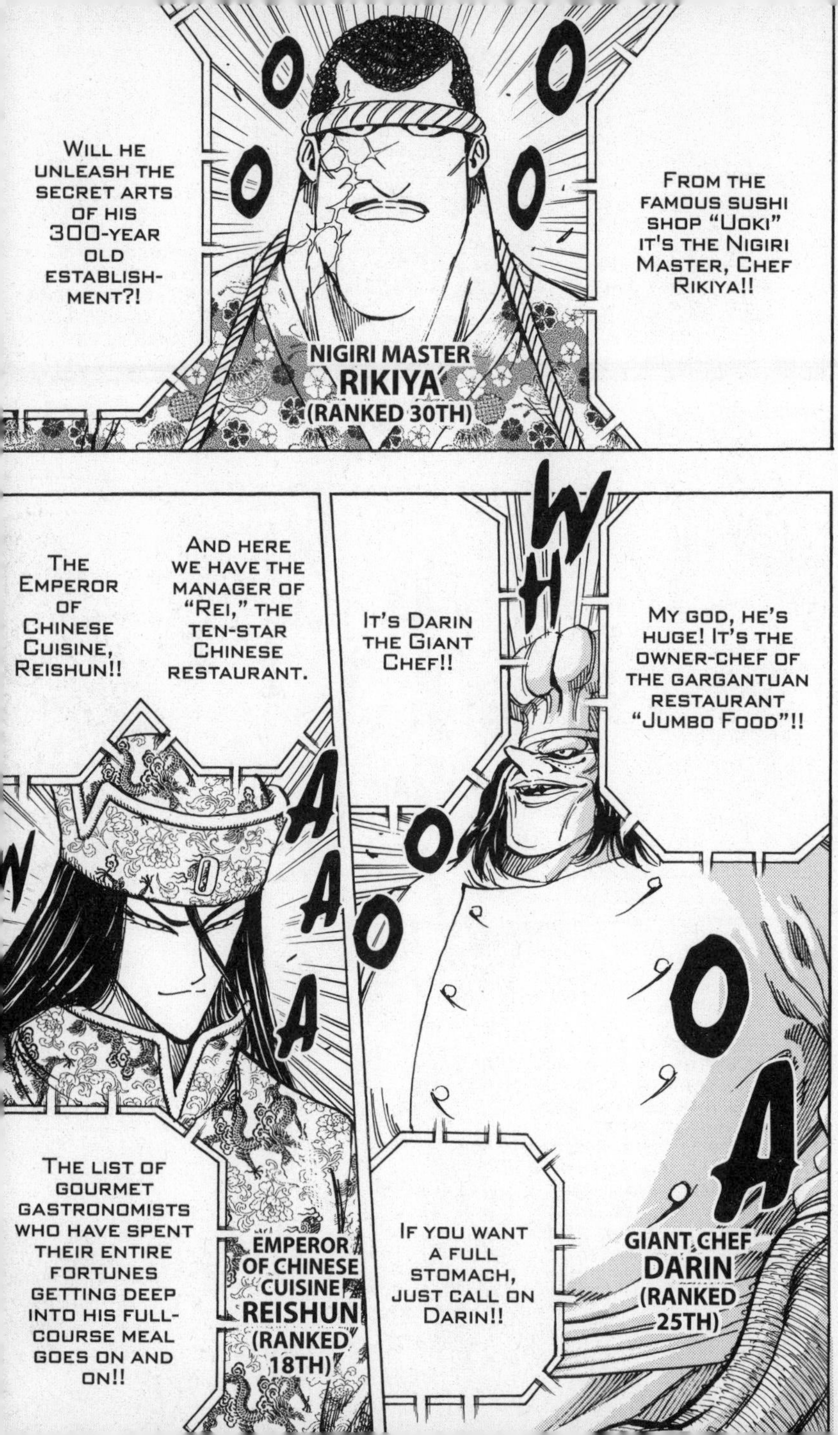

OOOO
From the famous sushi shop "Uoki" it's the Nigiri Master, Chef Rikiya!!
Will he unleash the secret arts of his 300-year old establish-ment?!
NIGIRI MASTER RIKIYA (RANKED 30TH)
WHOOOA
My god, he's huge! It's the owner-chef of the gargantuan restaurant "Jumbo Food"!!
It's Darin the Giant Chef!!
GIANT CHEF DARIN (RANKED 25TH)
If you want a full stomach, just call on Darin!!
AAA
And here we have the manager of "Rei," the ten-star Chinese restaurant.
The Emperor of Chinese Cuisine, Reishun!!
EMPEROR OF CHINESE CUISINE REISHUN (RANKED 18TH)
The list of gourmet gastronomists who have spent their entire fortunes getting deep into his full-course meal goes on and on!!

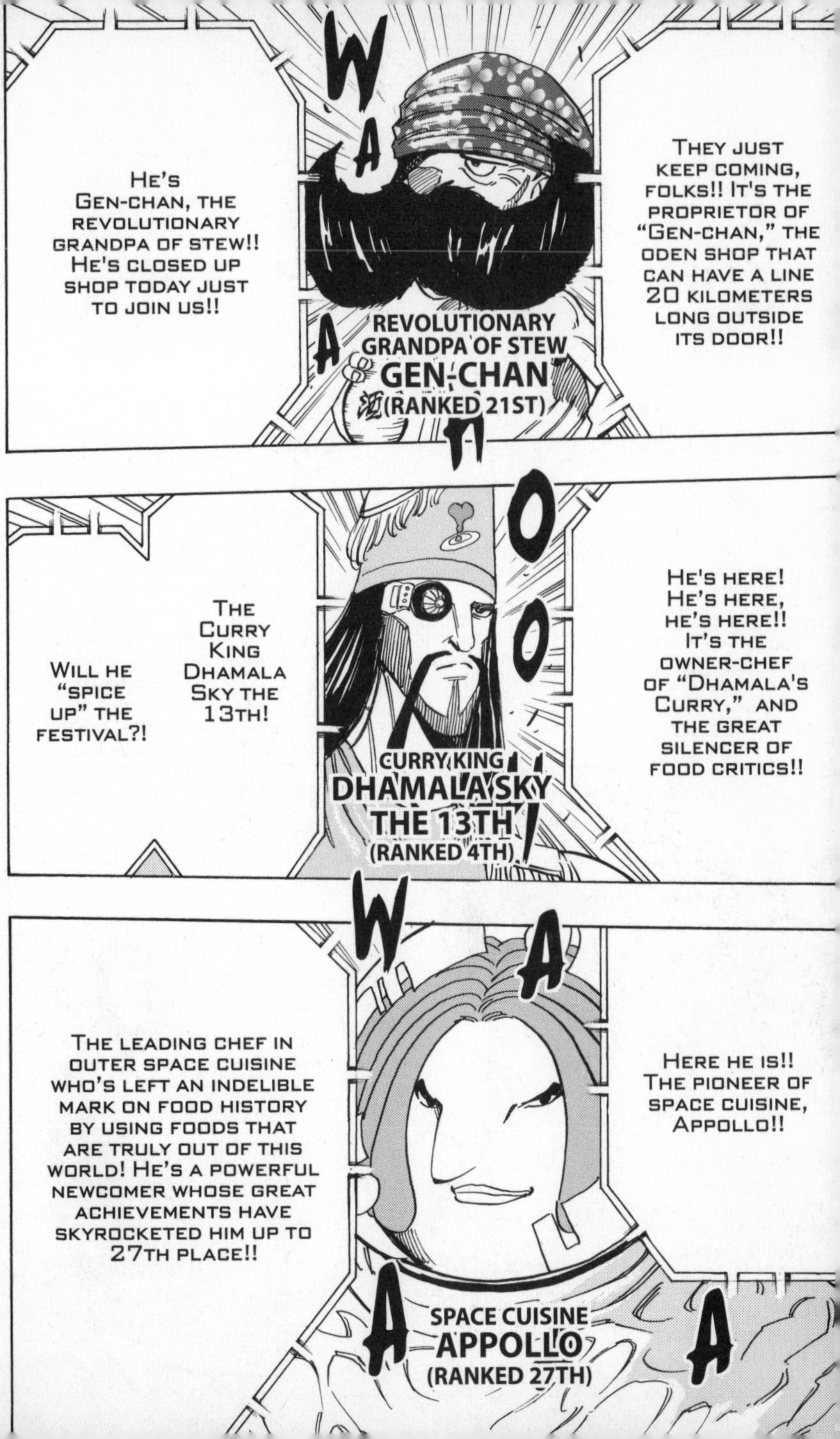
WA
They just keep coming, folks!! It's the proprietor of "Gen-chan," the oden shop that can have a line 20 kilometers long outside its door!!
Revolutionary Grandpa of Stew
Gen-chan
(Ranked 21st)
A
He's Gen-chan, the revolutionary grandpa of stew!! He's closed up shop today just to join us!!
H
O
O
He's here! He's here, he's here!! It's the owner-chef of "Dhamala's Curry," and the great silencer of food critics!!
Curry King
Dhamala Sky
the 13th
(Ranked 4th)
The Curry King Dhamala Sky the 13th!
Will he "spice up" the festival?!
W
A
Here he is!! The pioneer of space cuisine, Appollo!!
The leading chef in outer space cuisine who's left an indelible mark on food history by using foods that are truly out of this world! He's a powerful newcomer whose great achievements have skyrocketed him up to 27th place!!
A
Space Cuisine
Appollo
(Ranked 27th)
A

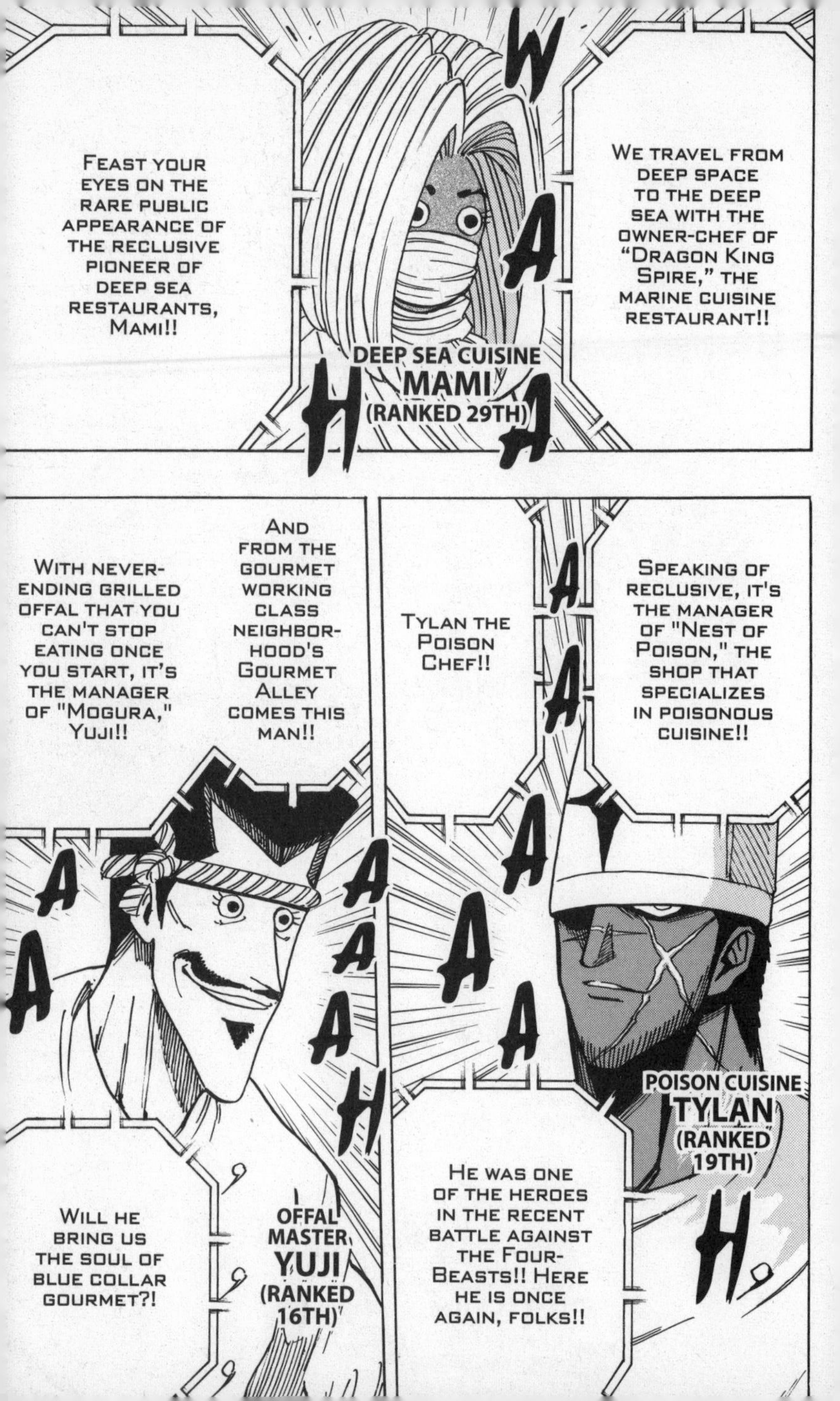
We travel from deep space to the deep sea with the owner-chef of "Dragon King Spire," the marine cuisine restaurant!!
WAAAH
Feast your eyes on the rare public appearance of the reclusive pioneer of deep sea restaurants, Mami!!
DEEP SEA CUISINE MAMI (RANKED 29TH)
Speaking of reclusive, it's the manager of "Nest of Poison," the shop that specializes in poisonous cuisine!!
Tylan the Poison Chef!!
AAAAAH
POISON CUISINE TYLAN (RANKED 19TH)
He was one of the heroes in the recent battle against the Four-Beasts!! Here he is once again, folks!!
And from the gourmet working class neighbor-hood's Gourmet Alley comes this man!!
With never-ending grilled offal that you can't stop eating once you start, it's the manager of "Mogura," Yuji!!
AAAAAH
OFFAL MASTER YUJI (RANKED 16TH)
Will he bring us the soul of blue collar gourmet?!

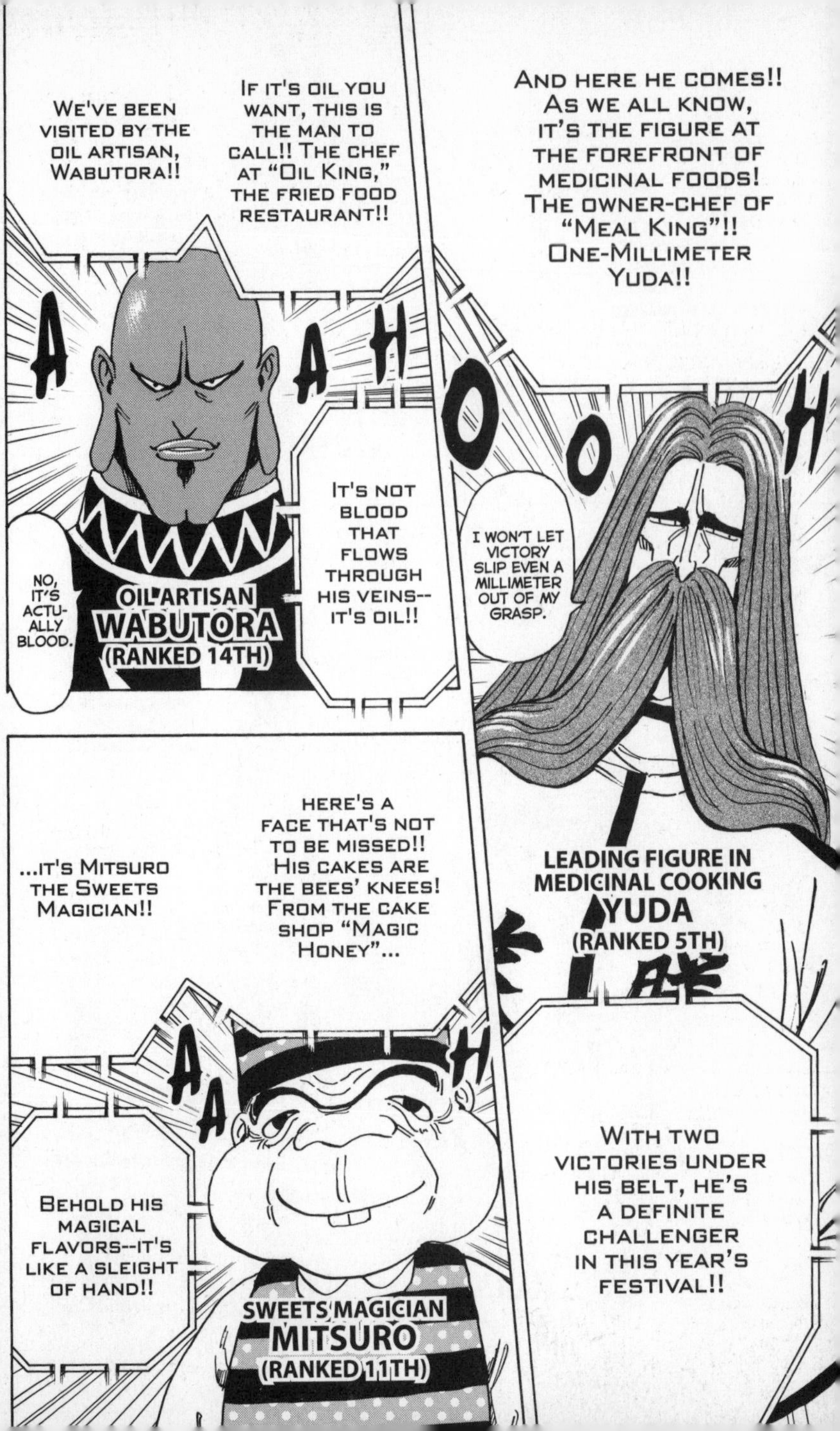
AND HERE HE COMES!! AS WE ALL KNOW, IT'S THE FIGURE AT THE FOREFRONT OF MEDICINAL FOODS! THE OWNER-CHEF OF "MEAL KING"!! ONE-MILLIMETER YUDA!!
I WON'T LET VICTORY SLIP EVEN A MILLIMETER OUT OF MY GRASP.
LEADING FIGURE IN MEDICINAL COOKING
YUDA
(RANKED 5TH)
WITH TWO VICTORIES UNDER HIS BELT, HE'S A DEFINITE CHALLENGER IN THIS YEAR'S FESTIVAL!!
IF IT'S OIL YOU WANT, THIS IS THE MAN TO CALL!! THE CHEF AT "OIL KING," THE FRIED FOOD RESTAURANT!!
WE'VE BEEN VISITED BY THE OIL ARTISAN, WABUTORA!!
IT'S NOT BLOOD THAT FLOWS THROUGH HIS VEINS--IT'S OIL!!
OIL ARTISAN
WABUTORA
(RANKED 14TH)
NO, IT'S ACTUALLY BLOOD.
HERE'S A FACE THAT'S NOT TO BE MISSED!! HIS CAKES ARE THE BEES' KNEES! FROM THE CAKE SHOP "MAGIC HONEY"...
...IT'S MITSURO THE SWEETS MAGICIAN!!
BEHOLD HIS MAGICAL FLAVORS--IT'S LIKE A SLEIGHT OF HAND!!
SWEETS MAGICIAN
MITSURO
(RANKED 11TH)

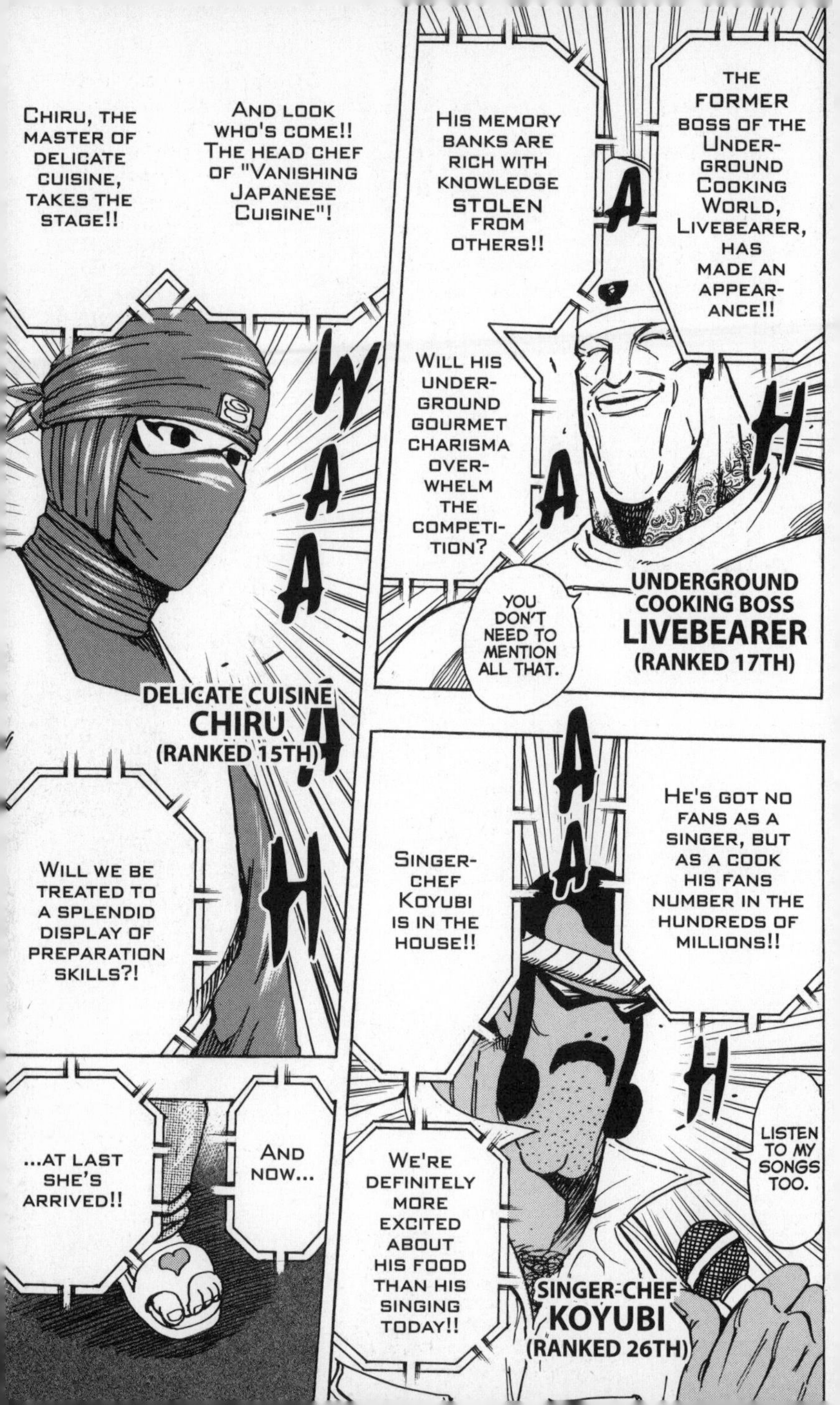
The former boss of the Under-ground Cooking World, Livebearer, has made an appear-ance!!
His memory banks are rich with knowledge stolen from others!!
A
Will his under-ground gourmet charisma over-whelm the competi-tion?
A
H
UNDERGROUND COOKING BOSS LIVEBEARER (RANKED 17TH)
You don't need to mention all that.
He's got no fans as a singer, but as a cook his fans number in the hundreds of millions!!
Singer-chef Koyubi is in the house!!
A
A
H
Listen to my songs too.
We're definitely more excited about his food than his singing today!!
SINGER-CHEF KOYUBI (RANKED 26TH)
Chiru, the master of delicate cuisine, takes the stage!!
And look who's come!! The head chef of "Vanishing Japanese Cuisine"!
W
A
A
DELICATE CUISINE CHIRU (RANKED 15TH)
A
H
Will we be treated to a splendid display of preparation skills?!
And now...
...at last she's arrived!!

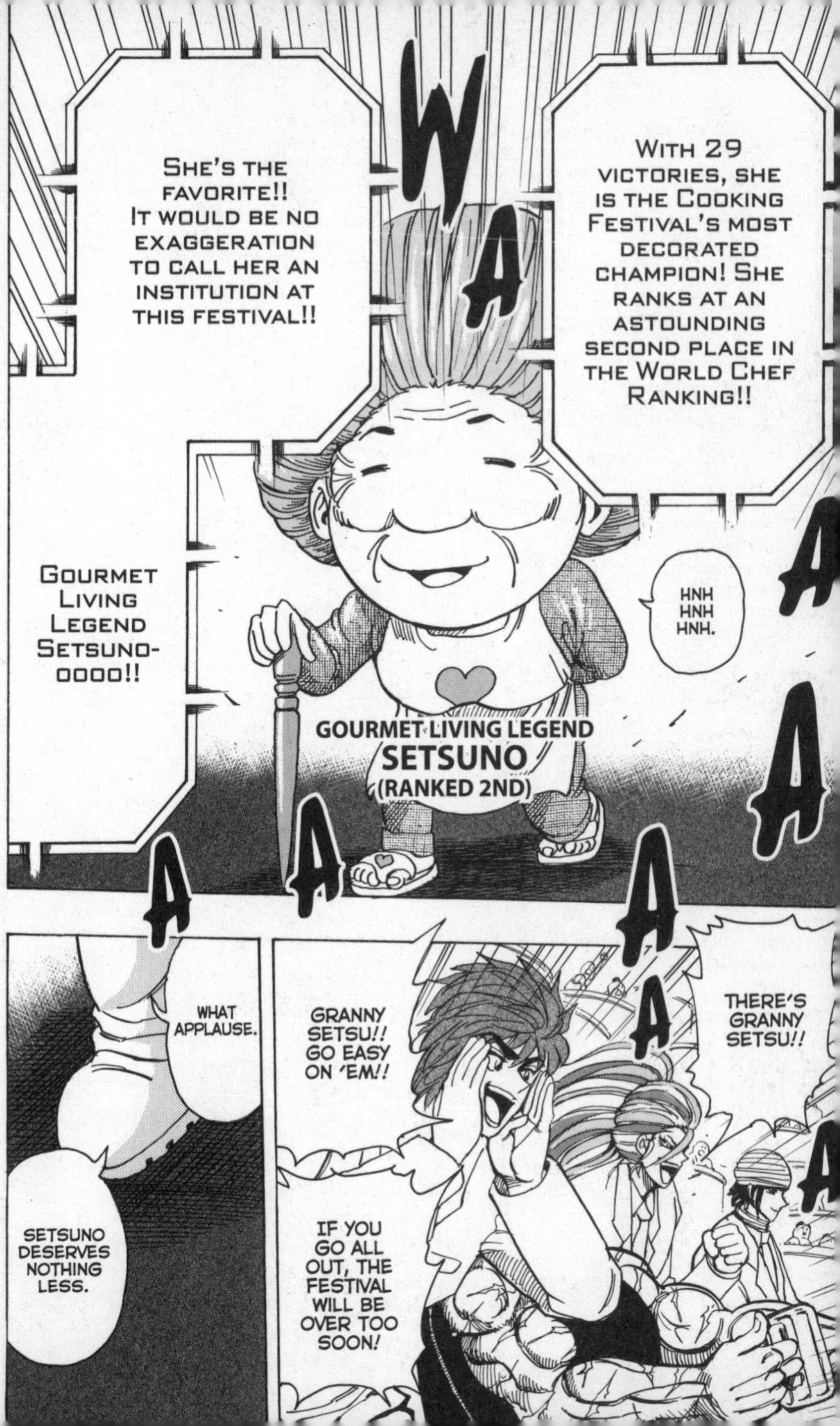
WAA
With 29 victories, she is the Cooking Festival's most decorated champion! She ranks at an astounding second place in the World Chef Ranking!!
She's the favorite!! It would be no exaggeration to call her an institution at this festival!!
Gourmet Living Legend Setsuno-oooo!!
HNH HNH HNH.
GOURMET LIVING LEGEND
SETSUNO
(RANKED 2ND)
AAAA
THERE'S GRANNY SETSU!!
GRANNY SETSU!! GO EASY ON 'EM!!
IF YOU GO ALL OUT, THE FESTIVAL WILL BE OVER TOO SOON!
WHAT APPLAUSE.
SETSUNO DESERVES NOTHING LESS.

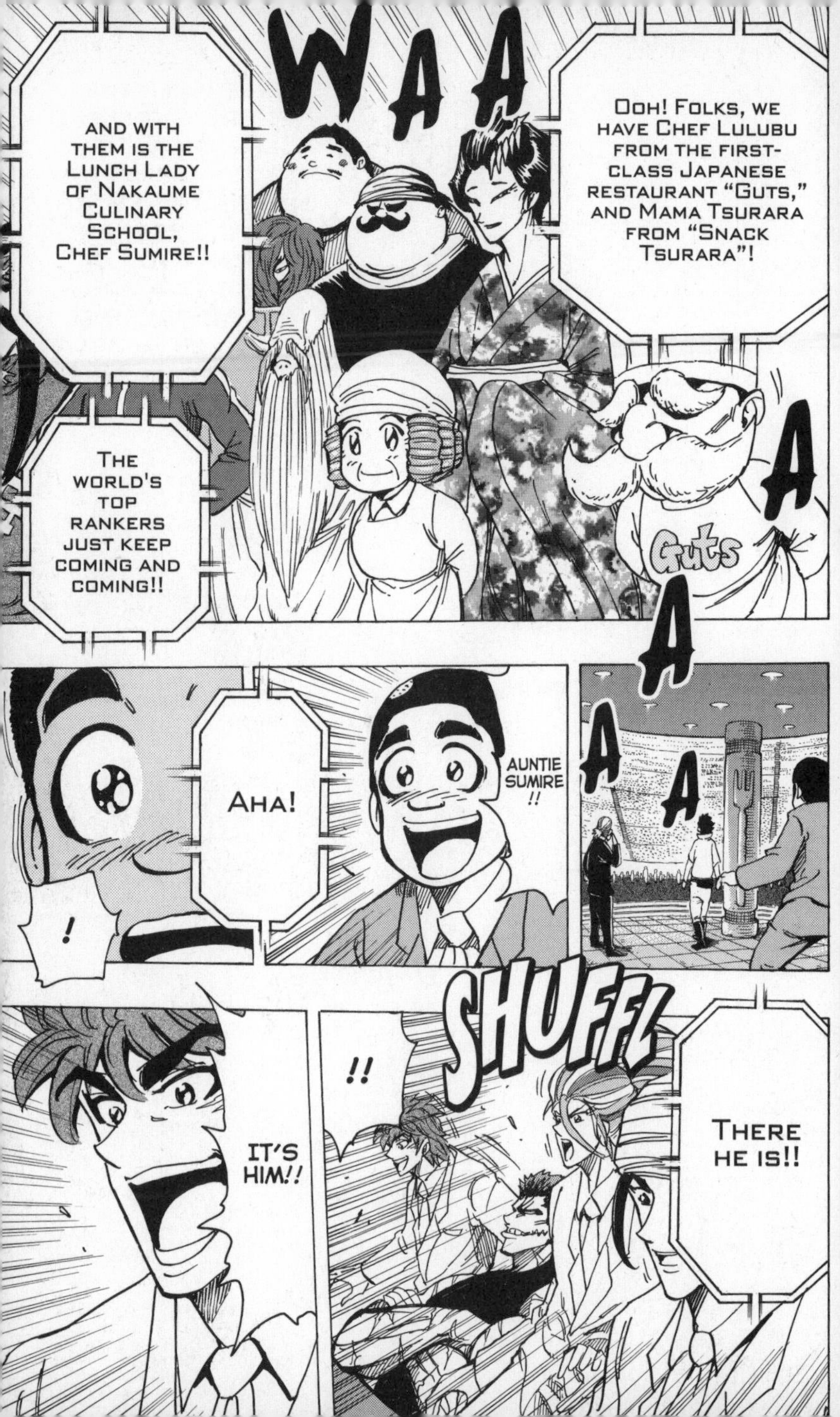
Ooh! Folks, we have Chef Lulubu from the first-class Japanese restaurant "Guts," and Mama Tsurara from "Snack Tsurara"!
WAAAAA
Guts
And with them is the Lunch Lady of Nakaume Culinary School, Chef Sumire!!
The world's top rankers just keep coming and coming!!
AAA
Auntie Sumire !!
Aha!
!
There he is!!
SHUFFL
!!
It's him!!

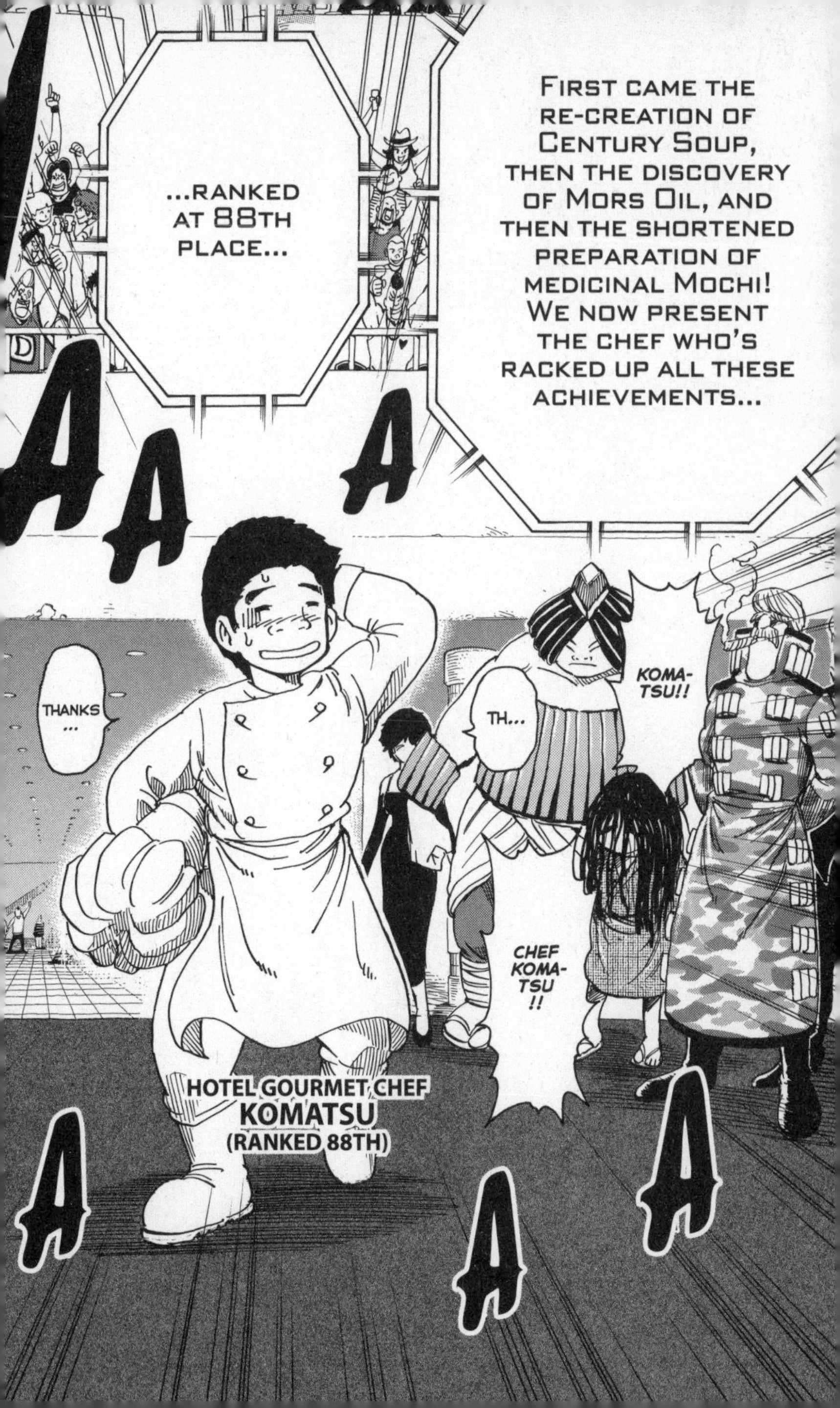
FIRST CAME THE RE-CREATION OF CENTURY SOUP, THEN THE DISCOVERY OF MORS OIL, AND THEN THE SHORTENED PREPARATION OF MEDICINAL MOCHI! WE NOW PRESENT THE CHEF WHO'S RACKED UP ALL THESE ACHIEVEMENTS...
...RANKED AT 88TH PLACE...
A
A
A
KOMA-TSU!!
TH...
THANKS...
CHEF KOMA-TSU!!
HOTEL GOURMET CHEF
KOMATSU
(RANKED 88TH)
A
A
A

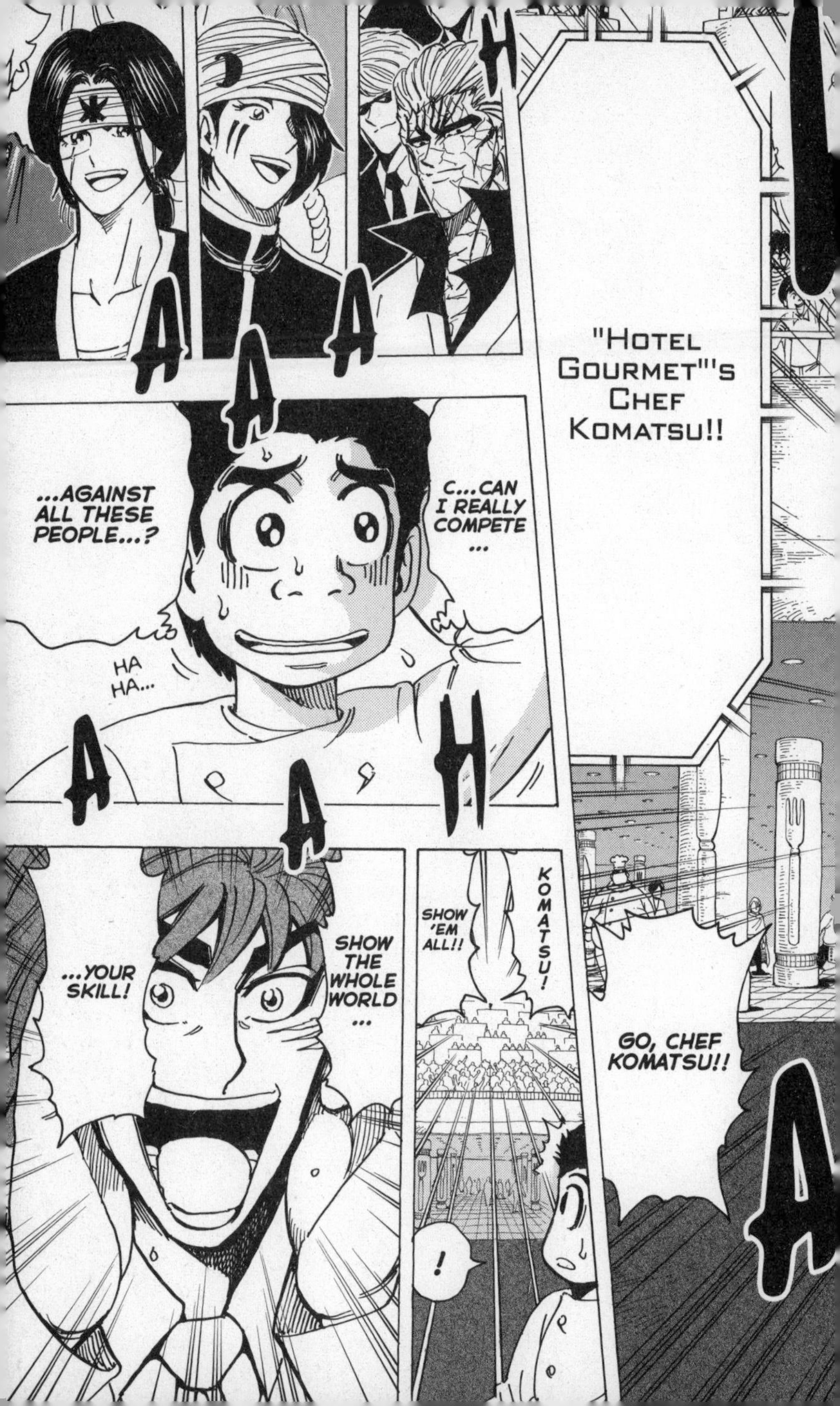
"HOTEL GOURMET"'s CHEF KOMATSU!!
GO, CHEF KOMATSU!!
C...CAN I REALLY COMPETE...
...AGAINST ALL THESE PEOPLE...?
HA HA...
KOMATSU!
SHOW 'EM ALL!!
!
SHOW THE WHOLE WORLD...
...YOUR SKILL!

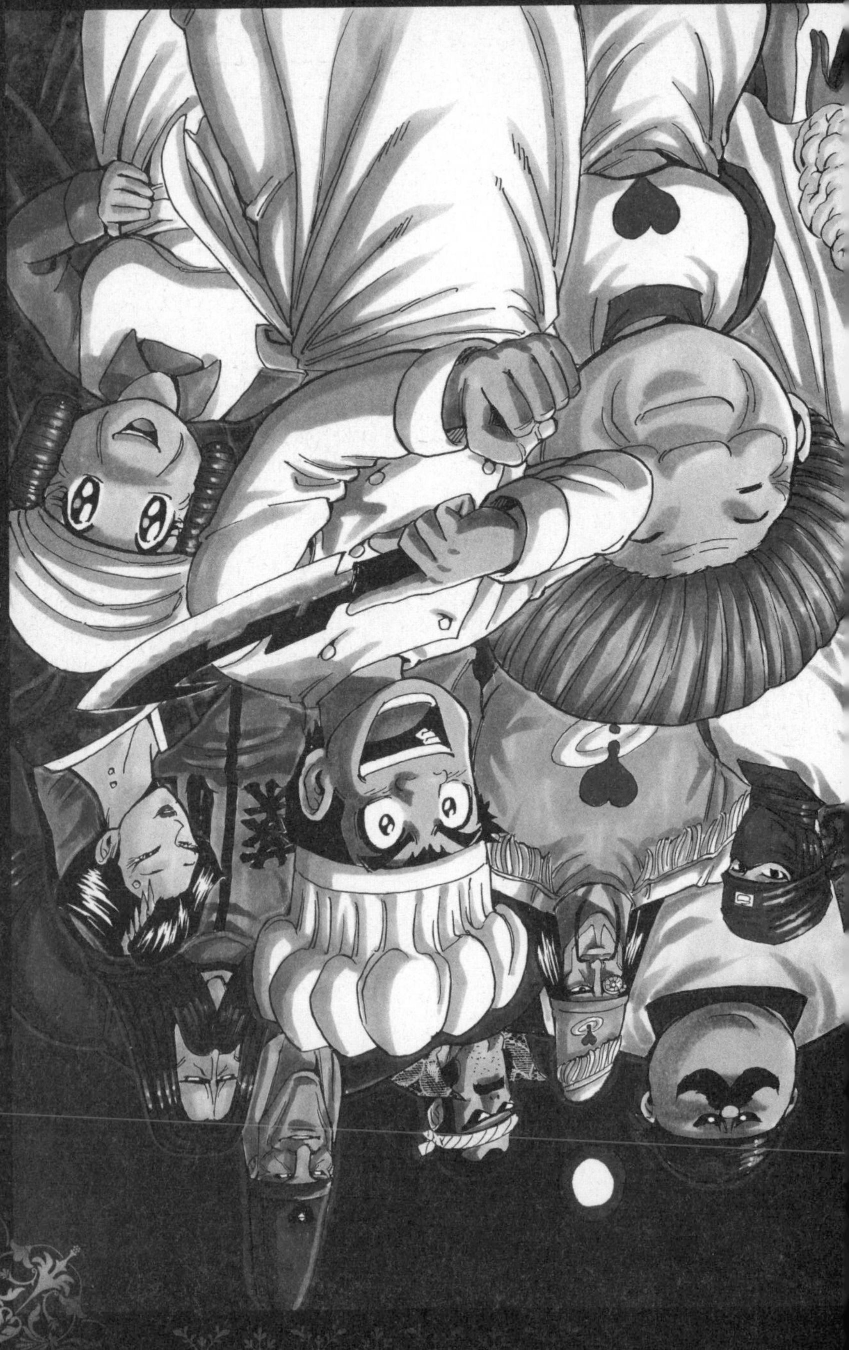

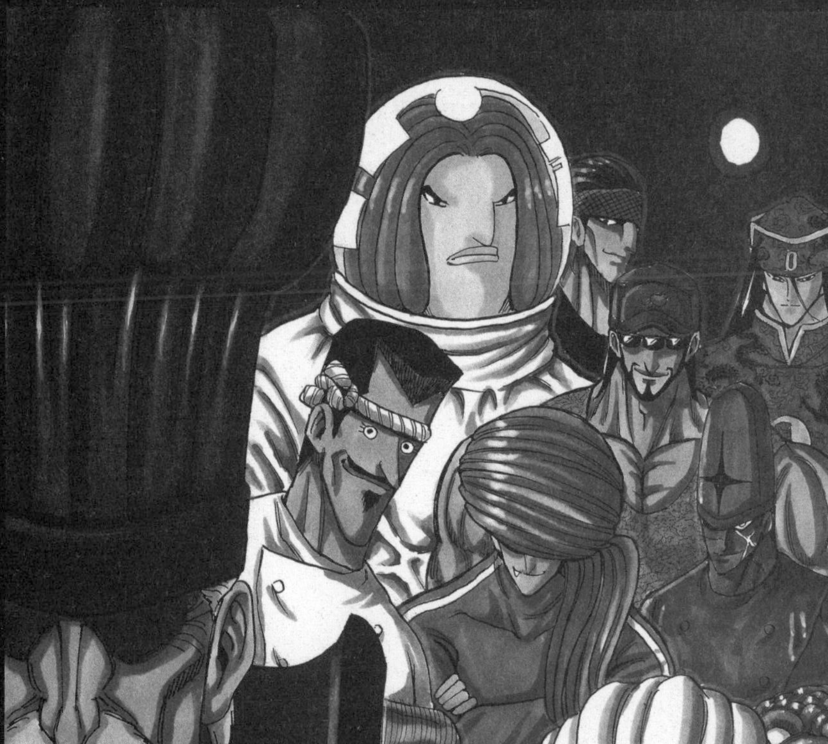
Guts

GOURMET 213: THE PRELIMINARIES BEGIN!!

TORIKO

GOURMET CHECKLIST

Vol. 245

MINERAL SHALLOT
(PLANT)

CAPTURE LEVEL: 1

HABITAT: THRIVES EVERYWHERE

LENGTH: 8 CM

HEIGHT: ---

WEIGHT: 80 G

PRICE: 150 YEN

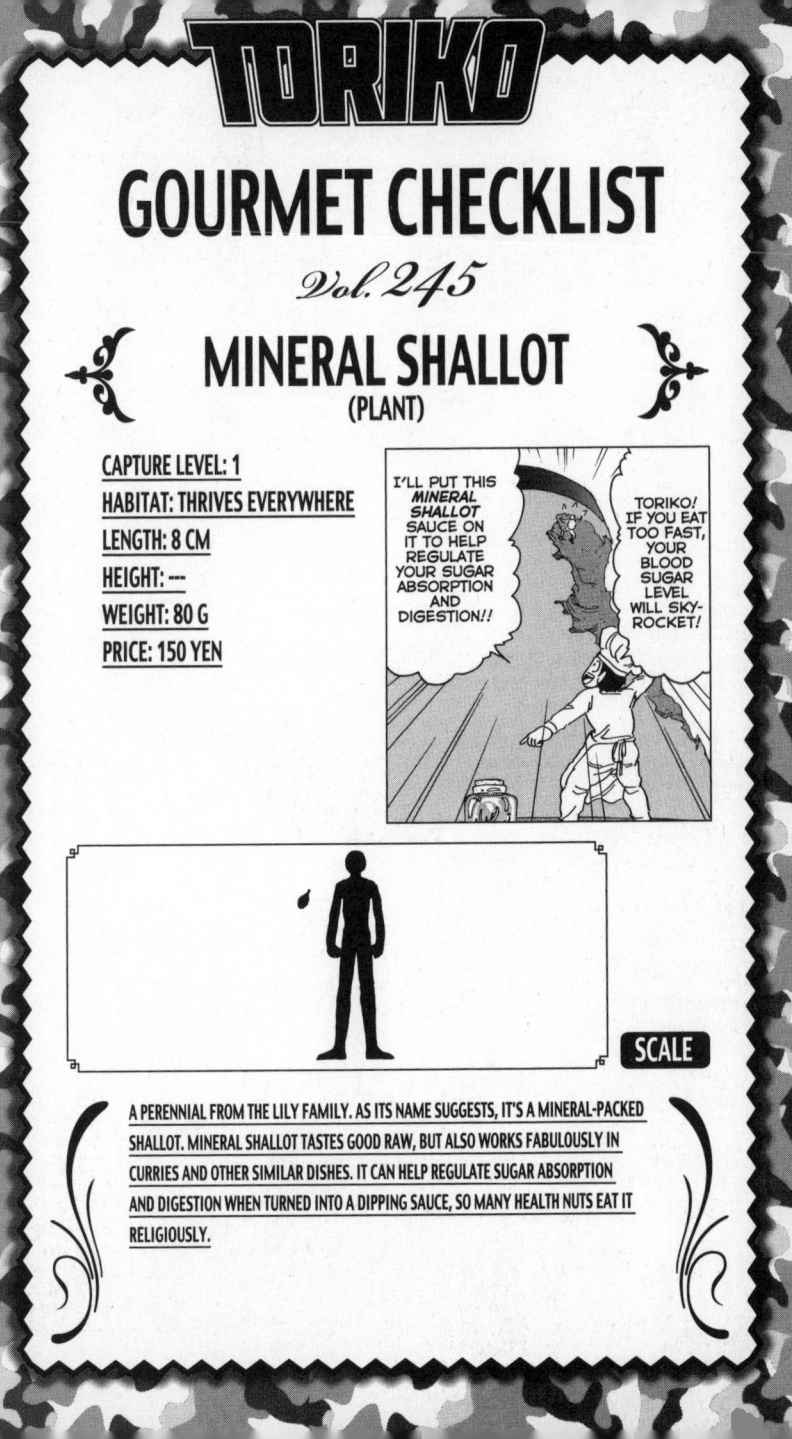

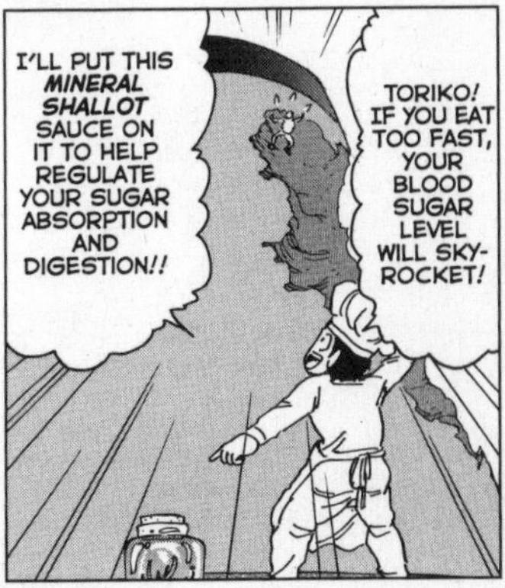
TORIKO! IF YOU EAT TOO FAST, YOUR BLOOD SUGAR LEVEL WILL SKY-ROCKET!
I'LL PUT THIS *MINERAL SHALLOT* SAUCE ON IT TO HELP REGULATE YOUR SUGAR ABSORPTION AND DIGESTION!!

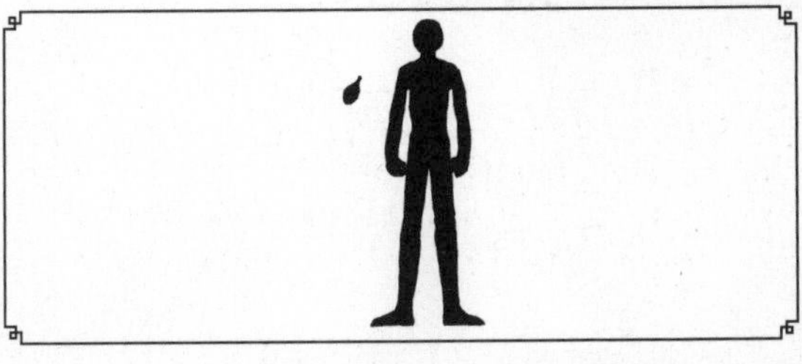

SCALE

A PERENNIAL FROM THE LILY FAMILY. AS ITS NAME SUGGESTS, IT'S A MINERAL-PACKED SHALLOT. MINERAL SHALLOT TASTES GOOD RAW, BUT ALSO WORKS FABULOUSLY IN CURRIES AND OTHER SIMILAR DISHES. IT CAN HELP REGULATE SUGAR ABSORPTION AND DIGESTION WHEN TURNED INTO A DIPPING SAUCE, SO MANY HEALTH NUTS EAT IT RELIGIOUSLY.

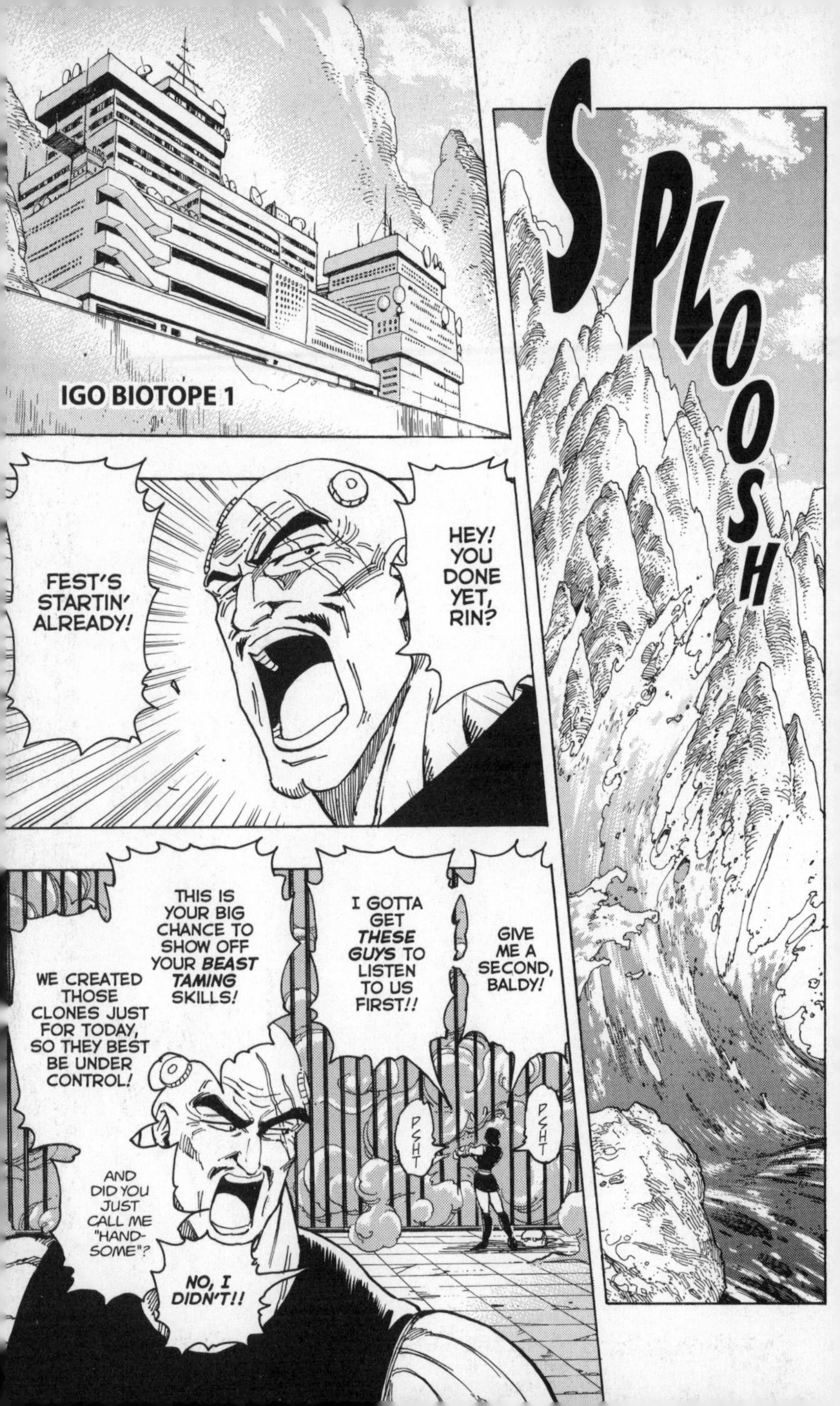
SPLOOSH
IGO BIOTOPE 1
HEY! YOU DONE YET, RIN?
FEST'S STARTIN' ALREADY!
GIVE ME A SECOND, BALDY!
I GOTTA GET *THESE GUYS* TO LISTEN TO US FIRST!!
THIS IS YOUR BIG CHANCE TO SHOW OFF YOUR *BEAST TAMING* SKILLS!
WE CREATED THOSE CLONES JUST FOR TODAY, SO THEY BEST BE UNDER CONTROL!
PSHT
PSHT
AND DID YOU JUST CALL ME "HAND-SOME"?
NO, I DIDN'T!!

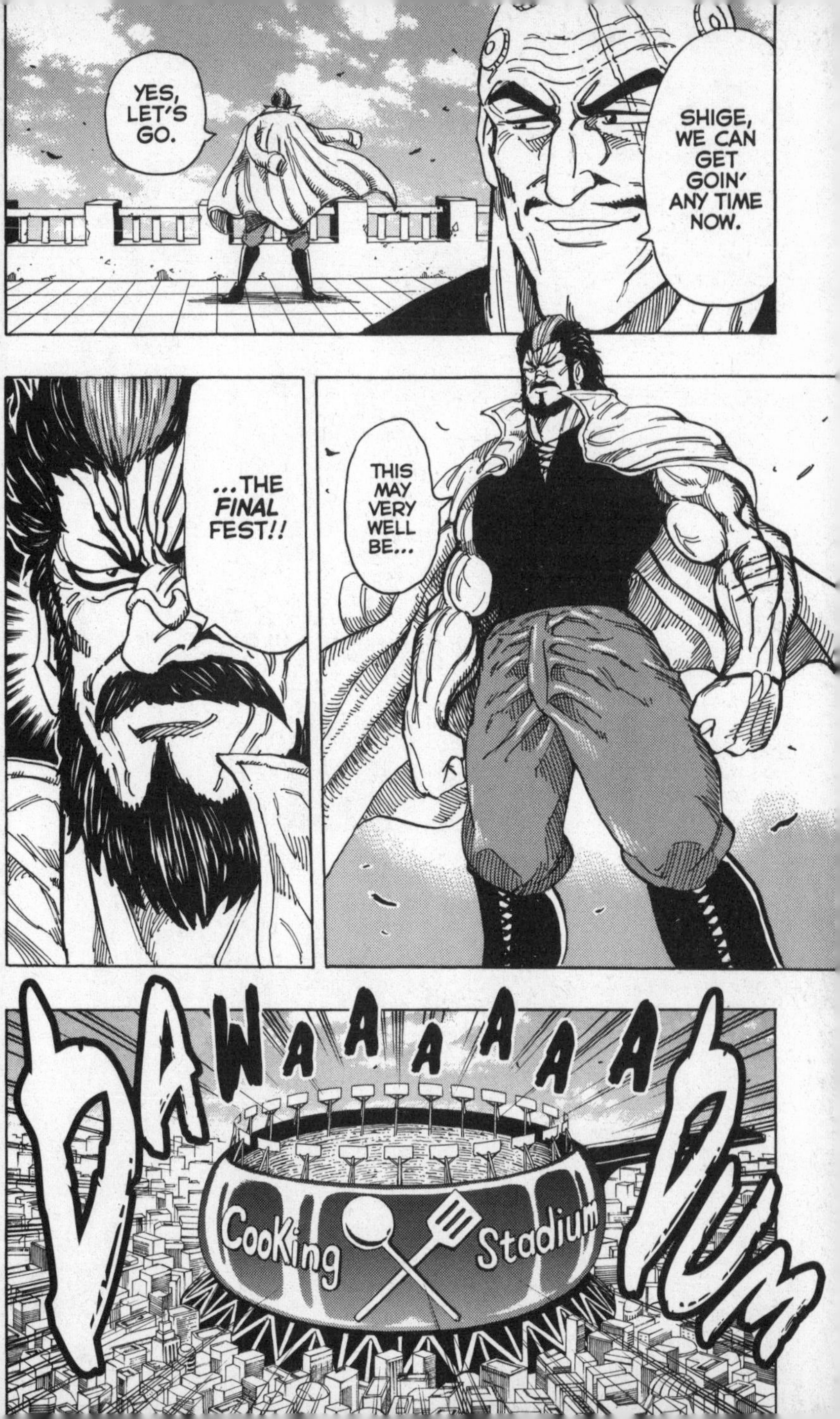
SHIGE, WE CAN GET GOIN' ANY TIME NOW.
YES, LET'S GO.
THIS MAY VERY WELL BE...
...THE *FINAL* FEST!!
DAWAAAAAAAAA DUM
Cooking Stadium

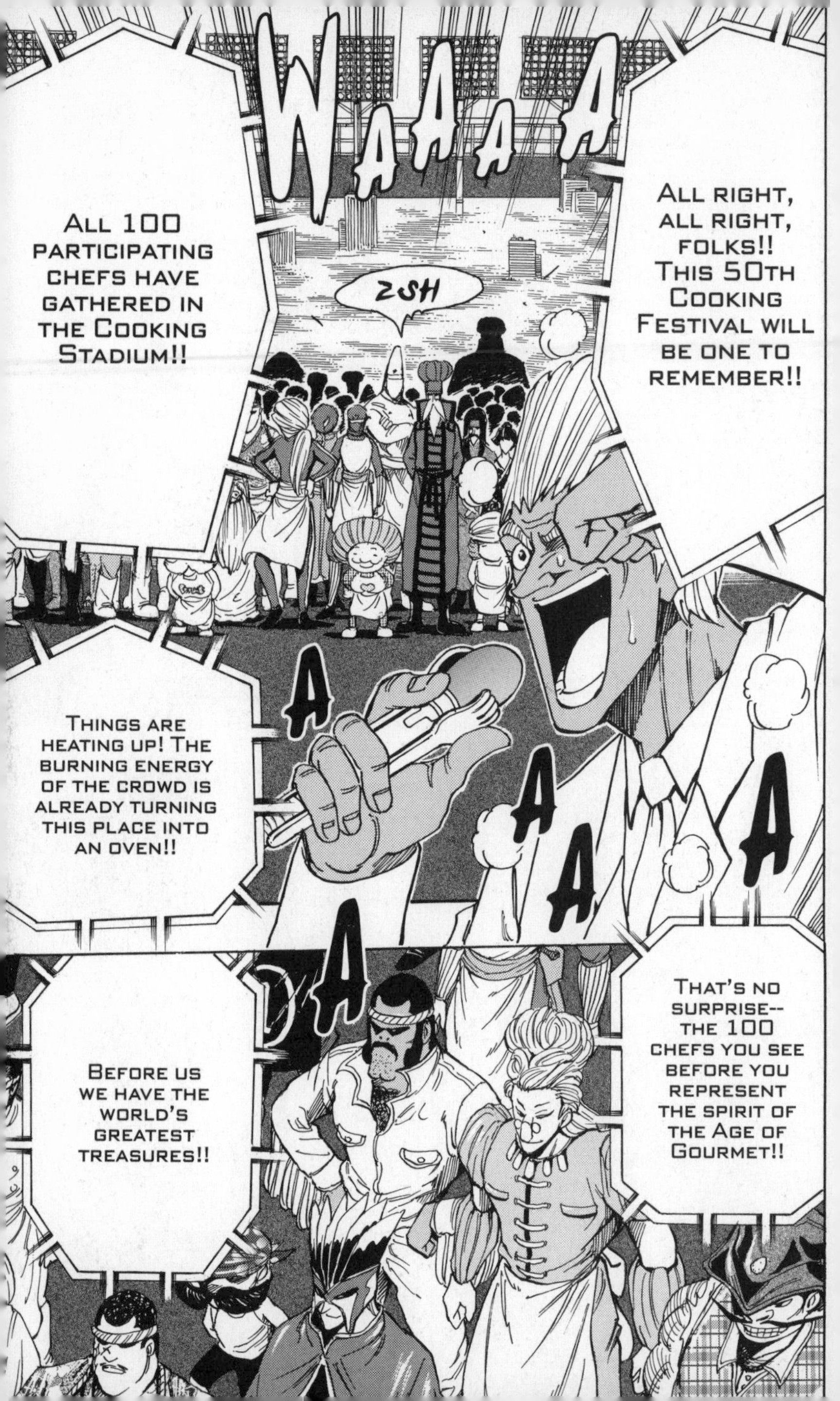
WAAAAA
ALL RIGHT, ALL RIGHT, FOLKS!! THIS 50TH COOKING FESTIVAL WILL BE ONE TO REMEMBER!!
ALL 100 PARTICIPATING CHEFS HAVE GATHERED IN THE COOKING STADIUM!!
ZSH
AAAA
THINGS ARE HEATING UP! THE BURNING ENERGY OF THE CROWD IS ALREADY TURNING THIS PLACE INTO AN OVEN!!
A
THAT'S NO SURPRISE-- THE 100 CHEFS YOU SEE BEFORE YOU REPRESENT THE SPIRIT OF THE AGE OF GOURMET!!
BEFORE US WE HAVE THE WORLD'S GREATEST TREASURES!!

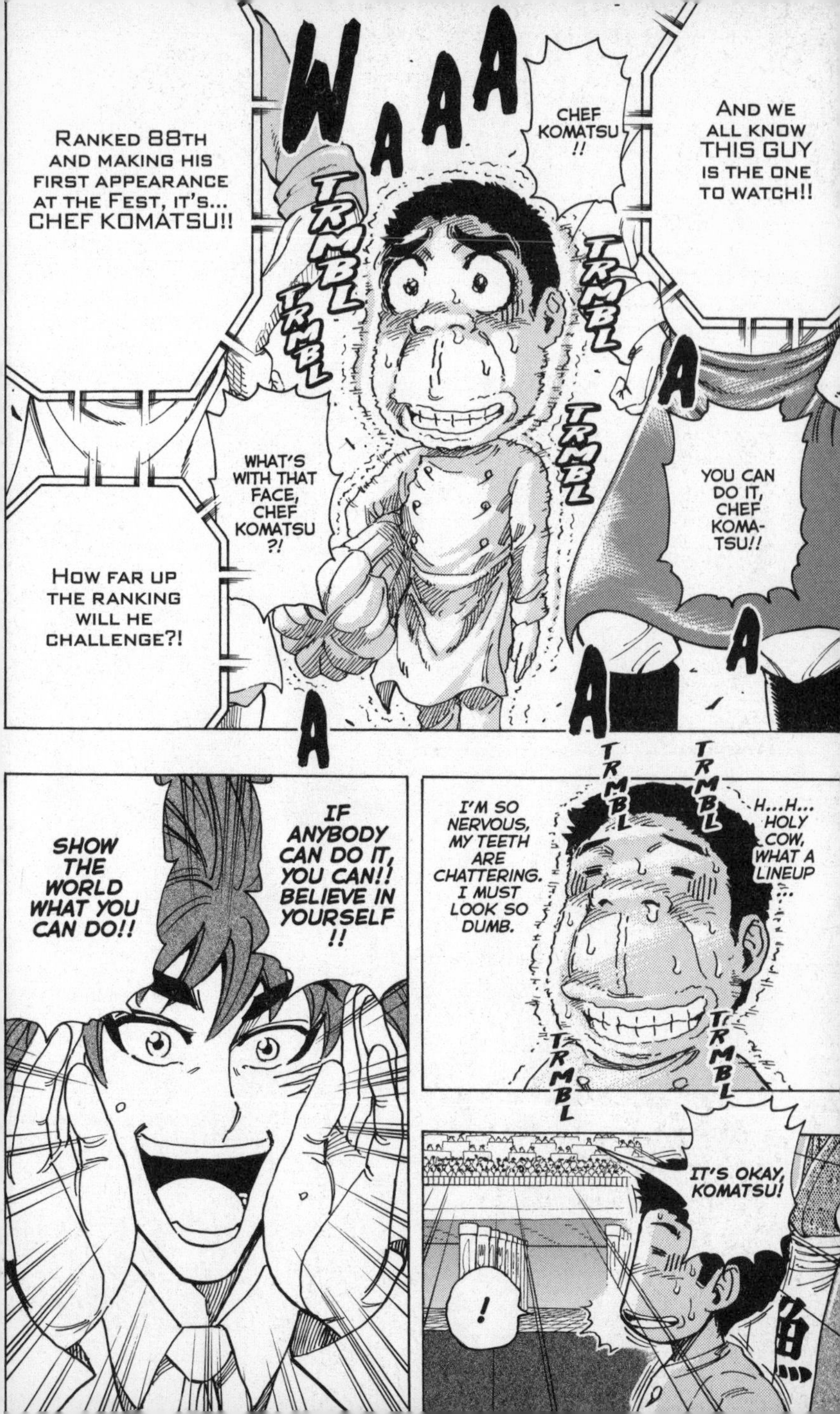
And we all know THIS GUY is the one to watch!!
CHEF KOMATSU!!
Ranked 88th and making his first appearance at the Fest, it's... CHEF KOMATSU!!
WAAAAAAA
TRMBL TRMBL
TRMBL
TRMBL
You can do it, Chef Koma-tsu!!
What's with that face, Chef Komatsu?!
How far up the ranking will he challenge?!
H...H... Holy cow, what a lineup...
TRMBL TRMBL
I'm so nervous, my teeth are chattering. I must look so dumb.
TRMBL TRMBL
If anybody can do it, you can!! Believe in yourself!!
Show the world what you can do!!
It's okay, Komatsu!
!

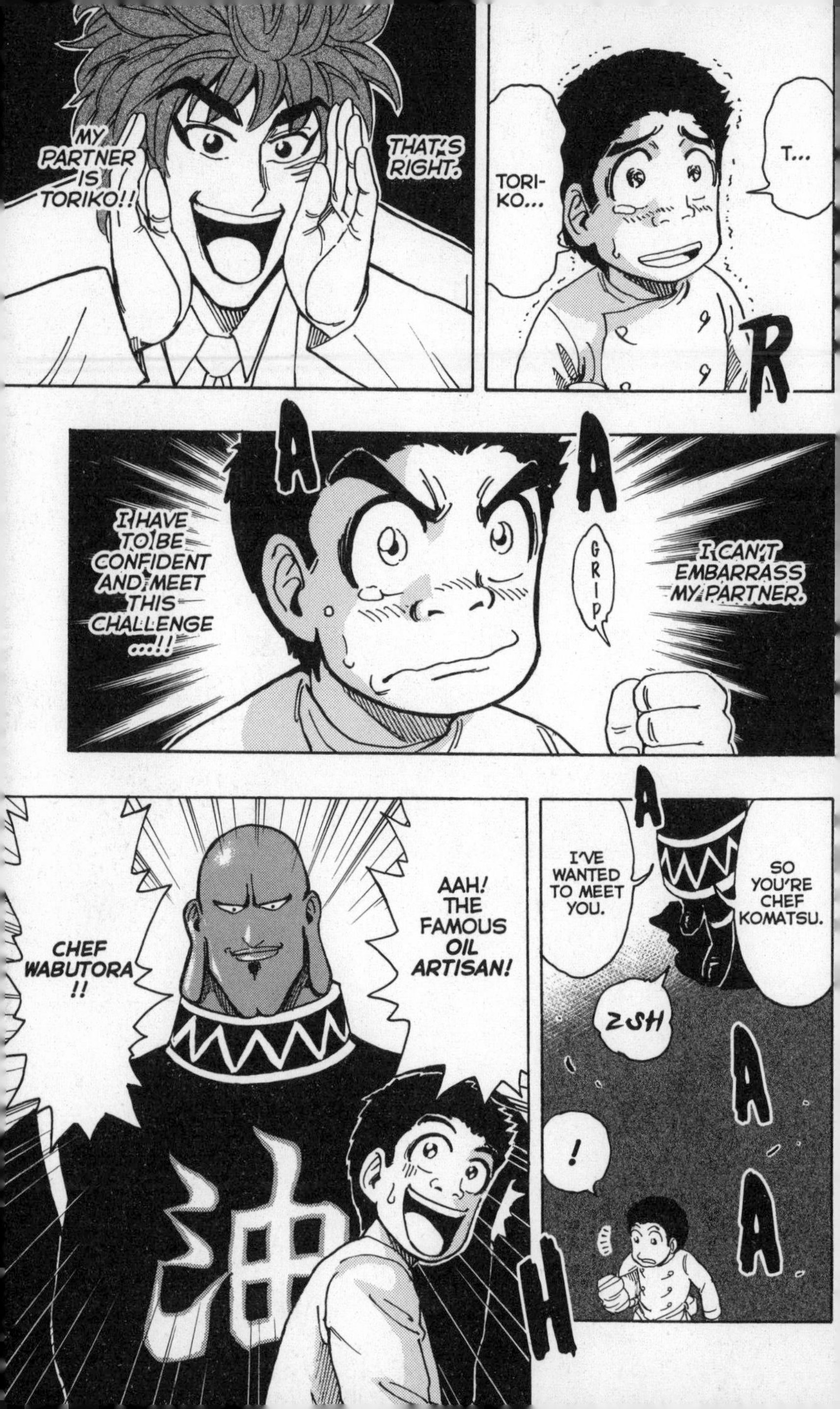
T...
TORI-KO...
THAT'S RIGHT.
MY PARTNER IS TORIKO!!
R
A
A
I CAN'T EMBARRASS MY PARTNER.
GRIP
I HAVE TO BE CONFIDENT AND MEET THIS CHALLENGE ...!!
A
SO YOU'RE CHEF KOMATSU.
I'VE WANTED TO MEET YOU.
ZSH
A
A
A
!
H
AAH! THE FAMOUS OIL ARTISAN!
CHEF WABUTORA!!

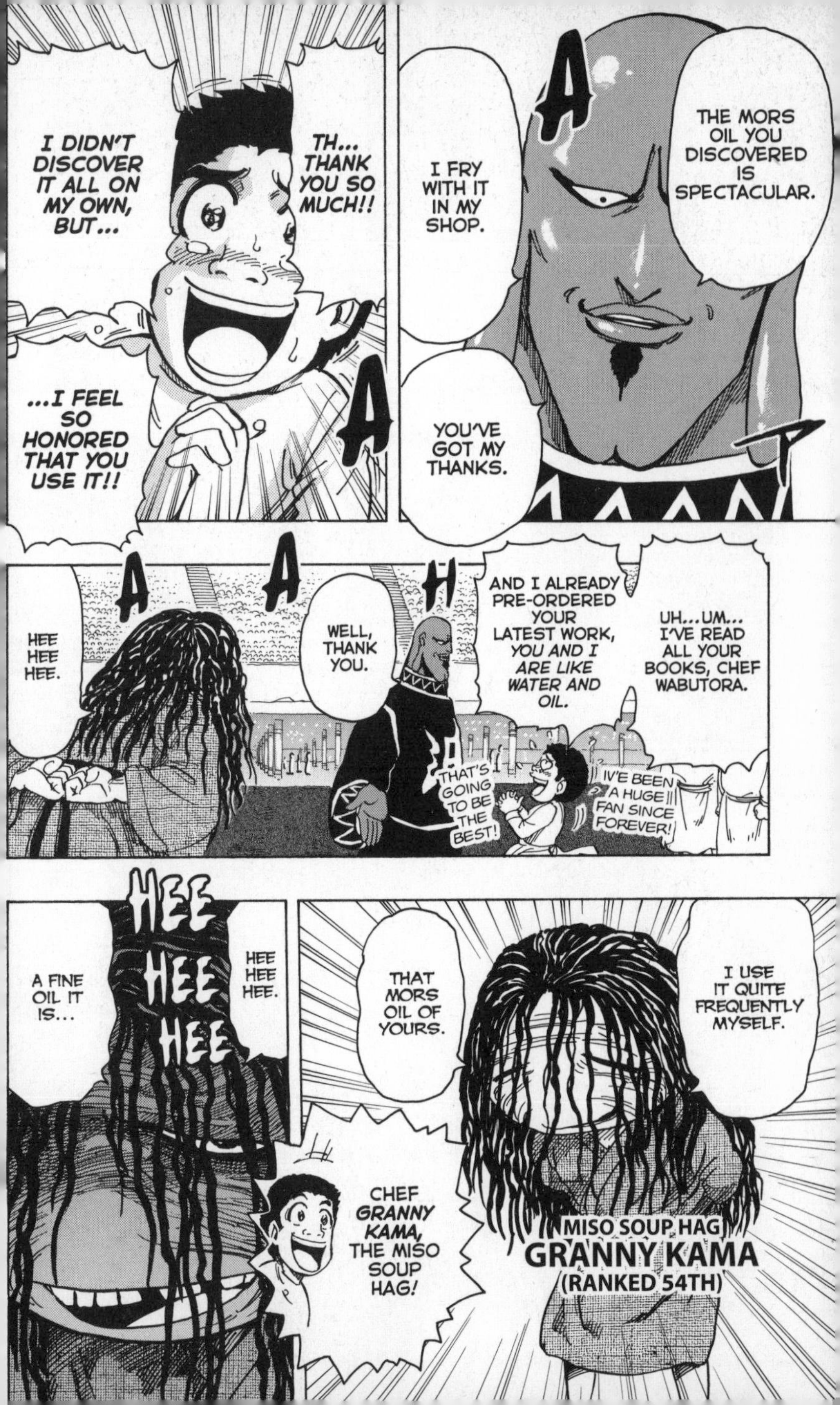
THE MORS OIL YOU DISCOVERED IS SPECTACULAR.
A
I FRY WITH IT IN MY SHOP.
YOU'VE GOT MY THANKS.
TH... THANK YOU SO MUCH!!
I DIDN'T DISCOVER IT ALL ON MY OWN, BUT...
...I FEEL SO HONORED THAT YOU USE IT!!
A
UH...UM... I'VE READ ALL YOUR BOOKS, CHEF WABUTORA.
AND I ALREADY PRE-ORDERED YOUR LATEST WORK, YOU AND I ARE LIKE WATER AND OIL.
I'VE BEEN A HUGE FAN SINCE FOREVER!
THAT'S GOING TO BE THE BEST!
H
WELL, THANK YOU.
A
A
HEE HEE HEE.
I USE IT QUITE FREQUENTLY MYSELF.
THAT MORS OIL OF YOURS.
MISO SOUP HAG
GRANNY KAMA
(RANKED 54TH)
CHEF GRANNY KAMA, THE MISO SOUP HAG!
HEE HEE HEE.
HEE HEE HEE
A FINE OIL IT IS...

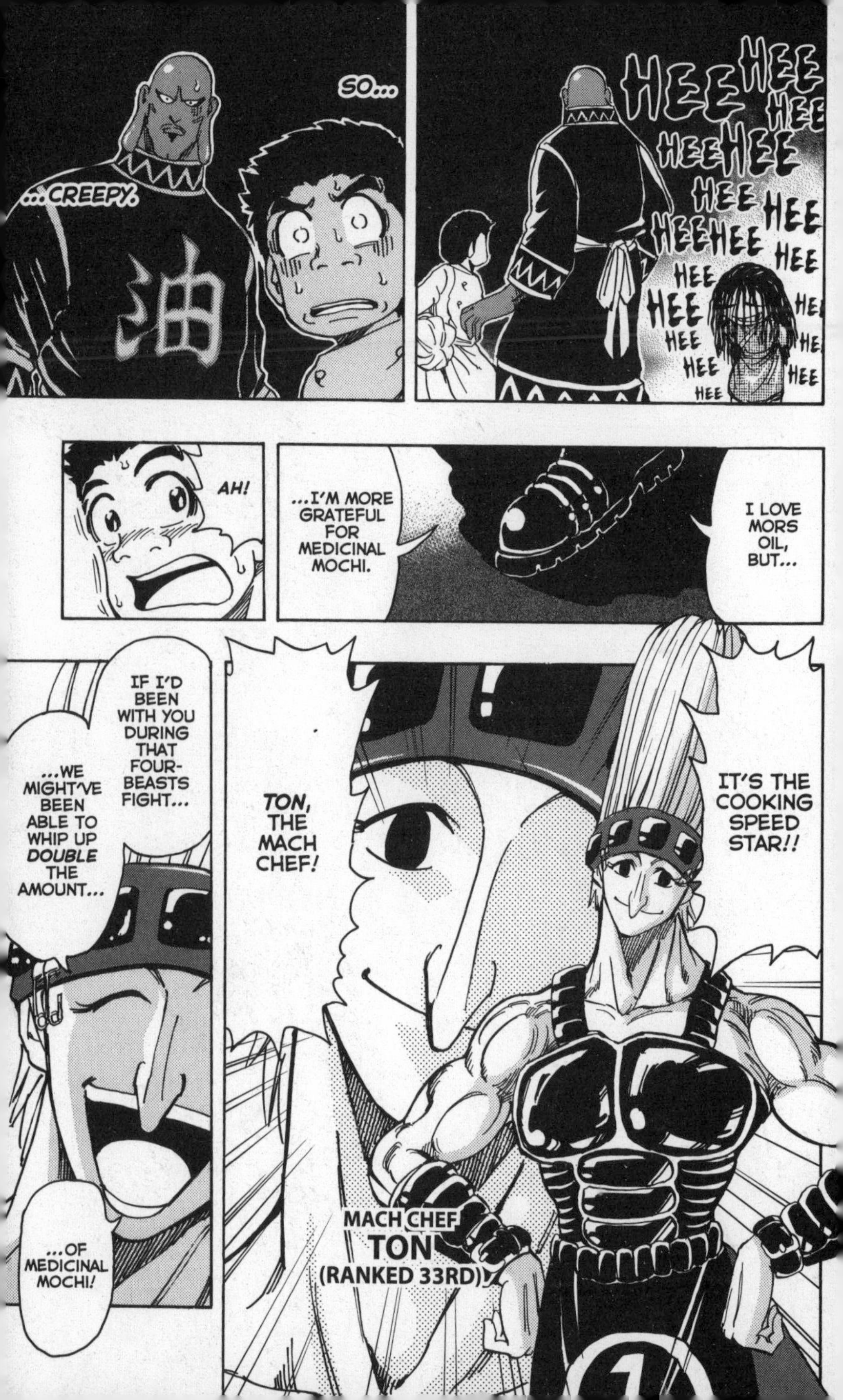
HEE HEE HEE HEE HEE HEE HEE HEE HEE HEE HEE HEE HEE HEE HEE HEE
SO...
...CREEPY.
I LOVE MORS OIL, BUT...
...I'M MORE GRATEFUL FOR MEDICINAL MOCHI.
AH!
IT'S THE COOKING SPEED STAR!!
TON, THE MACH CHEF!
MACH CHEF TON (RANKED 33RD)
IF I'D BEEN WITH YOU DURING THAT FOUR-BEASTS FIGHT...
...WE MIGHT'VE BEEN ABLE TO WHIP UP DOUBLE THE AMOUNT...
...OF MEDICINAL MOCHI!

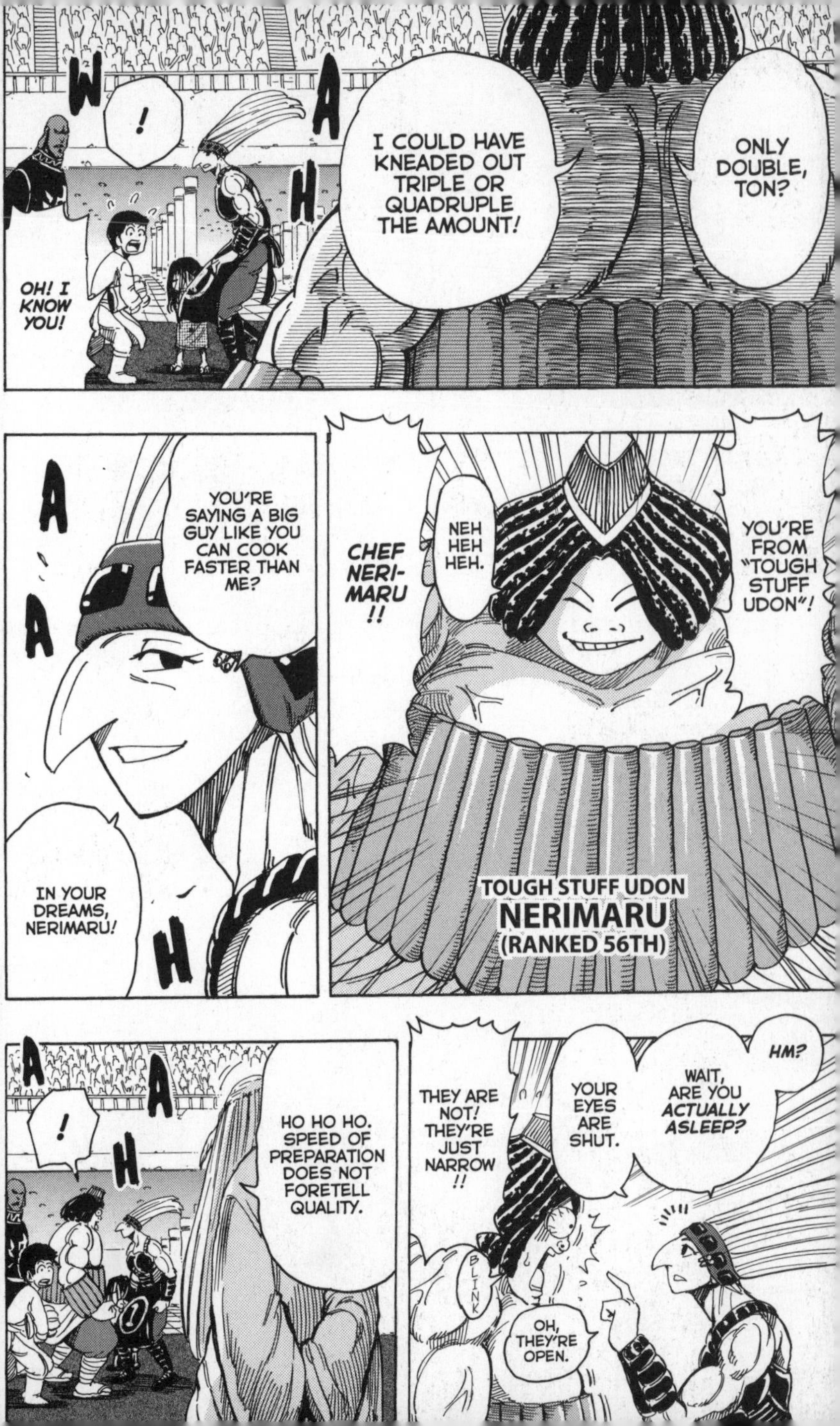
ONLY DOUBLE, TON?
I COULD HAVE KNEADED OUT TRIPLE OR QUADRUPLE THE AMOUNT!
W ! A H
OH! I KNOW YOU!
YOU'RE FROM "TOUGH STUFF UDON"!
NEH HEH HEH.
CHEF NERI-MARU !!
TOUGH STUFF UDON
NERIMARU
(RANKED 56TH)
YOU'RE SAYING A BIG GUY LIKE YOU CAN COOK FASTER THAN ME?
A A H
IN YOUR DREAMS, NERIMARU!
HM?
WAIT, ARE YOU ACTUALLY ASLEEP?
YOUR EYES ARE SHUT.
THEY ARE NOT! THEY'RE JUST NARROW !!
BLINK
OH, THEY'RE OPEN.
HO HO HO. SPEED OF PREPARATION DOES NOT FORETELL QUALITY.
A ! H A

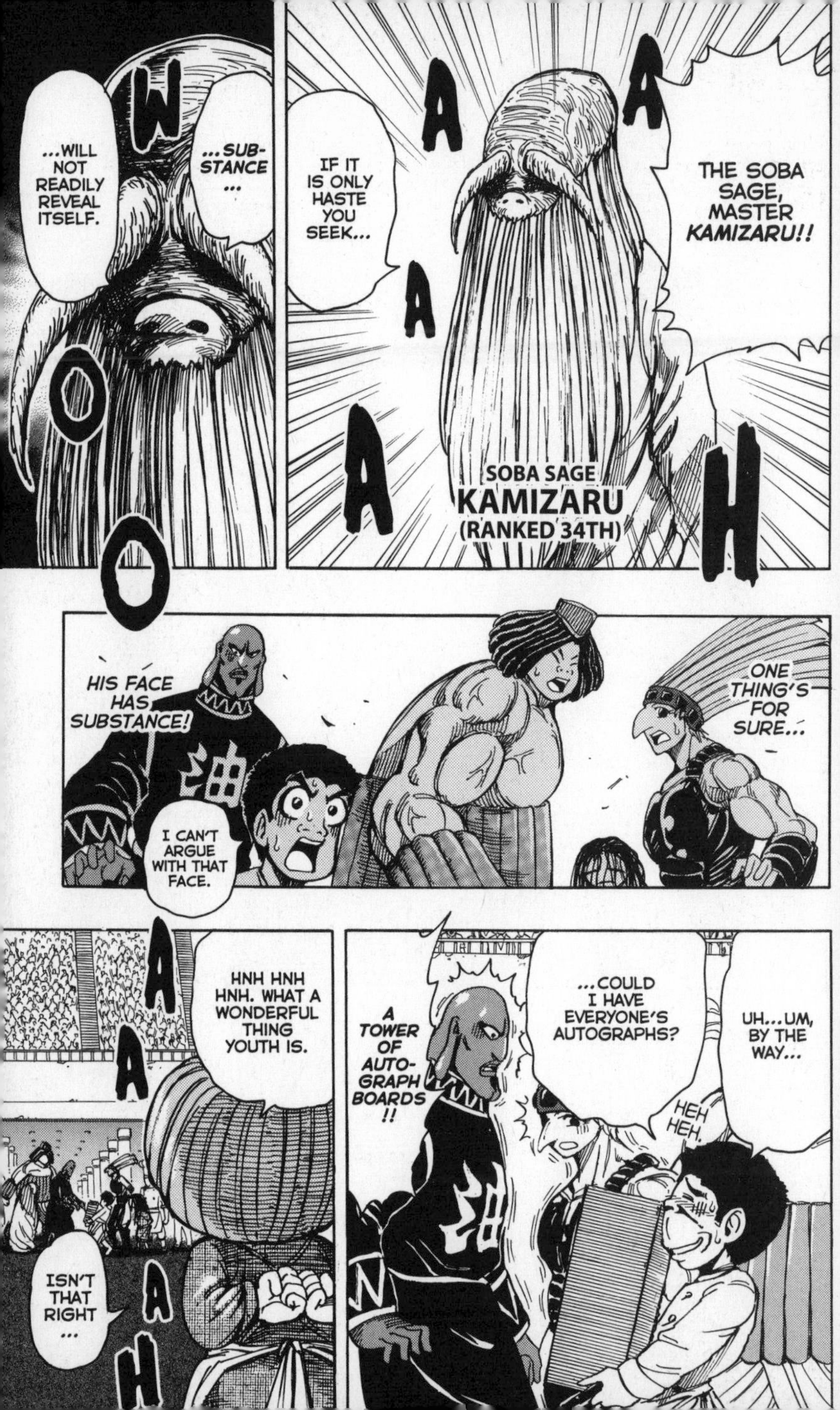
THE SOBA SAGE, MASTER KAMIZARU!!
SOBA SAGE KAMIZARU (RANKED 34TH)
H A A A
IF IT IS ONLY HASTE YOU SEEK...
A
...SUB-STANCE...
...WILL NOT READILY REVEAL ITSELF.
W O O O
ONE THING'S FOR SURE...
HIS FACE HAS SUBSTANCE!
I CAN'T ARGUE WITH THAT FACE.
UH...UM, BY THE WAY...
HEH HEH.
...COULD I HAVE EVERYONE'S AUTOGRAPHS?
A TOWER OF AUTO-GRAPH BOARDS!!
HNH HNH HNH. WHAT A WONDERFUL THING YOUTH IS.
ISN'T THAT RIGHT...
H A A A

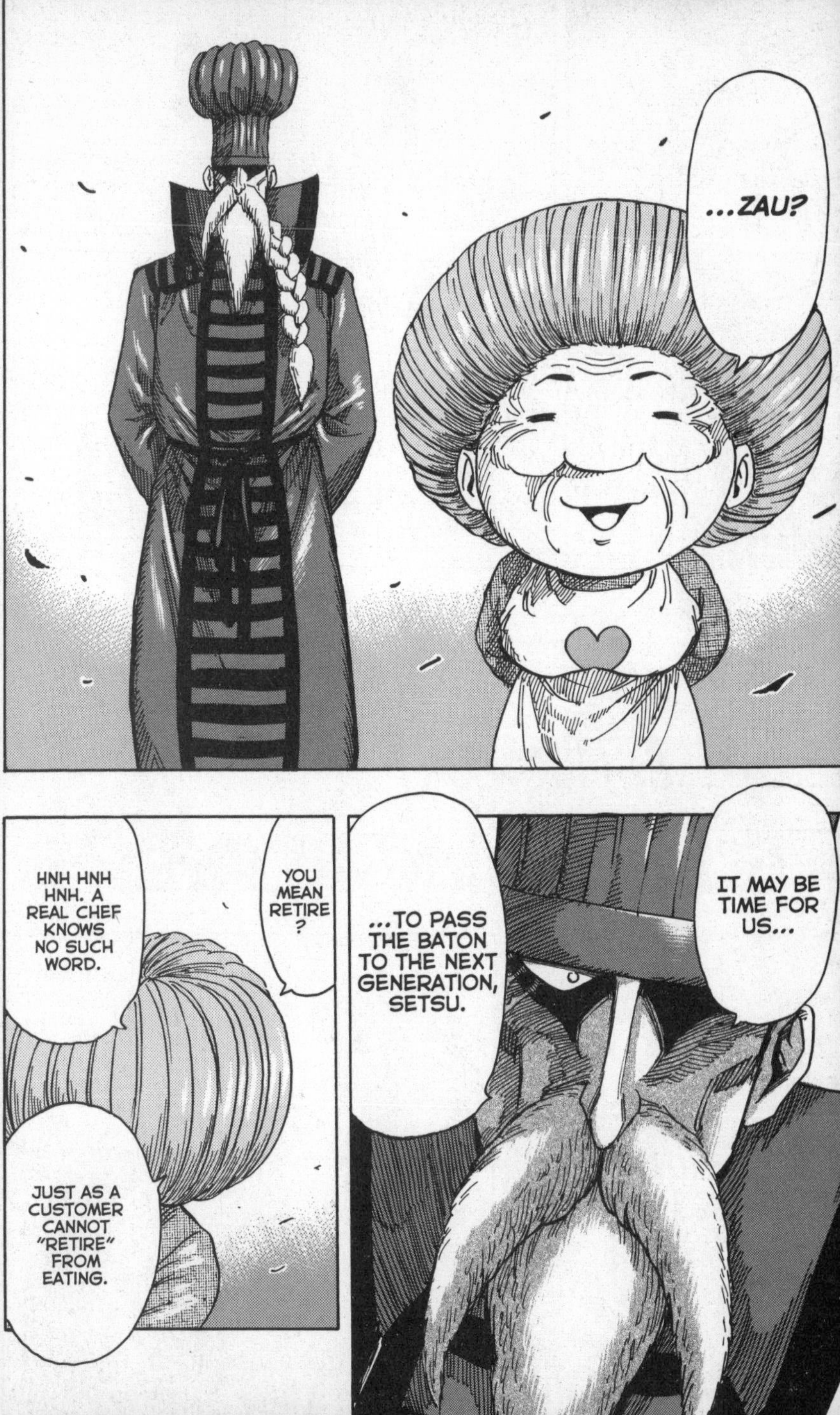
...ZAU?
IT MAY BE TIME FOR US...
...TO PASS THE BATON TO THE NEXT GENERATION, SETSU.
YOU MEAN RETIRE?
HNH HNH HNH. A REAL CHEF KNOWS NO SUCH WORD.
JUST AS A CUSTOMER CANNOT "RETIRE" FROM EATING.

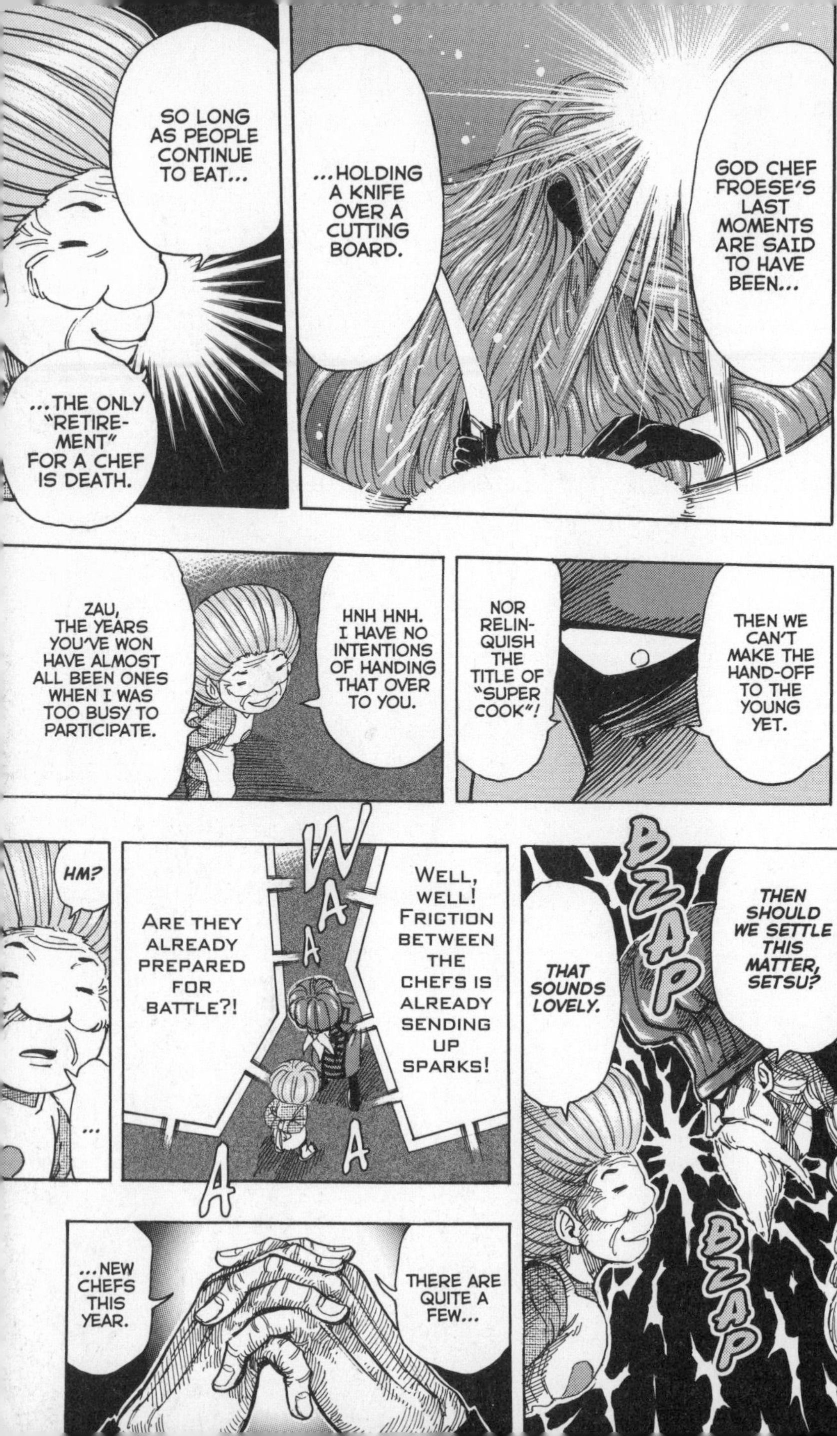
GOD CHEF FROESE'S LAST MOMENTS ARE SAID TO HAVE BEEN...
...HOLDING A KNIFE OVER A CUTTING BOARD.
SO LONG AS PEOPLE CONTINUE TO EAT...
...THE ONLY "RETIREMENT" FOR A CHEF IS DEATH.
THEN WE CAN'T MAKE THE HAND-OFF TO THE YOUNG YET.
NOR RELIN-QUISH THE TITLE OF "SUPER COOK"!
HNH HNH. I HAVE NO INTENTIONS OF HANDING THAT OVER TO YOU.
ZAU, THE YEARS YOU'VE WON HAVE ALMOST ALL BEEN ONES WHEN I WAS TOO BUSY TO PARTICIPATE.
BZAP
THEN SHOULD WE SETTLE THIS MATTER, SETSU?
THAT SOUNDS LOVELY.
BZAP
WAAAAA
WELL, WELL! FRICTION BETWEEN THE CHEFS IS ALREADY SENDING UP SPARKS!
ARE THEY ALREADY PREPARED FOR BATTLE?!
HM?
...
THERE ARE QUITE A FEW...
...NEW CHEFS THIS YEAR.

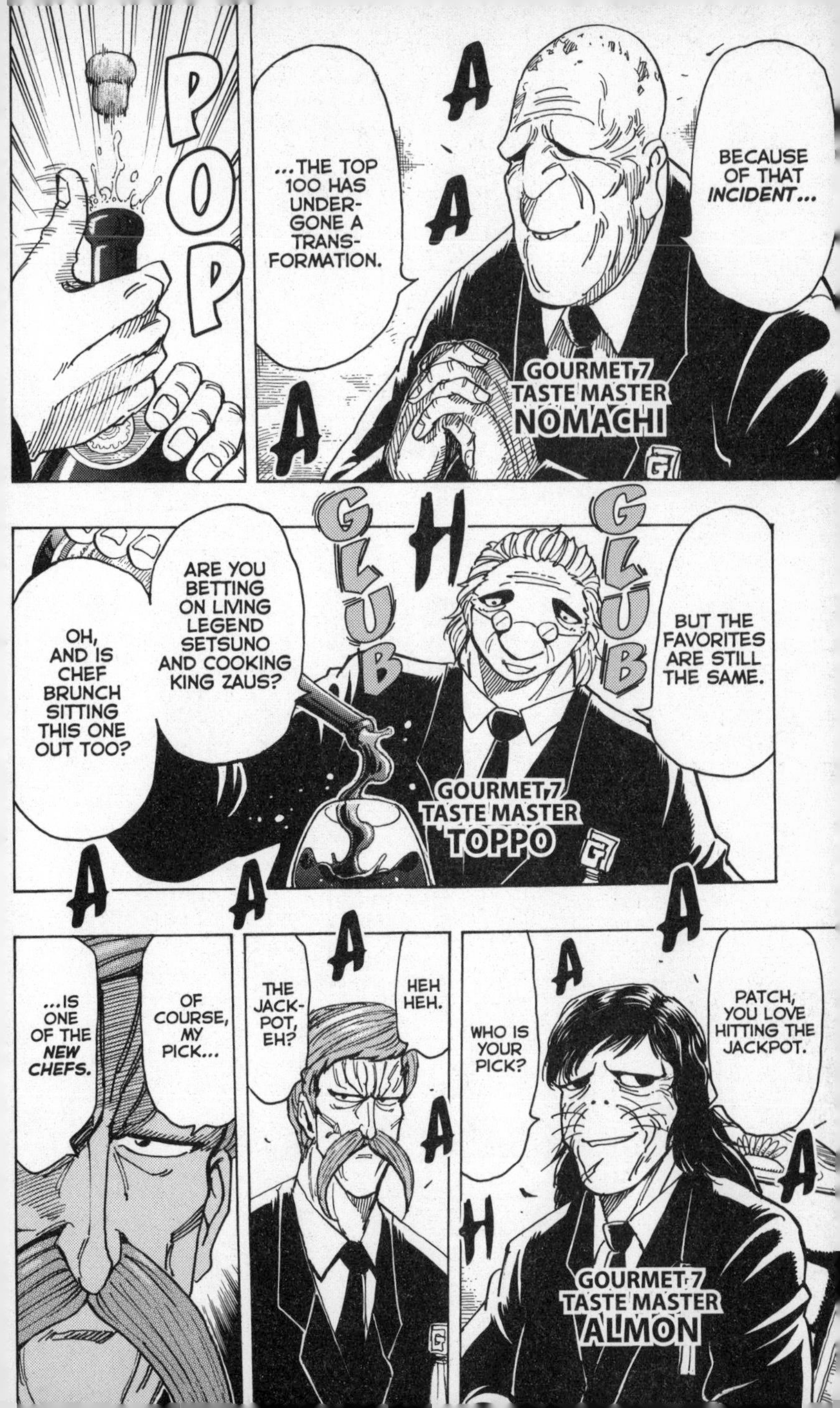
BECAUSE OF THAT INCIDENT...
...THE TOP 100 HAS UNDERGONE A TRANSFORMATION.
AAA
GOURMET 7 TASTE MASTER NOMACHI
POP
BUT THE FAVORITES ARE STILL THE SAME.
GLUB GLUB
H
GOURMET 7 TASTE MASTER TOPPO
ARE YOU BETTING ON LIVING LEGEND SETSUNO AND COOKING KING ZAUS?
OH, AND IS CHEF BRUNCH SITTING THIS ONE OUT TOO?
AAA
PATCH, YOU LOVE HITTING THE JACKPOT.
WHO IS YOUR PICK?
GOURMET 7 TASTE MASTER ALMON
AH
HEH HEH.
THE JACKPOT, EH?
AA
OF COURSE, MY PICK...
...IS ONE OF THE NEW CHEFS.
A

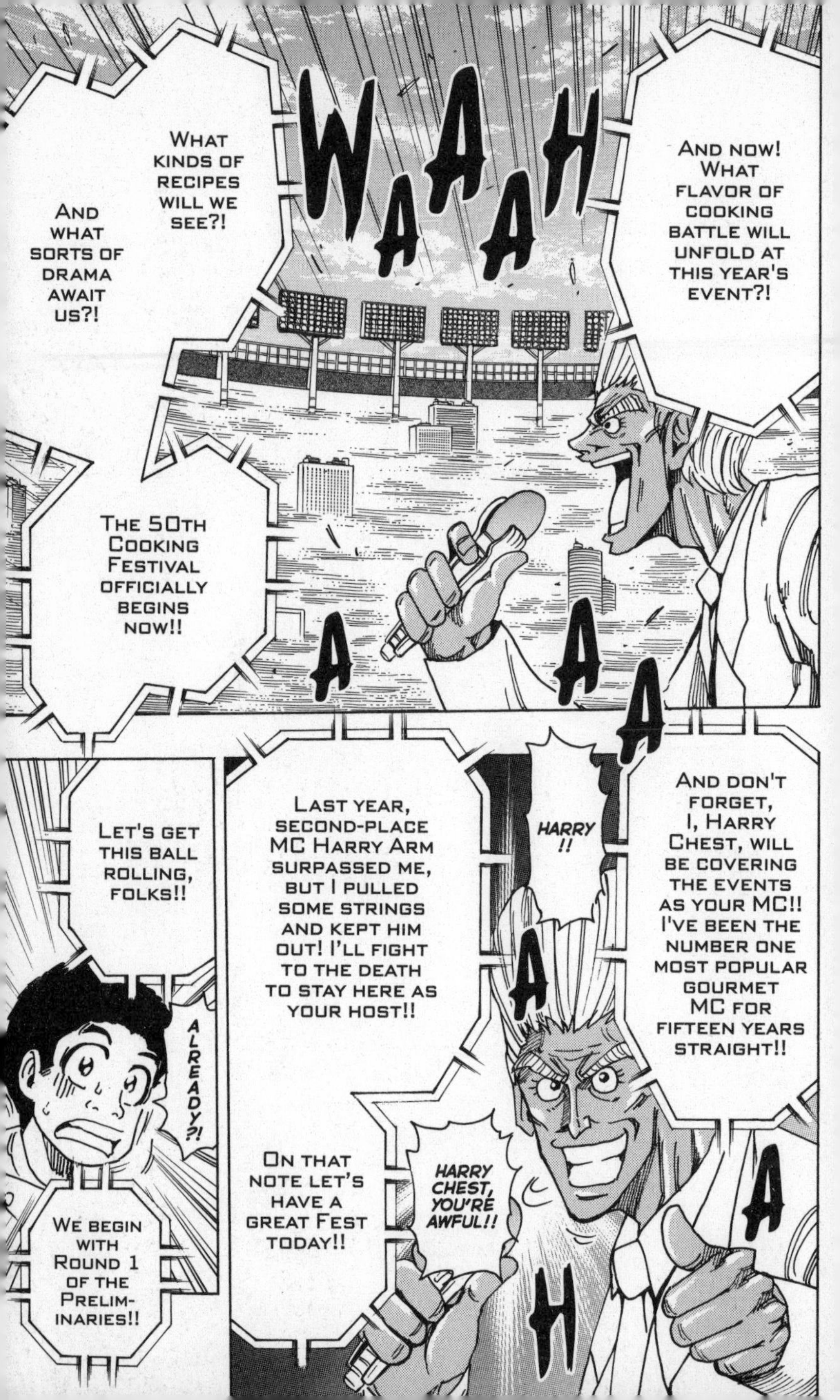
AND NOW! WHAT FLAVOR OF COOKING BATTLE WILL UNFOLD AT THIS YEAR'S EVENT?!
WAAAAH
WHAT KINDS OF RECIPES WILL WE SEE?!
AND WHAT SORTS OF DRAMA AWAIT US?!
THE 50TH COOKING FESTIVAL OFFICIALLY BEGINS NOW!!
AAA
AND DON'T FORGET, I, HARRY CHEST, WILL BE COVERING THE EVENTS AS YOUR MC!! I'VE BEEN THE NUMBER ONE MOST POPULAR GOURMET MC FOR FIFTEEN YEARS STRAIGHT!!
HARRY !!
LAST YEAR, SECOND-PLACE MC HARRY ARM SURPASSED ME, BUT I PULLED SOME STRINGS AND KEPT HIM OUT! I'LL FIGHT TO THE DEATH TO STAY HERE AS YOUR HOST!!
HARRY CHEST, YOU'RE AWFUL!!
ON THAT NOTE LET'S HAVE A GREAT FEST TODAY!!
AAH
LET'S GET THIS BALL ROLLING, FOLKS!!
ALREADY?!
WE BEGIN WITH ROUND 1 OF THE PRELIMINARIES!!

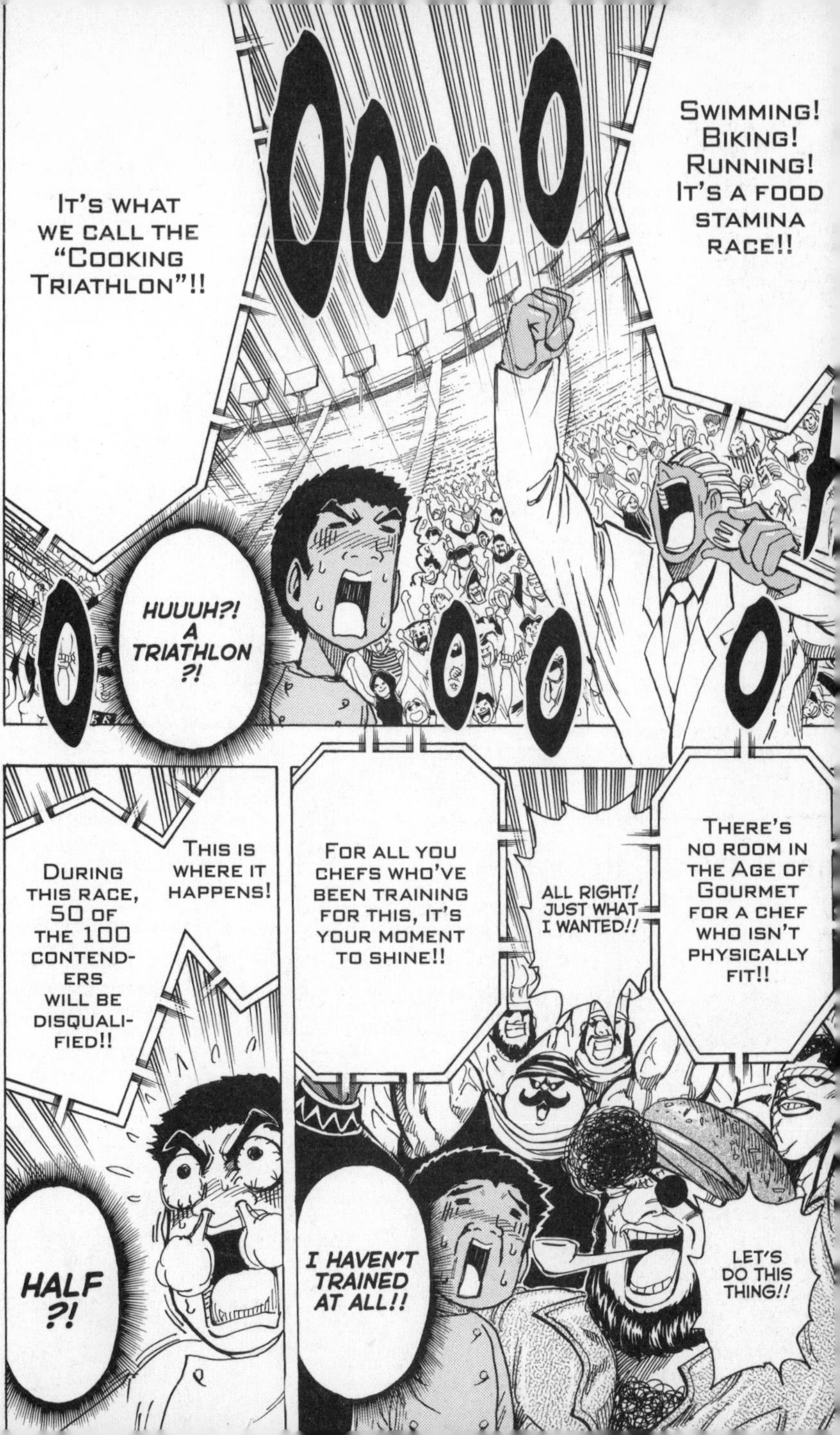
Swimming! Biking! Running! It's a food stamina race!!
OOOOO
It's what we call the "Cooking Triathlon"!!
O
HUUUH?! A TRIATHLON ?!
There's no room in the Age of Gourmet for a chef who isn't physically fit!!
ALL RIGHT! JUST WHAT I WANTED!!
For all you chefs who've been training for this, it's your moment to shine!!
This is where it happens!
During this race, 50 of the 100 contend-ers will be disquali-fied!!
LET'S DO THIS THING!!
I HAVEN'T TRAINED AT ALL!!
HALF ?!

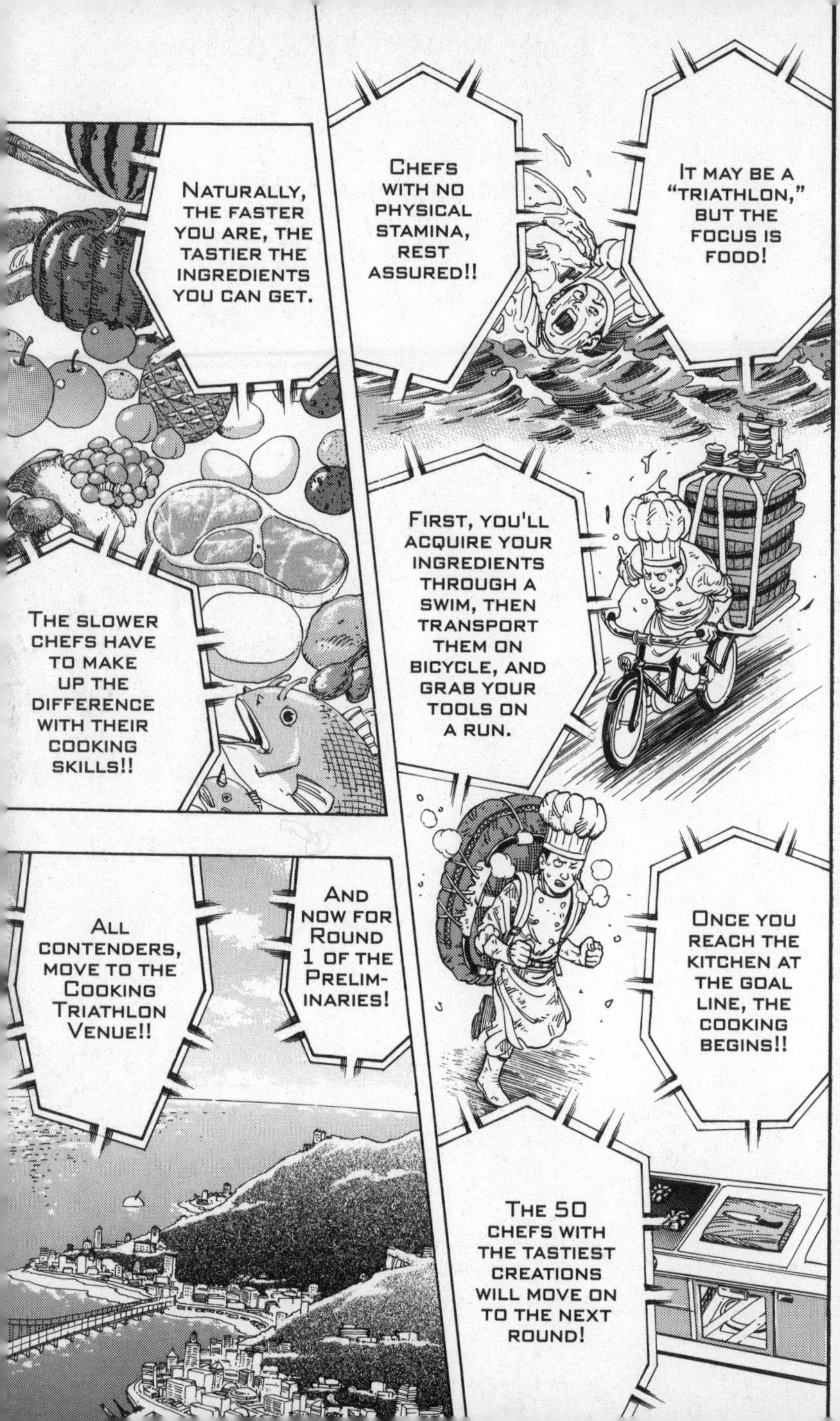
It may be a "triathlon," but the focus is food!
Chefs with no physical stamina, rest assured!!
First, you'll acquire your ingredients through a swim, then transport them on bicycle, and grab your tools on a run.
Once you reach the kitchen at the goal line, the cooking begins!!
The 50 chefs with the tastiest creations will move on to the next round!
Naturally, the faster you are, the tastier the ingredients you can get.
The slower chefs have to make up the difference with their cooking skills!!
And now for Round 1 of the Prelim-inaries!
All contenders, move to the Cooking Triathlon Venue!!

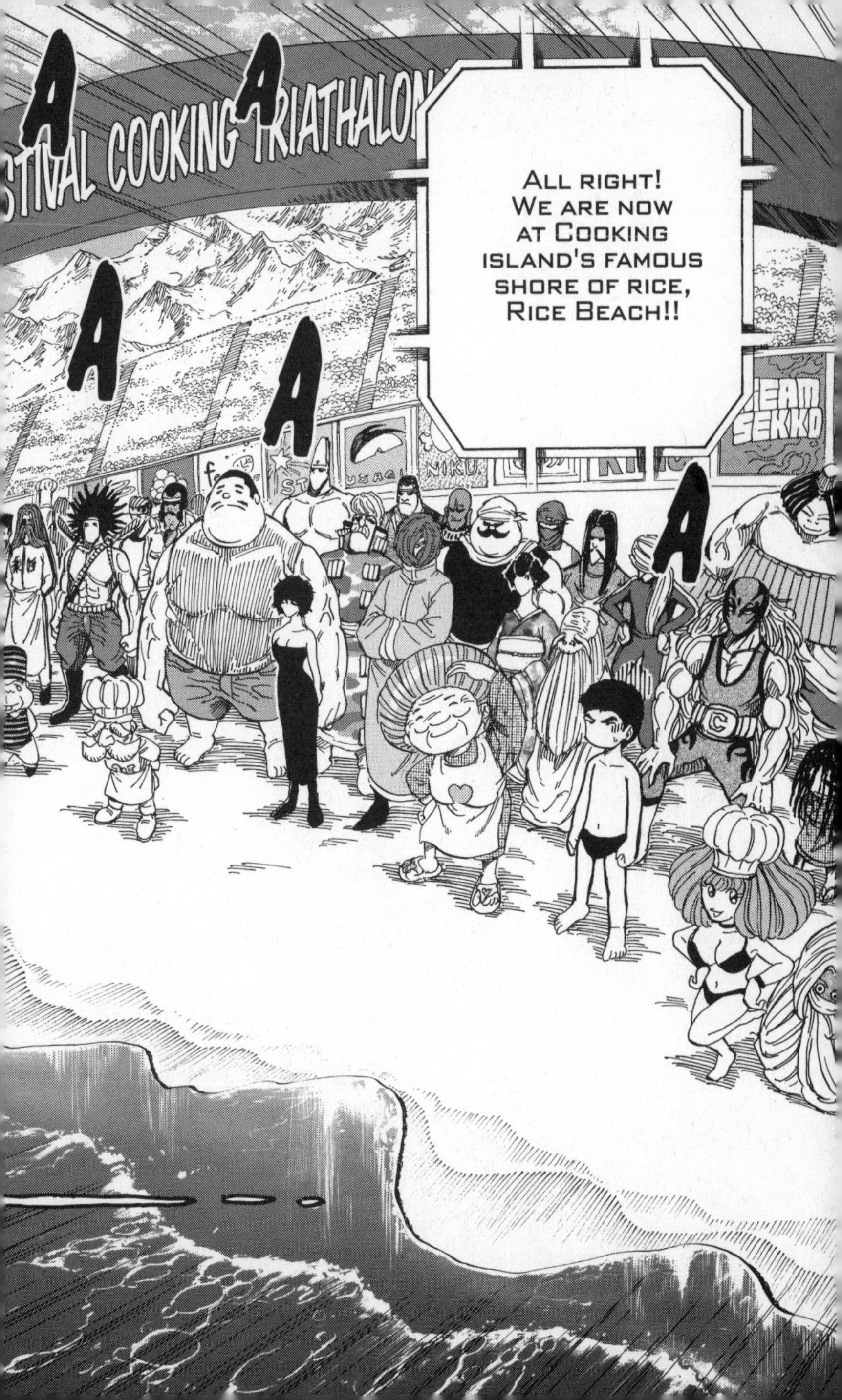
ALL RIGHT! WE ARE NOW AT COOKING ISLAND'S FAMOUS SHORE OF RICE, RICE BEACH!!
STIVAL COOKING TRIATHALON
A
A
A
A
A
TEAM SEKKO
NIKU
USAGI

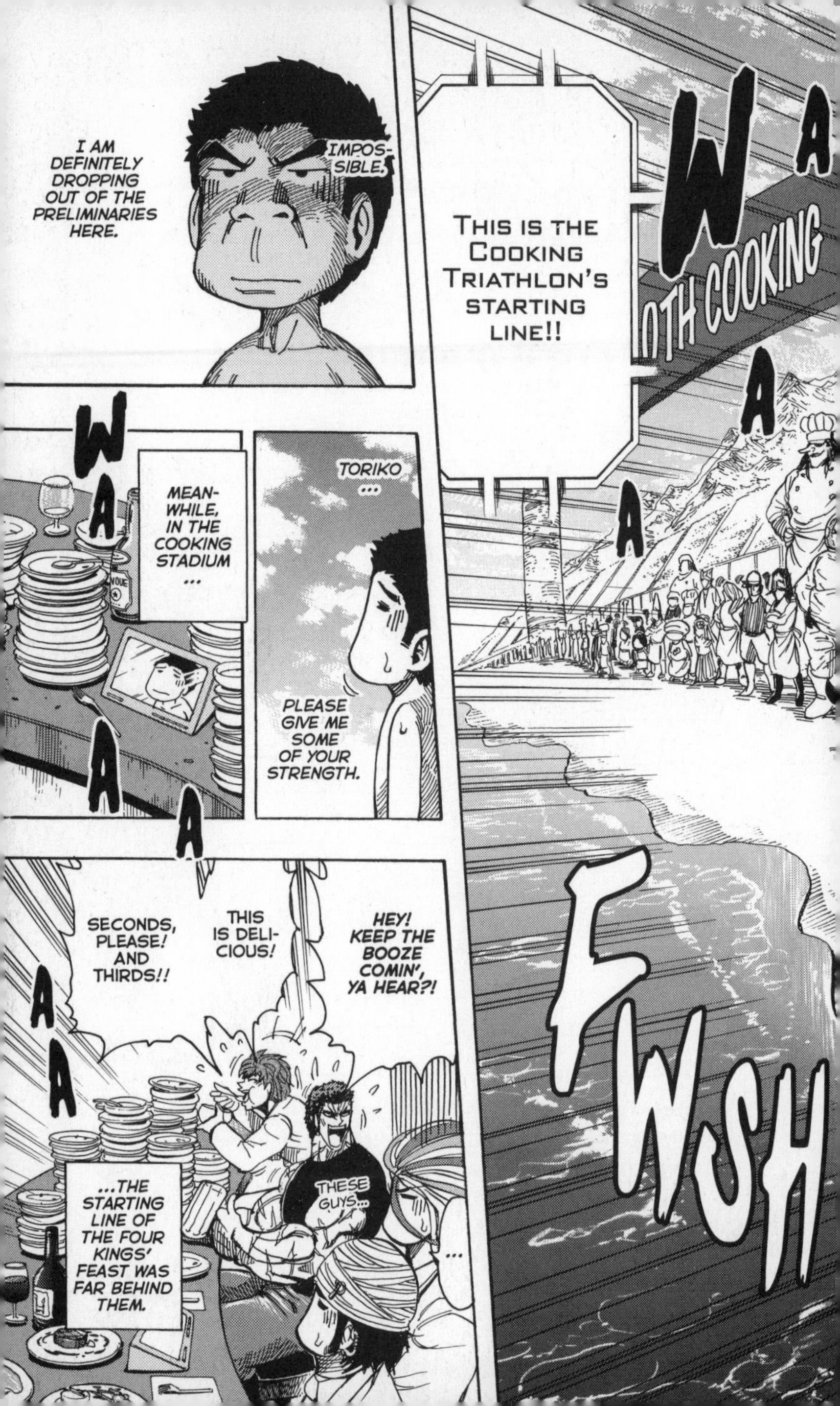
WAAAA
0TH COOKING
THIS IS THE COOKING TRIATHLON'S STARTING LINE!!
FWSH
I AM DEFINITELY DROPPING OUT OF THE PRELIMINARIES HERE.
IMPOS-SIBLE.
TORIKO...
PLEASE GIVE ME SOME OF YOUR STRENGTH.
WAAAA
MEAN-WHILE, IN THE COOKING STADIUM...
SECONDS, PLEASE! AND THIRDS!!
THIS IS DELI-CIOUS!
HEY! KEEP THE BOOZE COMIN', YA HEAR?!
THESE GUYS...
...
...THE STARTING LINE OF THE FOUR KINGS' FEAST WAS FAR BEHIND THEM.

TORIKO

GOURMET CHECKLIST

Vol. 246

SUMMER WHISKEY
(ALCOHOL)

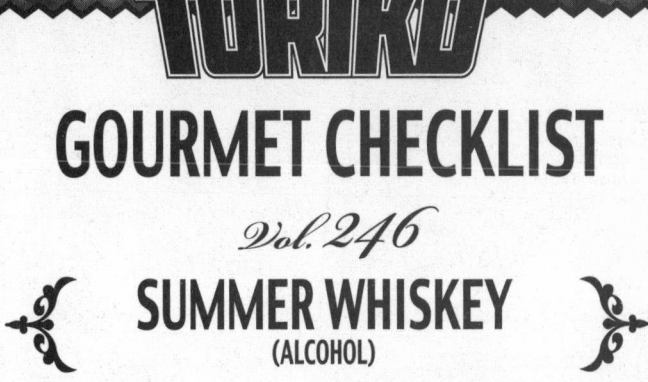

CAPTURE LEVEL: 90
HABITAT: MANMADE BUT STILL RARE
LENGTH: ---
HEIGHT: ---
WEIGHT: ---
PRICE: 15,000,000 YEN PER BOTTLE (2 LITERS)

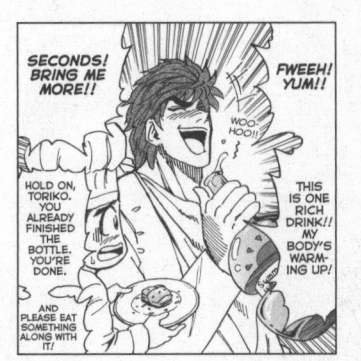

FWEEH! YUM!!
SECONDS! BRING ME MORE!!
WOO-HOO!!
THIS IS ONE RICH DRINK!! MY BODY'S WARM-ING UP!
HOLD ON, TORIKO. YOU ALREADY FINISHED THE BOTTLE. YOU'RE DONE.
AND PLEASE EAT SOMETHING ALONG WITH IT!

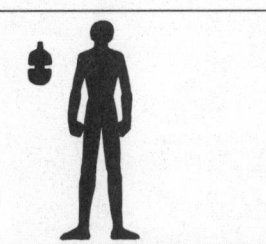

SCALE

SUMMER WHISKEY IS DISTILLED FROM SUN DURIAN (SAID TO BE A BLESSING FROM THE SUN) AND PLANET WATER (ONLY FOUND AT THE CENTER OF THE EARTH) OVER THREE WEEKS. AT 160 PROOF, SUMMER WHISKEY IS A STRONG DRINK THAT CAN OVERWHELM EVEN THE HARDIEST DRINKER. THE CONSUMPTION OF THIS DANGEROUS LIQUOR IS DISCOURAGED FOR ALL BUT THE STRONGEST DRINKERS.

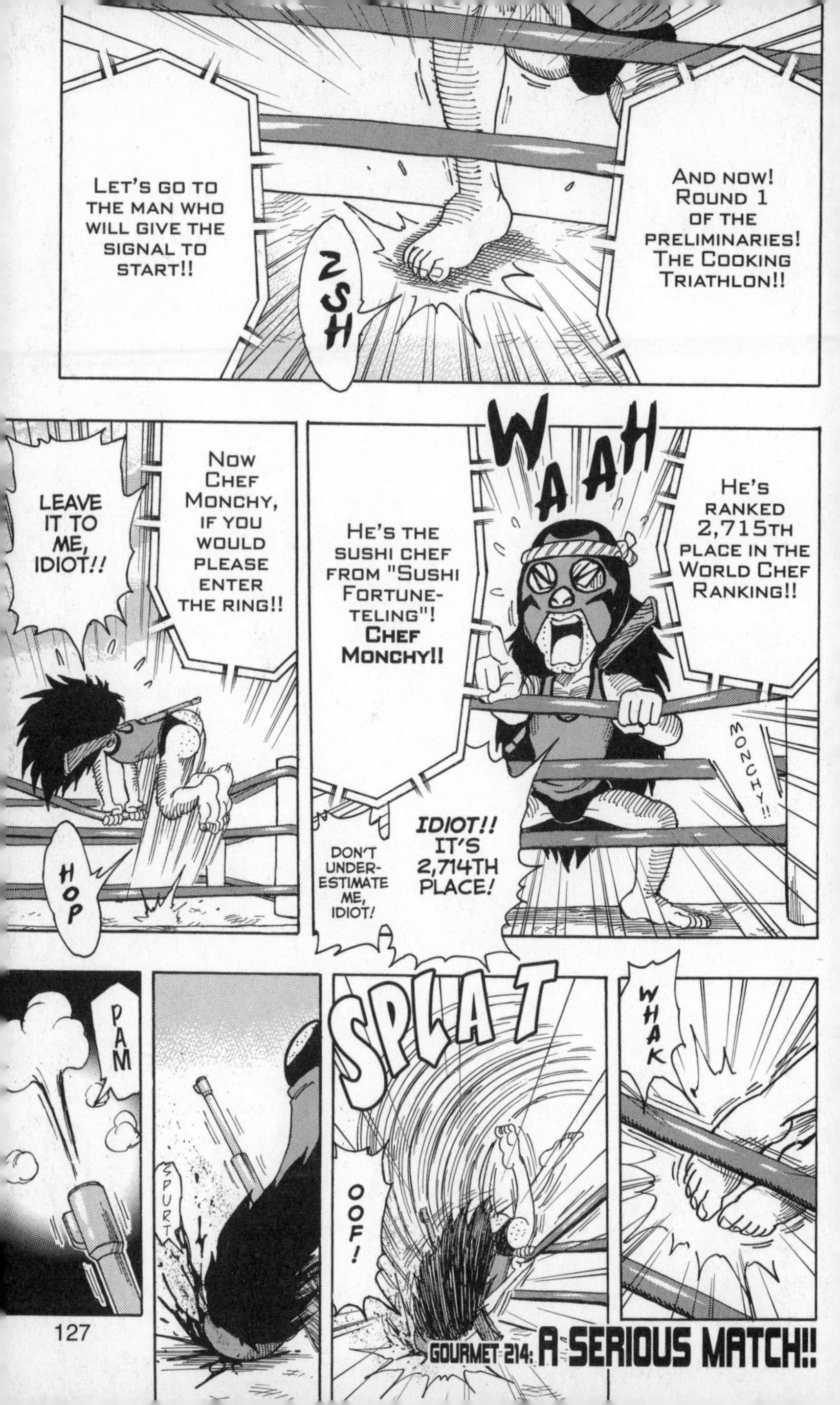
And now! Round 1 of the preliminaries! The Cooking Triathlon!!
Let's go to the man who will give the signal to start!!
ZSH
WAAH
He's ranked 2,715th place in the World Chef Ranking!!
He's the sushi chef from "Sushi Fortune-teling"! Chef Monchy!!
MONCHY!!
IDIOT!! IT'S 2,714TH PLACE!
Don't under-estimate me, idiot!
Now Chef Monchy, if you would please enter the ring!!
LEAVE IT TO ME, IDIOT!!
HOP
WHAK
SPLAT
OOF!
SPURT
PAM

GOURMET 214: A SERIOUS MATCH!!

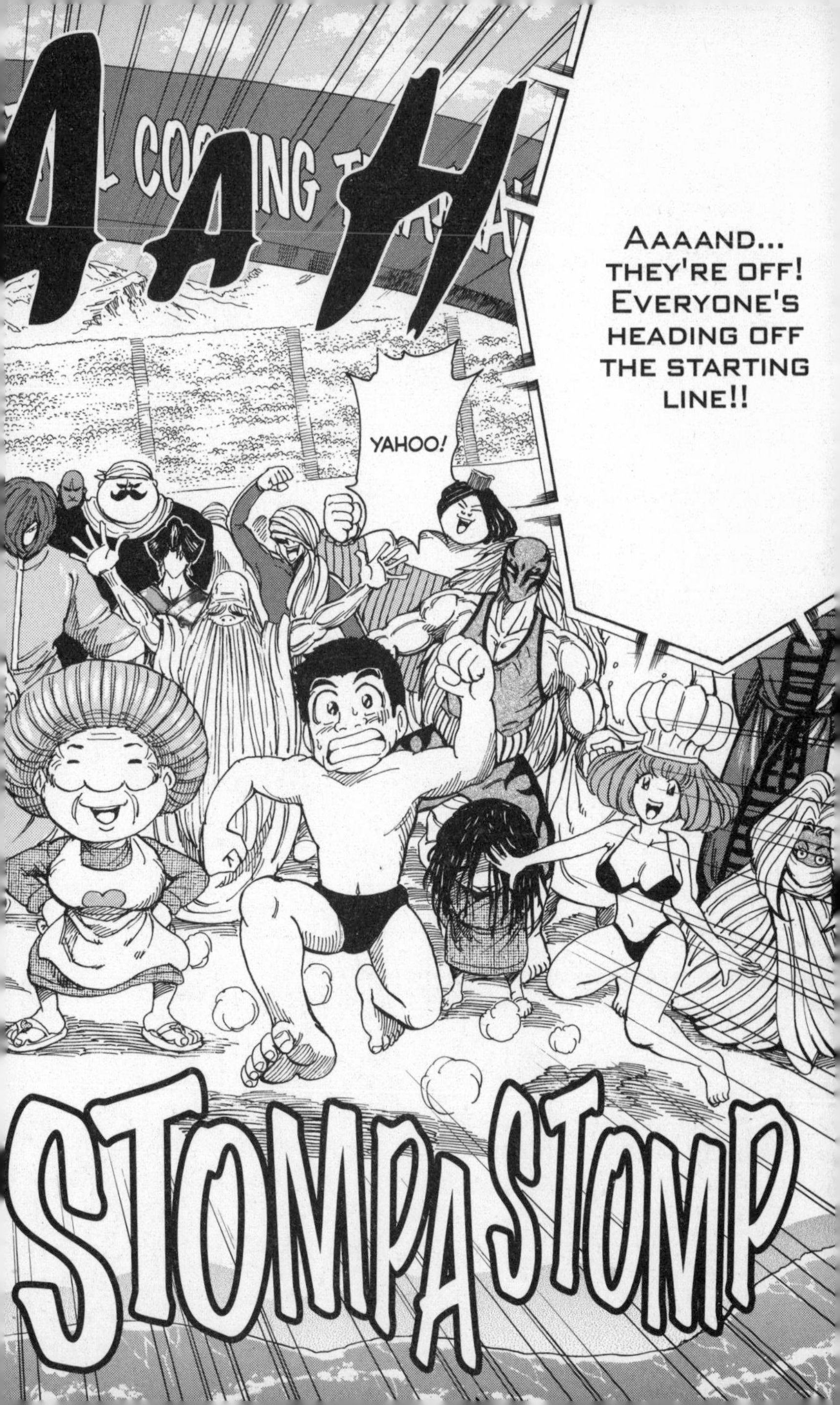
AAAH
AAAAND... THEY'RE OFF! EVERYONE'S HEADING OFF THE STARTING LINE!!
YAHOO!
STOMPA STOMP

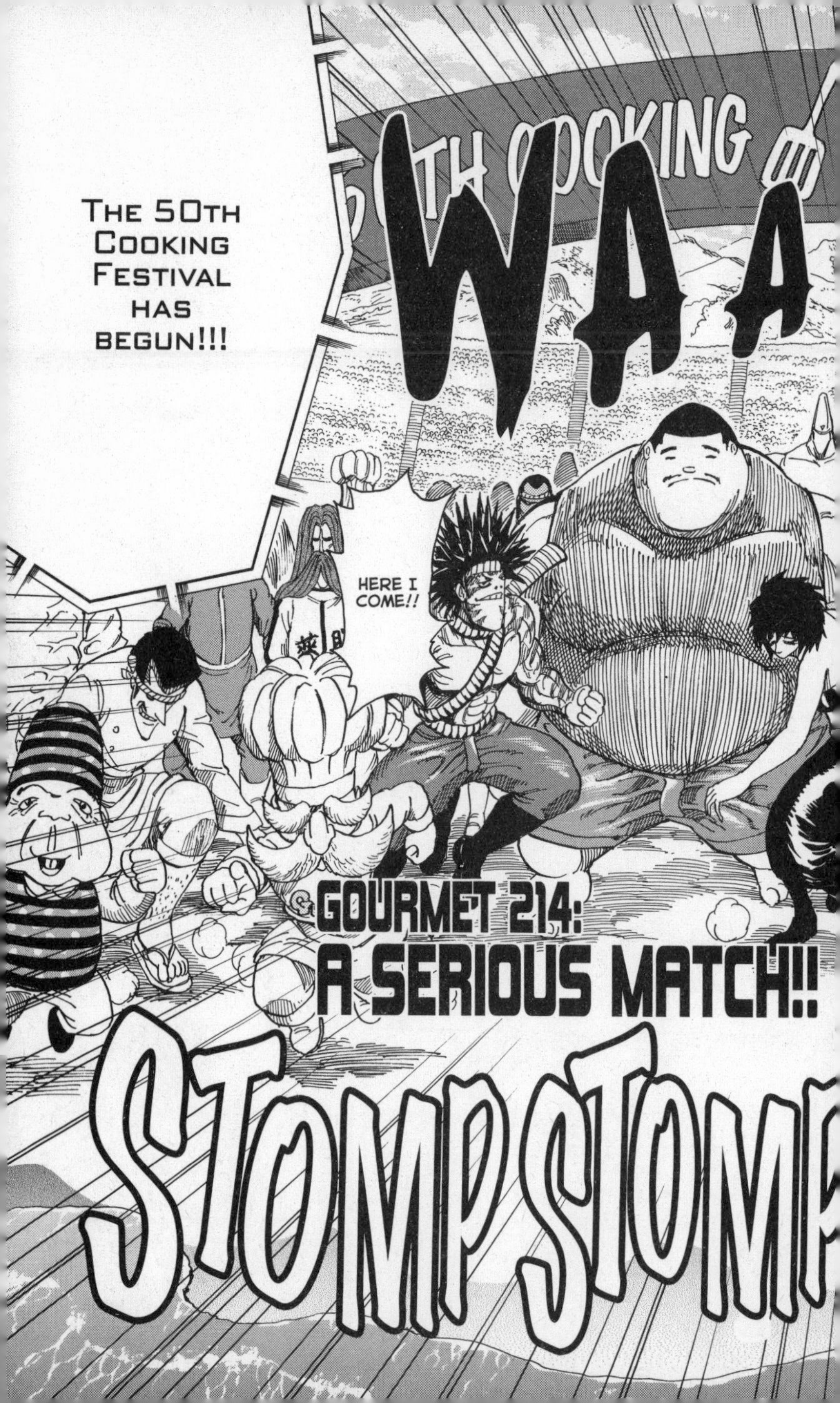
WAA
THE 50TH COOKING FESTIVAL HAS BEGUN!!!
HERE I COME!!
GOURMET 214:
A SERIOUS MATCH!!
STOMP STOMP

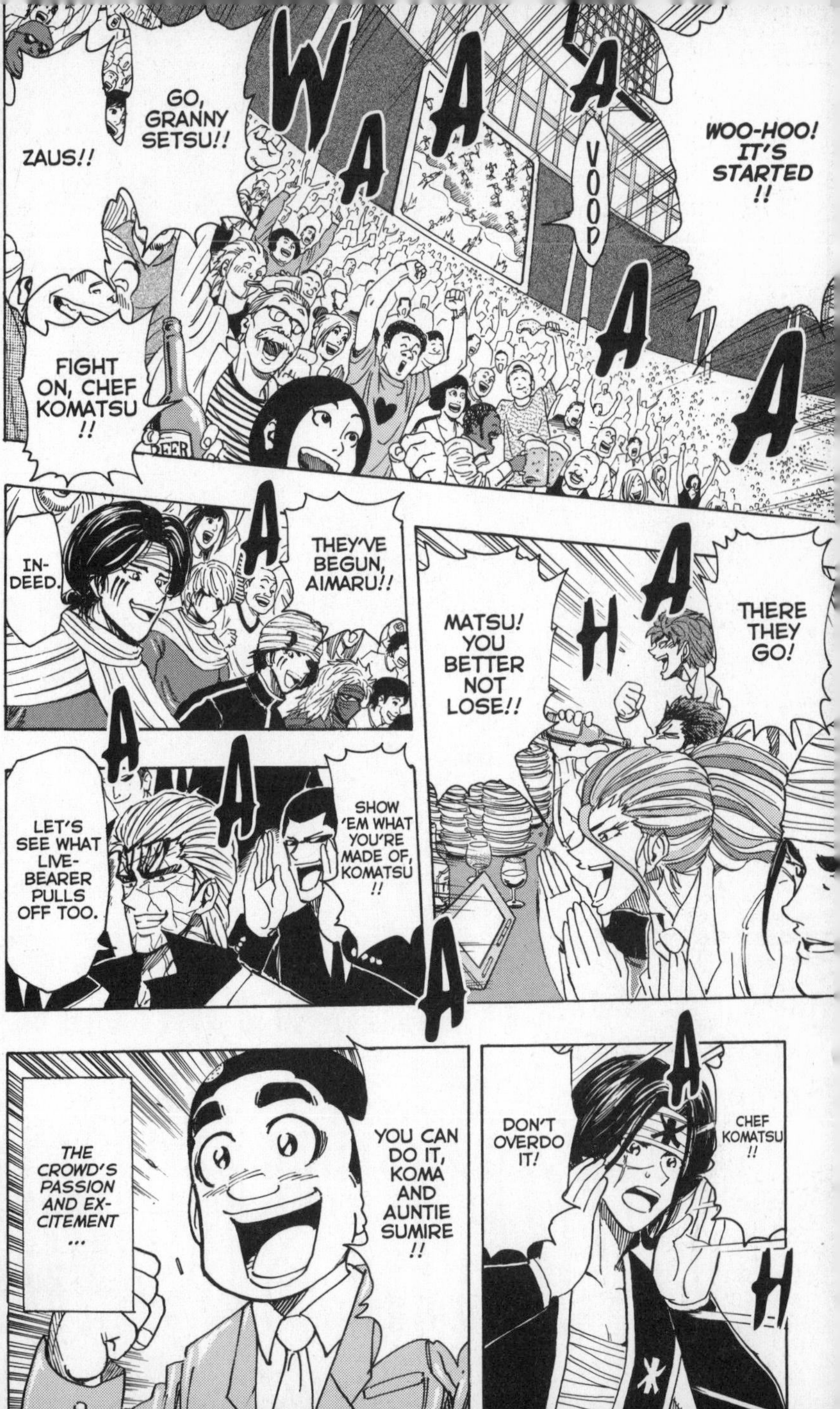
WOO-HOO! IT'S STARTED !!
VOOOP
WAAAAA
GO, GRANNY SETSU!!
ZAUS!!
FIGHT ON, CHEF KOMATSU !!
THERE THEY GO!
MATSU! YOU BETTER NOT LOSE!!
HAA
THEY'VE BEGUN, AIMARU!!
IN-DEED.
SHOW 'EM WHAT YOU'RE MADE OF, KOMATSU !!
LET'S SEE WHAT LIVE-BEARER PULLS OFF TOO.
AAA
CHEF KOMATSU !!
DON'T OVERDO IT!
HA
YOU CAN DO IT, KOMA AND AUNTIE SUMIRE !!
THE CROWD'S PASSION AND EX-CITEMENT ...

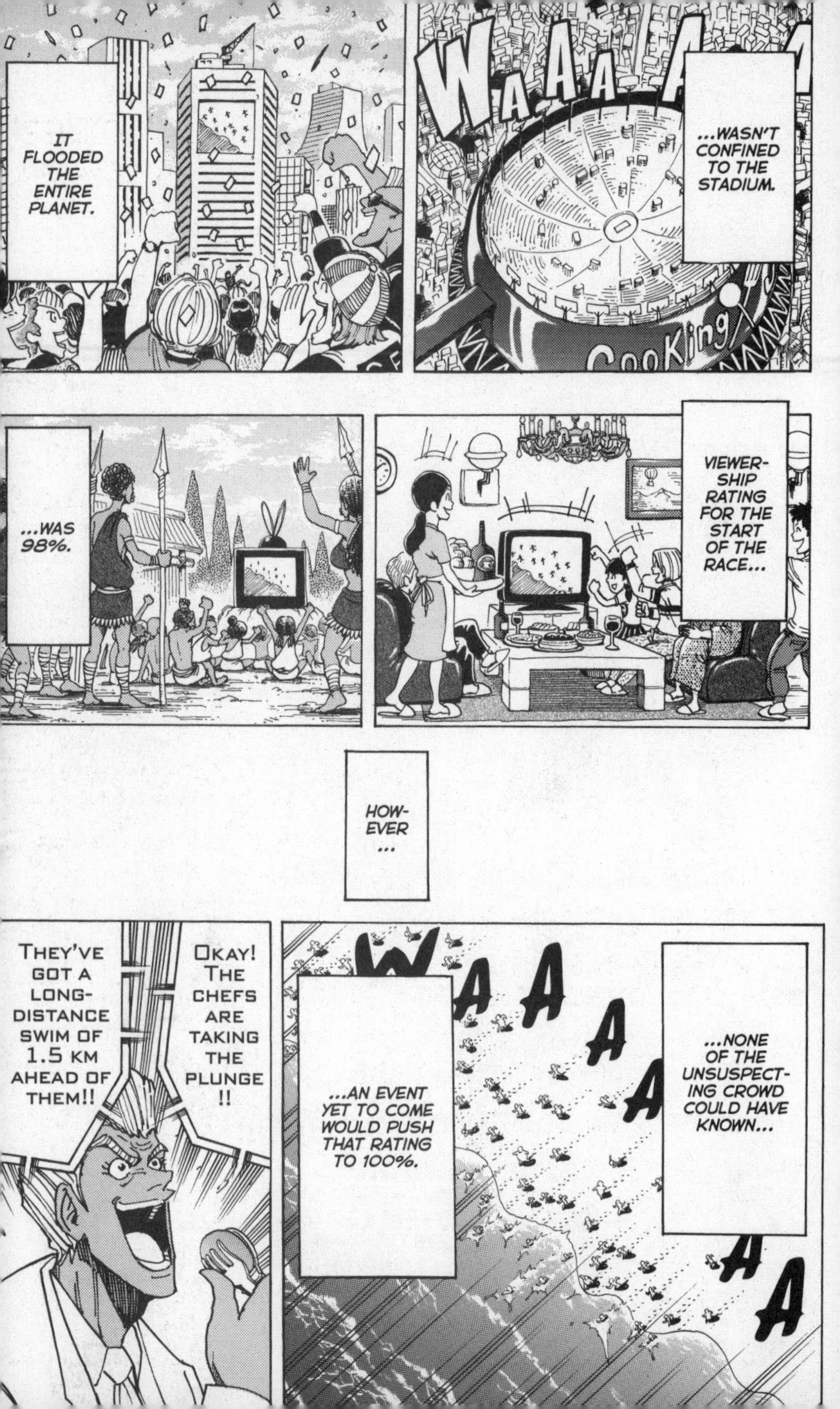
WAAAA
...WASN'T CONFINED TO THE STADIUM.
Cooking
IT FLOODED THE ENTIRE PLANET.
VIEWER-SHIP RATING FOR THE START OF THE RACE...
...WAS 98%.
HOW-EVER...
...NONE OF THE UNSUSPECT-ING CROWD COULD HAVE KNOWN...
WAAAAAAAA
...AN EVENT YET TO COME WOULD PUSH THAT RATING TO 100%.
OKAY! THE CHEFS ARE TAKING THE PLUNGE!!
THEY'VE GOT A LONG-DISTANCE SWIM OF 1.5 KM AHEAD OF THEM!!

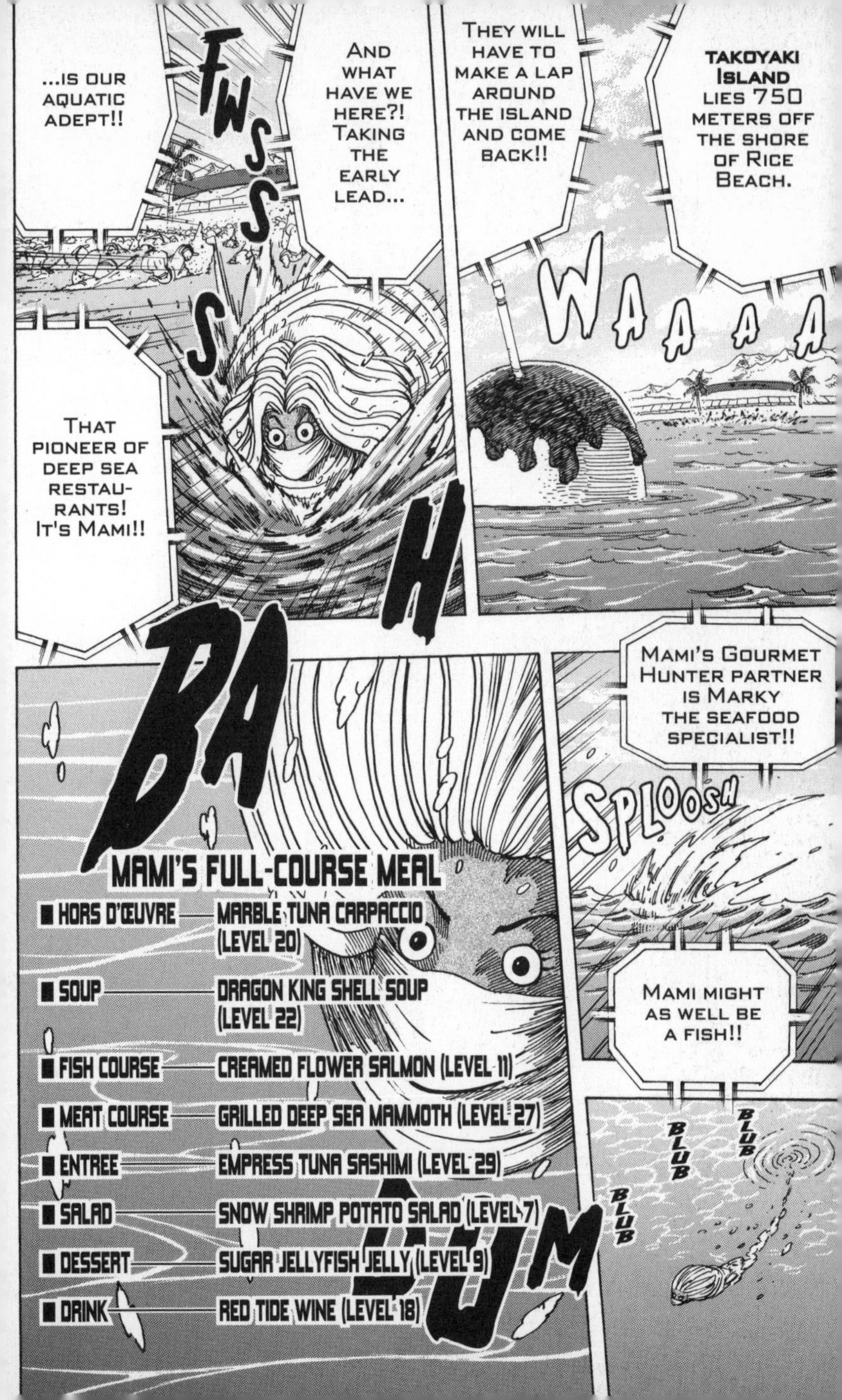
TAKOYAKI ISLAND LIES 750 METERS OFF THE SHORE OF RICE BEACH.
THEY WILL HAVE TO MAKE A LAP AROUND THE ISLAND AND COME BACK!!
WAAAAA
AND WHAT HAVE WE HERE?! TAKING THE EARLY LEAD...
FWSSS
...IS OUR AQUATIC ADEPT!!
THAT PIONEER OF DEEP SEA RESTAU-RANTS! IT'S MAMI!!
BAH
MAMI'S FULL-COURSE MEAL
■ HORS D'ŒUVRE — MARBLE TUNA CARPACCIO (LEVEL 20)
■ SOUP — DRAGON KING SHELL SOUP (LEVEL 22)
■ FISH COURSE — CREAMED FLOWER SALMON (LEVEL 11)
■ MEAT COURSE — GRILLED DEEP SEA MAMMOTH (LEVEL 27)
■ ENTREE — EMPRESS TUNA SASHIMI (LEVEL 29)
■ SALAD — SNOW SHRIMP POTATO SALAD (LEVEL 7)
■ DESSERT — SUGAR JELLYFISH JELLY (LEVEL 9)
■ DRINK — RED TIDE WINE (LEVEL 18)
DUM
MAMI'S GOURMET HUNTER PARTNER IS MARKY THE SEAFOOD SPECIALIST!!
SPLOOSH
MAMI MIGHT AS WELL BE A FISH!!
BLUB
BLUB
BLUB

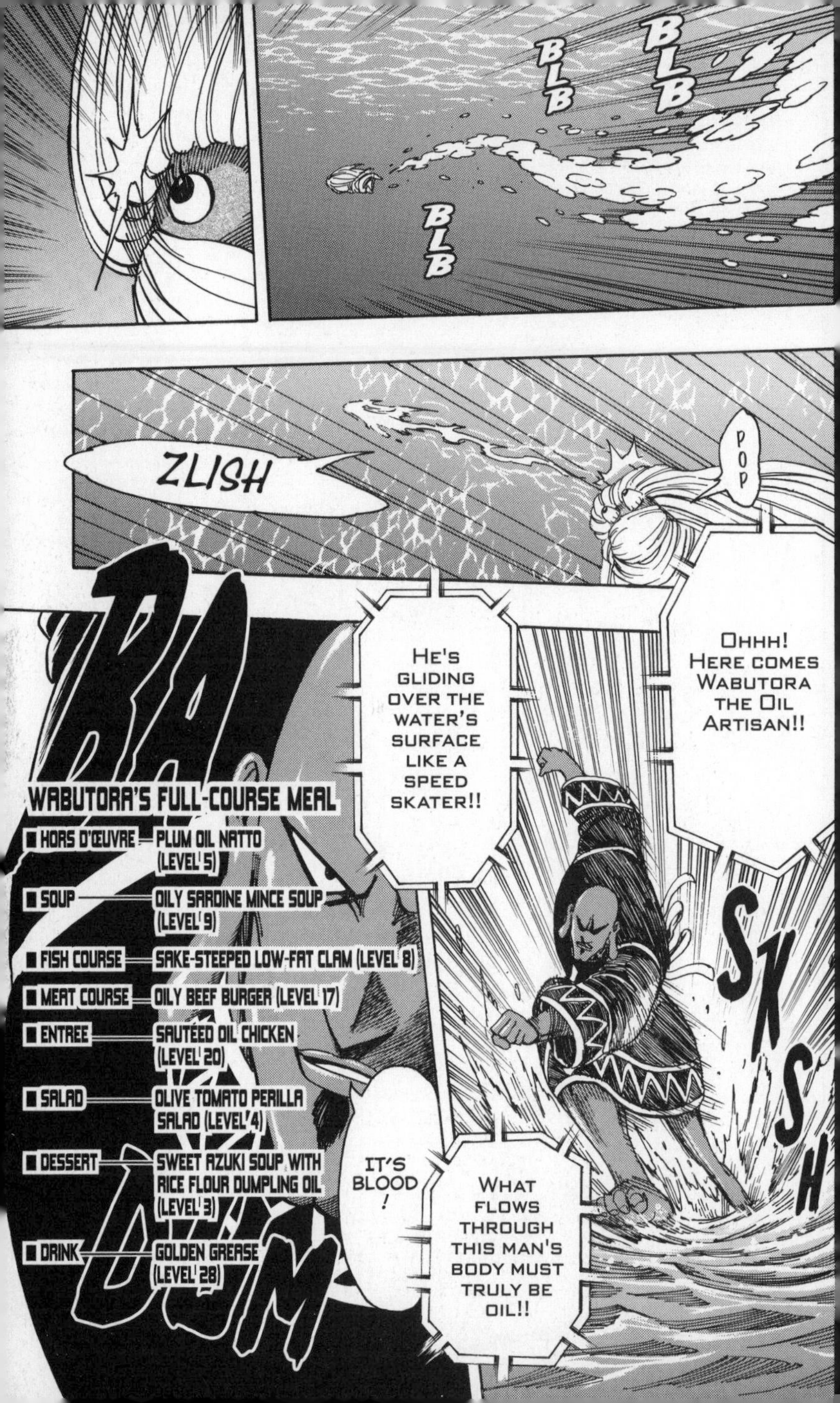
BLB BLB
BLB
POP
ZLISH
OHHH! HERE COMES WABUTORA THE OIL ARTISAN!!
HE'S GLIDING OVER THE WATER'S SURFACE LIKE A SPEED SKATER!!
SKSSH
BADUM
WABUTORA'S FULL-COURSE MEAL
■ HORS D'ŒUVRE — PLUM OIL NATTO (LEVEL 5)
■ SOUP — OILY SARDINE MINCE SOUP (LEVEL 9)
■ FISH COURSE — SAKE-STEEPED LOW-FAT CLAM (LEVEL 8)
■ MEAT COURSE — OILY BEEF BURGER (LEVEL 17)
■ ENTREE — SAUTÉED OIL CHICKEN (LEVEL 20)
■ SALAD — OLIVE TOMATO PERILLA SALAD (LEVEL 4)
■ DESSERT — SWEET AZUKI SOUP WITH RICE FLOUR DUMPLING OIL (LEVEL 3)
■ DRINK — GOLDEN GREASE (LEVEL 28)
WHAT FLOWS THROUGH THIS MAN'S BODY MUST TRULY BE OIL!!
IT'S BLOOD!

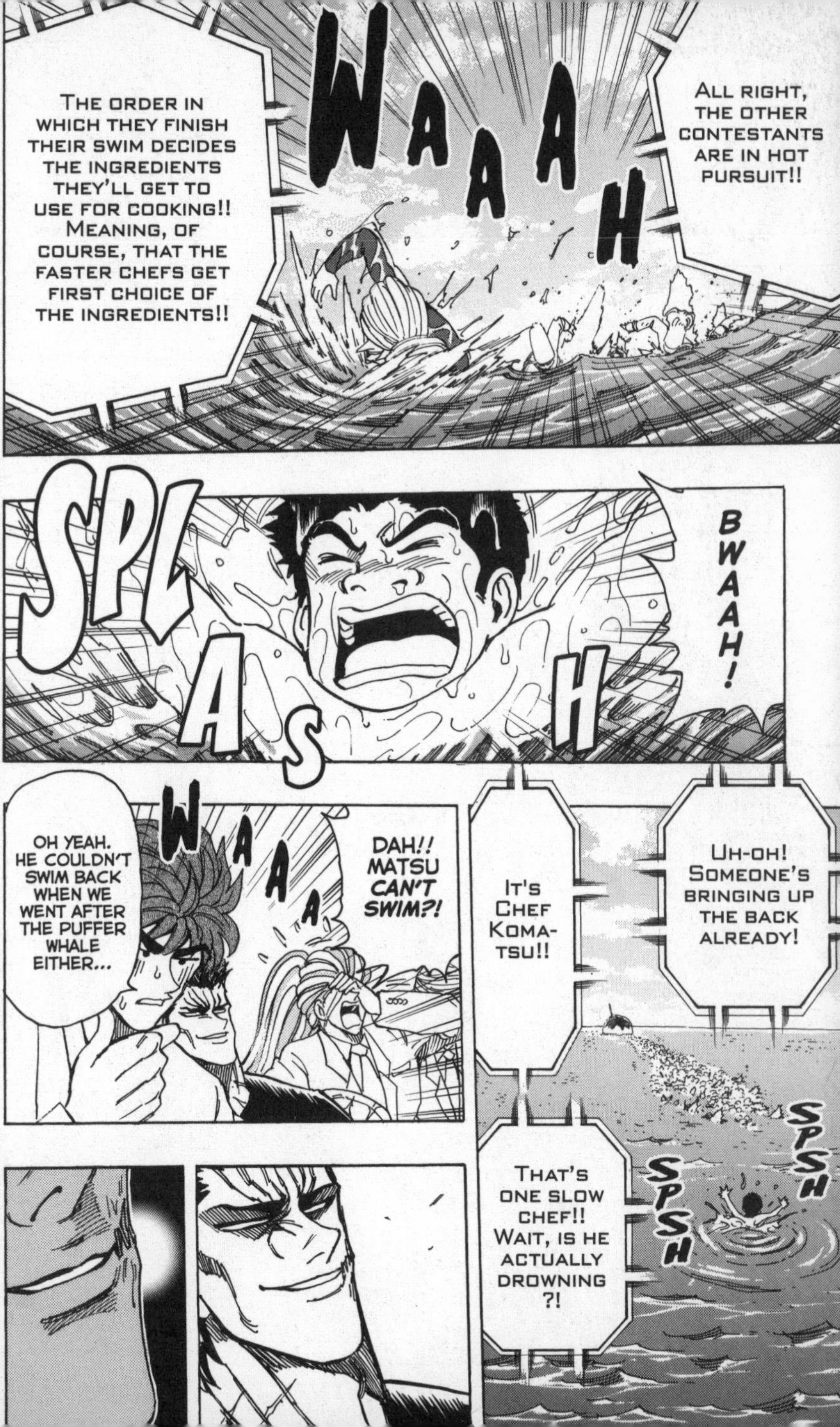
All right, the other contestants are in hot pursuit!!
WAAAAH
The order in which they finish their swim decides the ingredients they'll get to use for cooking!! Meaning, of course, that the faster chefs get first choice of the ingredients!!
BWAAAH!
SPLASH
Uh-oh! Someone's bringing up the back already!
It's Chef Koma-tsu!!
WAAAA
DAH!! Matsu can't swim?!
Oh yeah. He couldn't swim back when we went after the puffer whale either...
SPSH
SPSH
That's one slow chef!! Wait, is he actually drowning ?!

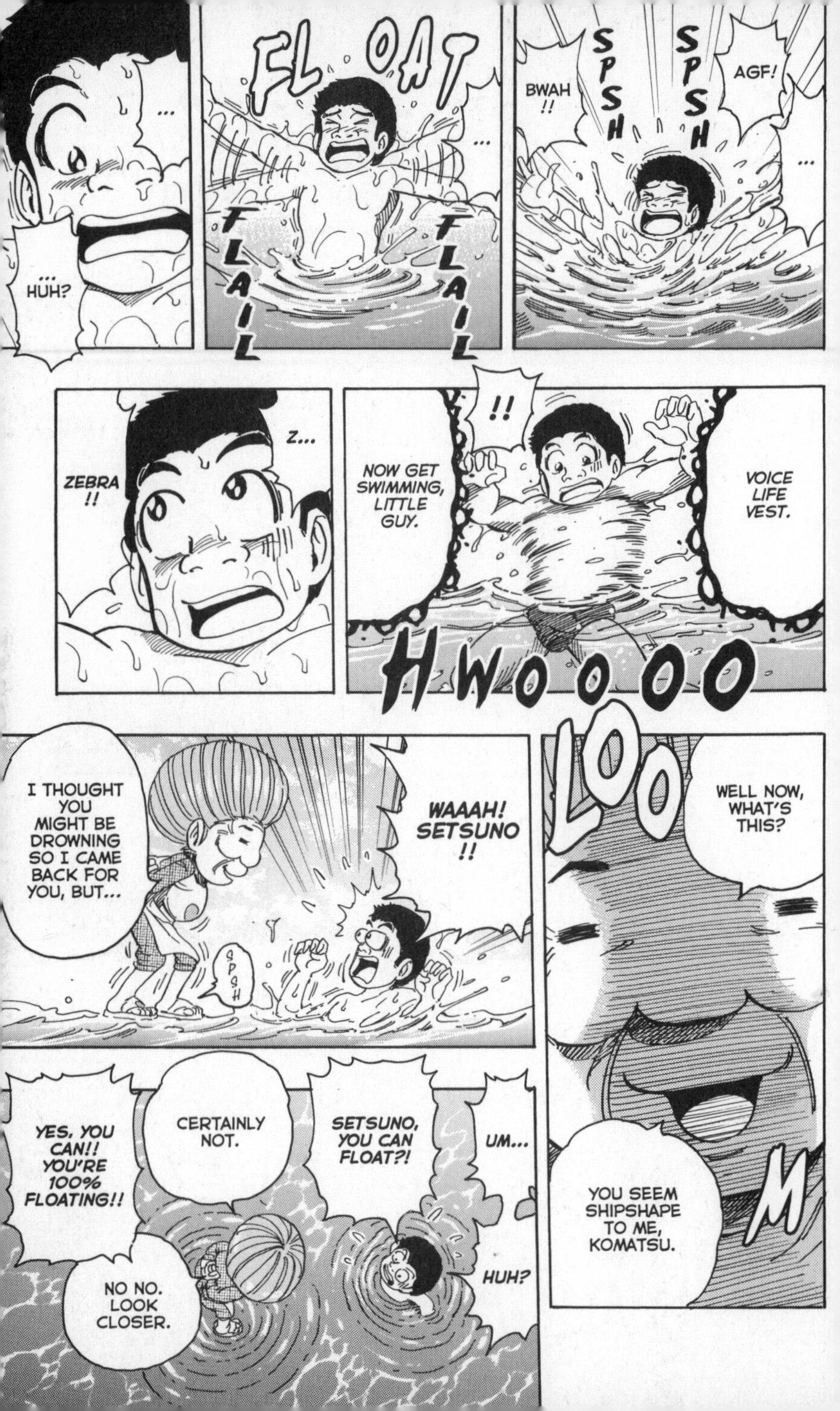
AGF!
SPSH
SPSH
BWAH !!
...
FL OAT
...
FLAIL
FLAIL
...
... HUH?
VOICE LIFE VEST.
!!
NOW GET SWIMMING, LITTLE GUY.
HWOOOO
Z...
ZEBRA !!
LOO
WELL NOW, WHAT'S THIS?
M
YOU SEEM SHIPSHAPE TO ME, KOMATSU.
WAAAH! SETSUNO !!
I THOUGHT YOU MIGHT BE DROWNING SO I CAME BACK FOR YOU, BUT...
SPSH
UM...
HUH?
SETSUNO, YOU CAN FLOAT?!
CERTAINLY NOT.
YES, YOU CAN!! YOU'RE 100% FLOATING!!
NO NO. LOOK CLOSER.

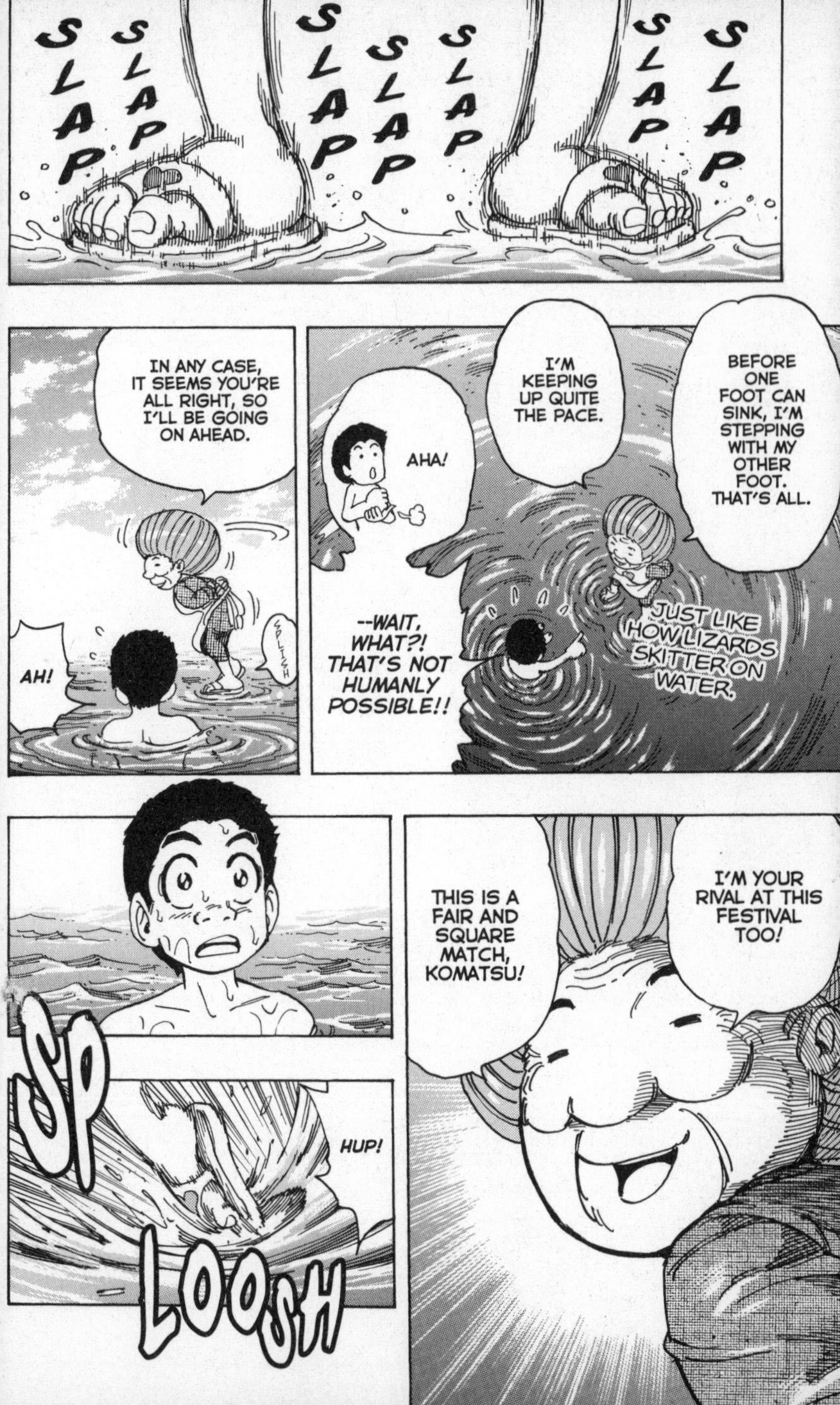
SLAP SLAP SLAP SLAP SLAP SLAP
BEFORE ONE FOOT CAN SINK, I'M STEPPING WITH MY OTHER FOOT. THAT'S ALL.
JUST LIKE HOW LIZARDS SKITTER ON WATER.
I'M KEEPING UP QUITE THE PACE.
AHA!
--WAIT, WHAT?! THAT'S NOT HUMANLY POSSIBLE!!
IN ANY CASE, IT SEEMS YOU'RE ALL RIGHT, SO I'LL BE GOING ON AHEAD.
SPLISH
AH!
I'M YOUR RIVAL AT THIS FESTIVAL TOO!
THIS IS A FAIR AND SQUARE MATCH, KOMATSU!
SPLOOSH
HUP!

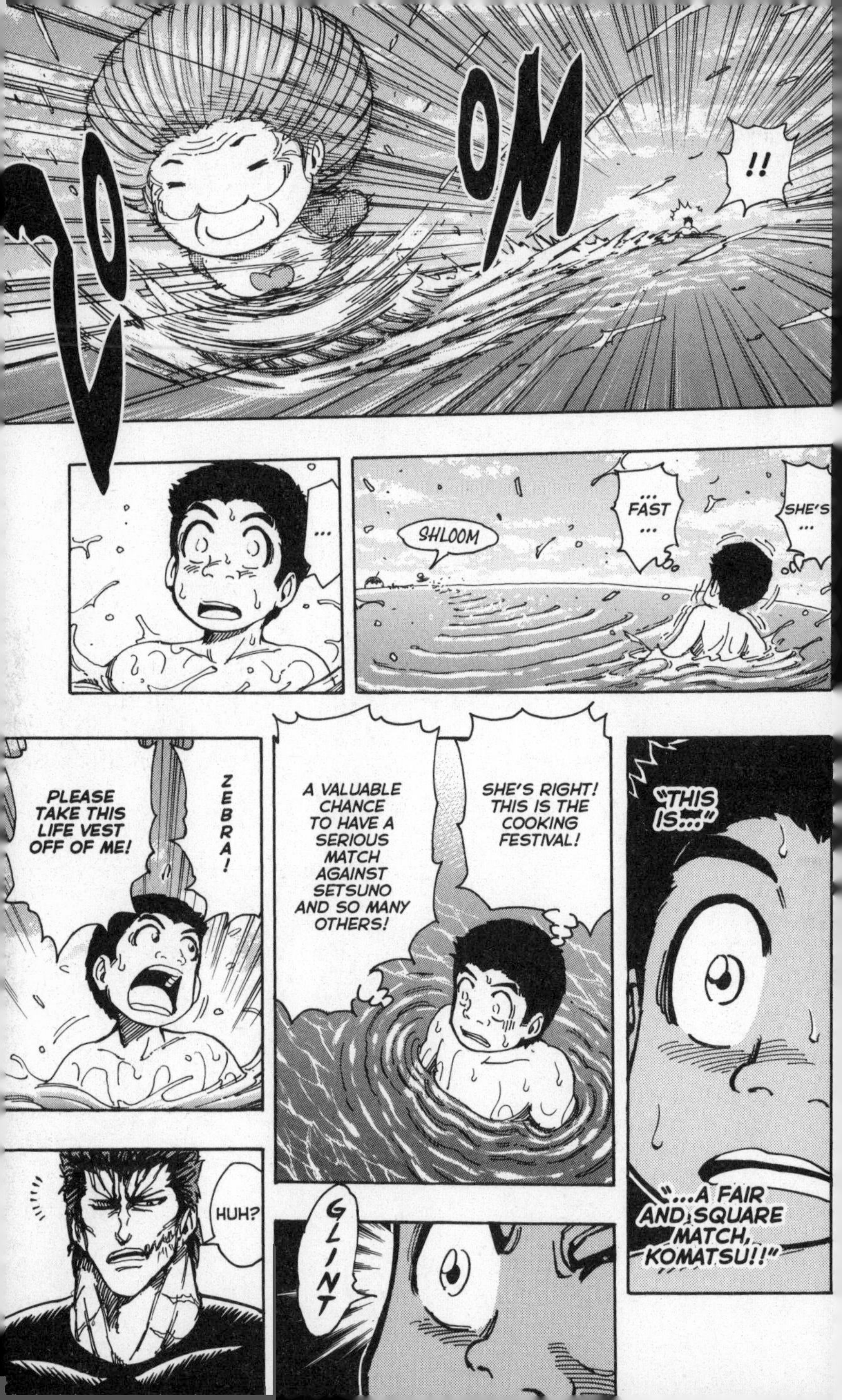
!!
ZOOM
SHE'S...
...FAST...
SHLOOM
...
"THIS IS..."
SHE'S RIGHT! THIS IS THE COOKING FESTIVAL!
A VALUABLE CHANCE TO HAVE A SERIOUS MATCH AGAINST SETSUNO AND SO MANY OTHERS!
ZEBRA!
PLEASE TAKE THIS LIFE VEST OFF OF ME!
"...A FAIR AND SQUARE MATCH, KOMATSU!!"
GLINT
HUH?

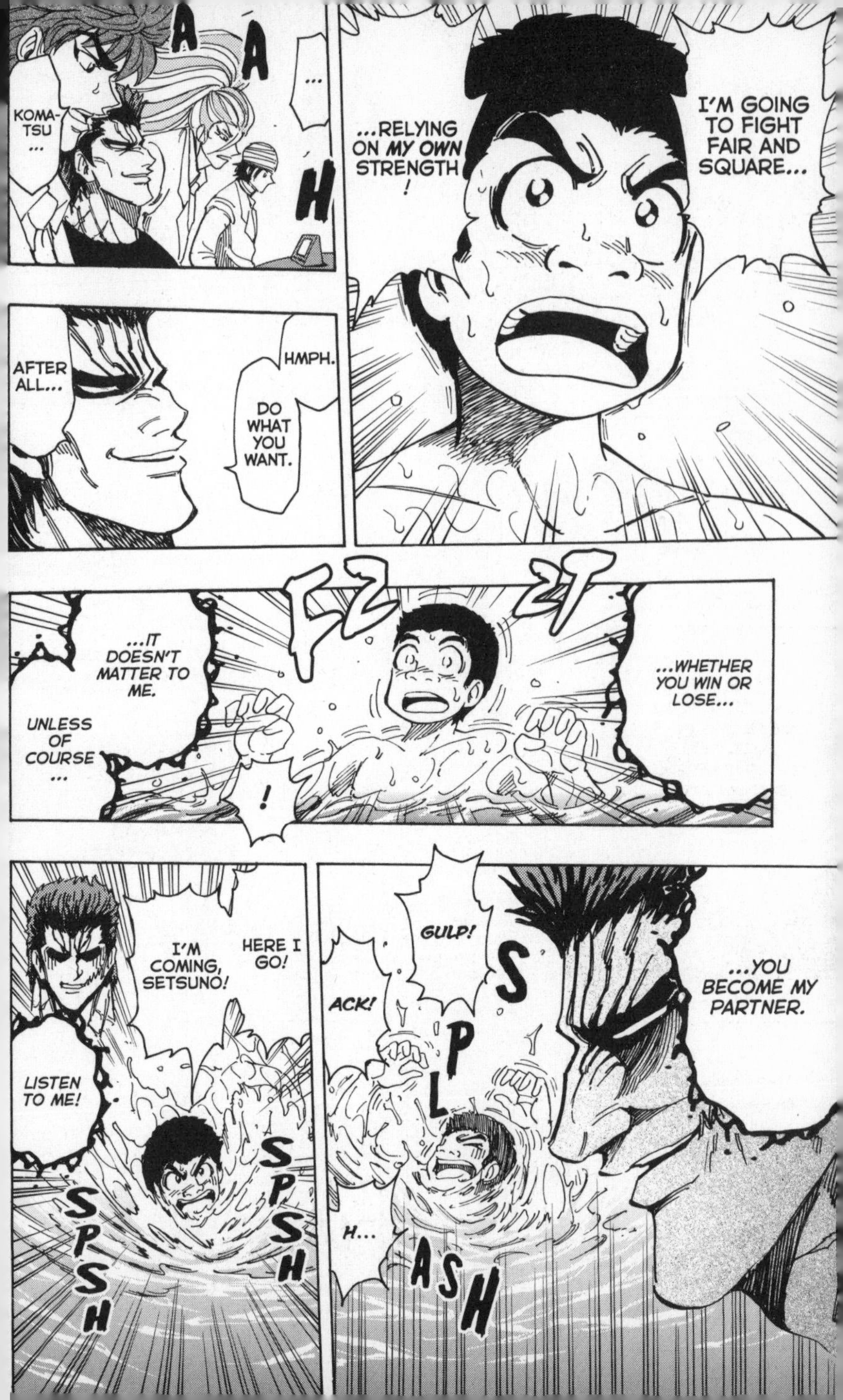
I'M GOING TO FIGHT FAIR AND SQUARE...
...RELYING ON MY OWN STRENGTH !
...
AAH
KOMA-TSU ...
HMPH.
AFTER ALL...
DO WHAT YOU WANT.
...WHETHER YOU WIN OR LOSE...
...IT DOESN'T MATTER TO ME.
UNLESS OF COURSE ...
!
...YOU BECOME MY PARTNER.
GULP!
SPLASH
ACK!
H...
HERE I GO!
I'M COMING, SETSUNO!
LISTEN TO ME!
SPSH
SPSH

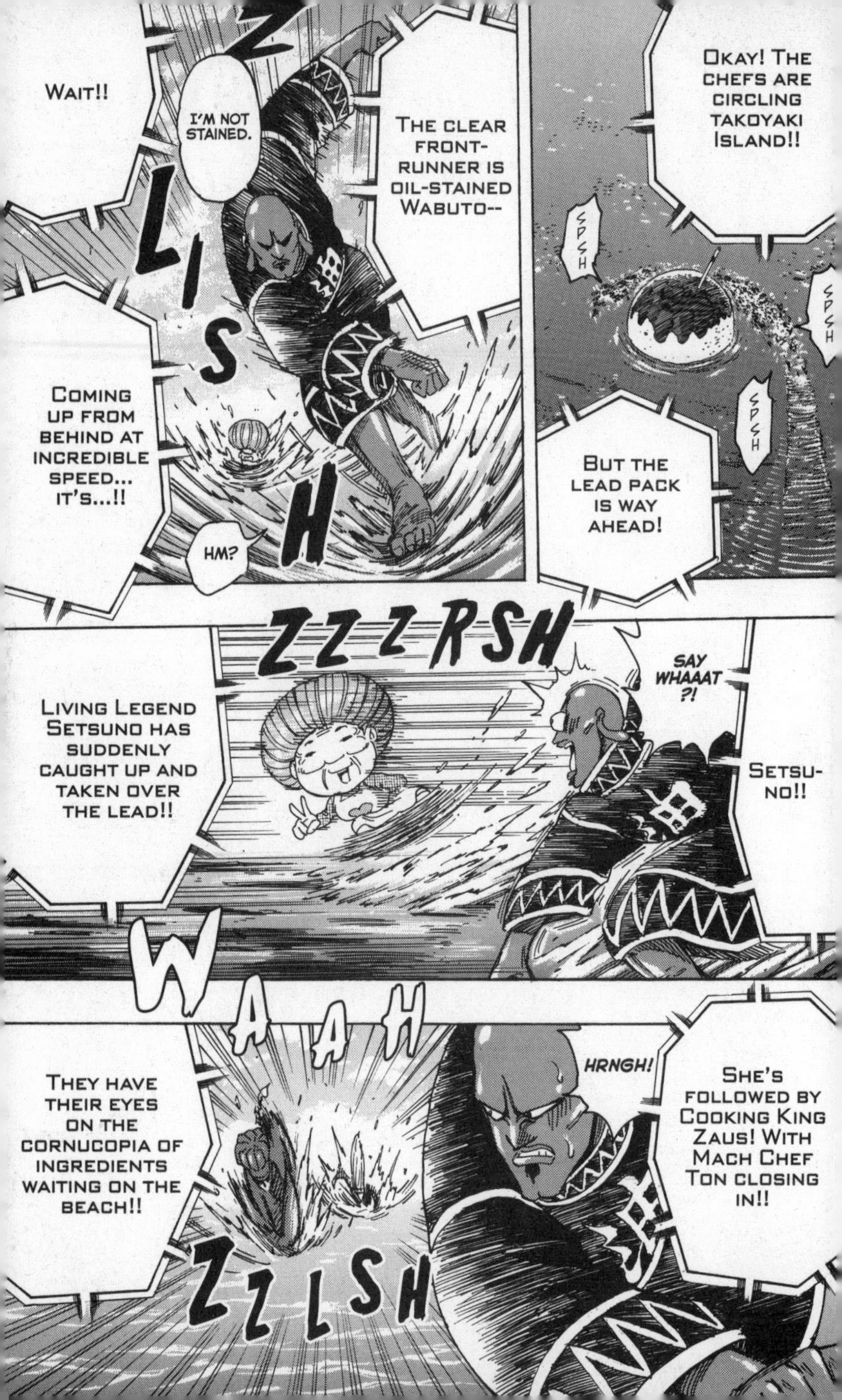
Okay! The chefs are circling Takoyaki Island!!
SPSH
SPSH
SPSH
But the lead pack is way ahead!
The clear front-runner is oil-stained Wabuto--
I'm not stained.
Wait!!
LISH
Coming up from behind at incredible speed... it's...!!
HM?
Setsu-no!!
SAY WHAAAT?!
ZZZRSH
Living Legend Setsuno has suddenly caught up and taken over the lead!!
WAAH
She's followed by Cooking King Zaus! With Mach Chef Ton closing in!!
HRNGH!
They have their eyes on the cornucopia of ingredients waiting on the beach!!
ZZLSH

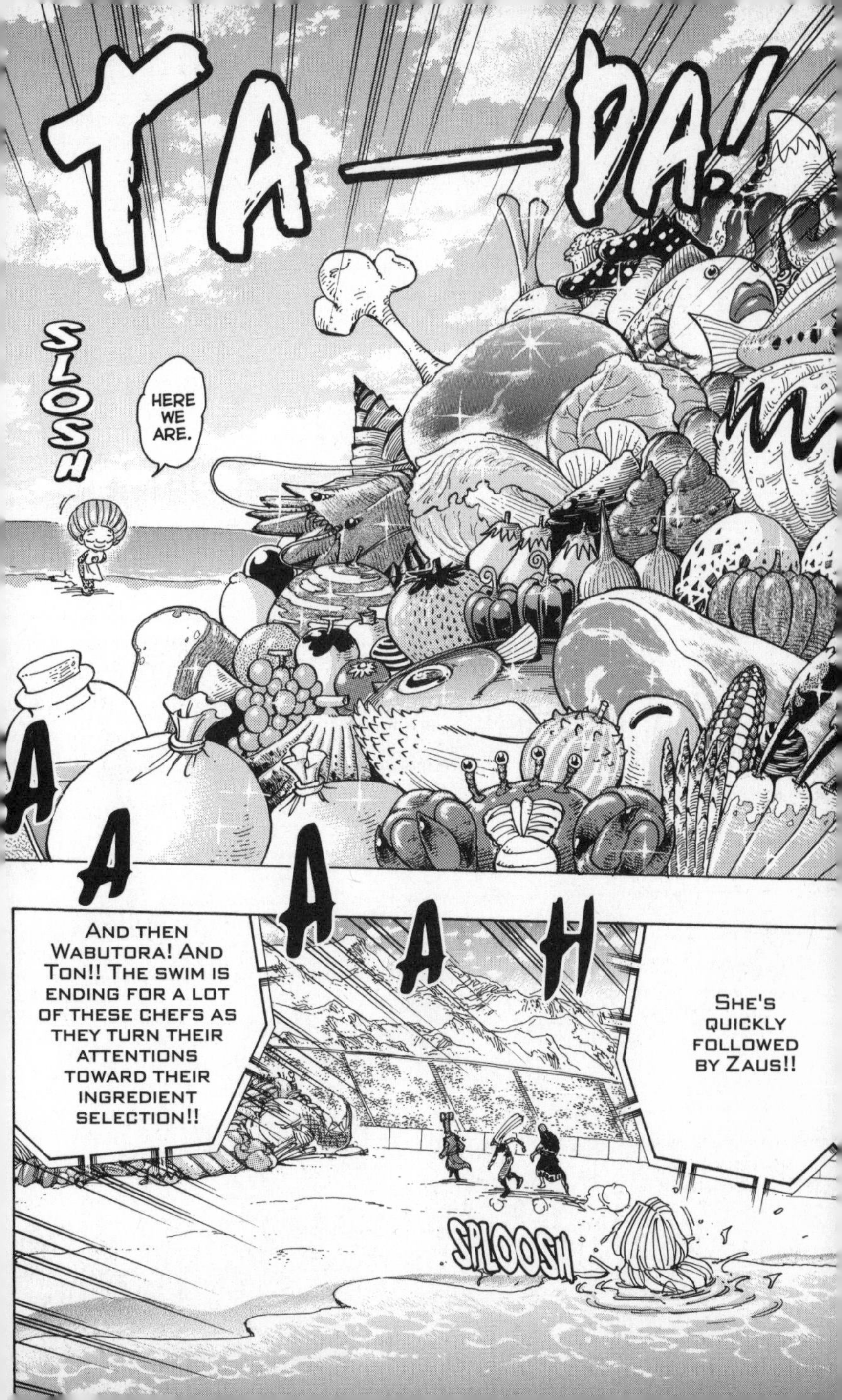
TA—DA!
SLOSH
HERE WE ARE.
AAAAH
She's quickly followed by Zaus!!
And then Wabutora! And Ton!! The swim is ending for a lot of these chefs as they turn their attentions toward their ingredient selection!!
SPLOOSH

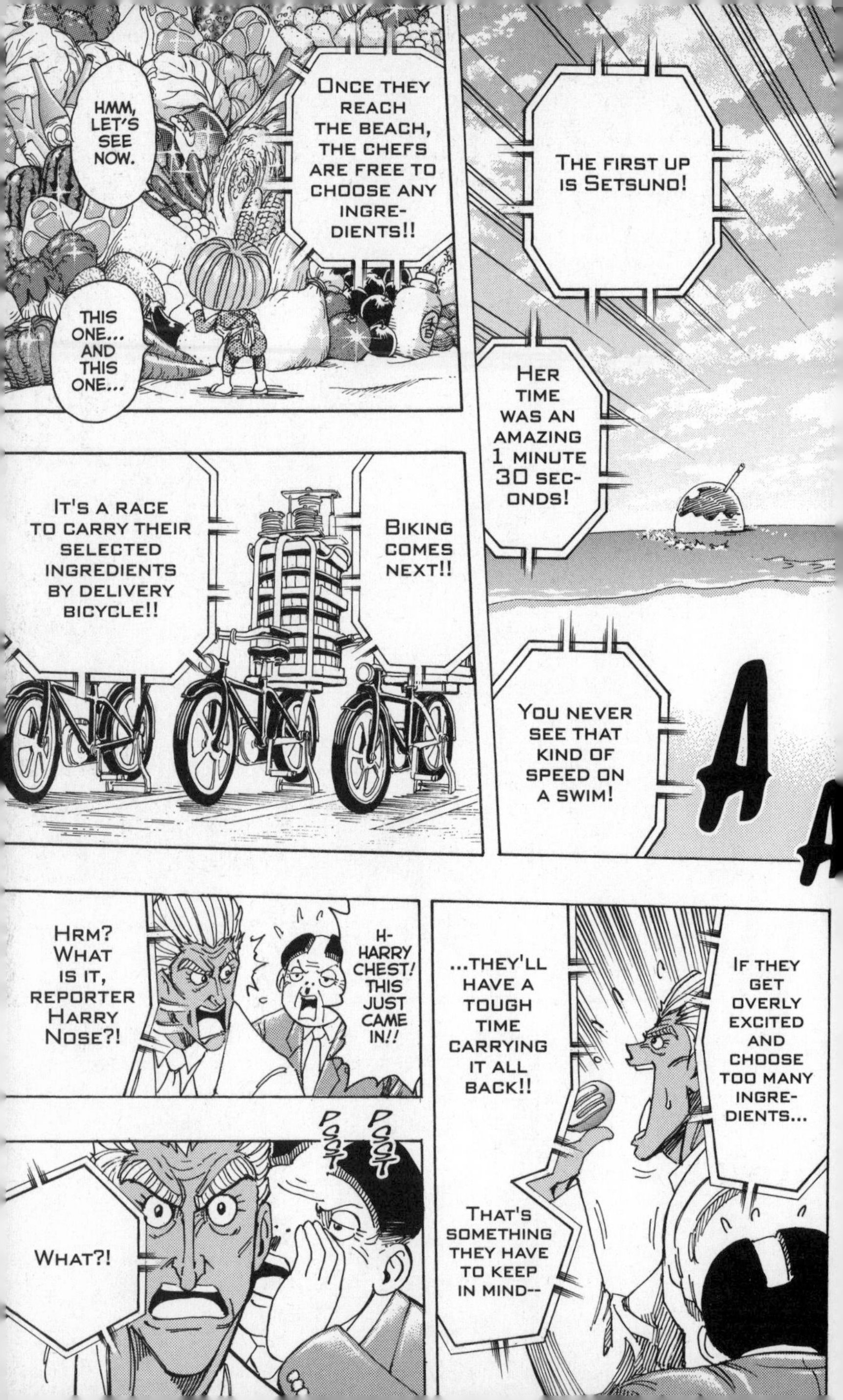
The first up is Setsuno!
Her time was an amazing 1 minute 30 seconds!
You never see that kind of speed on a swim!
A
A
Once they reach the beach, the chefs are free to choose any ingredients!!
Hmm, let's see now.
This one... and this one...
Biking comes next!!
It's a race to carry their selected ingredients by delivery bicycle!!
If they get overly excited and choose too many ingredients...
...they'll have a tough time carrying it all back!!
That's something they have to keep in mind--
H-Harry Chest! This just came in!!
Hrm? What is it, reporter Harry Nose?!
Psst
Psst
What?!

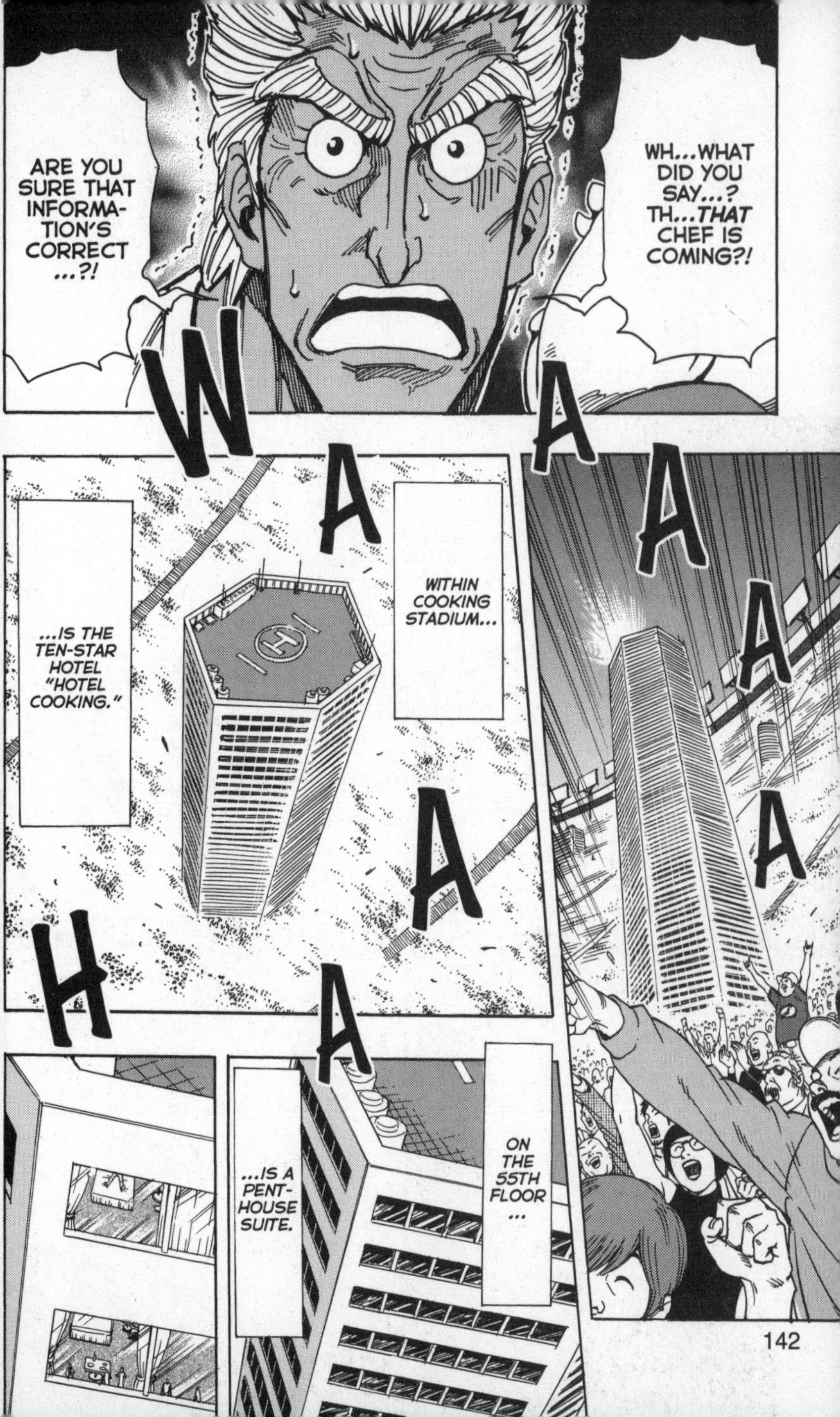
WH...WHAT DID YOU SAY...? TH...*THAT* CHEF IS COMING?!
ARE YOU SURE THAT INFORMATION'S CORRECT ...?!
WAAAAAAAAHH
WITHIN COOKING STADIUM...
...IS THE TEN-STAR HOTEL "HOTEL COOKING."
ON THE 55TH FLOOR ...
...IS A PENT-HOUSE SUITE.

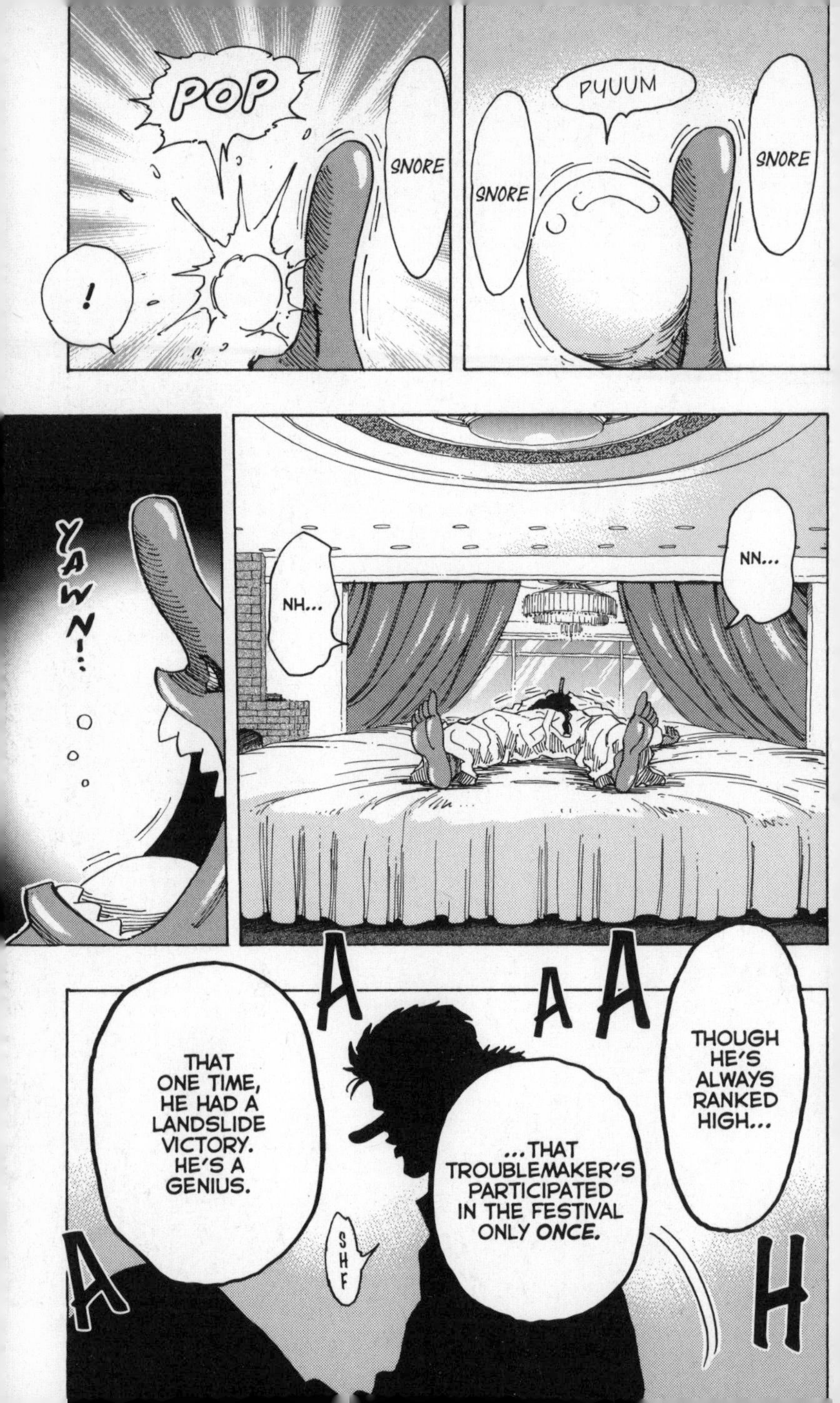
SNORE
PYUUM
SNORE
SNORE
POP
!
NN...
NH...
YAWN!..
THOUGH HE'S ALWAYS RANKED HIGH...
...THAT TROUBLEMAKER'S PARTICIPATED IN THE FESTIVAL ONLY ONCE.
SHF
THAT ONE TIME, HE HAD A LANDSLIDE VICTORY. HE'S A GENIUS.
AAAAH

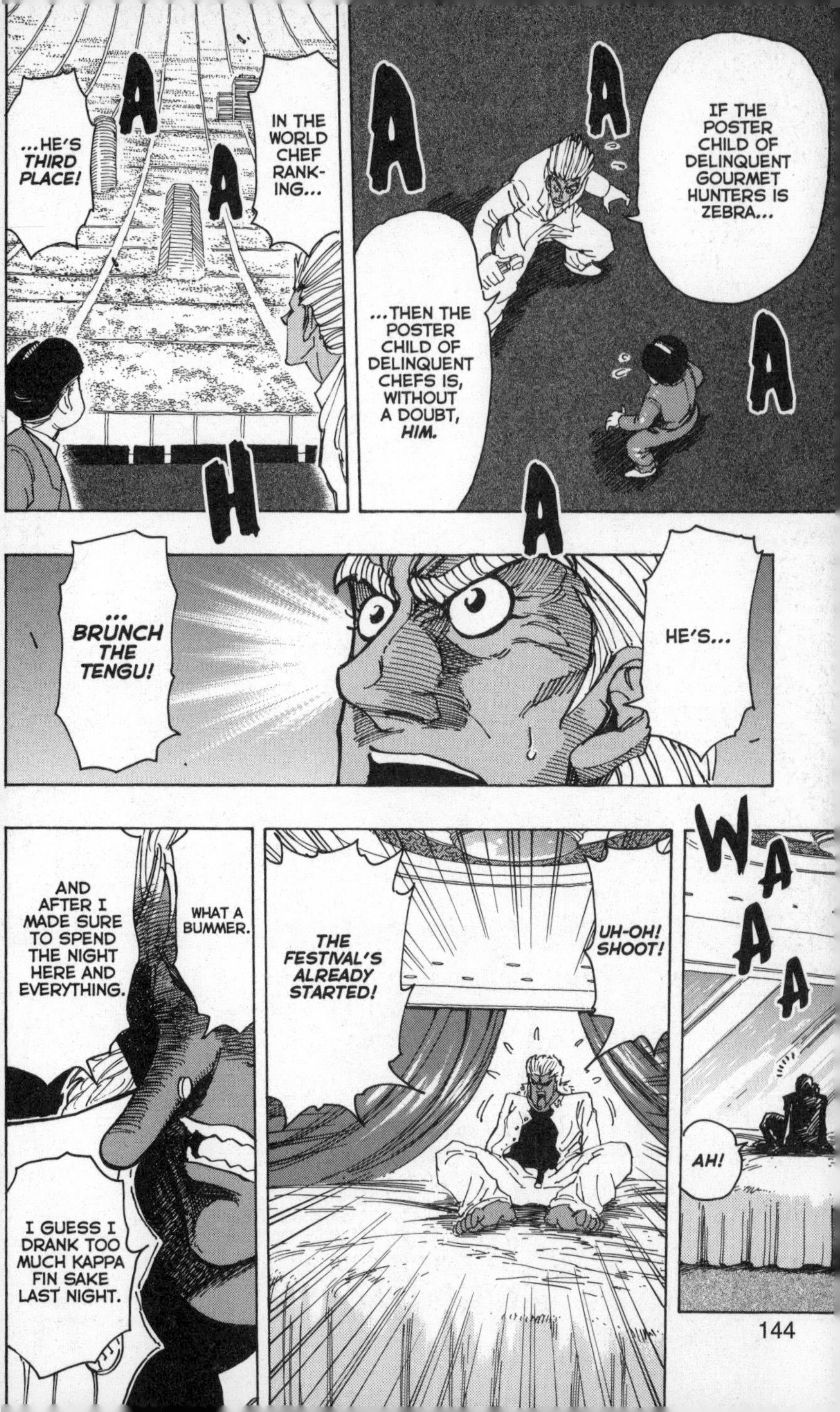
IF THE POSTER CHILD OF DELINQUENT GOURMET HUNTERS IS ZEBRA...
...THEN THE POSTER CHILD OF DELINQUENT CHEFS IS, WITHOUT A DOUBT, *HIM.*
IN THE WORLD CHEF RANK-ING...
...HE'S *THIRD PLACE!*
AAAAAH
HE'S...
...*BRÜNCH THE TENGU!*
WAAAA
AH!
UH-OH! SHOOT!
THE FESTIVAL'S ALREADY STARTED!
WHAT A BUMMER.
AND AFTER I MADE SURE TO SPEND THE NIGHT HERE AND EVERYTHING.
I GUESS I DRANK TOO MUCH KAPPA FIN SAKE LAST NIGHT.

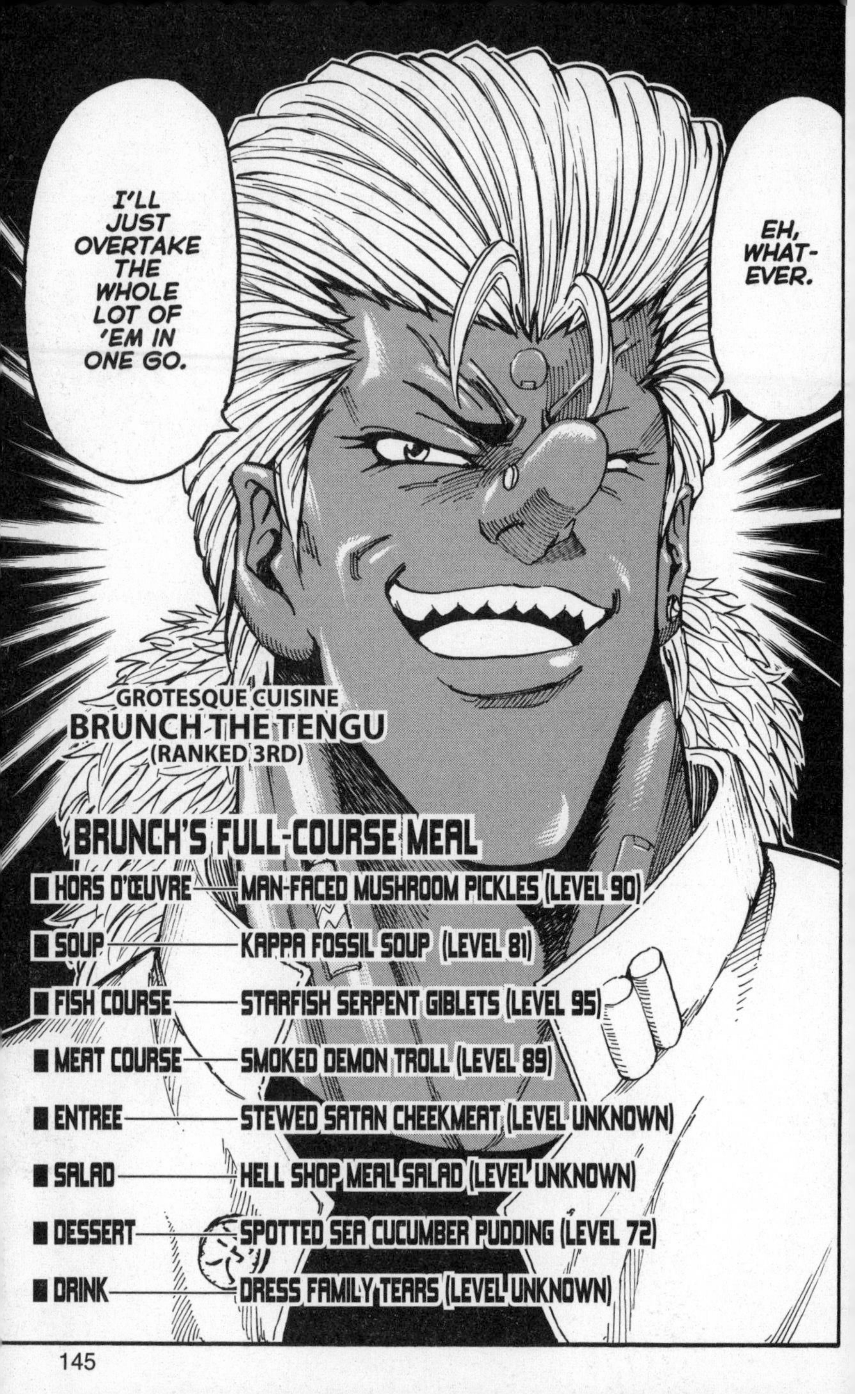
EH, WHAT-EVER.
I'LL JUST OVERTAKE THE WHOLE LOT OF 'EM IN ONE GO.
GROTESQUE CUISINE
BRUNCH THE TENGU
(RANKED 3RD)
BRUNCH'S FULL-COURSE MEAL
HORS D'ŒUVRE — MAN-FACED MUSHROOM PICKLES (LEVEL 90)
SOUP — KAPPA FOSSIL SOUP (LEVEL 81)
FISH COURSE — STARFISH SERPENT GIBLETS (LEVEL 95)
MEAT COURSE — SMOKED DEMON TROLL (LEVEL 89)
ENTREE — STEWED SATAN CHEEKMEAT (LEVEL UNKNOWN)
SALAD — HELL SHOP MEAL SALAD (LEVEL UNKNOWN)
DESSERT — SPOTTED SEA CUCUMBER PUDDING (LEVEL 72)
DRINK — DRESS FAMILY TEARS (LEVEL UNKNOWN)

TORIKO

GOURMET CHECKLIST

Vol. 247

BULLET ACORN
(TREE NUT)

CAPTURE LEVEL: 23
HABITAT: WASTELANDS
LENGTH: 7 CM
HEIGHT: ---
WEIGHT: 250 G
PRICE: 1,500 YEN PER NUT

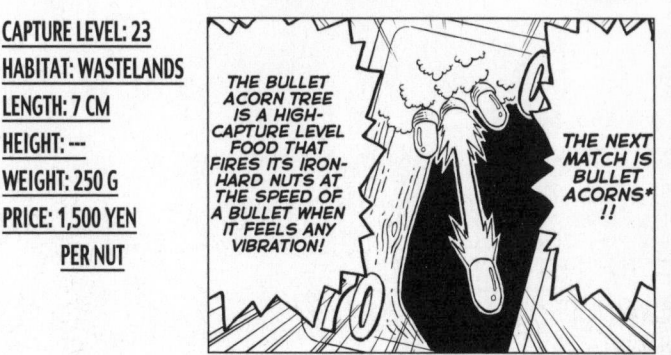

THE NEXT MATCH IS BULLET ACORNS* !!
THE BULLET ACORN TREE IS A HIGH-CAPTURE LEVEL FOOD THAT FIRES ITS IRON-HARD NUTS AT THE SPEED OF A BULLET WHEN IT FEELS ANY VIBRATION!
TO

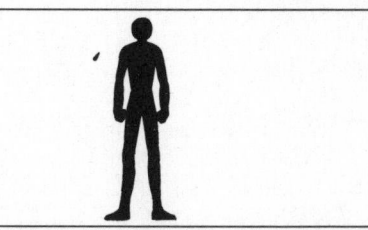

SCALE

THIS IRON-HARD NUT IS SHOT AT THE SPEED OF A BULLET WHEN ITS TREE FEELS ANY VIBRATION. THE MOMENT IT HITS THE GROUND IT SPROUTS A POISONOUS BUD, SO IF YOU WANT TO EAT IT YOU HAVE TO CATCH IT MIDAIR. THAT'S NO BREEZY FEAT, HENCE BULLET ACORN'S HIGH CAPTURE LEVEL. EVERY YEAR IN BULLET ACORN SEASON, PEOPLE DIE FROM STRAY ACORNS, AND THE AREA SURROUNDING THE TREES IS CLASSIFIED AS A DANGER ZONE.

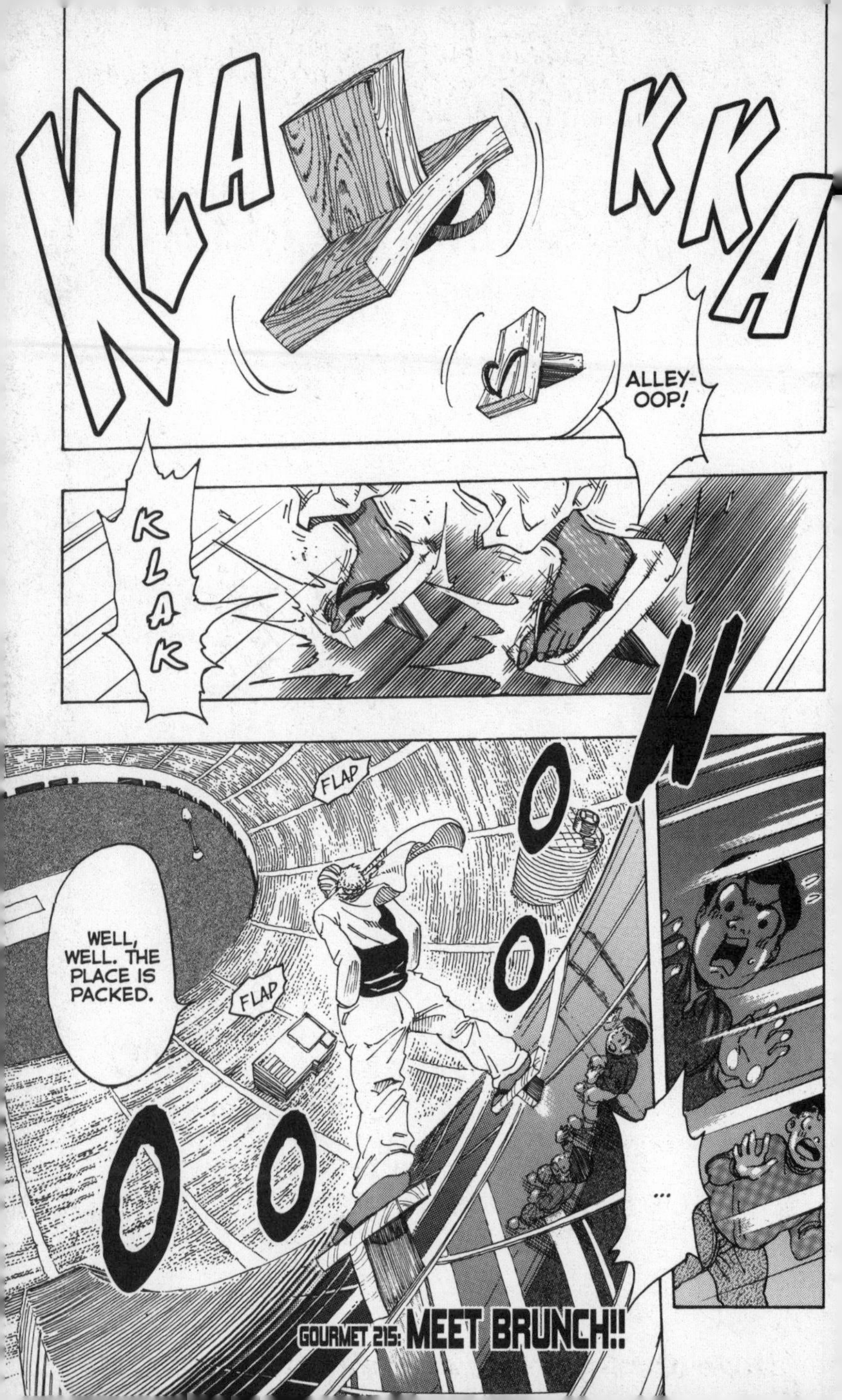
KLAKKA
ALLEY-OOP!
KLAK
WOOOO
WELL, WELL. THE PLACE IS PACKED.
FLAP
FLAP
...
GOURMET 215: MEET BRUNCH!!

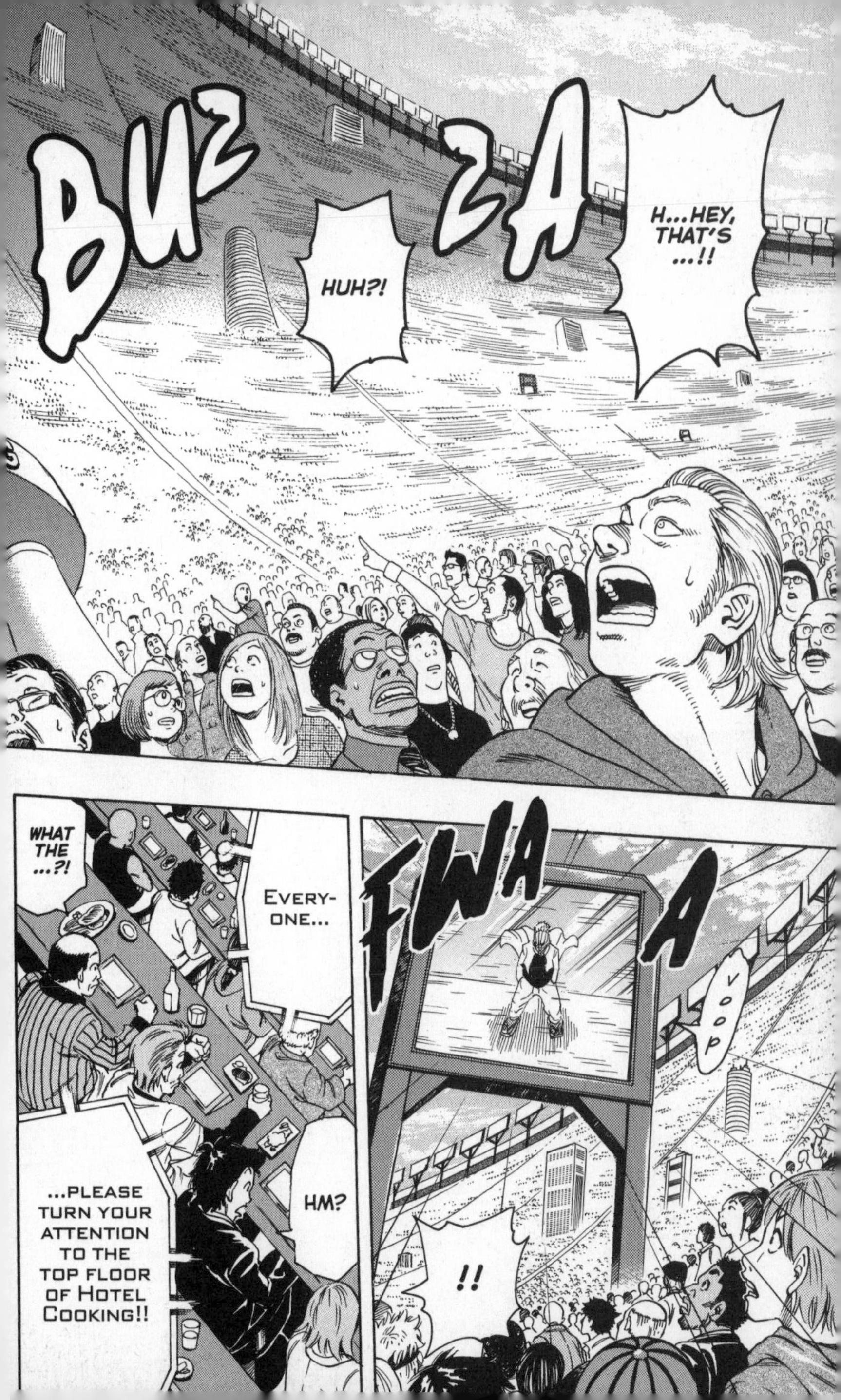
H...HEY, THAT'S ...!!
BUZ ZA
HUH?!
FWA A
VOOP
!!
EVERY-ONE...
WHAT THE ...?!
HM?
...PLEASE TURN YOUR ATTENTION TO THE TOP FLOOR OF HOTEL COOKING!!

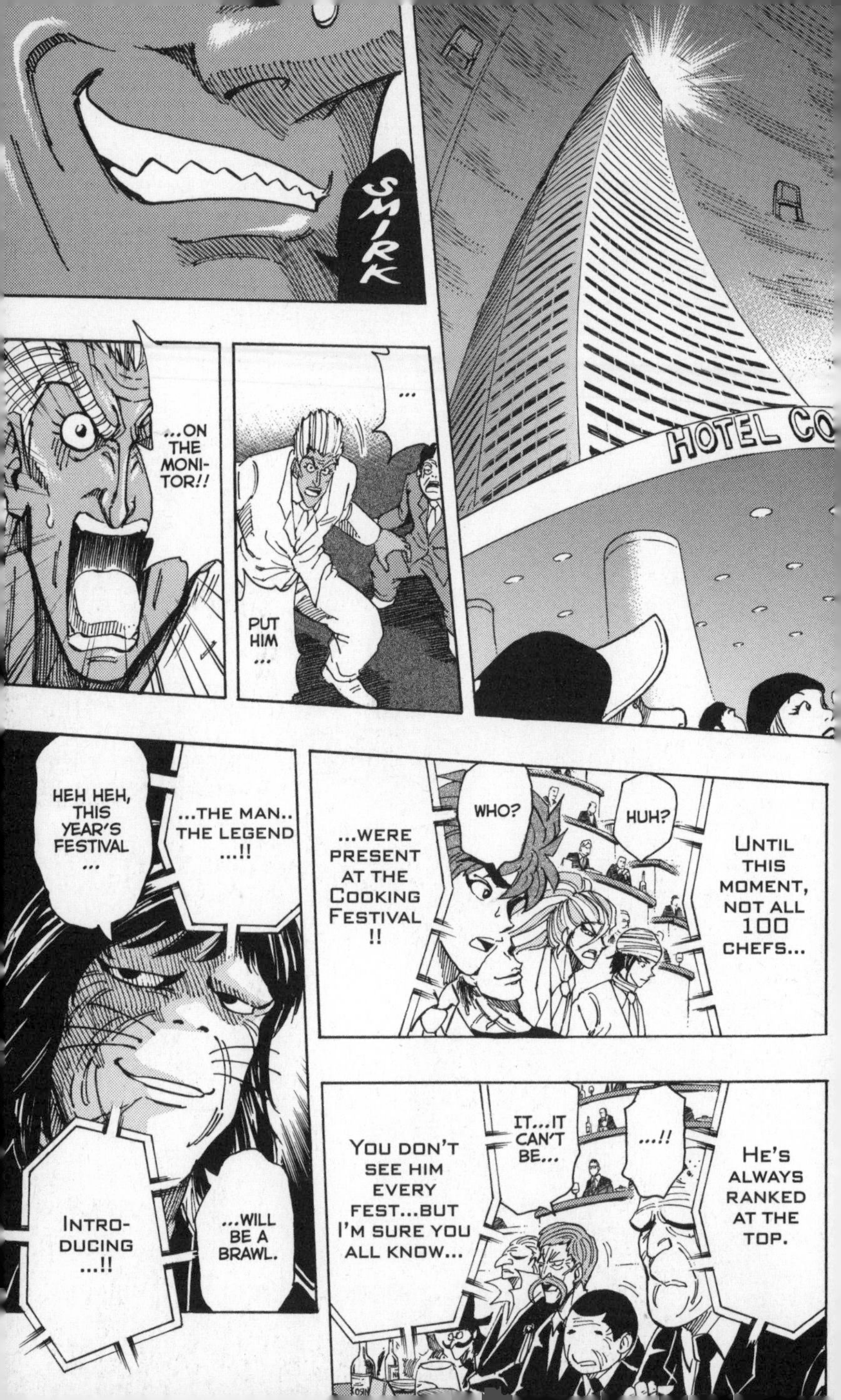
HOTEL CO
SMIRK
...
PUT HIM...
...ON THE MONI-TOR!!
UNTIL THIS MOMENT, NOT ALL 100 CHEFS...
HUH?
WHO?
...WERE PRESENT AT THE COOKING FESTIVAL!!
HE'S ALWAYS RANKED AT THE TOP.
...!!
IT...IT CAN'T BE...
YOU DON'T SEE HIM EVERY FEST...BUT I'M SURE YOU ALL KNOW...
...THE MAN.. THE LEGEND...!!
HEH HEH, THIS YEAR'S FESTIVAL...
...WILL BE A BRAWL.
INTRO-DUCING...!!

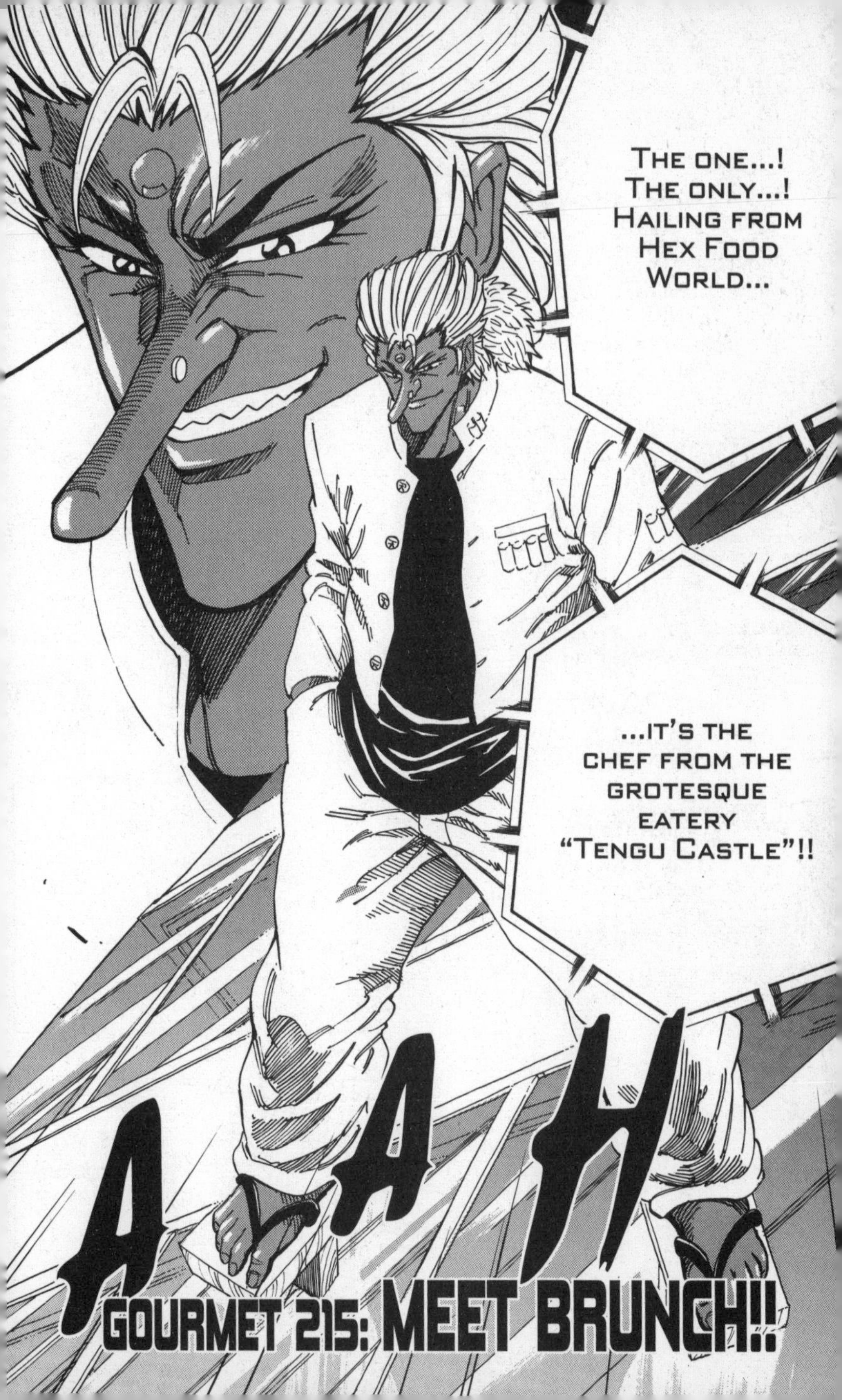
THE ONE...! THE ONLY...! HAILING FROM HEX FOOD WORLD...
...IT'S THE CHEF FROM THE GROTESQUE EATERY "TENGU CASTLE"!!
AAH
GOURMET 215: MEET BRUNCH!!

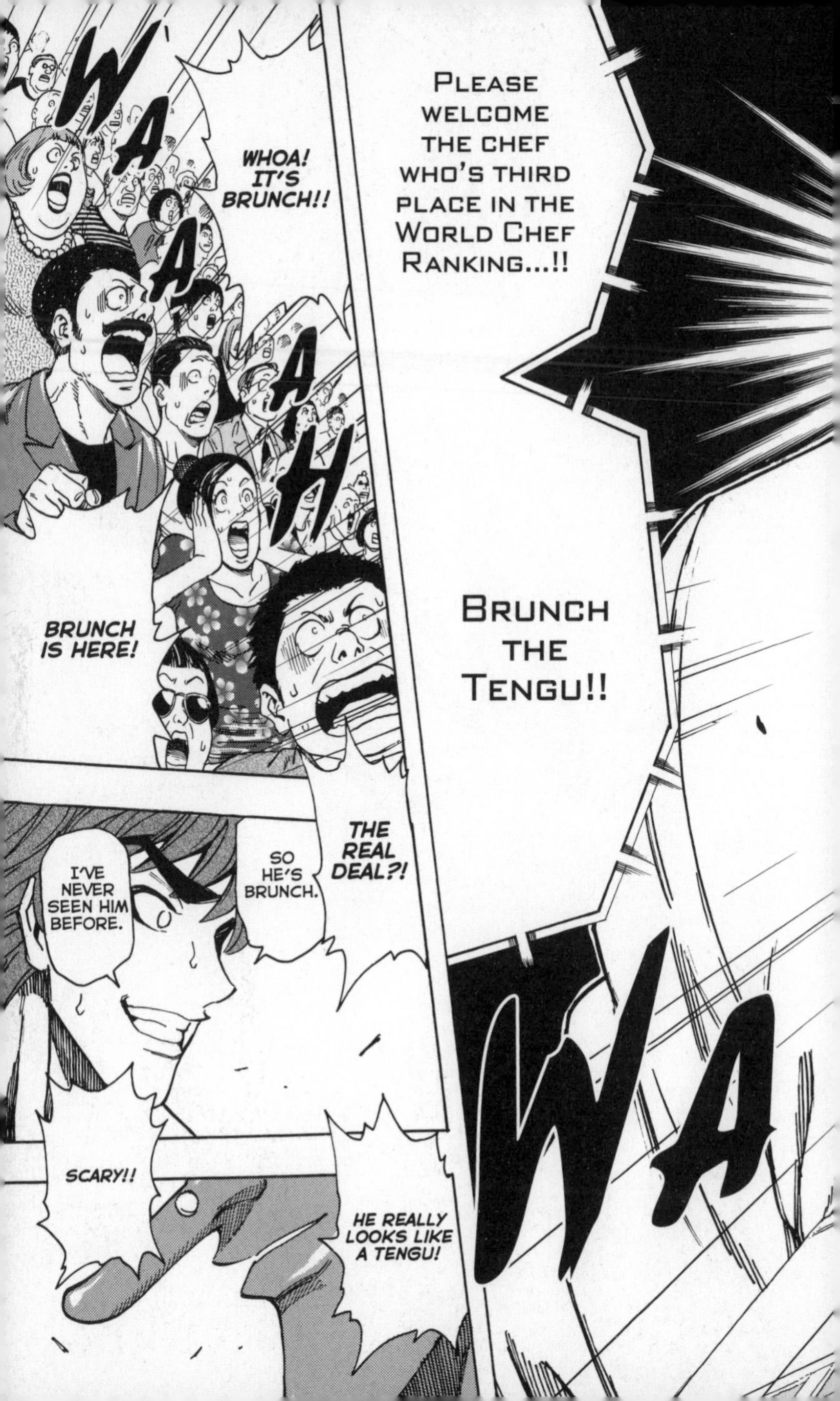
PLEASE WELCOME THE CHEF WHO'S THIRD PLACE IN THE WORLD CHEF RANKING...!!
BRUNCH THE TENGU!!
WA
WAAAH
WHOA! IT'S BRUNCH!!
BRUNCH IS HERE!
THE REAL DEAL?!
SO HE'S BRUNCH.
I'VE NEVER SEEN HIM BEFORE.
SCARY!!
HE REALLY LOOKS LIKE A TENGU!

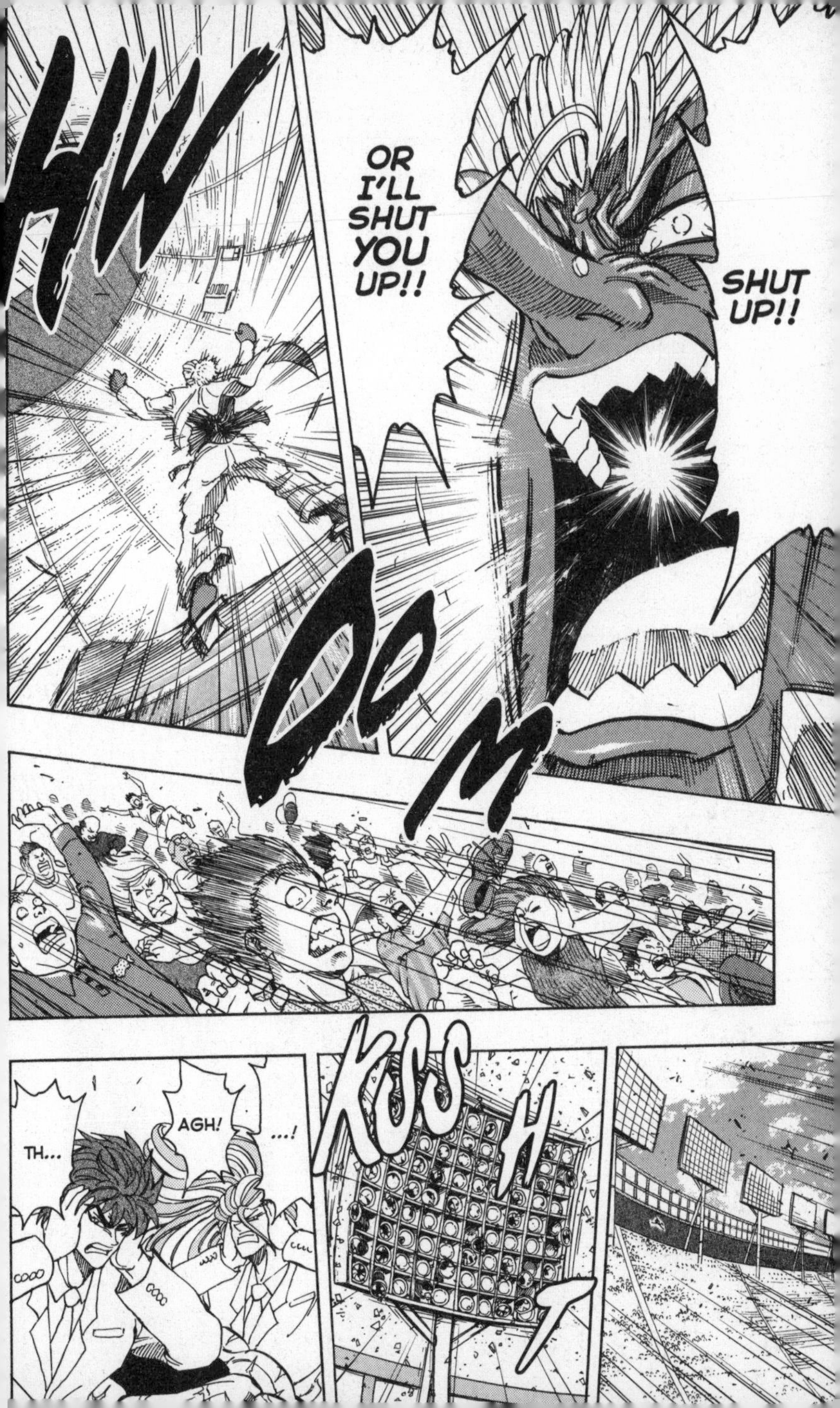
SHUT UP!!
OR I'LL SHUT YOU UP!!
FWW
DOOM
KSSH
...!
AGH!
TH...

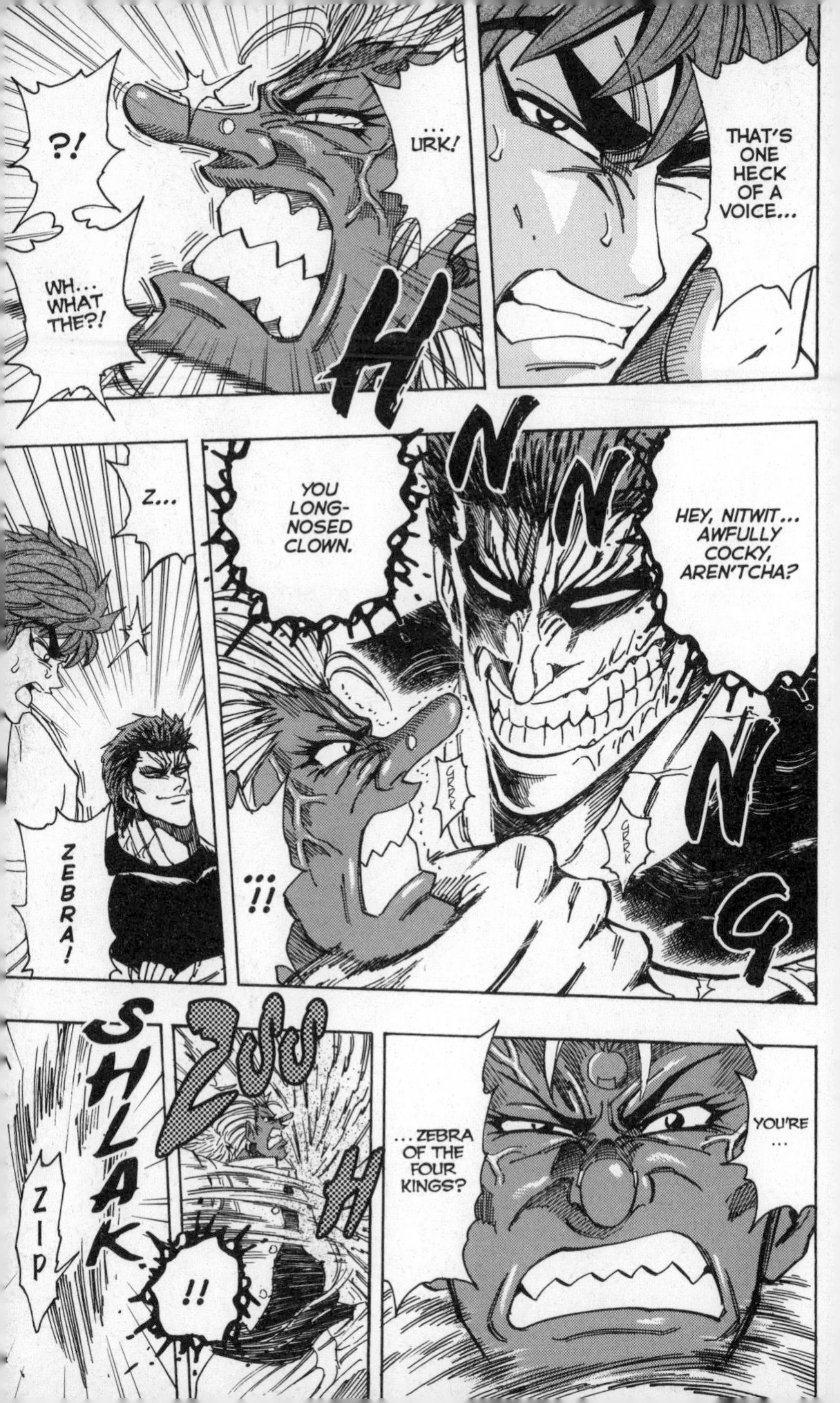
THAT'S ONE HECK OF A VOICE...
... URK!
?!
WH... WHAT THE?!
HNNNNG
HEY, NITWIT... AWFULLY COCKY, AREN'TCHA?
YOU LONG-NOSED CLOWN.
GRRK
GRRK
...!!
Z...
ZEBRA!
YOU'RE ...
...ZEBRA OF THE FOUR KINGS?
ZUUH
SHLAK
ZIP
!!

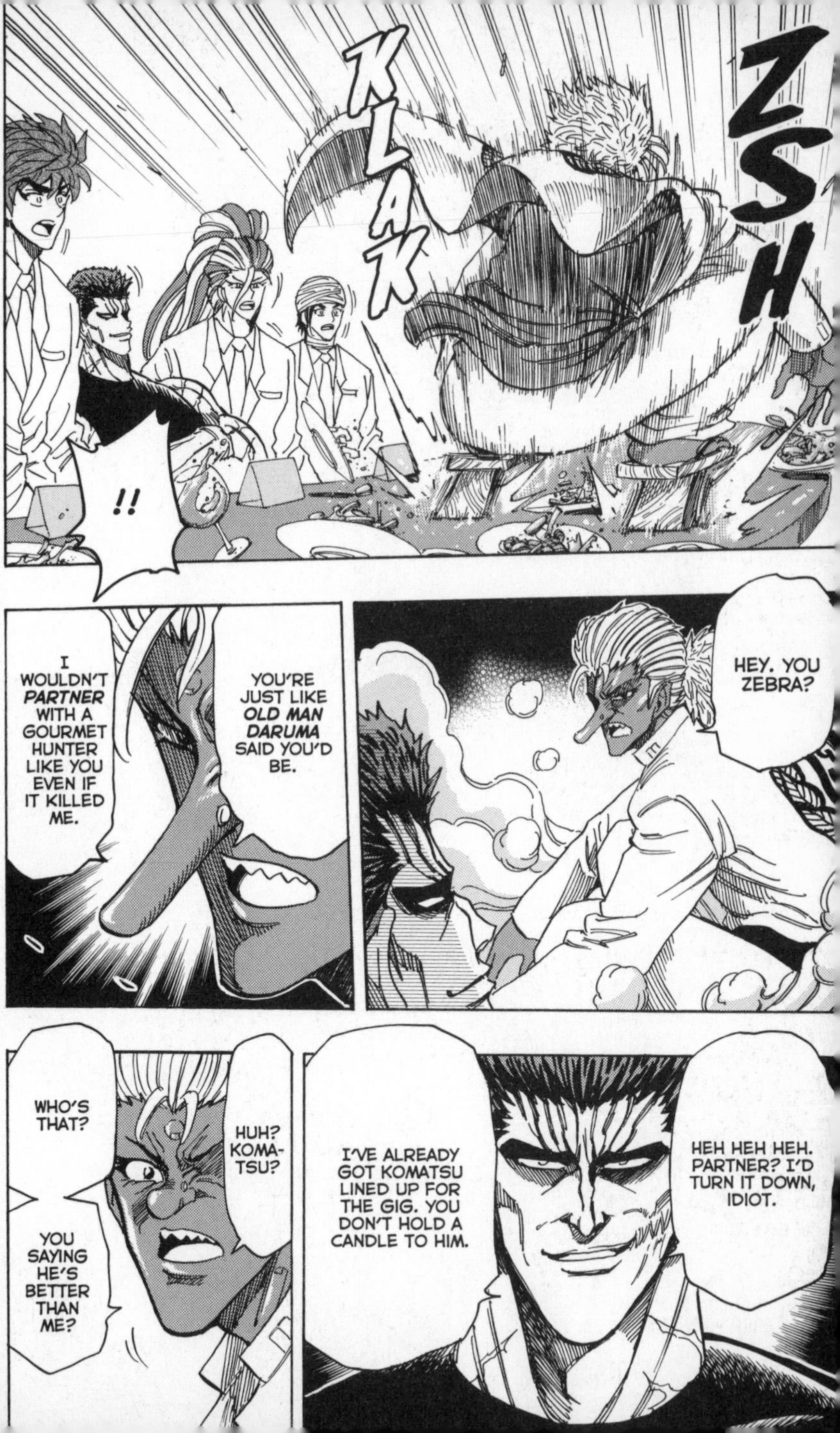
ZSH
KLAK
!!
HEY. YOU ZEBRA?
YOU'RE JUST LIKE OLD MAN DARUMA SAID YOU'D BE.
I WOULDN'T PARTNER WITH A GOURMET HUNTER LIKE YOU EVEN IF IT KILLED ME.
HEH HEH HEH. PARTNER? I'D TURN IT DOWN, IDIOT.
I'VE ALREADY GOT KOMATSU LINED UP FOR THE GIG. YOU DON'T HOLD A CANDLE TO HIM.
HUH? KOMA-TSU?
WHO'S THAT?
YOU SAYING HE'S BETTER THAN ME?

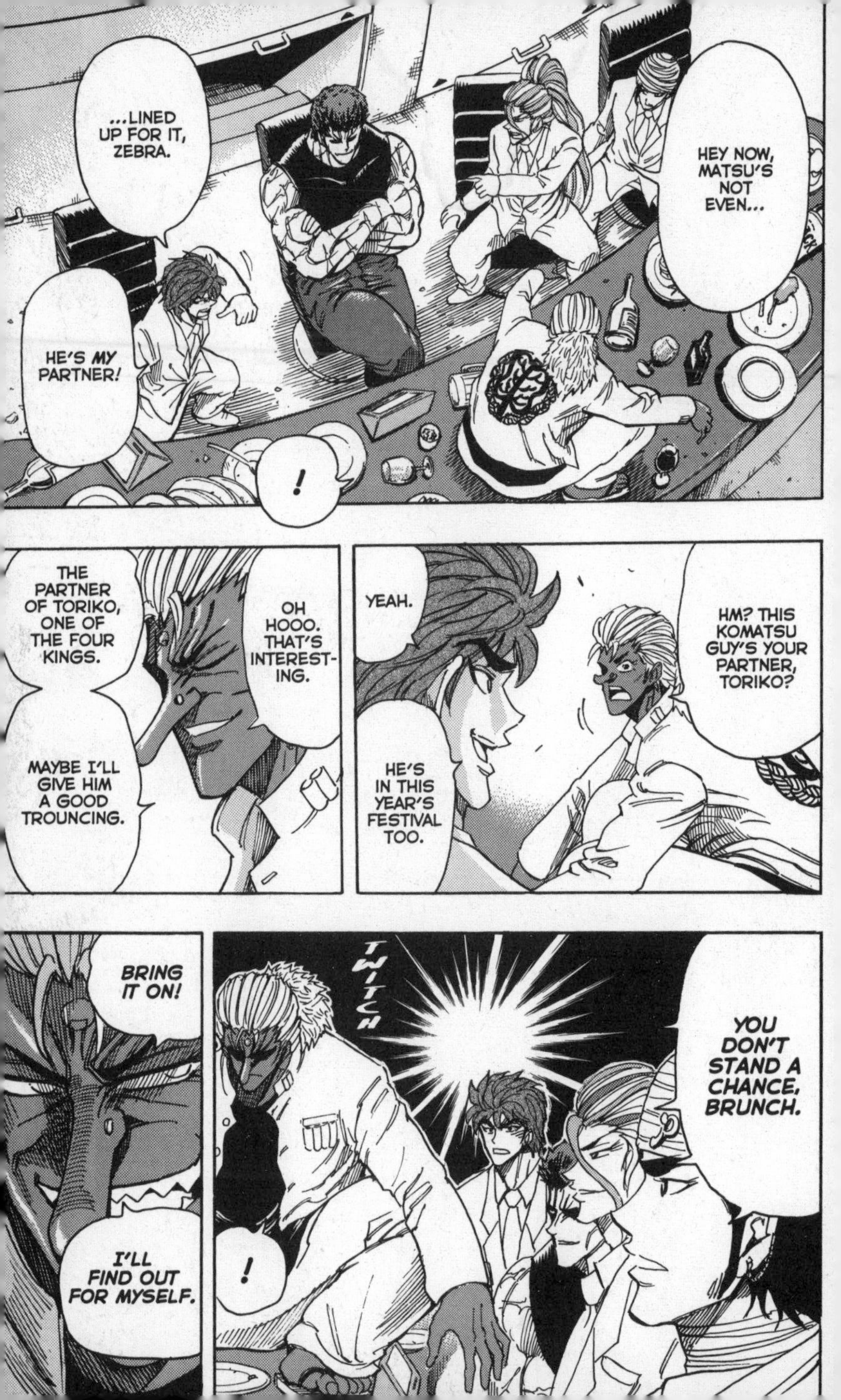
HEY NOW, MATSU'S NOT EVEN...
...LINED UP FOR IT, ZEBRA.
HE'S MY PARTNER!
!
HM? THIS KOMATSU GUY'S YOUR PARTNER, TORIKO?
YEAH.
HE'S IN THIS YEAR'S FESTIVAL TOO.
OH HOOO. THAT'S INTEREST-ING.
THE PARTNER OF TORIKO, ONE OF THE FOUR KINGS.
MAYBE I'LL GIVE HIM A GOOD TROUNCING.
YOU DON'T STAND A CHANCE, BRUNCH.
TWITCH
!
BRING IT ON!
I'LL FIND OUT FOR MYSELF.

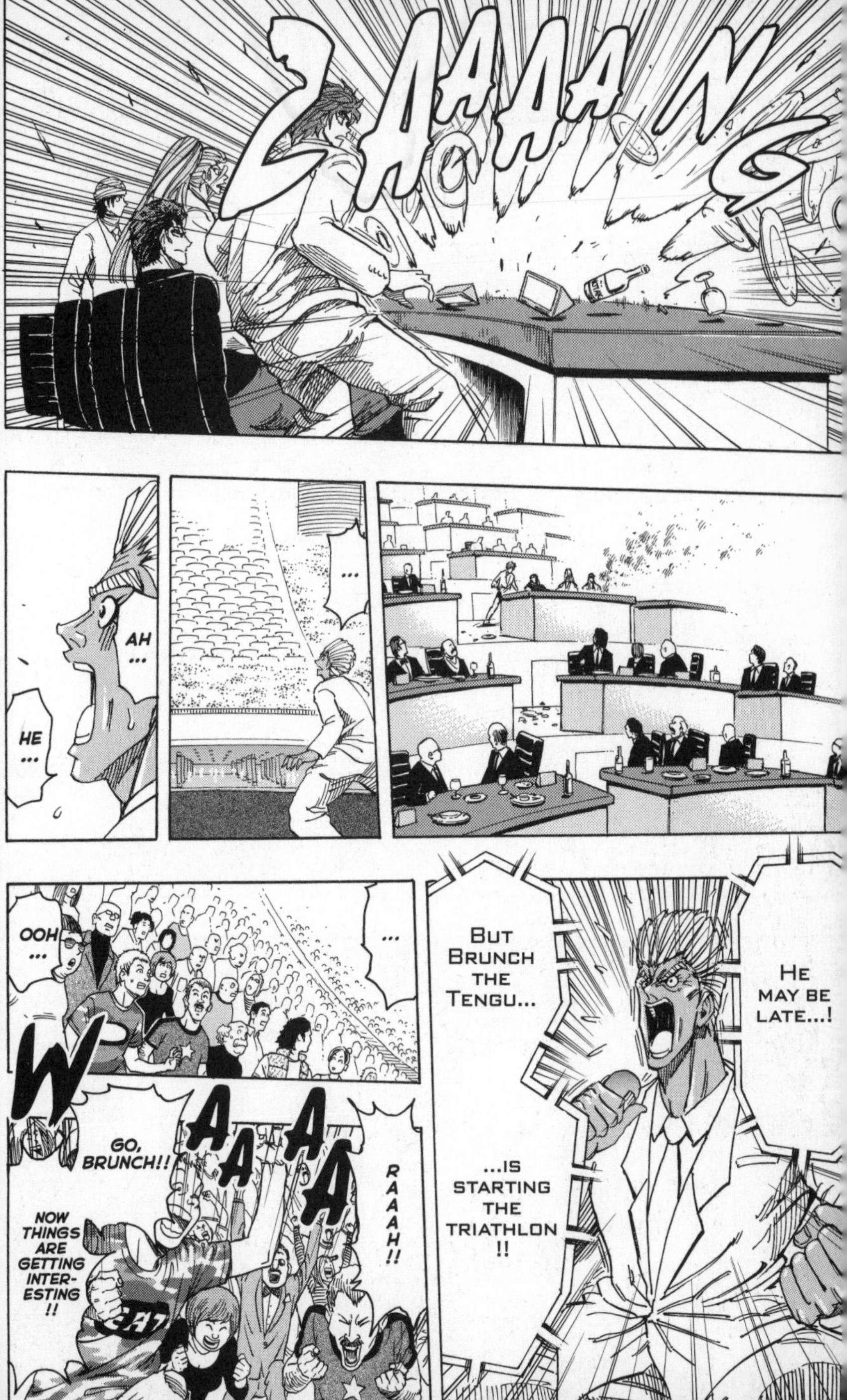
ZAAAAANG
...
AH...
HE...
He may be late...!
But Brunch the Tengu...
...is starting the triathlon!!
...
OOH...
WAAAA
RAAAAH!!
GO, BRUNCH!!
NOW THINGS ARE GETTING INTER-ESTING!!

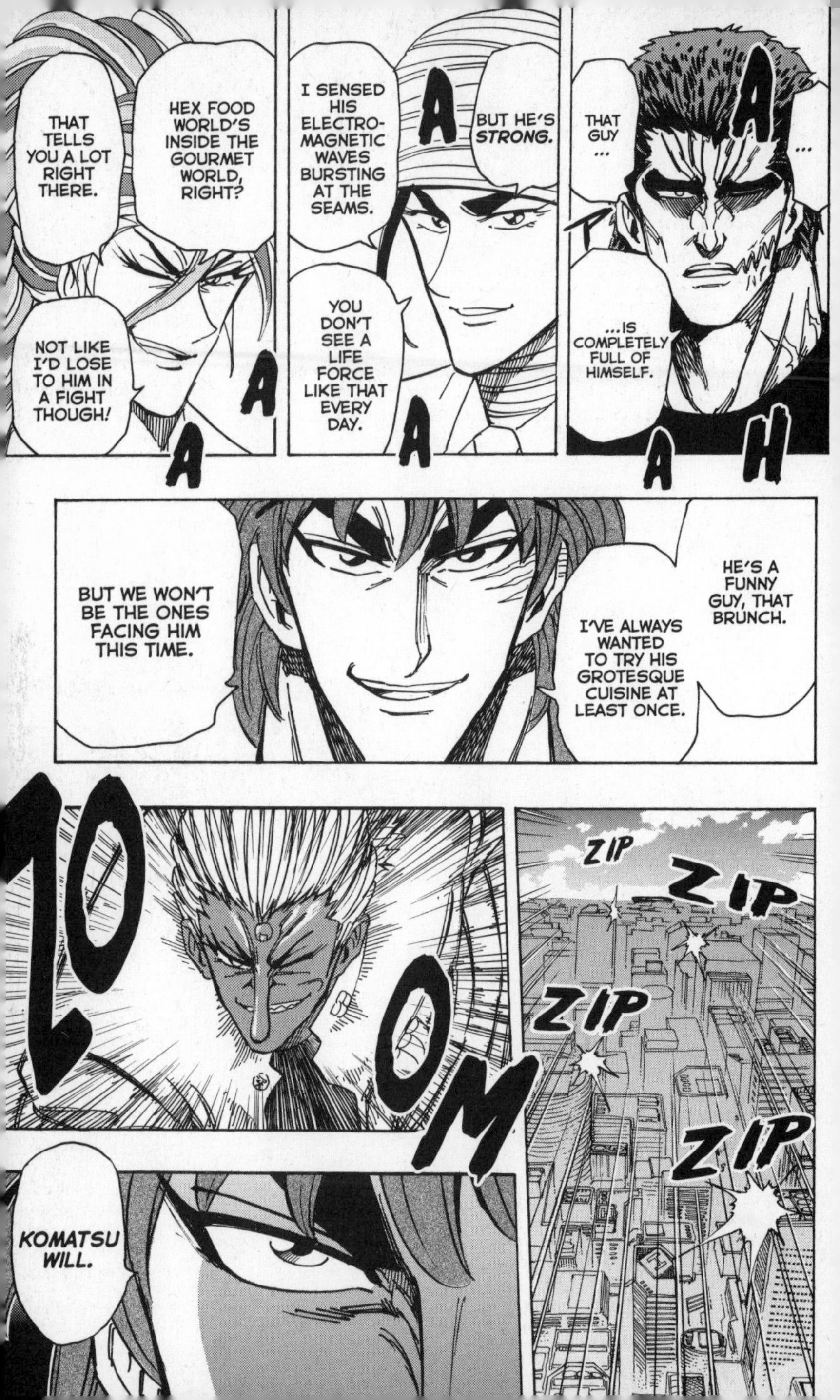
THAT GUY ...
...
...IS COMPLETELY FULL OF HIMSELF.
BUT HE'S *STRONG.*
I SENSED HIS ELECTRO-MAGNETIC WAVES BURSTING AT THE SEAMS.
YOU DON'T SEE A LIFE FORCE LIKE THAT EVERY DAY.
HEX FOOD WORLD'S INSIDE THE GOURMET WORLD, RIGHT?
THAT TELLS YOU A LOT RIGHT THERE.
NOT LIKE I'D LOSE TO HIM IN A FIGHT THOUGH!
AAAAAH
HE'S A FUNNY GUY, THAT BRUNCH.
I'VE ALWAYS WANTED TO TRY HIS GROTESQUE CUISINE AT LEAST ONCE.
BUT WE WON'T BE THE ONES FACING HIM THIS TIME.
ZIP
ZIP
ZIP
ZIP
ZOOM
KOMATSU WILL.

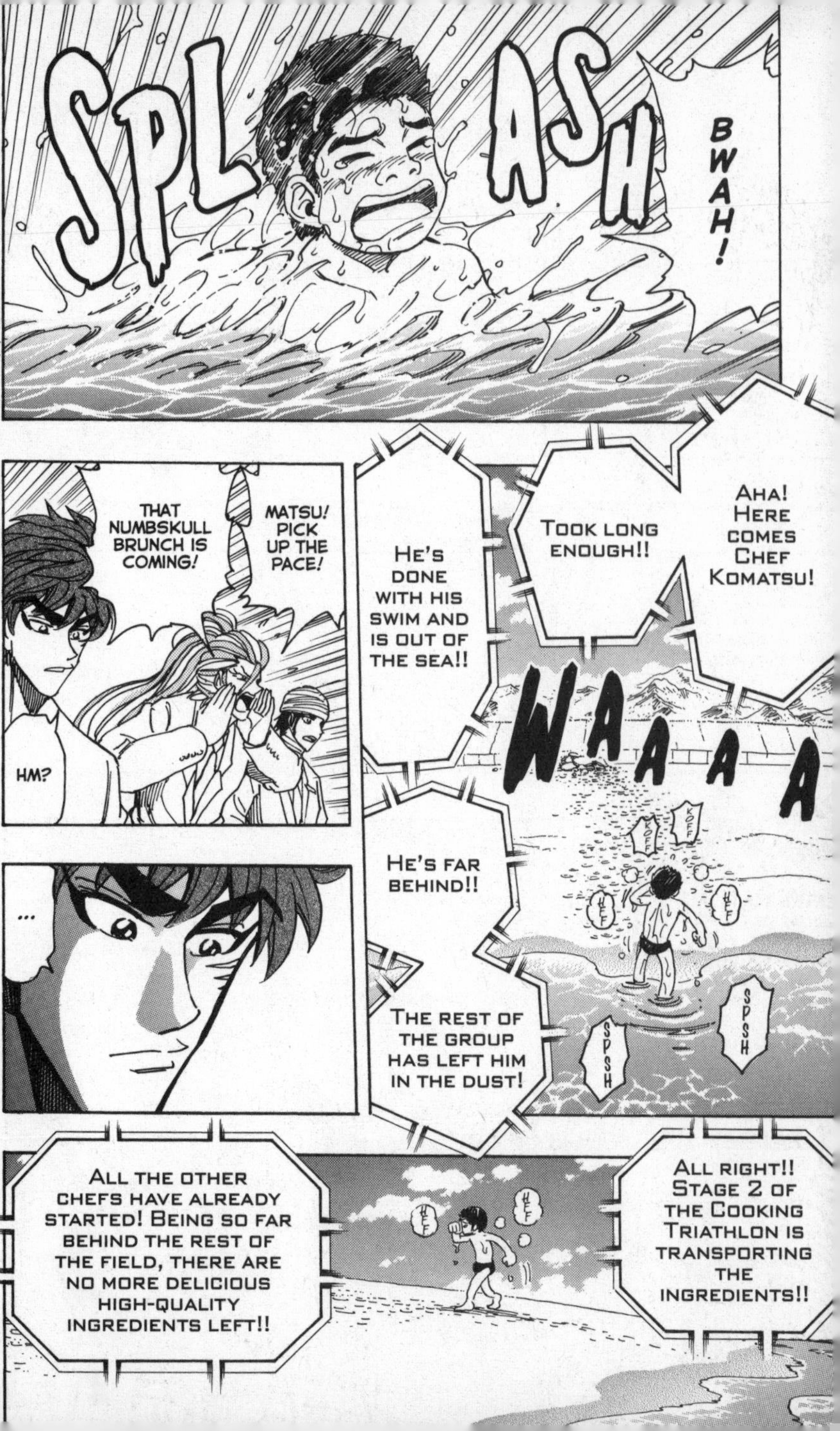
SPLASH
BWAH!
AHA! HERE COMES CHEF KOMATSU!
TOOK LONG ENOUGH!!
HE'S DONE WITH HIS SWIM AND IS OUT OF THE SEA!!
WAAAAA
KOFF
KOFF
HEF
HEF
HE'S FAR BEHIND!!
SPSH
SPSH
THE REST OF THE GROUP HAS LEFT HIM IN THE DUST!
MATSU! PICK UP THE PACE!
THAT NUMBSKULL BRUNCH IS COMING!
HM?
...
ALL RIGHT!! STAGE 2 OF THE COOKING TRIATHLON IS TRANSPORTING THE INGREDIENTS!!
HEF
HEF
ALL THE OTHER CHEFS HAVE ALREADY STARTED! BEING SO FAR BEHIND THE REST OF THE FIELD, THERE ARE NO MORE DELICIOUS HIGH-QUALITY INGREDIENTS LEFT!!

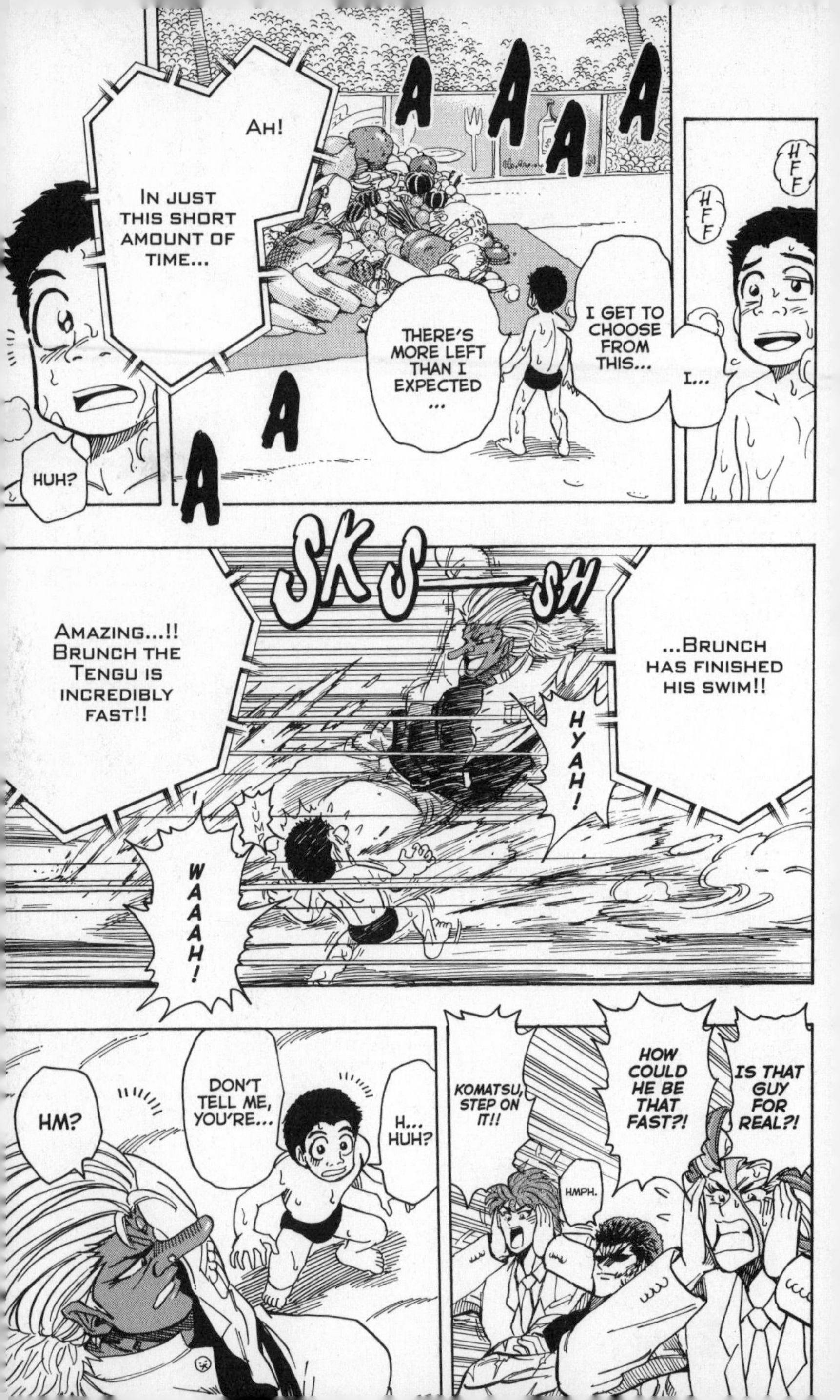
HFF
HFF
I...
I GET TO CHOOSE FROM THIS...
THERE'S MORE LEFT THAN I EXPECTED ...
AAAAAAA
AH!
IN JUST THIS SHORT AMOUNT OF TIME...
HUH?
SKSSH
...BRUNCH HAS FINISHED HIS SWIM!!
AMAZING...!! BRUNCH THE TENGU IS INCREDIBLY FAST!!
HYAH!
JUMP
WAAAAH!
IS THAT GUY FOR REAL?!
HOW COULD HE BE THAT FAST?!
KOMATSU, STEP ON IT!!
HMPH.
H... HUH?
DON'T TELL ME, YOU'RE...
HM?

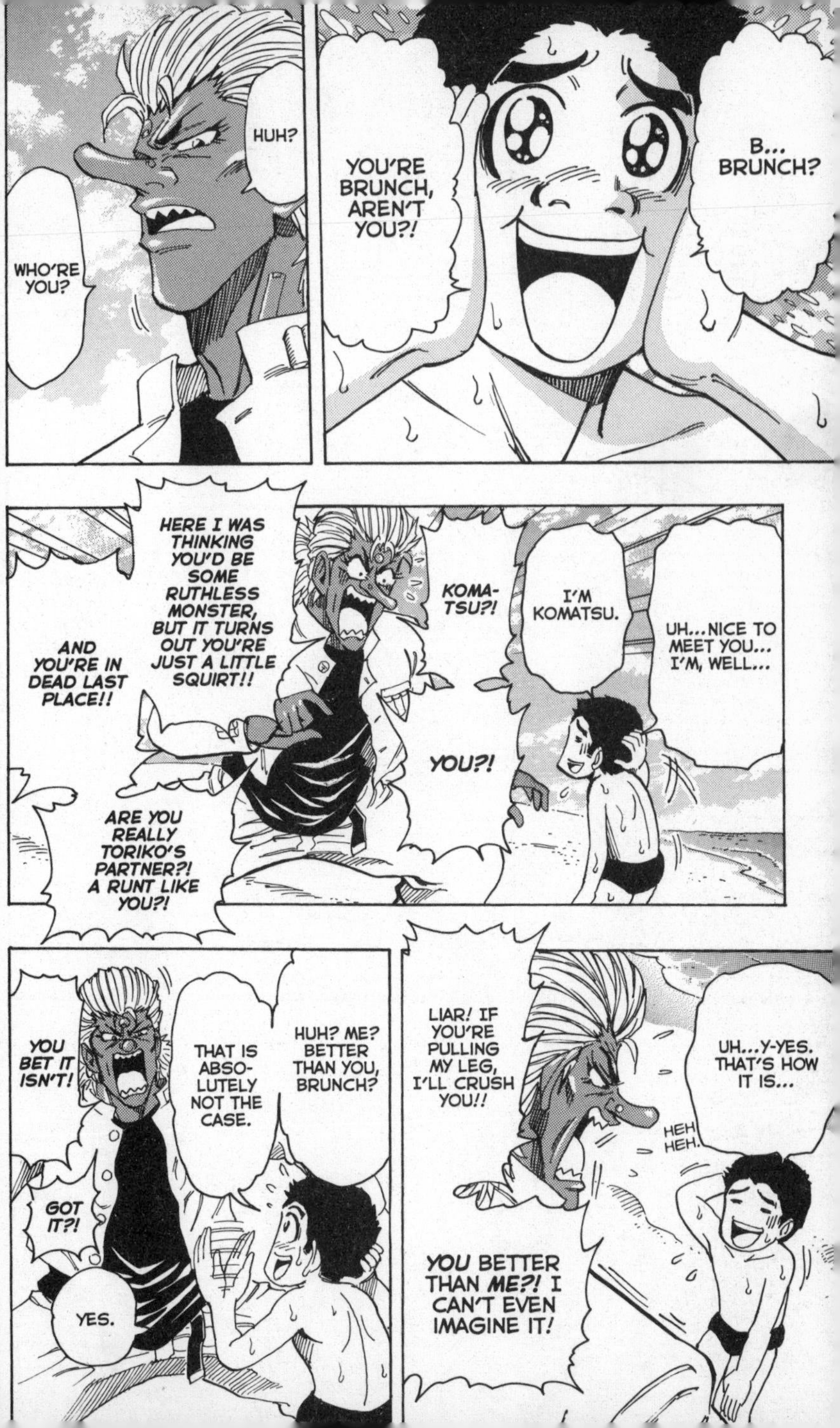
B... BRUNCH?
YOU'RE BRUNCH, AREN'T YOU?!
HUH?
WHO'RE YOU?
UH...NICE TO MEET YOU... I'M, WELL...
I'M KOMATSU.
KOMA-TSU?!
YOU?!
HERE I WAS THINKING YOU'D BE SOME RUTHLESS MONSTER, BUT IT TURNS OUT YOU'RE JUST A LITTLE SQUIRT!!
AND YOU'RE IN DEAD LAST PLACE!!
ARE YOU REALLY TORIKO'S PARTNER?! A RUNT LIKE YOU?!
UH...Y-YES. THAT'S HOW IT IS...
HEH HEH.
LIAR! IF YOU'RE PULLING MY LEG, I'LL CRUSH YOU!!
YOU BETTER THAN ME?! I CAN'T EVEN IMAGINE IT!
HUH? ME? BETTER THAN YOU, BRUNCH?
THAT IS ABSO-LUTELY NOT THE CASE.
YOU BET IT ISN'T!
GOT IT?!
YES.

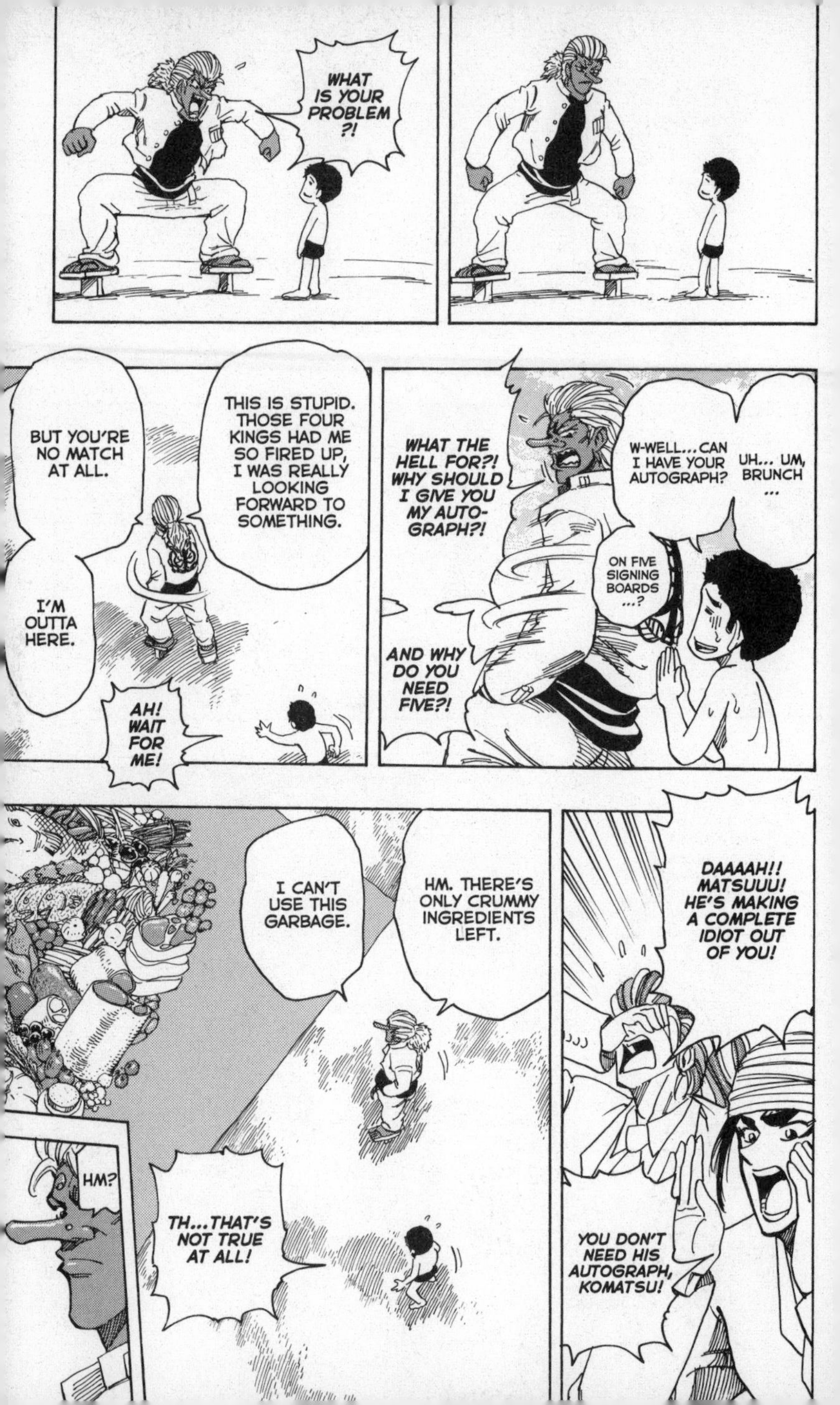
WHAT IS YOUR PROBLEM ?!
W-WELL...CAN I HAVE YOUR AUTOGRAPH?
UH... UM, BRUNCH ...
ON FIVE SIGNING BOARDS ...?
WHAT THE HELL FOR?! WHY SHOULD I GIVE YOU MY AUTO-GRAPH?!
AND WHY DO YOU NEED FIVE?!
THIS IS STUPID. THOSE FOUR KINGS HAD ME SO FIRED UP, I WAS REALLY LOOKING FORWARD TO SOMETHING.
BUT YOU'RE NO MATCH AT ALL.
I'M OUTTA HERE.
AH! WAIT FOR ME!
DAAAAH!! MATSUUU! HE'S MAKING A COMPLETE IDIOT OUT OF YOU!
YOU DON'T NEED HIS AUTOGRAPH, KOMATSU!
HM. THERE'S ONLY CRUMMY INGREDIENTS LEFT.
I CAN'T USE THIS GARBAGE.
TH...THAT'S NOT TRUE AT ALL!
HM?

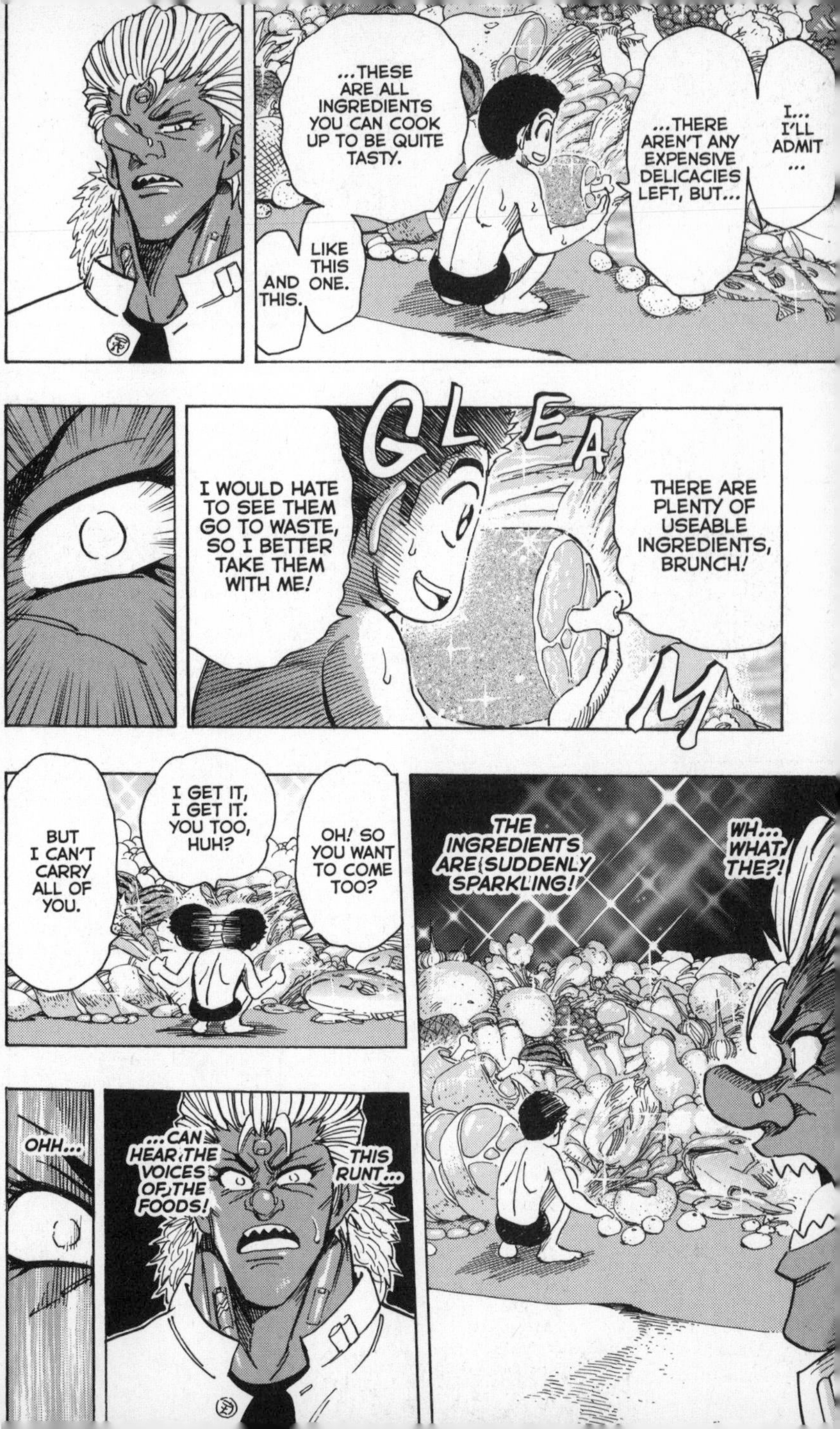
I... I'LL ADMIT ...
...THERE AREN'T ANY EXPENSIVE DELICACIES LEFT, BUT...
...THESE ARE ALL INGREDIENTS YOU CAN COOK UP TO BE QUITE TASTY.
LIKE THIS ONE.
AND THIS.
THERE ARE PLENTY OF USEABLE INGREDIENTS, BRUNCH!
GLEAM
I WOULD HATE TO SEE THEM GO TO WASTE, SO I BETTER TAKE THEM WITH ME!
WH... WHAT THE?!
THE INGREDIENTS ARE SUDDENLY SPARKLING!
OH! SO YOU WANT TO COME TOO?
I GET IT, I GET IT. YOU TOO, HUH?
BUT I CAN'T CARRY ALL OF YOU.
THIS RUNT...
...CAN HEAR THE VOICES OF THE FOODS!
OHH...

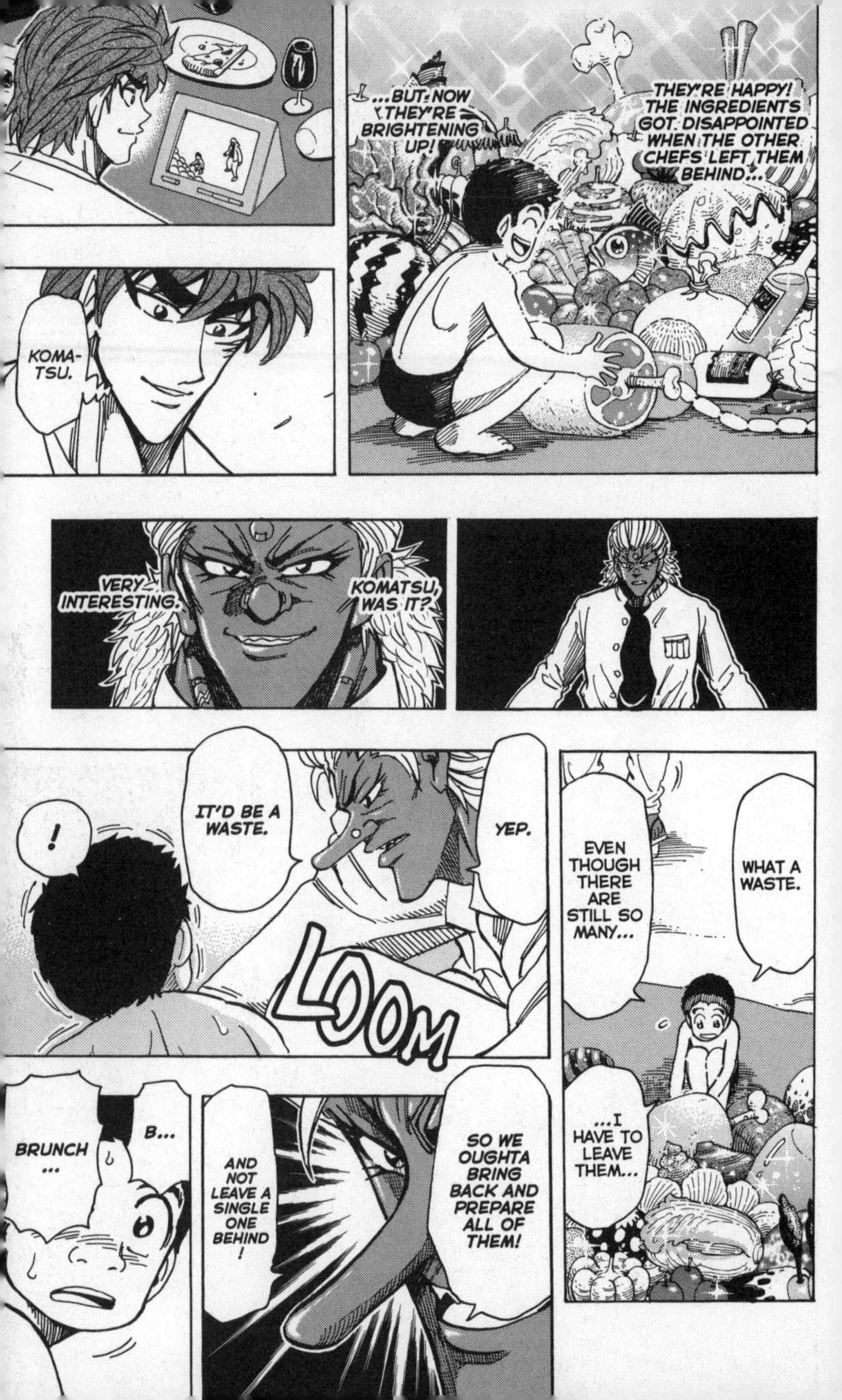
THEY'RE HAPPY! THE INGREDIENTS GOT DISAPPOINTED WHEN THE OTHER CHEFS LEFT THEM BEHIND...
...BUT NOW THEY'RE BRIGHTENING UP!
KOMA-TSU.
KOMATSU, WAS IT?
VERY INTERESTING.
WHAT A WASTE.
EVEN THOUGH THERE ARE STILL SO MANY...
...I HAVE TO LEAVE THEM...
YEP.
IT'D BE A WASTE.
!
LOOM
SO WE OUGHTA BRING BACK AND PREPARE ALL OF THEM!
AND NOT LEAVE A SINGLE ONE BEHIND!
B...
BRUNCH...

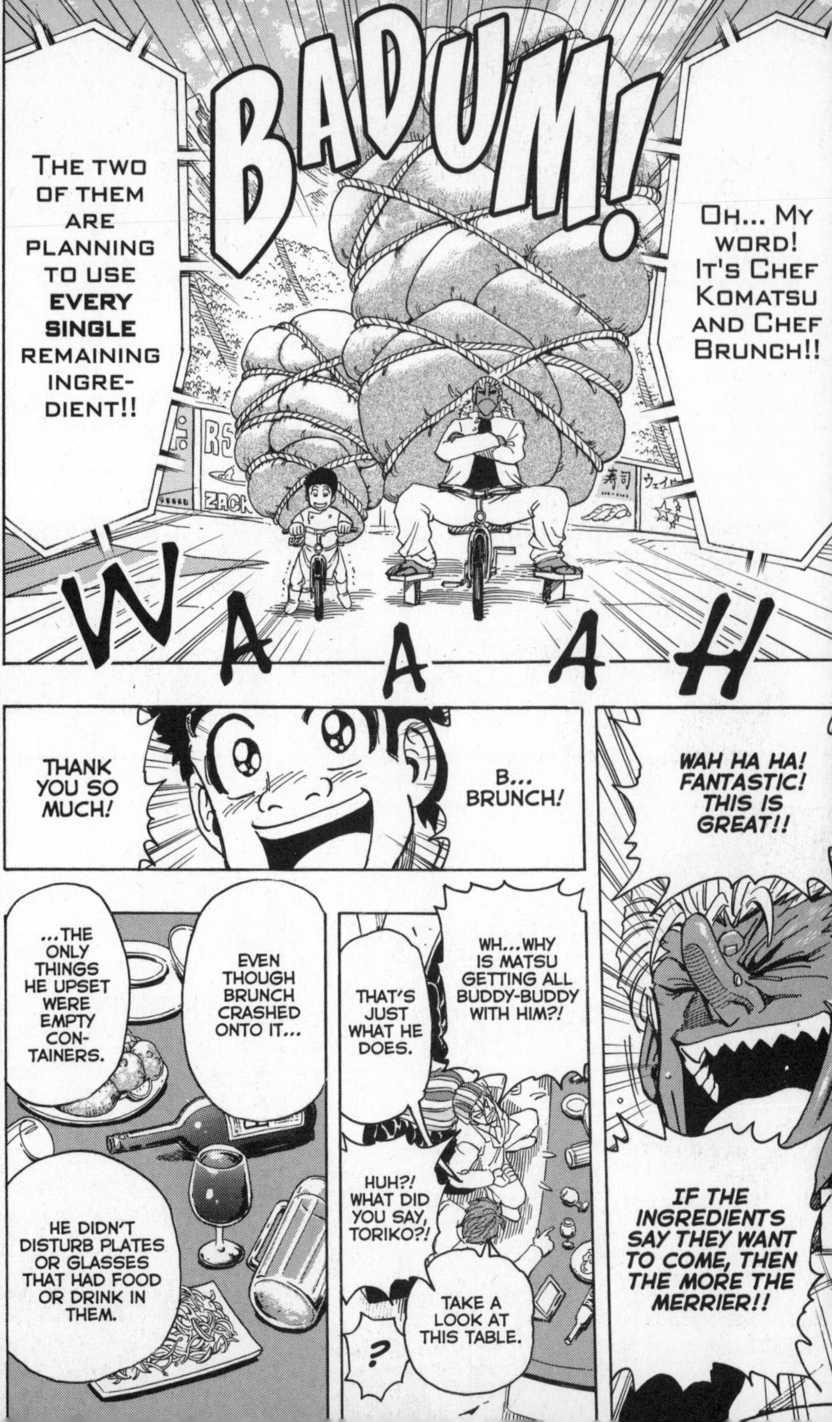
OH... MY WORD! IT'S CHEF KOMATSU AND CHEF BRUNCH!!
BADUM!
THE TWO OF THEM ARE PLANNING TO USE **EVERY SINGLE** REMAINING INGRE- DIENT!!
WAAAH
WAH HA HA! FANTASTIC! THIS IS GREAT!!
IF THE INGREDIENTS SAY THEY WANT TO COME, THEN THE MORE THE MERRIER!!
B... BRUNCH!
THANK YOU SO MUCH!
WH...WHY IS MATSU GETTING ALL BUDDY-BUDDY WITH HIM?!
THAT'S JUST WHAT HE DOES.
HUH?! WHAT DID YOU SAY, TORIKO?!
TAKE A LOOK AT THIS TABLE.
?
EVEN THOUGH BRUNCH CRASHED ONTO IT...
...THE ONLY THINGS HE UPSET WERE EMPTY CON- TAINERS.
HE DIDN'T DISTURB PLATES OR GLASSES THAT HAD FOOD OR DRINK IN THEM.

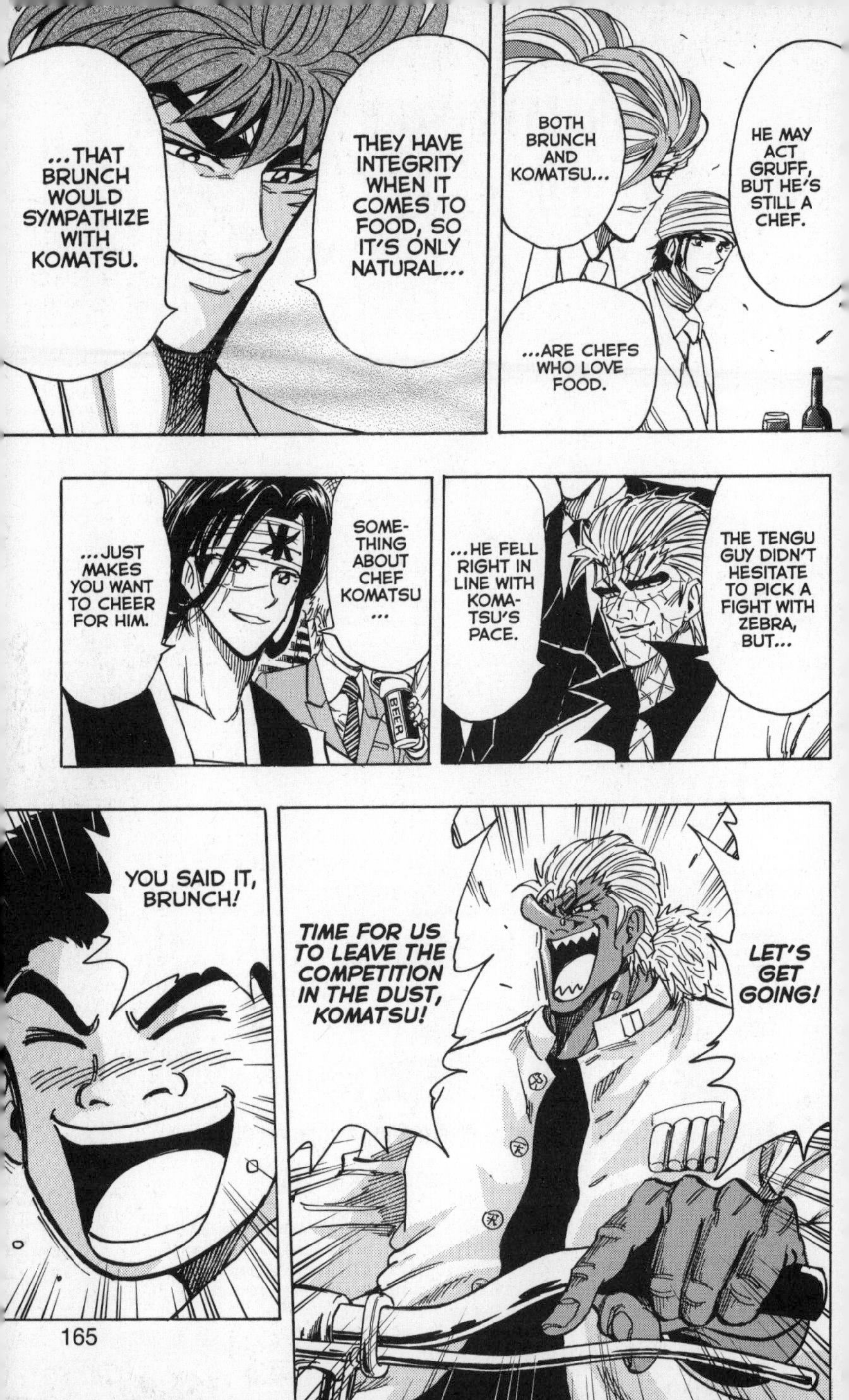
HE MAY ACT GRUFF, BUT HE'S STILL A CHEF.
BOTH BRUNCH AND KOMATSU...
...ARE CHEFS WHO LOVE FOOD.
THEY HAVE INTEGRITY WHEN IT COMES TO FOOD, SO IT'S ONLY NATURAL...
...THAT BRUNCH WOULD SYMPATHIZE WITH KOMATSU.
THE TENGU GUY DIDN'T HESITATE TO PICK A FIGHT WITH ZEBRA, BUT...
...HE FELL RIGHT IN LINE WITH KOMA-TSU'S PACE.
SOME-THING ABOUT CHEF KOMATSU...
...JUST MAKES YOU WANT TO CHEER FOR HIM.
LET'S GET GOING!
TIME FOR US TO LEAVE THE COMPETITION IN THE DUST, KOMATSU!
YOU SAID IT, BRUNCH!

CHARACTER PROFILE

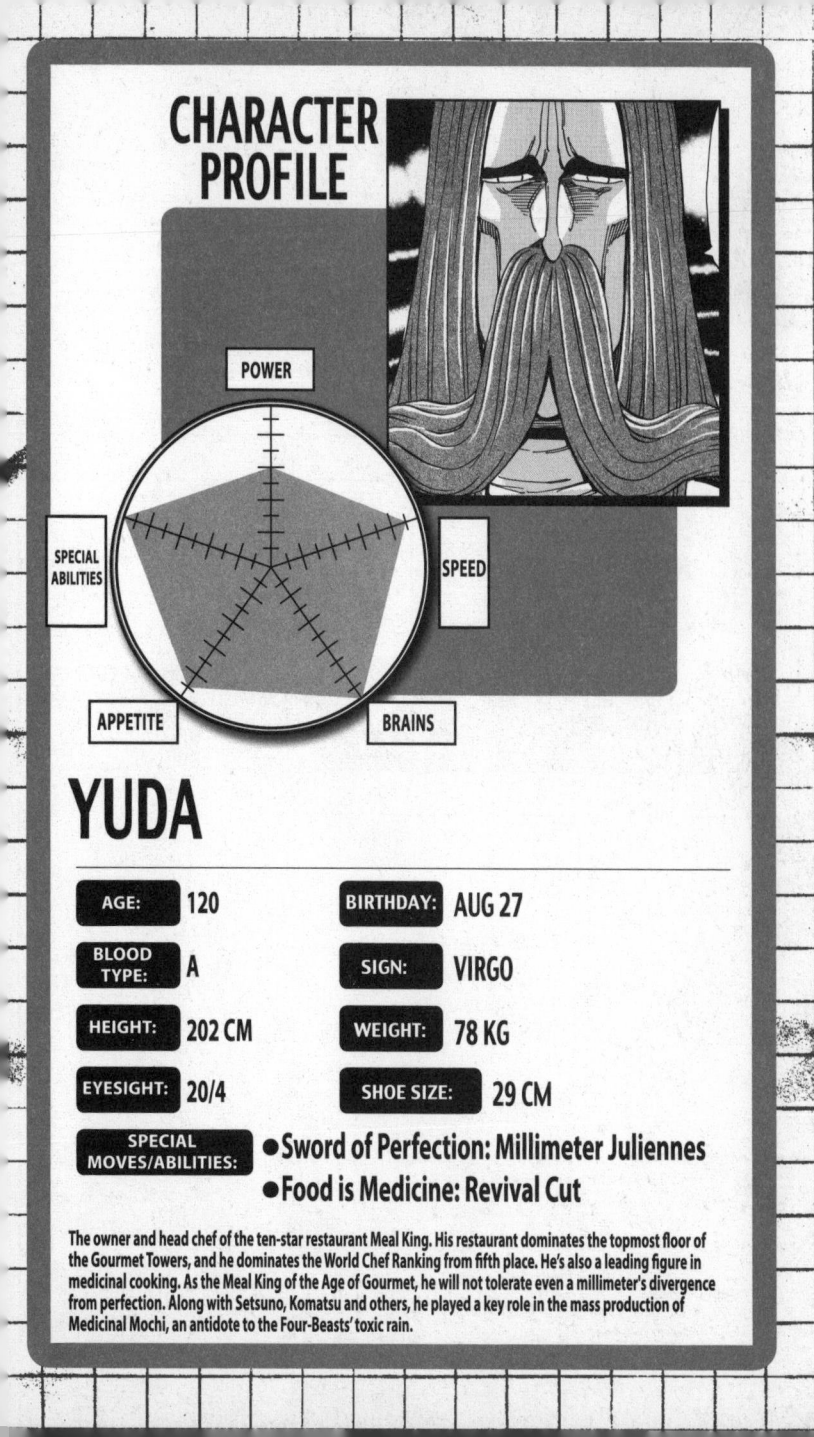

POWER

SPECIAL ABILITIES

SPEED

APPETITE

BRAINS

YUDA

AGE:	120	**BIRTHDAY:**	AUG 27
BLOOD TYPE:	A	**SIGN:**	VIRGO
HEIGHT:	202 CM	**WEIGHT:**	78 KG
EYESIGHT:	20/4	**SHOE SIZE:**	29 CM

SPECIAL MOVES/ABILITIES:
- Sword of Perfection: Millimeter Juliennes
- Food is Medicine: Revival Cut

The owner and head chef of the ten-star restaurant Meal King. His restaurant dominates the topmost floor of the Gourmet Towers, and he dominates the World Chef Ranking from fifth place. He's also a leading figure in medicinal cooking. As the Meal King of the Age of Gourmet, he will not tolerate even a millimeter's divergence from perfection. Along with Setsuno, Komatsu and others, he played a key role in the mass production of Medicinal Mochi, an antidote to the Four-Beasts' toxic rain.

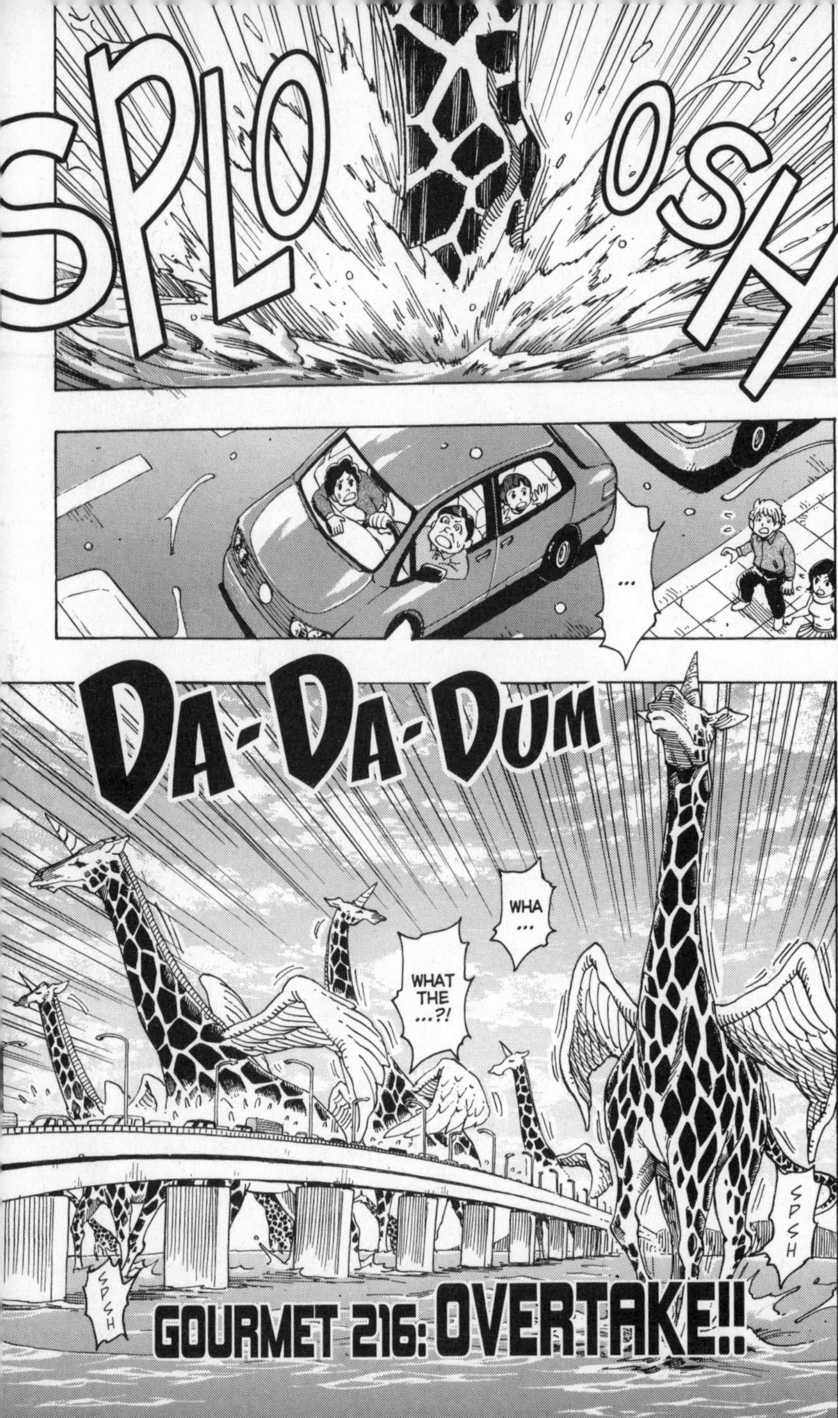
SPLOOSH
...
DA-DA-DUM
WHA ...
WHAT THE ...?!
SPSH
SPSH

GOURMET 216: OVERTAKE!!

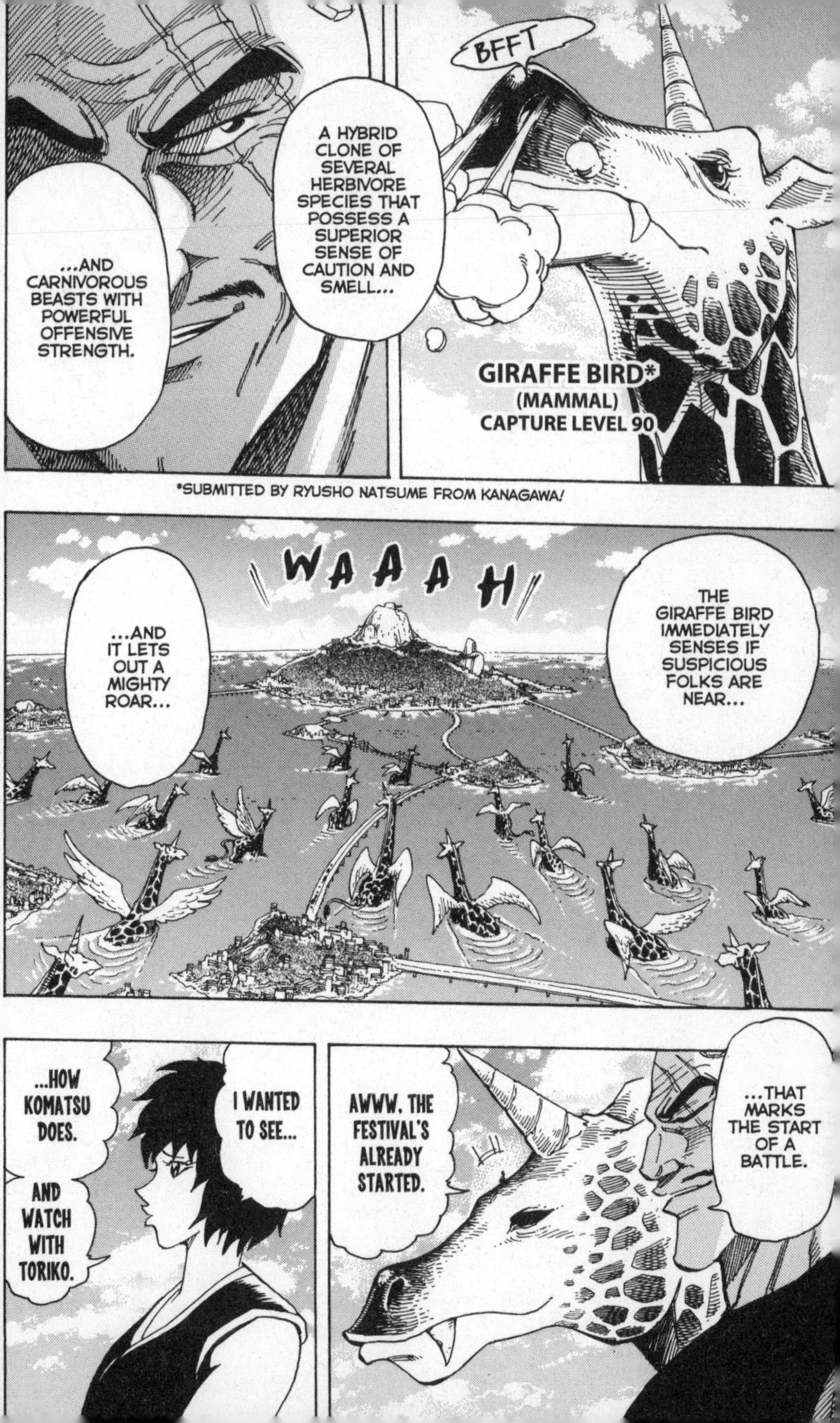
BFFT
A HYBRID CLONE OF SEVERAL HERBIVORE SPECIES THAT POSSESS A SUPERIOR SENSE OF CAUTION AND SMELL...
GIRAFFE BIRD* (MAMMAL) CAPTURE LEVEL 90
...AND CARNIVOROUS BEASTS WITH POWERFUL OFFENSIVE STRENGTH.
*SUBMITTED BY RYUSHO NATSUME FROM KANAGAWA!
THE GIRAFFE BIRD IMMEDIATELY SENSES IF SUSPICIOUS FOLKS ARE NEAR...
WAAAH
...AND IT LETS OUT A MIGHTY ROAR...
...THAT MARKS THE START OF A BATTLE.
AWWW, THE FESTIVAL'S ALREADY STARTED.
I WANTED TO SEE...
...HOW KOMATSU DOES.
AND WATCH WITH TORIKO.

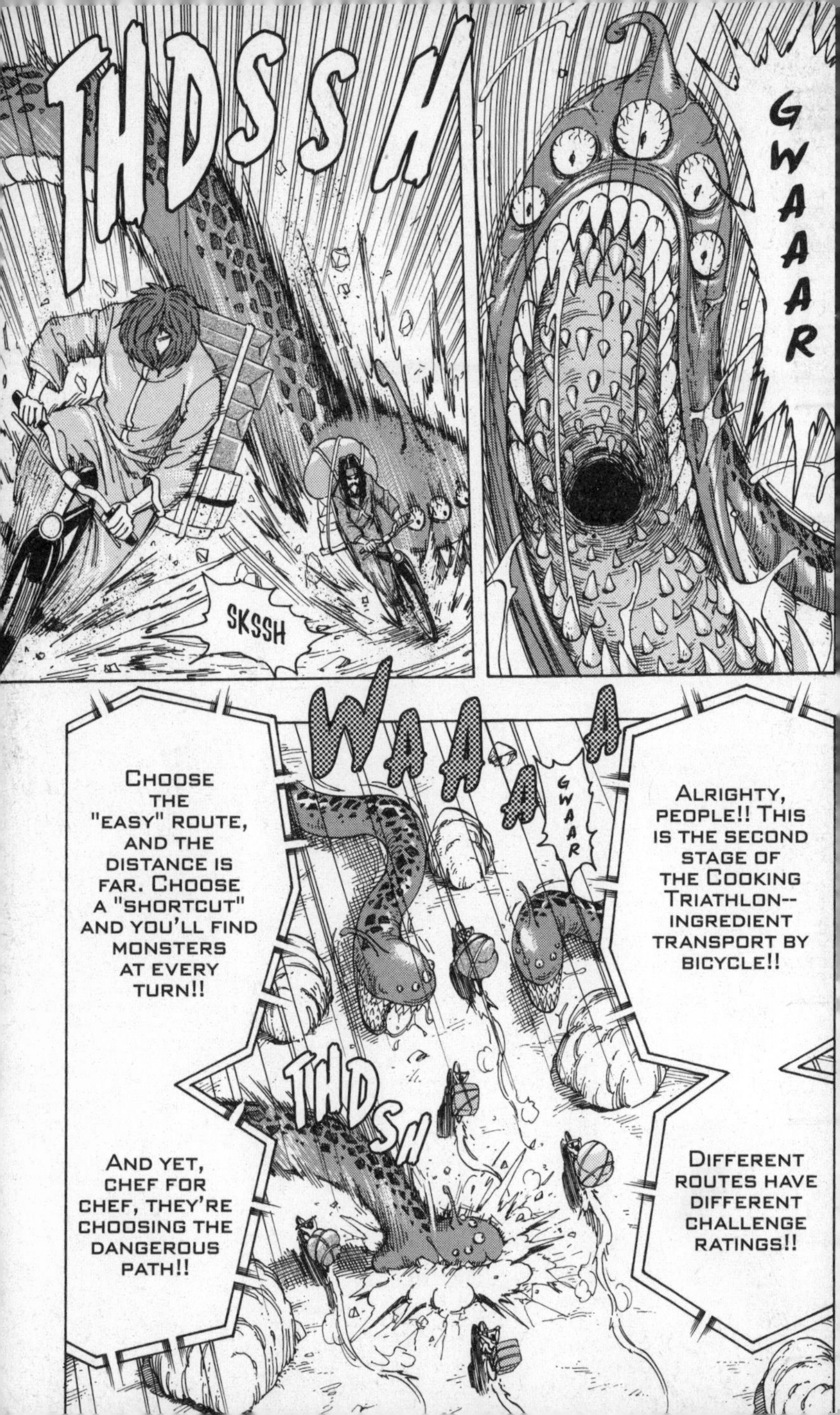
GWAAAR
THDSSH
SKSSH
WAAAA
GWAAR
ALRIGHTY, PEOPLE!! THIS IS THE SECOND STAGE OF THE COOKING TRIATHLON-- INGREDIENT TRANSPORT BY BICYCLE!!
CHOOSE THE "EASY" ROUTE, AND THE DISTANCE IS FAR. CHOOSE A "SHORTCUT" AND YOU'LL FIND MONSTERS AT EVERY TURN!!
THDSH
DIFFERENT ROUTES HAVE DIFFERENT CHALLENGE RATINGS!!
AND YET, CHEF FOR CHEF, THEY'RE CHOOSING THE DANGEROUS PATH!!

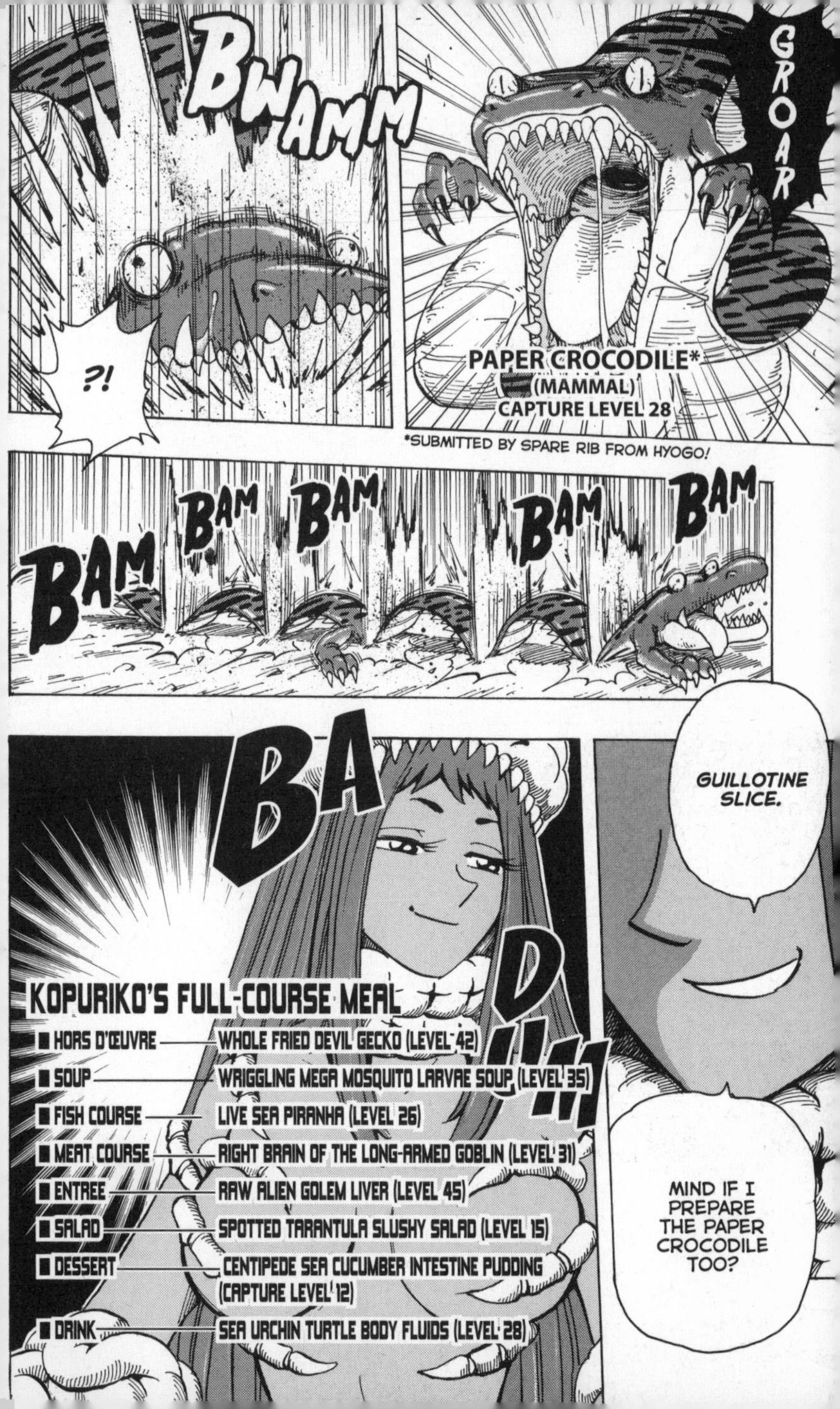
GROAR
PAPER CROCODILE*
(MAMMAL)
CAPTURE LEVEL 28
*SUBMITTED BY SPARE RIB FROM HYOGO!
BWAMM
?!
BAM BAM BAM BAM BAM
GUILLOTINE SLICE.
MIND IF I PREPARE THE PAPER CROCODILE TOO?
BADUM!!!
KOPURIKO'S FULL-COURSE MEAL
■ HORS D'ŒUVRE — WHOLE FRIED DEVIL GECKO (LEVEL 42)
■ SOUP — WRIGGLING MEGA MOSQUITO LARVAE SOUP (LEVEL 35)
■ FISH COURSE — LIVE SEA PIRANHA (LEVEL 26)
■ MEAT COURSE — RIGHT BRAIN OF THE LONG-ARMED GOBLIN (LEVEL 31)
■ ENTREE — RAW ALIEN GOLEM LIVER (LEVEL 45)
■ SALAD — SPOTTED TARANTULA SLUSHY SALAD (LEVEL 15)
■ DESSERT — CENTIPEDE SEA CUCUMBER INTESTINE PUDDING (CAPTURE LEVEL 12)
■ DRINK — SEA URCHIN TURTLE BODY FLUIDS (LEVEL 28)

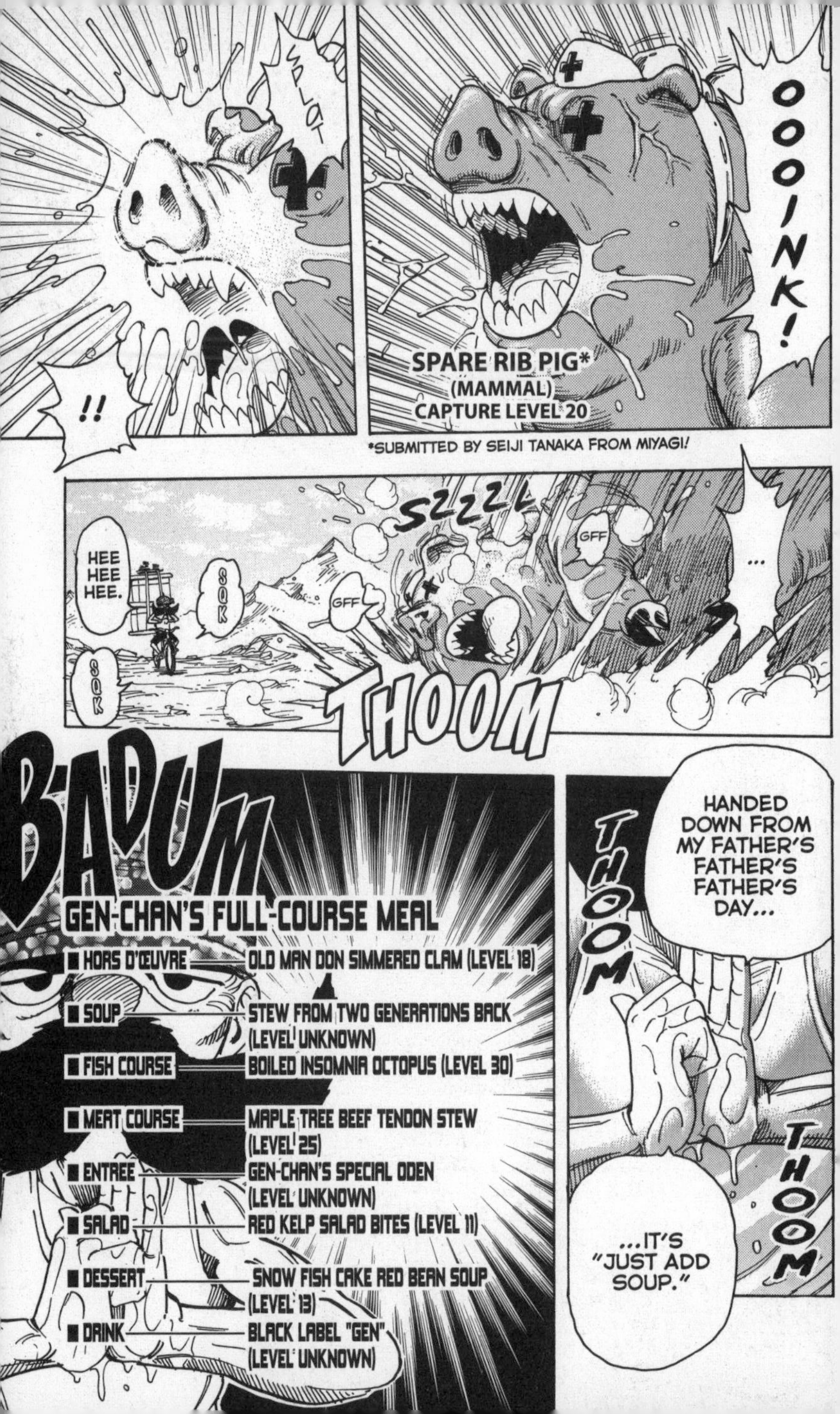
OOOINK!
SPARE RIB PIG*
(MAMMAL)
CAPTURE LEVEL 20
*SUBMITTED BY SEIJI TANAKA FROM MIYAGI!
SPLOT
!!
...
GFF
SZZZL
GFF
SQK
HEE HEE HEE.
SQK
THOOM
HANDED DOWN FROM MY FATHER'S FATHER'S FATHER'S DAY...
THOOM
...IT'S "JUST ADD SOUP."
THOOM
BADUM
GEN-CHAN'S FULL-COURSE MEAL
■ HORS D'ŒUVRE — OLD MAN DON SIMMERED CLAM (LEVEL 18)
■ SOUP — STEW FROM TWO GENERATIONS BACK (LEVEL UNKNOWN)
■ FISH COURSE — BOILED INSOMNIA OCTOPUS (LEVEL 30)
■ MEAT COURSE — MAPLE TREE BEEF TENDON STEW (LEVEL 25)
■ ENTREE — GEN-CHAN'S SPECIAL ODEN (LEVEL UNKNOWN)
■ SALAD — RED KELP SALAD BITES (LEVEL 11)
■ DESSERT — SNOW FISH CAKE RED BEAN SOUP (LEVEL 13)
■ DRINK — BLACK LABEL "GEN" (LEVEL UNKNOWN)

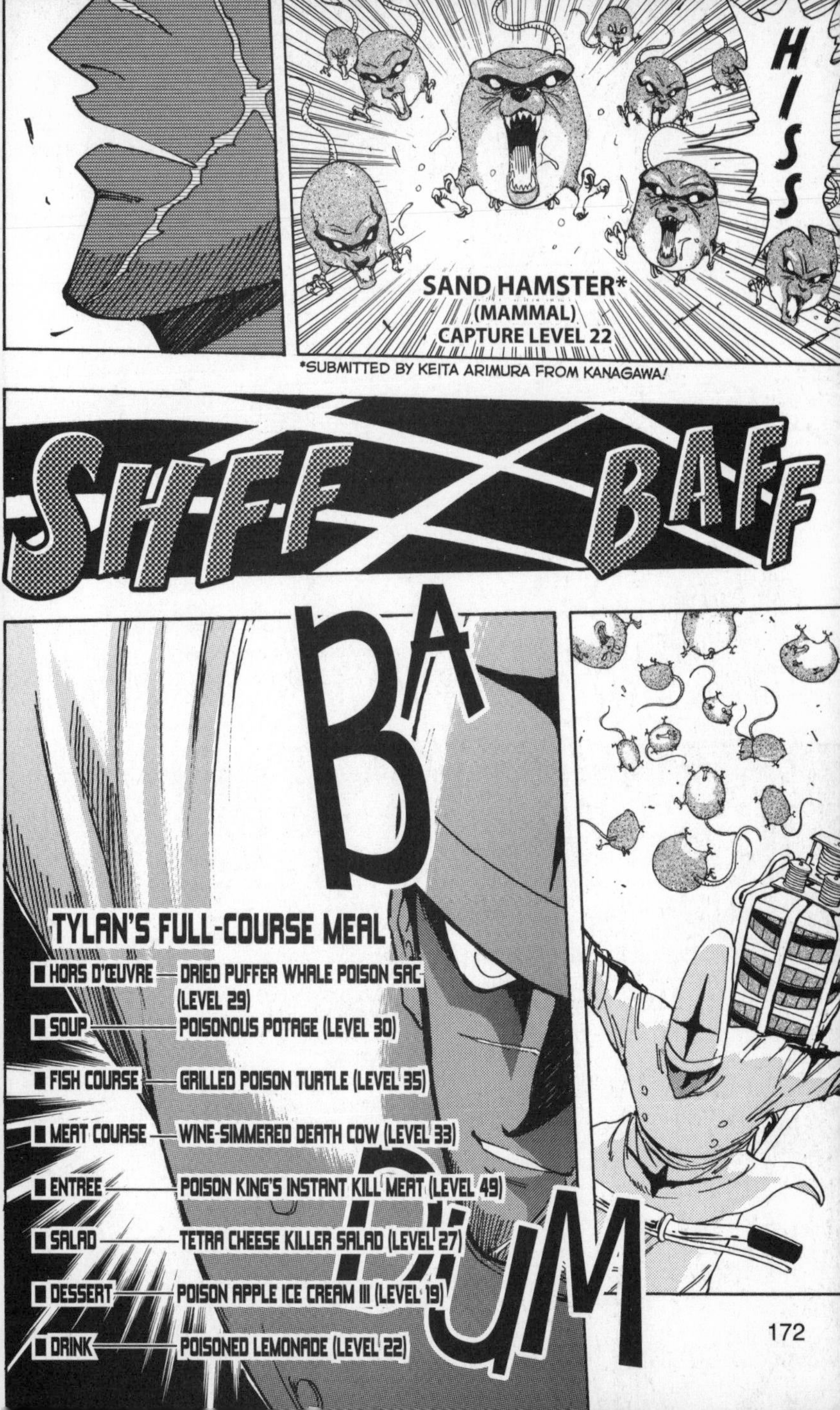
HISS
SAND HAMSTER*
(MAMMAL)
CAPTURE LEVEL 22
*SUBMITTED BY KEITA ARIMURA FROM KANAGAWA!
SH-F-F
BA-F-F
BA
DUM
TYLAN'S FULL-COURSE MEAL
■ HORS D'ŒUVRE — DRIED PUFFER WHALE POISON SAC (LEVEL 29)
■ SOUP — POISONOUS POTAGE (LEVEL 30)
■ FISH COURSE — GRILLED POISON TURTLE (LEVEL 35)
■ MEAT COURSE — WINE-SIMMERED DEATH COW (LEVEL 33)
■ ENTREE — POISON KING'S INSTANT KILL MEAT (LEVEL 49)
■ SALAD — TETRA CHEESE KILLER SALAD (LEVEL 27)
■ DESSERT — POISON APPLE ICE CREAM III (LEVEL 19)
■ DRINK — POISONED LEMONADE (LEVEL 22)

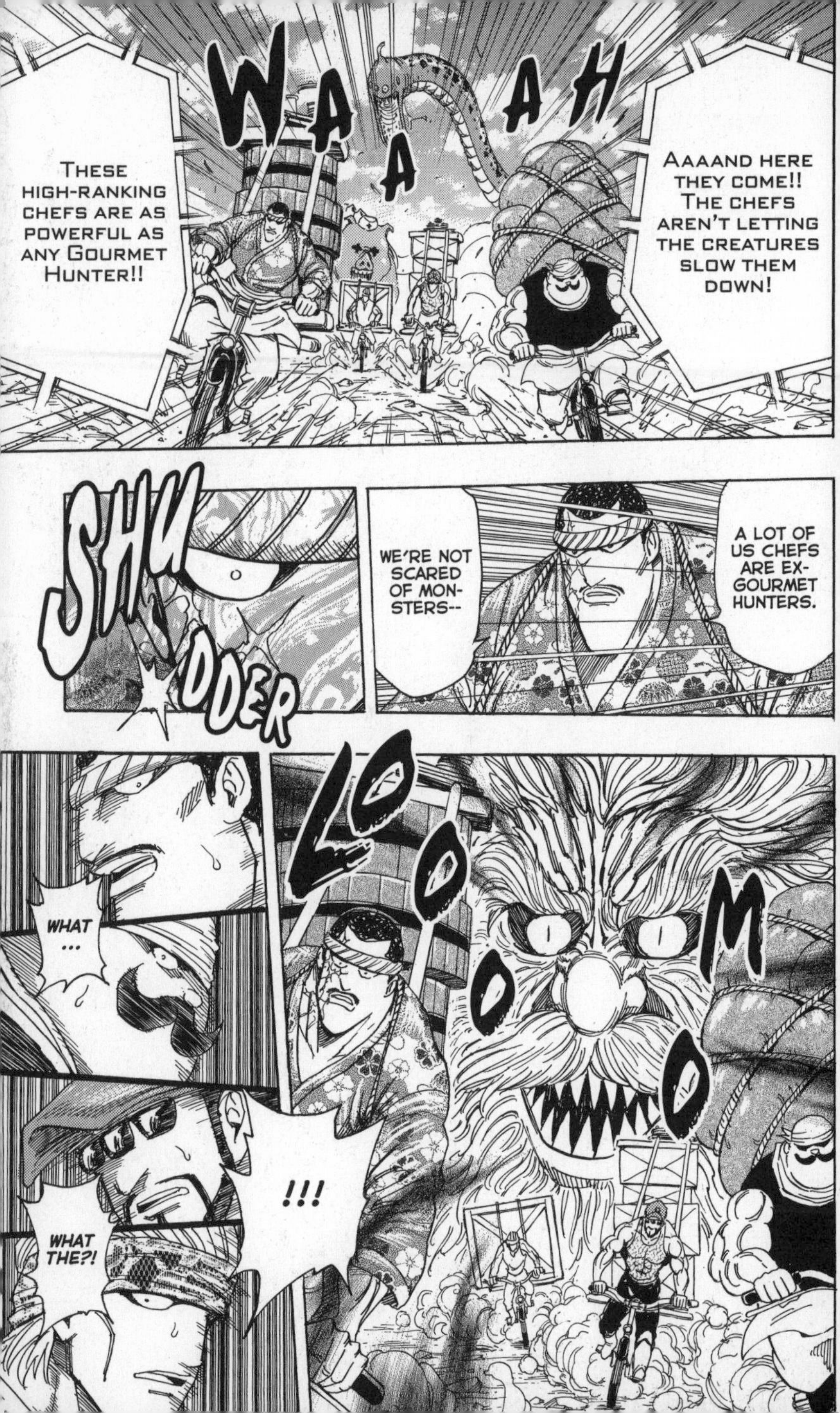
Aaaand here they come!! The chefs aren't letting the creatures slow them down!
WAAAH
These high-ranking chefs are as powerful as any Gourmet Hunter!!
A lot of us chefs are ex-gourmet hunters.
We're not scared of mon-sters--
SHUDDER
LOOOOOM
!!!
What...
What the?!

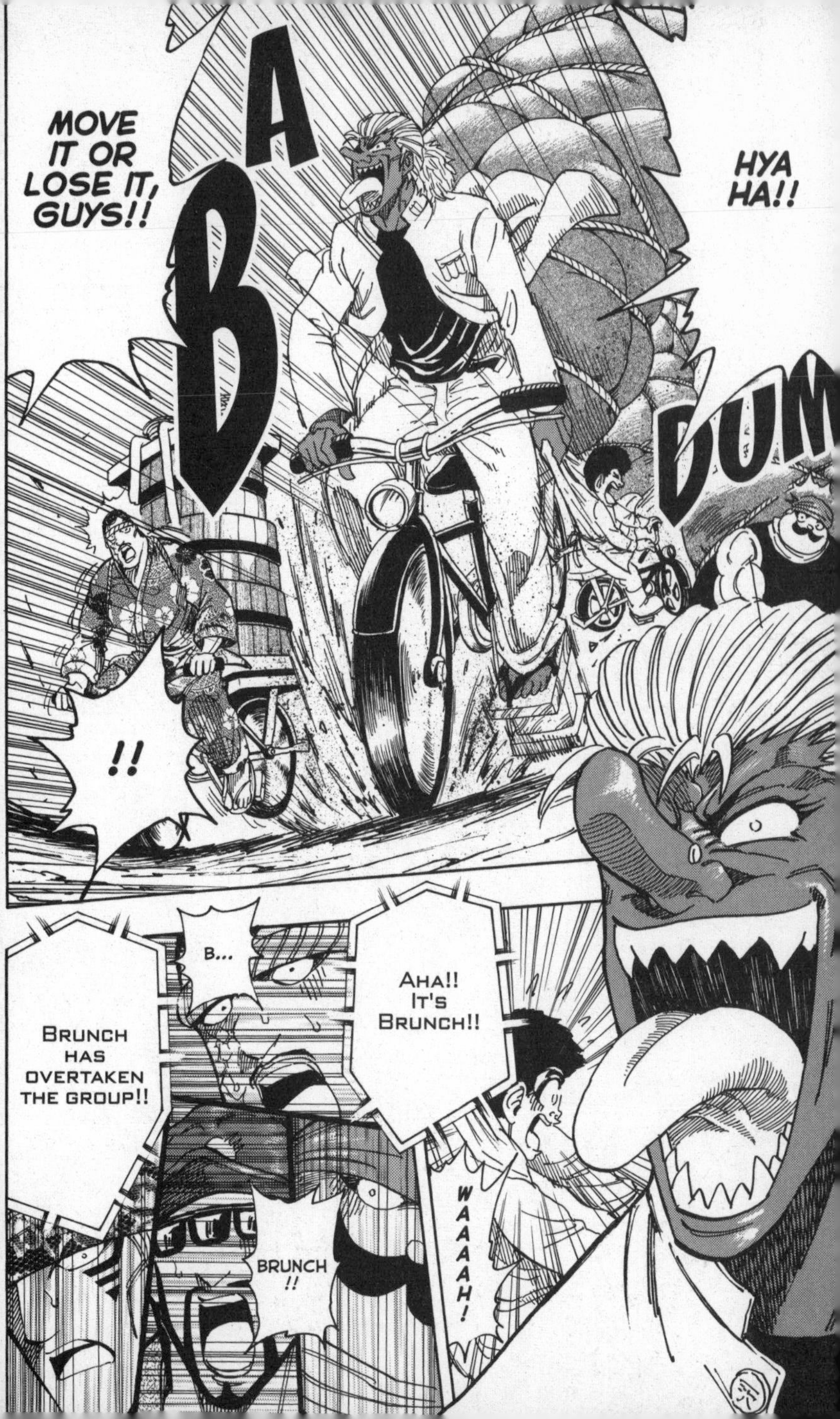
HYA HA!!
MOVE IT OR LOSE IT, GUYS!!
BA
BUM
!!
WAAAAAH!
AHA!! IT'S BRUNCH!!
B...
BRUNCH HAS OVERTAKEN THE GROUP!!
BRUNCH !!

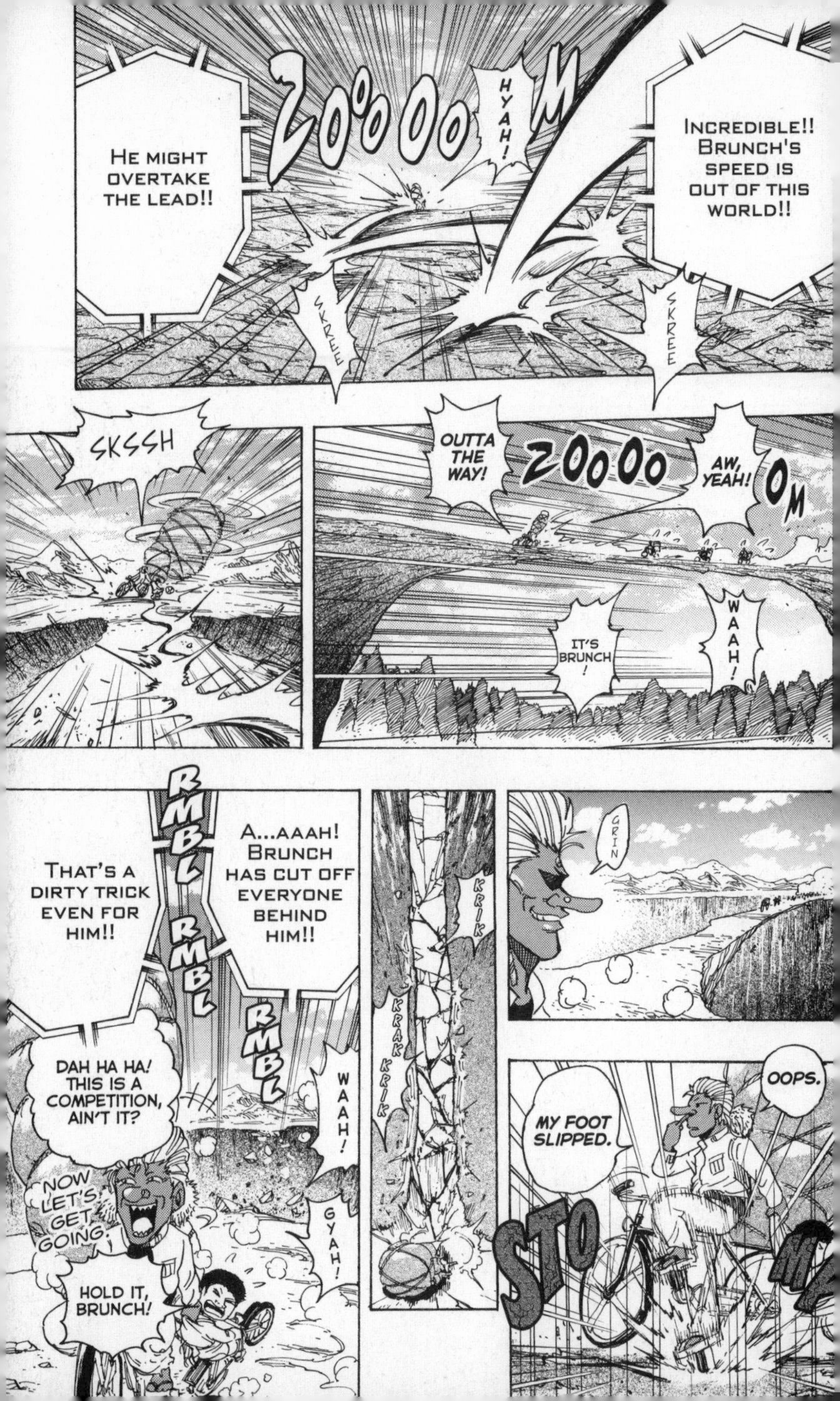
INCREDIBLE!! BRUNCH'S SPEED IS OUT OF THIS WORLD!!
ZOOOOOM
HYAH!
HE MIGHT OVERTAKE THE LEAD!!
SKREE
SKREE
AW, YEAH!
ZOOOOOM
OUTTA THE WAY!
WAAH!
IT'S BRUNCH!
SKSSH
GRIN
OOPS.
MY FOOT SLIPPED.
STOMP
KRIK
KRAK KRIK
A...AAAH! BRUNCH HAS CUT OFF EVERYONE BEHIND HIM!!
THAT'S A DIRTY TRICK EVEN FOR HIM!!
RMBL RMBL RMBL
DAH HA HA! THIS IS A COMPETITION, AIN'T IT?
WAAH!
NOW LET'S GET GOING.
GYAH!
HOLD IT, BRUNCH!

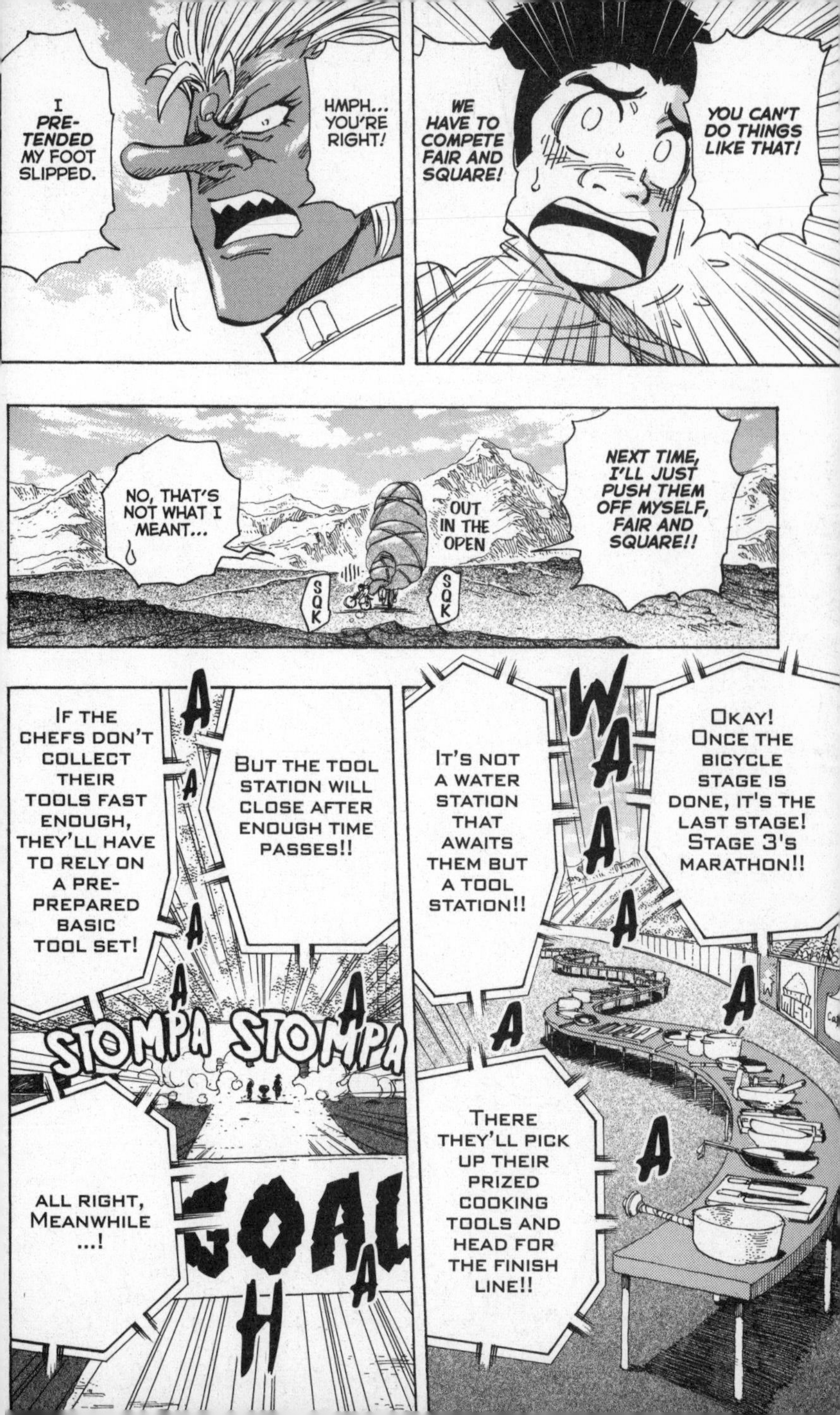
YOU CAN'T DO THINGS LIKE THAT!
WE HAVE TO COMPETE FAIR AND SQUARE!
HMPH... YOU'RE RIGHT!
I PRETENDED MY FOOT SLIPPED.
NEXT TIME, I'LL JUST PUSH THEM OFF MYSELF, FAIR AND SQUARE!!
OUT IN THE OPEN
SQK
SQK
NO, THAT'S NOT WHAT I MEANT...
WAAAA
OKAY! ONCE THE BICYCLE STAGE IS DONE, IT'S THE LAST STAGE! STAGE 3'S MARATHON!!
IT'S NOT A WATER STATION THAT AWAITS THEM BUT A TOOL STATION!!
THERE THEY'LL PICK UP THEIR PRIZED COOKING TOOLS AND HEAD FOR THE FINISH LINE!!
AAA
BUT THE TOOL STATION WILL CLOSE AFTER ENOUGH TIME PASSES!!
IF THE CHEFS DON'T COLLECT THEIR TOOLS FAST ENOUGH, THEY'LL HAVE TO RELY ON A PRE-PREPARED BASIC TOOL SET!
AAAAA
STOMPA STOMPA
GOAL
AAH
ALL RIGHT, MEANWHILE ...!

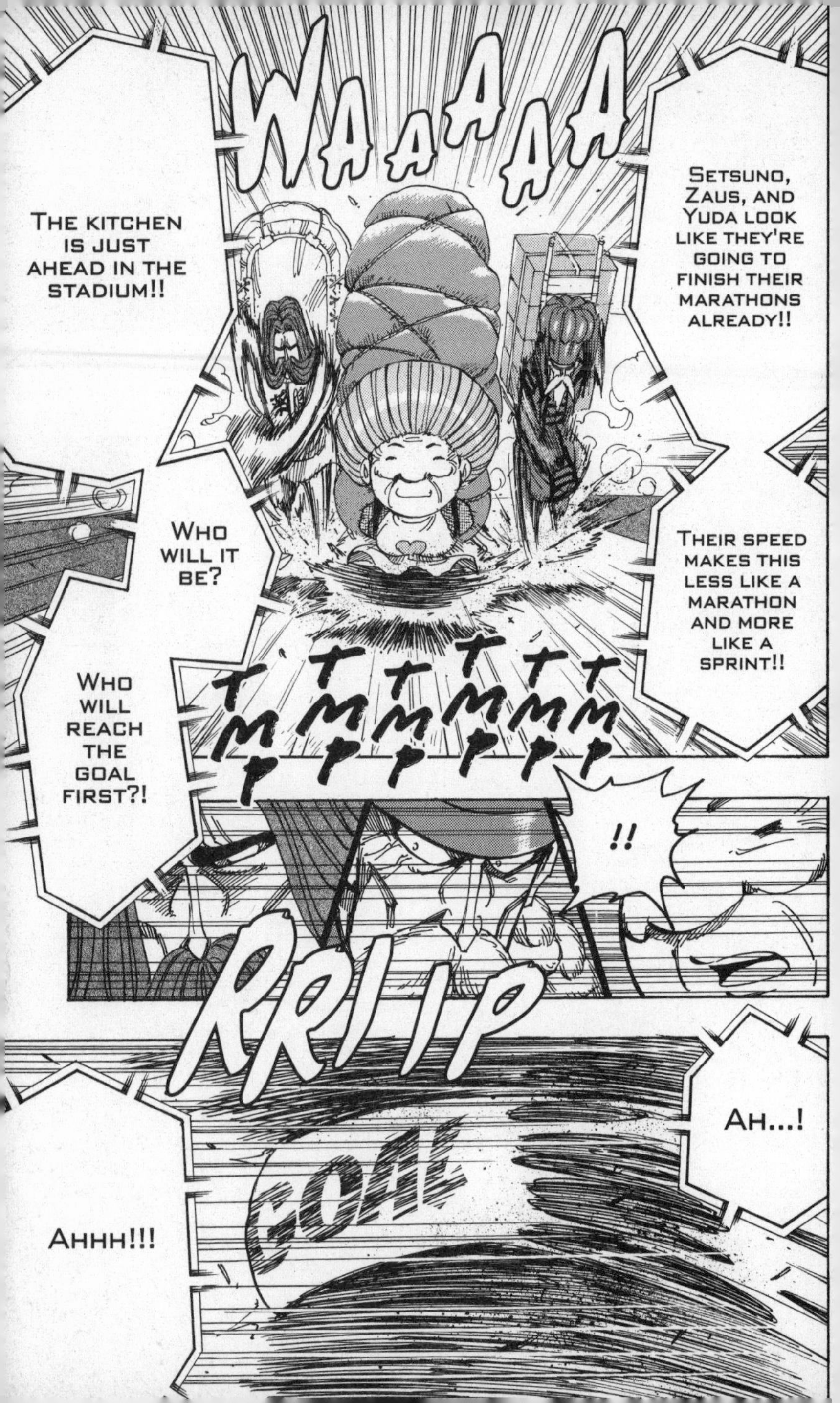
WAAAAA
SETSUNO, ZAUS, AND YUDA LOOK LIKE THEY'RE GOING TO FINISH THEIR MARATHONS ALREADY!!
THE KITCHEN IS JUST AHEAD IN THE STADIUM!!
THEIR SPEED MAKES THIS LESS LIKE A MARATHON AND MORE LIKE A SPRINT!!
WHO WILL IT BE?
TMPTMPTMPTMPTMPTMP
WHO WILL REACH THE GOAL FIRST?!
!!
RRIIP
AH...!
GOAL
AHHH!!!

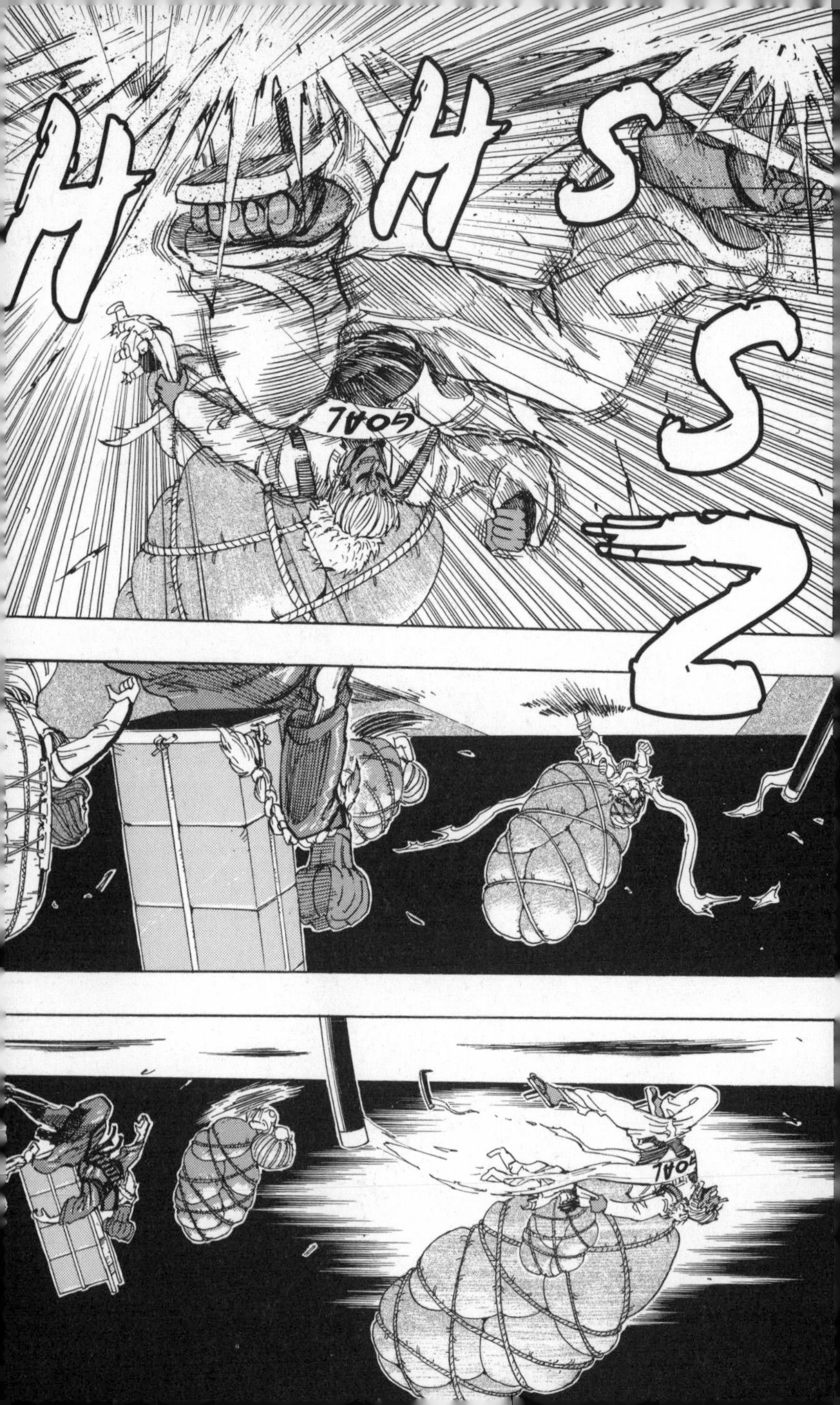
HHSSZ
GOAL
GOAL

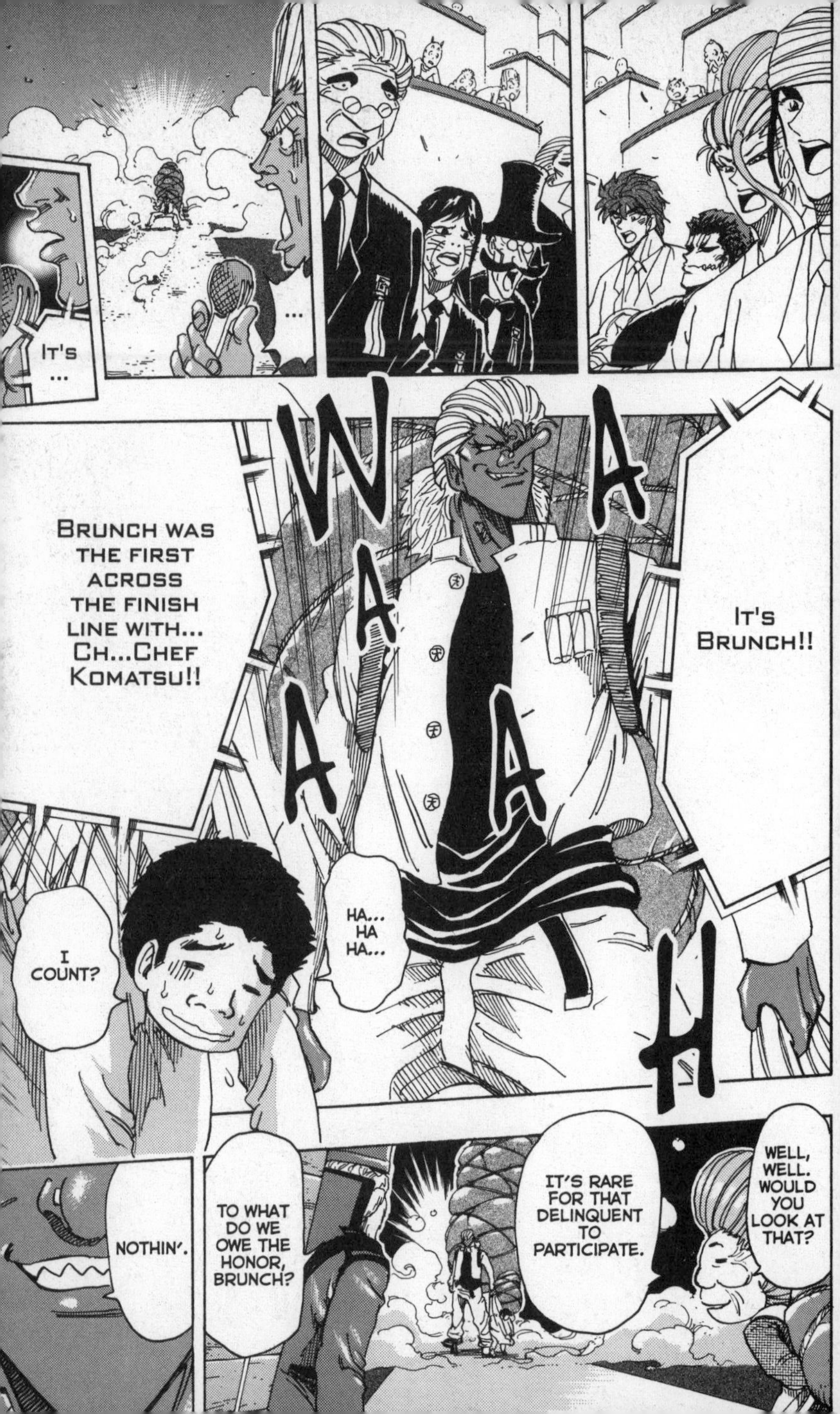
...
IT'S ...
IT'S BRUNCH!!
WAAAAH
BRUNCH WAS THE FIRST ACROSS THE FINISH LINE WITH... CH...CHEF KOMATSU!!
HA... HA HA...
I COUNT?
WELL, WELL. WOULD YOU LOOK AT THAT?
IT'S RARE FOR THAT DELINQUENT TO PARTICIPATE.
TO WHAT DO WE OWE THE HONOR, BRUNCH?
NOTHIN'.

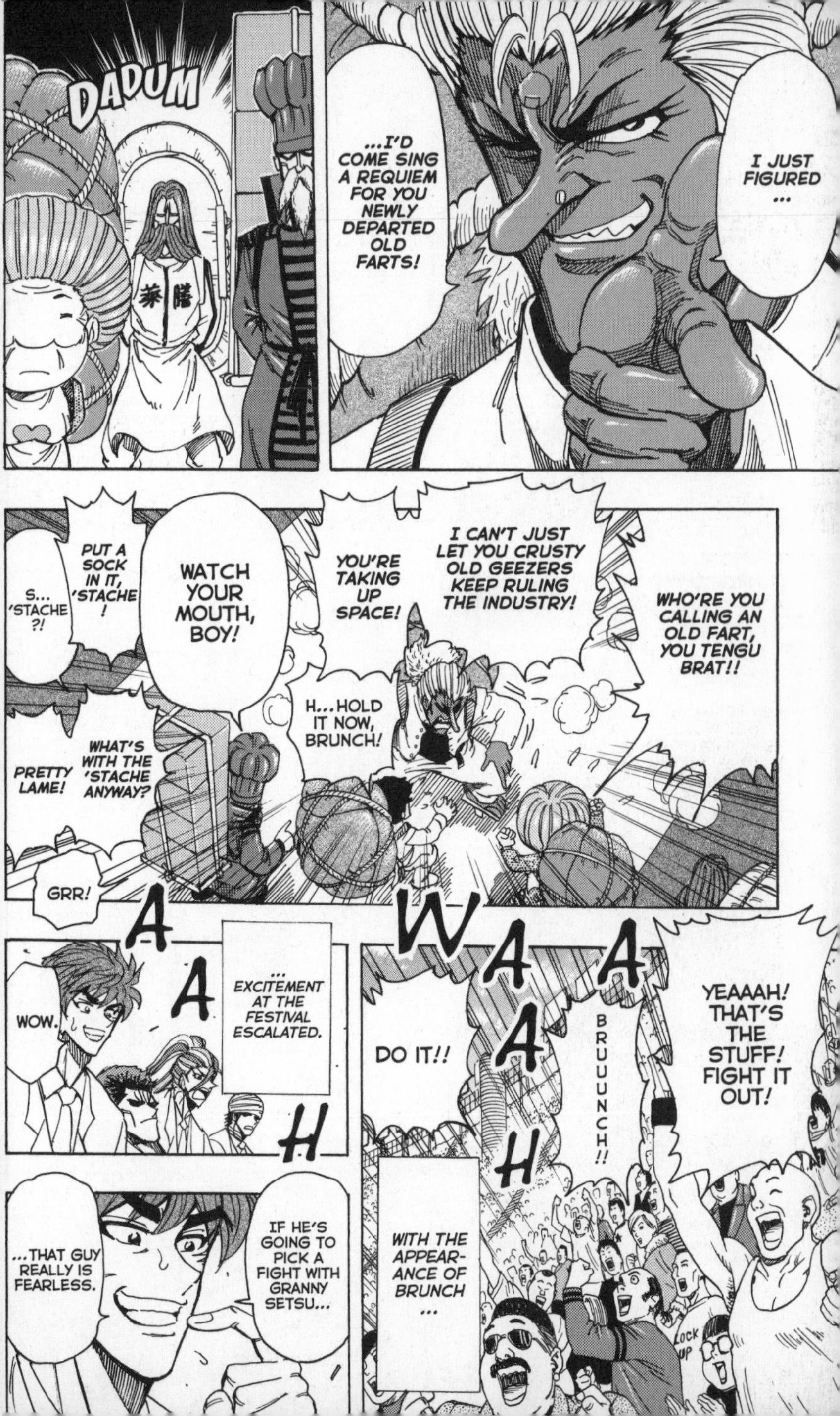
I JUST FIGURED ...
...I'D COME SING A REQUIEM FOR YOU NEWLY DEPARTED OLD FARTS!
DADUM
WHO'RE YOU CALLING AN OLD FART, YOU TENGU BRAT!!
I CAN'T JUST LET YOU CRUSTY OLD GEEZERS KEEP RULING THE INDUSTRY!
YOU'RE TAKING UP SPACE!
H...HOLD IT NOW, BRUNCH!
WATCH YOUR MOUTH, BOY!
PUT A SOCK IN IT, 'STACHE!
S... 'STACHE?!
WHAT'S WITH THE 'STACHE ANYWAY?
PRETTY LAME!
GRR!
WAAAAAAH
YEAAAH! THAT'S THE STUFF! FIGHT IT OUT!
BRUUUNCH!!
DO IT!!
WITH THE APPEAR-ANCE OF BRUNCH ...
LOCK UP
WOW.
... EXCITEMENT AT THE FESTIVAL ESCALATED.
IF HE'S GOING TO PICK A FIGHT WITH GRANNY SETSU...
...THAT GUY REALLY IS FEARLESS.

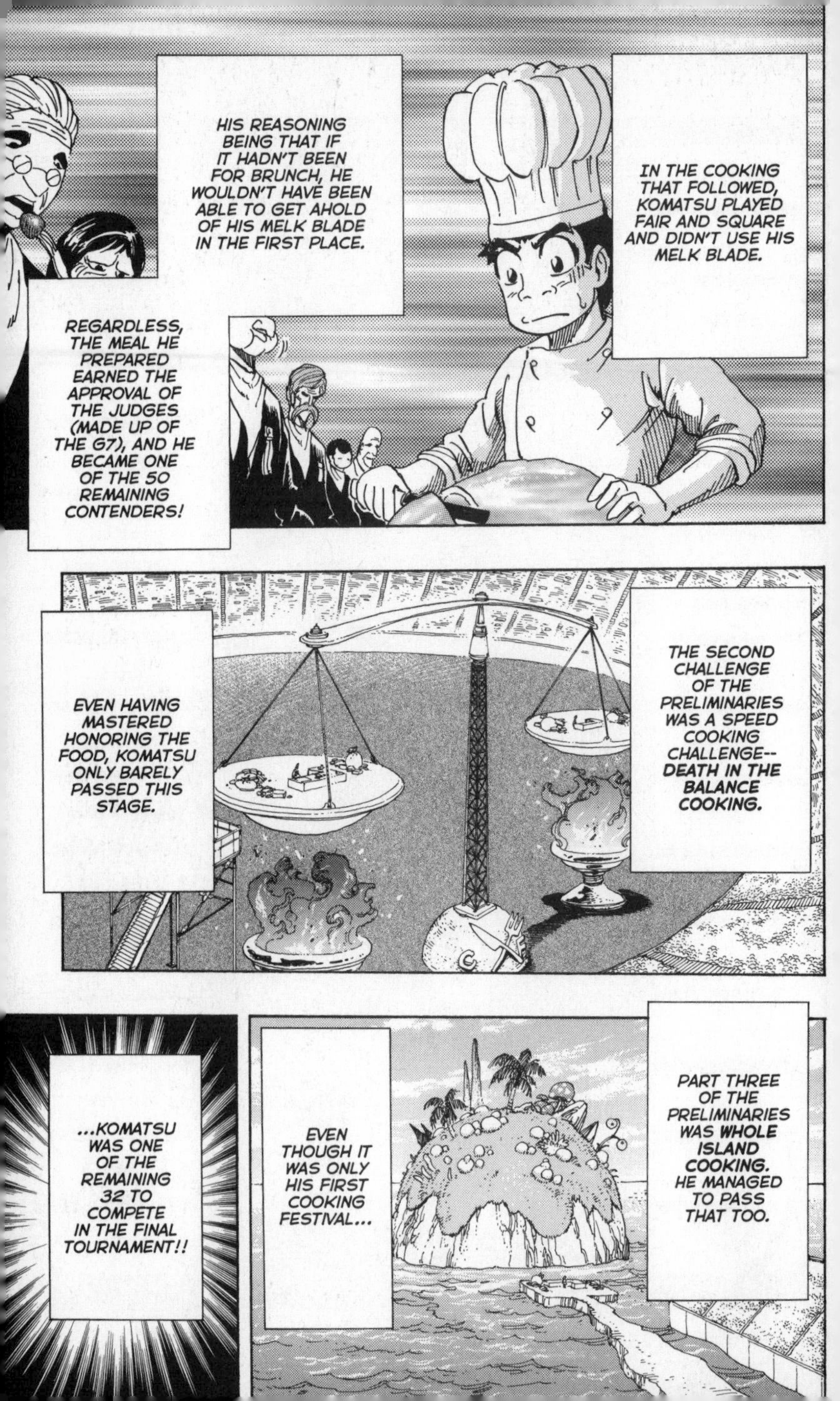
IN THE COOKING THAT FOLLOWED, KOMATSU PLAYED FAIR AND SQUARE AND DIDN'T USE HIS MELK BLADE.
HIS REASONING BEING THAT IF IT HADN'T BEEN FOR BRUNCH, HE WOULDN'T HAVE BEEN ABLE TO GET AHOLD OF HIS MELK BLADE IN THE FIRST PLACE.
REGARDLESS, THE MEAL HE PREPARED EARNED THE APPROVAL OF THE JUDGES (MADE UP OF THE G7), AND HE BECAME ONE OF THE 50 REMAINING CONTENDERS!
THE SECOND CHALLENGE OF THE PRELIMINARIES WAS A SPEED COOKING CHALLENGE--DEATH IN THE BALANCE COOKING.
EVEN HAVING MASTERED HONORING THE FOOD, KOMATSU ONLY BARELY PASSED THIS STAGE.
PART THREE OF THE PRELIMINARIES WAS WHOLE ISLAND COOKING. HE MANAGED TO PASS THAT TOO.
EVEN THOUGH IT WAS ONLY HIS FIRST COOKING FESTIVAL...
...KOMATSU WAS ONE OF THE REMAINING 32 TO COMPETE IN THE FINAL TOURNAMENT!!

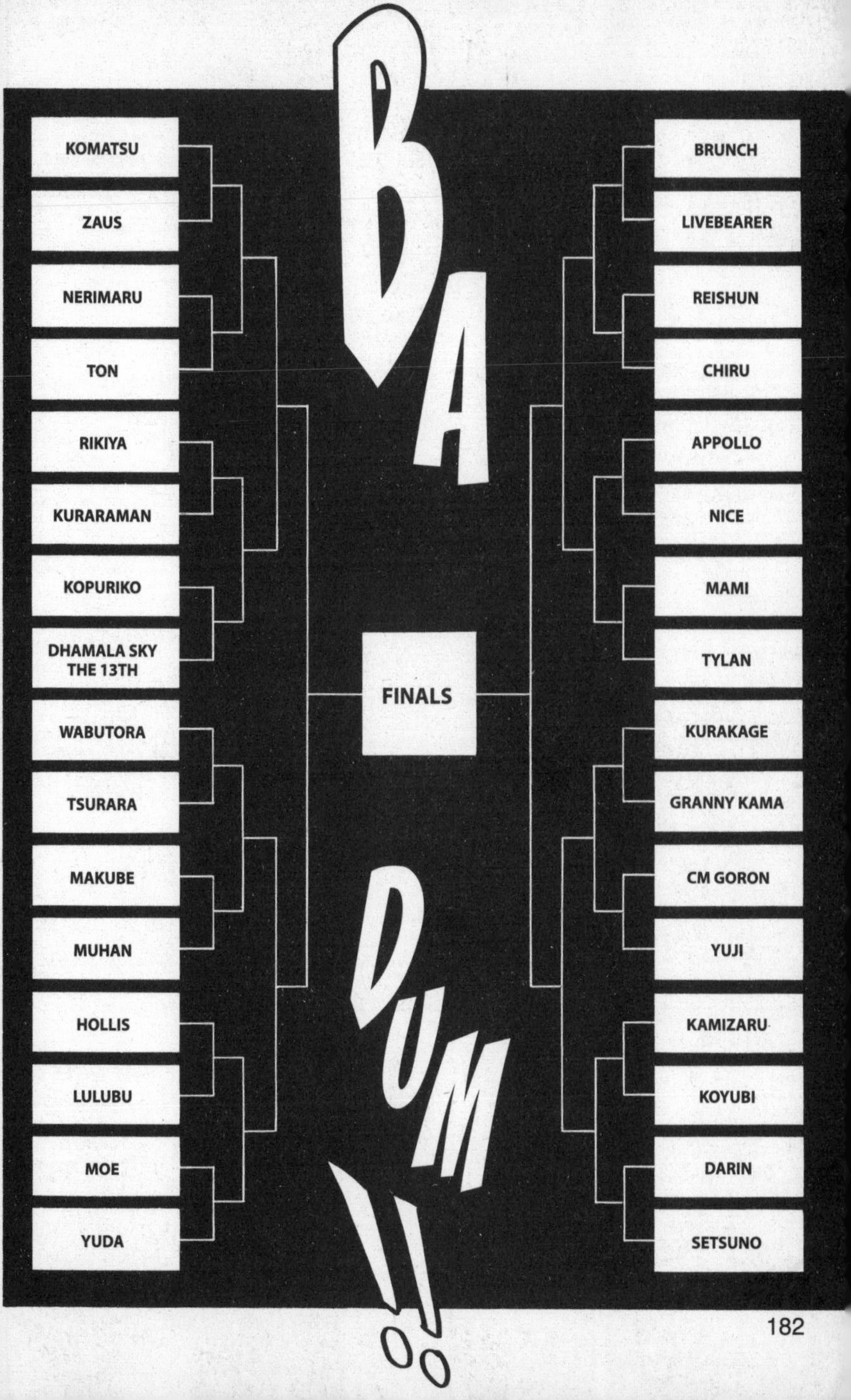
BA
DUM!!
BRUNCH
LIVEBEARER
REISHUN
CHIRU
APPOLLO
NICE
MAMI
TYLAN
KURAKAGE
GRANNY KAMA
CM GORON
YUJI
KAMIZARU
KOYUBI
DARIN
SETSUNO
FINALS
KOMATSU
ZAUS
NERIMARU
TON
RIKIYA
KURARAMAN
KOPURIKO
DHAMALA SKY THE 13TH
WABUTORA
TSURARA
MAKUBE
MUHAN
HOLLIS
LULUBU
MOE
YUDA

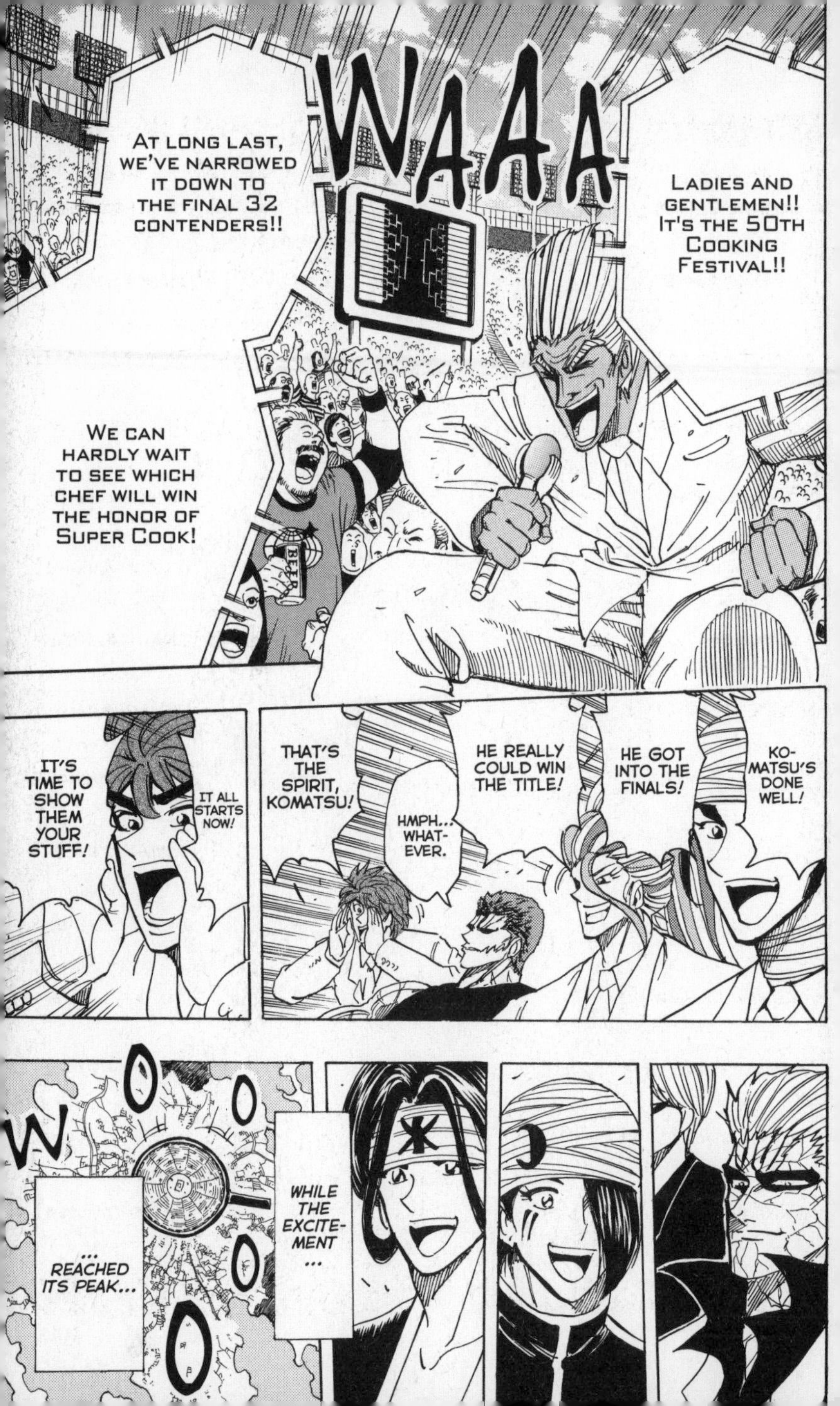
Ladies and gentlemen!! It's the 50th Cooking Festival!!
WAAA
At long last, we've narrowed it down to the final 32 contenders!!
We can hardly wait to see which chef will win the honor of Super Cook!
Ko-matsu's done well!
He got into the finals!
He really could win the title!
That's the spirit, Komatsu!
Hmph... whatever.
It's time to show them your stuff!
It all starts now!
While the excite-ment ...
... reached its peak...
WOOOOO

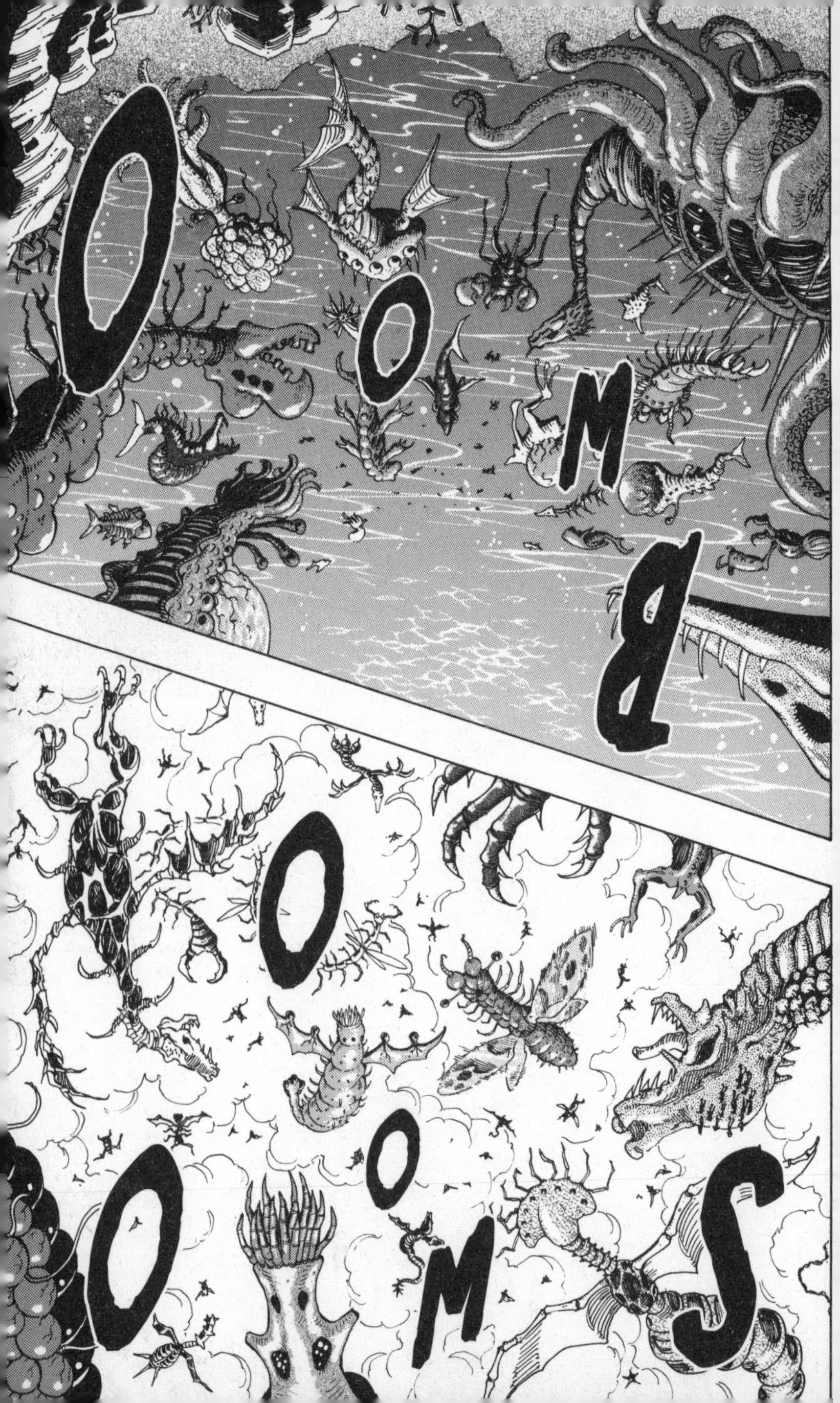
OOMB
OOOMS

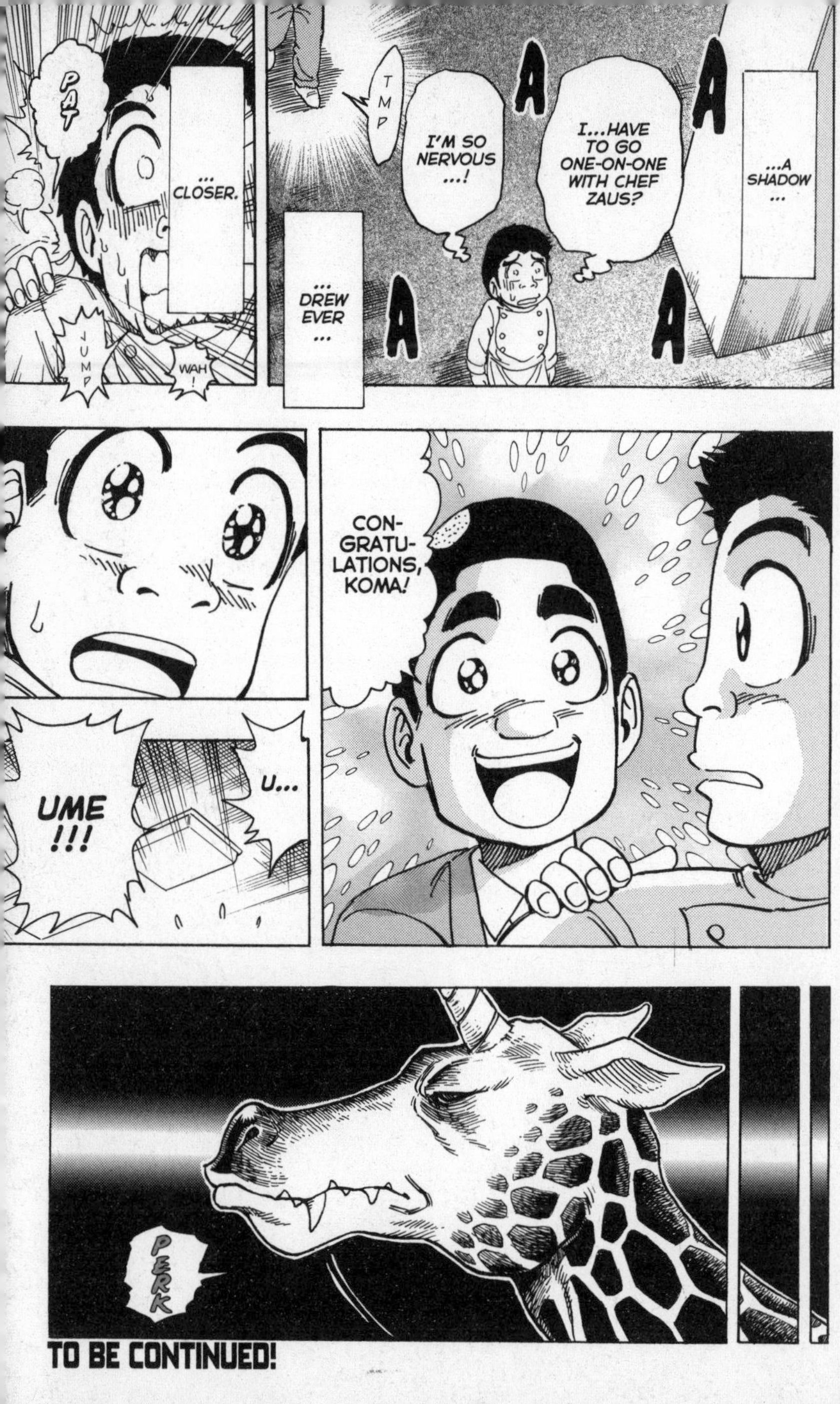
...A SHADOW ...
A
A
I...HAVE TO GO ONE-ON-ONE WITH CHEF ZAUS?
A
A
I'M SO NERVOUS ...!
TMP
... DREW EVER ...
... CLOSER.
PAT
JUMP
WAH !
CON-GRATU-LATIONS, KOMA!
U...
UME !!!
PERK

TO BE CONTINUED!

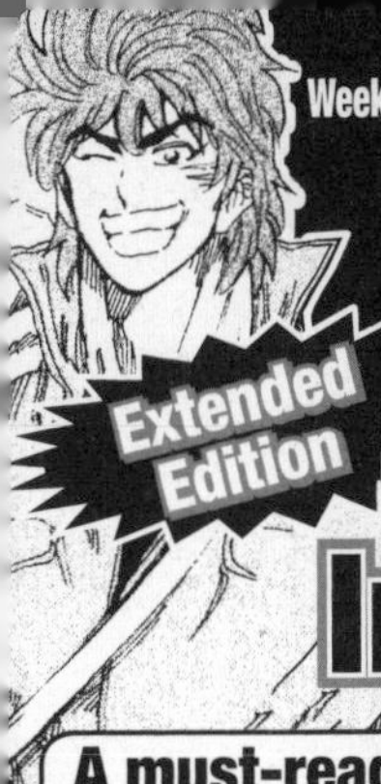

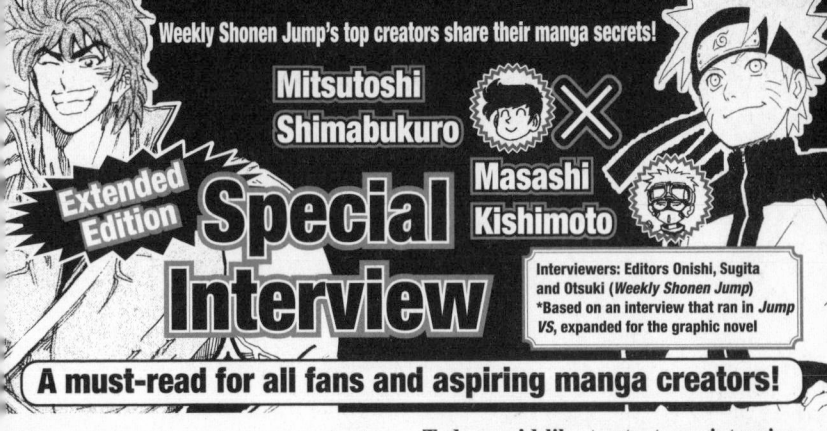

Weekly Shonen Jump's top creators share their manga secrets!

Mitsutoshi Shimabukuro × Masashi Kishimoto

Extended Edition

Special Interview

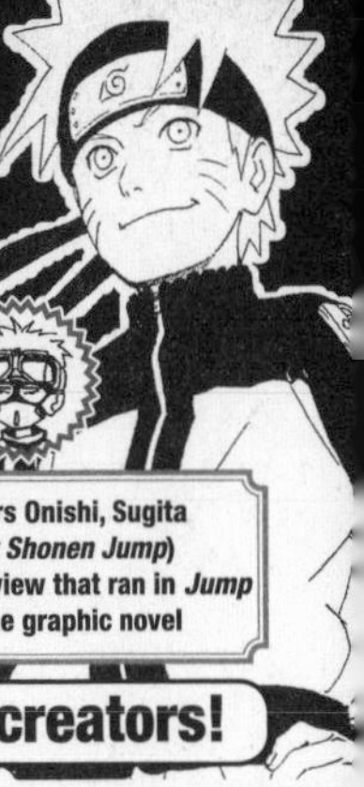

Interviewers: Editors Onishi, Sugita and Otsuki (*Weekly Shonen Jump*)
*Based on an interview that ran in *Jump VS*, expanded for the graphic novel

A must-read for all fans and aspiring manga creators!

Today we'd like to start our interview with you two leading figures of shonen manga by discussing the phrase "the golden standard in shonen manga." Let's get right to the point. What does it mean to you?

Masashi Kishimoto: I'll start by talking about the "standard." When I began *Naruto*, I don't think anyone considered it a standard.

Mitsutoshi Shimabukuro: I still don't consider *Toriko* a standard of manga either (*laugh*). If I had to pick the standard, I guess I'd say *Dragon Ball*.

What sets it apart?

Kishimoto: *Dragon Ball* doesn't really use drama. Instead of calling it the standard in shonen manga, it might be more accurate to call it the standard in shonen battle manga.

When you say "drama" are you referring to the kind of "human drama" where characters' pasts and feelings are delved into?

Kishimoto: That's right. *Dragon Ball* rarely goes into the past and moves forward organically. At the beginning, I thought *Toriko* would go down the same path as *Dragon Ball*.

Shimabukuro: That's probably because when I created *Toriko* I set out to make something like *Dragon Ball* (*laugh*).

But *One Piece* is full of human drama, isn't it?

Kishimoto: *Naruto* has plenty of drama in it, but *Toriko* doesn't really push the drama aspect and instead introduces all these larger-than-life creatures and disturbing enemies. It's always doing the unexpected. In that sense, I think *Toriko* is a lot like *Dragon Ball*.

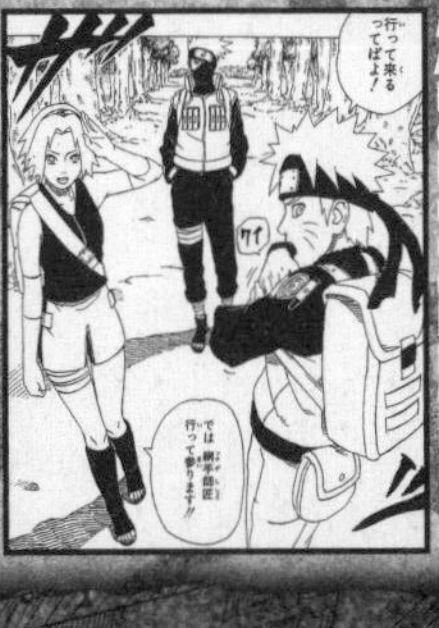

Naruto
A young boy named Naruto dreams of becoming Hokage and battles to develop his ninja skills! Masashi Kishimoto's masterpiece, currently running in *Jump*.

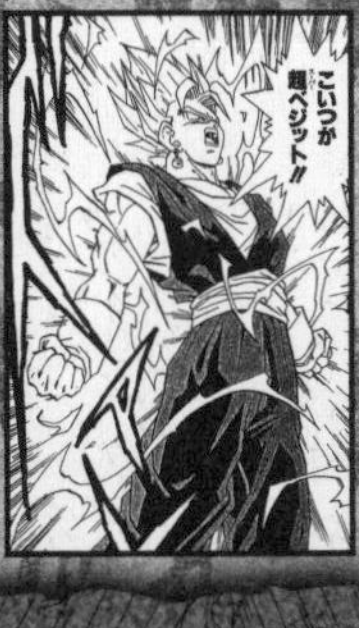

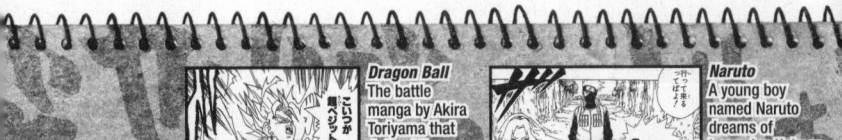

Dragon Ball
The battle manga by Akira Toriyama that defined the genre and laid the foundation of *Jump*'s first generation. Still wildly popular even though it's no longer running in *Jump*.

Kishimoto: Also, when the camera angles are mediocre. When it's always the same angle and same position, a work can lack real dynamism. Looking at *Toriko*, I notice a lot of crane shots interspersed with close-ups of characters' faces, so it tells me that he really thought this through. That in itself makes it stand out quite a bit.

Shimabukuro: This is of course true for the drawings, but the story, too, has to be well thought out. Especially in a battle manga, it's important to make the reason for the characters' fighting easy to understand. In the case of *Toriko*, I made the goal "fighting to eat," which I think is pretty easy to grasp.

Everyone eats, so it's intuitive.

Shimabukuro: I still need to work out some of the characters' motivations, but I think the eating one was a good place to start.

MANGA INFLUENCES

Before you became manga artists, were there any people or works that inspired you?

Kishimoto: To be frank, there were tons (*laugh*).

Shimabukuro: Same for me. I think I was inspired by movies, novels and games. Manga, in particular, was a huge part of my life.

Assuming that being the standard also means that something is popular, then one could say that battle manga are the standard of *Weekly Shonen Jump*. Some depict human drama like *Naruto* and *One Piece*, and others like *Toriko* and *Dragon Ball* emphasize shock and surprise. You could say there are two kinds of standards.

Moving on, when you draw shonen manga, what sort of things are you particularly conscious of?

Kishimoto: I guess the first thing I keep in mind is readability—showing things in a way that will be easy to understand. What that means for the art is choosing the best camera position and angles, and considering which expressions will convey information best to the readers.

Say you're looking at a one-shot by a new manga artist. What do you notice first?

Kishimoto: I tend to muse that if only they'd dug a little deeper during their meetings with their editor and in the storyboard stage, then they could've made it more interesting. For example, this includes works where the whole setup of the story is explained through words alone. I think that normally explanation should be shown slowly and carefully over a number of chapters with various episodes.

Shimabukuro: It can feel like such a waste, because the art itself can be really good.

Camera
This refers to the point of view in a manga. The word comes from the camera used in film.

Storyboard
A manga artist's rough planning of the chapter. It details the number of panels and their layout, as well as the characters' positioning on any given page. They're drawn before meeting with one's editor.

Crane Shot
A shot drawn as if from a high vantage point. Seeing things from above gives the reader a sense of "seeing the whole picture." Also called a "bird's eye view."

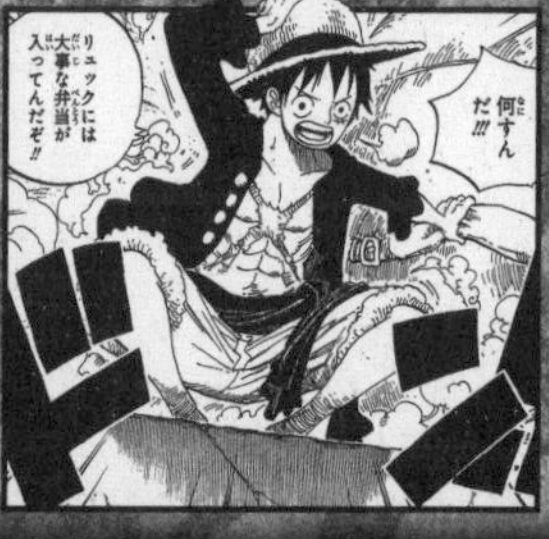
リュックには大事な弁当が入ってんだぞ!!
何すんだ!!!

One Piece
A pirate adventure starring Luffy, a boy who wants to become the king of the pirates, and his friends. Written by Eiichiro Oda, it has sold 280 million copies as of 2013.

Shimabukuro: Even when I go to the *Jump* New Year's party, I can't match the other creators' faces to their names.

Kishimoto: Shimabukuro is the second *Jump* creator that I've gotten to have an in-depth conversation with through an interview like this. The last time was with Togashi Sensei. But none since then.

Shimabukuro: Younger manga creators might find it difficult to strike up a conversation with someone like Oda or Kishimoto. Unless an editor introduces them or something.

Kishimoto: That might be it. But speaking of Togashi Sensei, I learned a lot from him when *Naruto* was starting.

Back then, both *Hunter x Hunter* and *Naruto* had the same editor, right?

Kishimoto: Yep. Togashi Sensei has a lot of experience, and is really good at directing scenes. That's why studying *Hunter x Hunter* taught me a lot. If you wanted to talk about the standard in battle manga, perhaps you should have talked to him (*laugh*).

Shimabukuro: Togashi Sensei is often called a gifted auteur, composing a vivid world and story with the manga medium.

Kishimoto: During our interview, Togashi Sensei said that he's always striving to outdo reader expectations. He said that he outright

Kishimoto: When I was a kid, if I hadn't read *Jump* I would be completely out of the loop when my friends were talking. That's how big it was.

Shimabukuro: But there were the two camps of *Jump* readers—magazine vs. graphic novels. When the magazine readers would be talking about the latest developments, the graphic novel readers would get mad at them and shout "No spoilers!" (*laugh*). In those days, the Internet didn't have as big a presence, so you were most likely to hear a spoiler while talking with your friends.

Out of the many influences it seems like you had, what's the first one that comes to mind?

Shimabukuro: For me, I think it all started with reading *Ultimate Muscle* in *Jump*. I was also very influenced by the anime. As a kid, you become a fan of something through the anime first, right?

Kishimoto: I think that was true for me too. I used to watch *Dr. Slump*.

How about since becoming manga artists? What are some people or works that have influenced you?

Kishimoto: There are definitely a lot of works that influenced me, but in terms of people, I guess I haven't met all that many.

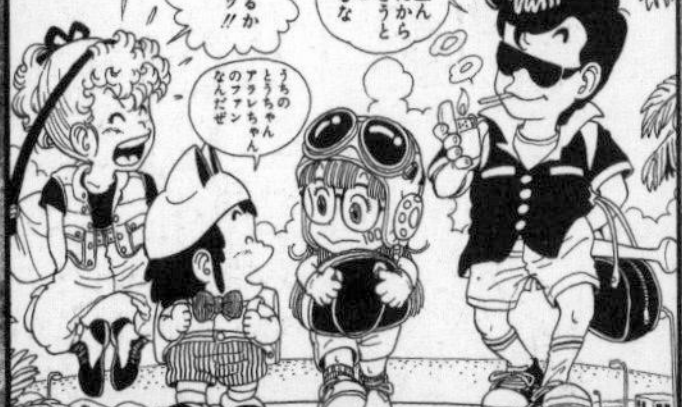
高校生んなったからどうどうとタバコすえるな
すえるかアホッ!!
うちのとうちゃんアラレちゃんのファンなんだぜ

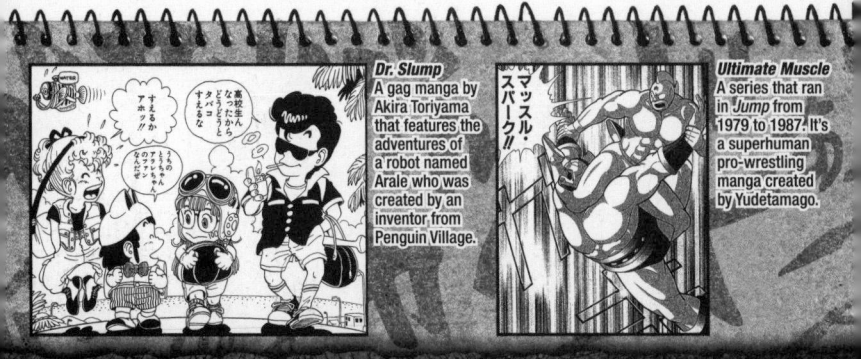

Dr. Slump
A gag manga by Akira Toriyama that features the adventures of a robot named Arale who was created by an inventor from Penguin Village.

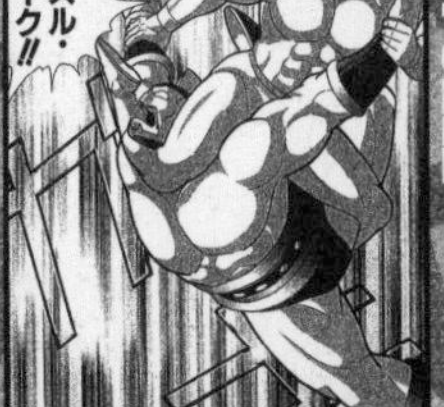
マッスル・スパーク!!

Ultimate Muscle
A series that ran in *Jump* from 1979 to 1987. It's a superhuman pro-wrestling manga created by Yudetamago.

Shimabukuro: When the second one-shot of *Seikimatsu Leader Den Takeshi* was greenlit, I suddenly had 30 pages to do and only two weeks before the deadline.

Thirty pages in two weeks is quite the workload.

Shimabukuro: Yeah. I got the call when I was at my parents' house for New Year's and immediately agreed to do the project. As I recall, it consisted of two chapters, and I got the roughs for the first chapter done on the flight to Tokyo. Because I did that, I got hooked up with a serialization.

So you're saying that even though it was hard, you're glad you did it?

Shimabukuro: I see challenges as opportunities. If I were to say "I've got other plans," then there's no telling when my next chance would be. I have to pour everything I've got into every minute and second and stick to my guns.

It's up to us to take advantage of the opportunities that come our way. So tell me, how old were you when your first professional work was published?

Kishimoto: I was 25, I guess.

Shimabukuro: I think I was around 22 years old. At the time, I wanted to get a story serialized as soon as possible. I was in a real rush.

avoids orthodox plot turns. Like presenting options A and B, but then having the character choose the not-there option of C.

It does make the readers' hearts race when things develop in a way they never saw coming.

Kishimoto: At the time, when asked what he does when it gets out of hand, he said, "Even when the story goes in an unexpected direction, there's still a sense that everything will come around in the end."

Shimabukuro: I see. That must be the wisdom of experience.

Kishimoto: Exactly. It's a way only a veteran could think. Even if a newbie tried to emulate that, it probably wouldn't come out right. It's a lot like what you've said about characters coming to you out of the blue, Shimabukuro.

Shimabukuro: Though that's only happened once (*laugh*). With Takeshi.

Kishimoto: But still, talking like this to you and Togashi Sensei leaves me feeling like I've got a lot of growing to do. It's stimulating.

CHALLENGE...OR CHANCE?

It's not out of the ordinary for a newly serialized manga artist to be expected to churn out a lot of work very quickly. What were your experiences like?

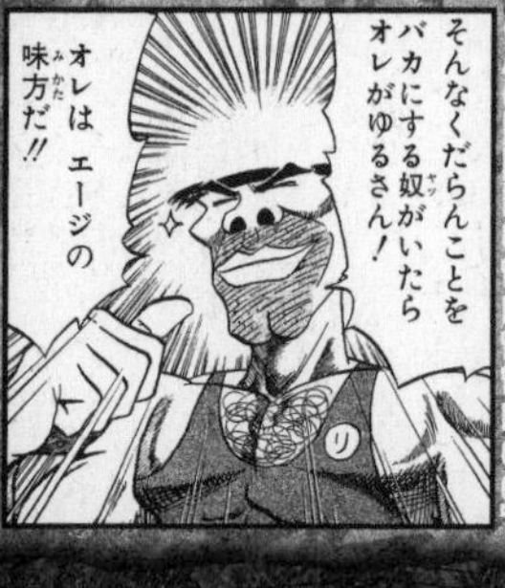

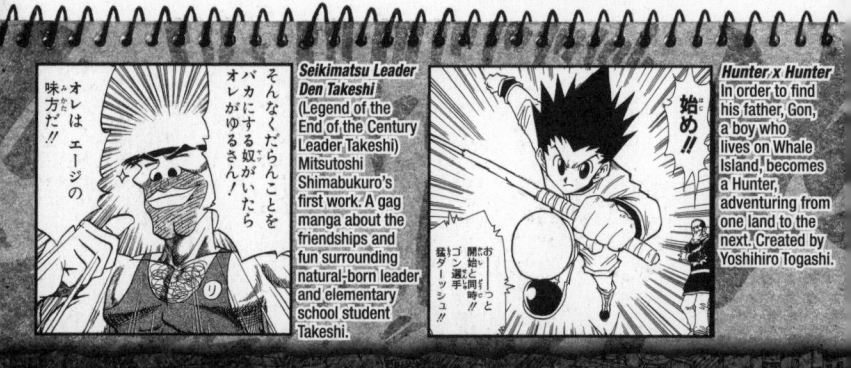

そんなくだらんことを
バカにする奴がいたら
オレがゆるさん!
オレは エージの
味方だ!!

Seikimatsu Leader Den Takeshi (Legend of the End of the Century Leader Takeshi) Mitsutoshi Shimabukuro's first work. A gag manga about the friendships and fun surrounding natural-born leader and elementary school student Takeshi.

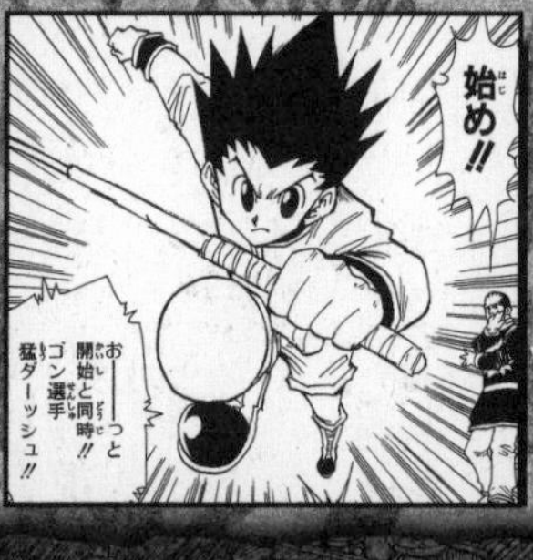

始め!!
おーーっと
開始と同時!!
ゴン選手
猛ダッシュ!!

Hunter x Hunter In order to find his father, Gon, a boy who lives on Whale Island, becomes a Hunter, adventuring from one land to the next. Created by Yoshihiro Togashi.

then, there was another guy named Yamakawa, and both he and Oda were so talented that even my editor told me that I should read their works.

Shimabukuro: Back then, gag was in. Usuta was serializing *Sexy Commando Gaiden: Sugoi yo!! Masaru-san* and Oguri was serializing *Hanasaka Tenshi Tenten-kun*, so the genre was alive. I'm a little sad that gag is on the decline. I wish there were more newbies creating gag manga. Like Sawai's *Bobobo-bo Bo-bobo*. It would be nice to have more high-energy gag manga like that coming out.

A MANGA ARTIST'S LIFE

Shimabukuro: Kishimoto, when did you move to Tokyo? Right after graduating from college?

Kishimoto: No, I first drew in my house. I came to Tokyo after my serialization was greenlit, and I went apartment hunting with my editor.

Shimabukuro: That must've been tough at first.

Kishimoto: Actually, I had a lucky break. Usually, when you're chosen for serialization, you have to start right away, but in my case, there happened to be a delay, so I had time to accumulate some storyboards before it started. I had a backlog of the first eight chapters before I started serialization.

At age 22, you were in a rush?

Shimabukuro: I sure was. At the time, I knew a guy called Kita who was drawing a manga called *Makuhari*. He was about 26 when he started the serialization for that. Looking at newbies these days, that's pretty normal, but since I was only around 20 at the time, I thought he was such an old man. I think he felt that way too because I remember him saying, "If this doesn't work out, I'm through."

Kishimoto: When I started serialization, I also felt like I was way behind. Shimabukuro was younger than me and Oda, who's my same age, had started serializing his work two years ahead of me.

Shimabukuro: Thinking back on it now, 25 or 26 isn't a late age to start at all. But Oda even received an award at a pretty young age. I mean, he was still in high school. He was this newcomer that everyone was taking their hats off for.

What do you think of Oda Sensei?

Shimabukuro: He really is special. First off, his manga is interesting. It has been ever since he was only doing one-shots.

Kishimoto: I've also read many of Oda's works, including the one that won him the Hop Step Award. Don't other newbies' award-winning works strike you too? When I read them, I'm so entertained and impressed. Back

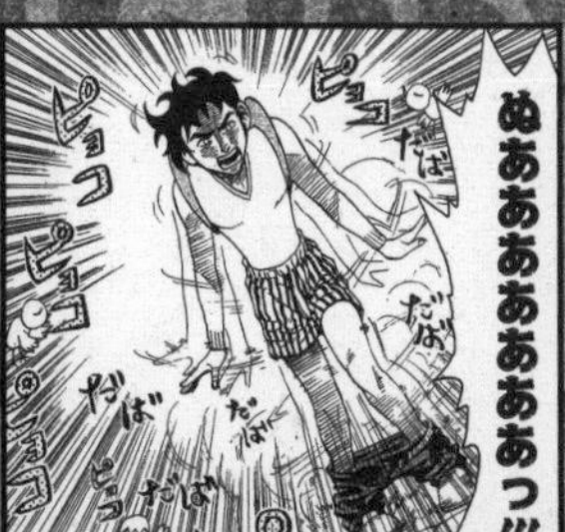
ぬあああああああっ!!!

Sexy Commando Gaiden: Sugoi yo!! Masaru-san
(Sexy Commando Side Story: That's Amazing, Masaru!)
Kyosuke Usuta's first serialized work. Though the title says *gaiden* (side story), it isn't a spin-off. Known for its unique and surreal gags.

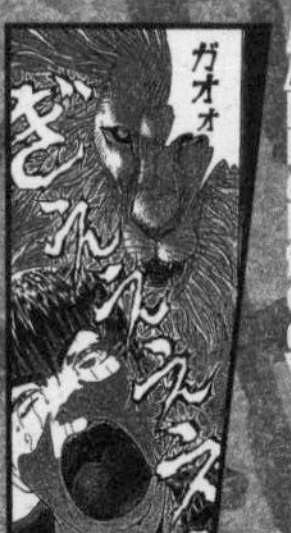
ガオォ

Makuhari
A gag manga set in a high school in the Makuhari area of Chiba Prefecture. It features parodies of other *Jump* series. Created by Yasuaki Kita.

Shimabukuro: Why crackers? (*laugh*)

Kishimoto: I don't know the details, but I guess he considers "yummy treats" a stimulating influence on his world too.

Shimabukuro: Even if I'm not that stoic, there are times I want to cut off the outside world and concentrate. Back in the day, novelists would confine themselves to hotels to write, and that must be exactly why.

Kishimoto: If I see my family even once, it's hard for me to get back into "work mode."

Shimabukuro: When I go from "normal" to "work mode," it does take quite a bit of time to get back into the swing of things. And when I've taken a long break, I completely forget how I'm supposed to focus again.

Kishimoto: On the flip side, when I'm immersed in manga, whether I'm in bed or on the john, or even in the bathtub, I can't get manga out of my head. Sometimes I'll be thinking in the tub and realize, "Wait, have I washed myself yet? Or do I still need to do that?" (*laugh*)

Shimabukuro: That's focus! (*laugh*) But it's true that great ideas can come to you in the bathtub.

Kishimoto: That's why I keep a notepad by the tub. So that I can write down ideas before I forget them. It's also why I forget if I've washed my hair and stuff.

Shimabukuro: That is a lucky break. They really pile on the work when you start. All newbies ever want is time.

Kishimoto: To be honest, if I hadn't had time to prepare that backlog I might've found myself in a pinch. Because of the extra time, I was able to tweak and adjust all these little things before I submitted the final drafts.

Shimabukuro: If you have difficulty producing manga at the beginning, those first 15 weeks or so can be this constant state of being out of breath. When I started, I felt like I was fighting for my life. I had to think about my pages 24/7. I never relaxed.

Having to focus on work without even time to sleep is something that manga artists probably have in common with movie directors and composers.

Shimabukuro: That's probably true. I recently read a book by composer Joe Hisaishi, who scores movies and other works. When he gets a job he'll hole himself up in the studio for about a month, completely blocking out the outside world to create his music. I guess Hayao Miyazaki's the same way.

Kishimoto: I think Togashi Sensei's the same way too. He's said that he pulls the blinds and shuts out the world to create his own world. While eating crackers.

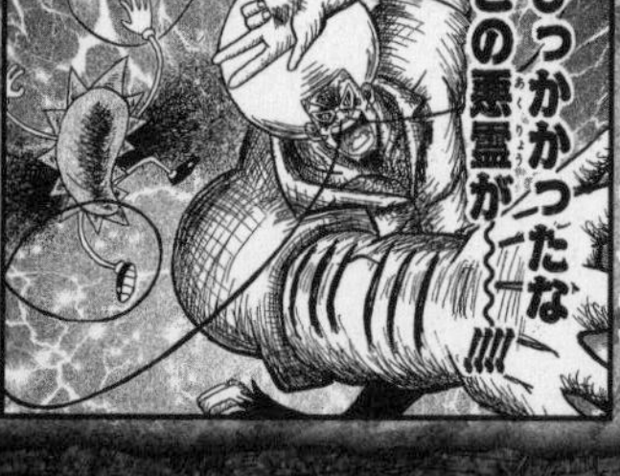
ひっかかったな
この悪霊が～～～!!!!

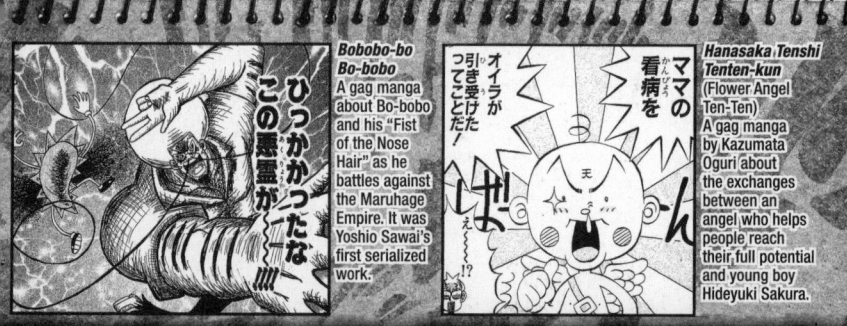

Bobobo-bo Bo-bobo
A gag manga about Bo-bobo and his "Fist of the Nose Hair" as he battles against the Maruhage Empire. It was Yoshio Sawai's first serialized work.

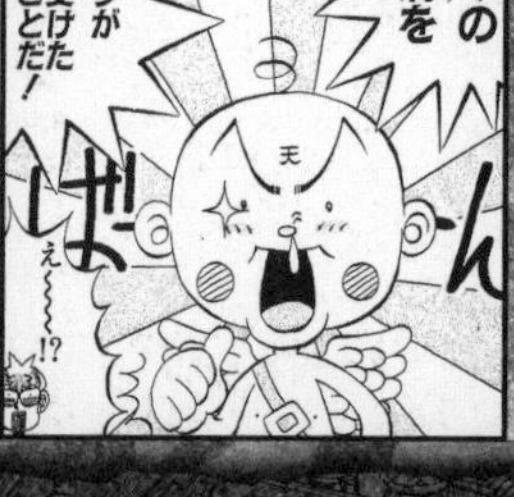
ママの看病を
オイラが引き受けたってことだ!
え～～～!?

Hanasaka Tenshi Tenten-kun
(Flower Angel Ten-Ten)
A gag manga by Kazumata Oguri about the exchanges between an angel who helps people reach their full potential and young boy Hideyuki Sakura.

Shimabukuro: It'd be similar, if it was just about drawing manga. But I'd never had experience hiring somebody. Still, I think I have been lucky. I've never had any major problems.

Kishimoto: I think I've had it good too. I've heard stories about one big manga artist's assistant who asked him to make him ramen (*laugh*).

Shimabukuro: He should have made it himself (*laugh*). I wonder if he thought he'd get in trouble for making it.

TORIKO SECRETS

Kishimoto: Are there any interesting things that never made it into *Toriko*?

Shimabukuro: Hmm. At first, Mellow Cola was going to go into Toriko's Full-Course Meal.

Kishimoto: Oh, really? You're talking about that food they went into the pyramid to retrieve, right?

Shimabukuro: Yeah, that one. Since soda's a popular drink with kids, I figured it'd be the perfect thing to add to Toriko's Full-Course Meal, but I got stuck with the storyboards so I figured I'd just drop that one.

Kishimoto: I'm surprised to hear that (*laugh*).

Shimabukuro: So on the spur of the moment, I decided to make it part of Zebra's Full-Course Meal instead.

Kishimoto: I was wondering where they'd find the Cola, so it really fascinated me that it ended up being monster tears.

Shimabukuro: That arc didn't really move the story along much. I guess that's also why I added it to Zebra's Full-Course Meal.

Shimabukuro: Who cares about it at that point, right? (*laugh*)

HITTING A WALL

Since becoming a manga artist, have you faced any struggles besides creating your manga?

Shimabukuro: I took on some assistants after the serialization began, but since I'd never had assistants before, I didn't know how to instruct them. It was difficult.

Kishimoto: I also had a really tough time with that.

Any anecdotes to share?

Kishimoto: Well, one time I hired on some assistants to help out for three days. At the end of those three days, the work still wasn't finished. Because I'd promised it'd only last three days, I let those assistants leave. Then I had to hire different assistants to finish the work.

Shimabukuro: The first assistant I had told me, "I have a part time job to go to, so I'm outta here," and then left (*laugh*).

Kishimoto: Wow, that's incredible (*laugh*).

Shimabukuro: My editor was pissed and made them quit their other job. After that they stayed on as a regular to help me. But at first I didn't know what was asking too much or what I should make allowances for, so that was tough. I think it would've done me some good if I'd had experience being an assistant somewhere else.

Kishimoto: That's definitely a wall you have to get over when first starting a serialization.

Is creating manga different when you've got a whole team of assistants to keep track of, compared to when you were alone?

JUST LOOK AT IT!

SO THIS IS THE WORLD'S BEST COLA!

EVEN THE HARROWING BATTLE THEY'D JUST FOUGHT SEEMED DULL IN COMPARISON.

The Salamander Sphinx is the boss of Gourmet Pyramid. When you make attacks in a certain order, it cries cola tears.

Shimabukuro: When it comes to creating a hook that will bring people back, I want to make it as shocking and impactful as possible.

Kishimoto: And it is! But then, when you're drawing for the next week, you panic about how you're going to tie it all together, and the explanation gets so long. And when that happens, it's not very effective at all.

Shimabukuro: But part of it is expressing your intention to go in that particular direction. If I had all the time in the world, I would stop there and really think through all the different aspects.

Kishimoto: Shimabukuro, you draw an awful lot of crazy environments. Like Gourmet Casino, Gourmet Shrine or food stalls.

Shimabukuro: The assistants help me a lot with that. And on that note, I would say that the backgrounds in *Naruto* are a lot more difficult to draw, wouldn't you say?

Kishimoto: There are things like busy street scenes in *Naruto*. So I understand how difficult these things get.

Kishimoto: Still, I think the way you show the story unfolding is so good, Shimabukuro. Like in the arc where they went fishing behind the waterfall. Since the fish would die of shock if they saw a strong person, having it be Komatsu was so clever. When did you think that up?

Shimabukuro: I decided that just before writing it. I figured I should give Komatsu his time to shine.

Kishimoto: So you stumbled upon that idea by instinct. And didn't a GT Robot-looking creature called a Nitro make an appearance in the pyramid? Had you always intended on the GT Robots being robots?

Shimabukuro: I'd always planned on the GT Robots being robots, only with the operators being a lot more mysterious.

Kishimoto: I also found it interesting that the Four-Beasts was actually just one creature. Your ideas really come out of left field, Shimabukuro.

I GOT SOME SHINING GOURAMI!

SORRY FOR THE WAIT!

The Shining Gourami requires special preparation. It's so docile that its taste sours in the presence of a strong creature.

Shimabukuro: I had twelve hours before I'd be late for my deadline, and I didn't even have any storyboards. I had no hope of making it that week.

Kishimoto: I get the feeling that you could run into that problem with gag manga.

Shimabukuro: So when I was pressed up against the wall, I decided, "I'll make a gag out of the fact that I'm having my assistants do it." And that became the chapter.

Kishimoto: When I read it, I laughed myself silly (*laugh*). Also, since the *seikimatsu* in the title means "End of the Century," when the new millennium rolled around, you had to change the title, didn't you?

Shimabukuro: But illustrations of the world are important. Since scenery shots express what the Age of Gourmet is all about, they may be difficult, but you've just got to draw them.

Kishimoto: Even though they take a lot of time, they're where the world of the series grows. Shimabukuro, are you quick with your pages?

Shimabukuro: Not at all. When I was drawing *Takeshi*, I was super slow. I even missed a deadline once.

There was one chapter where all your assistants worked together to draw it, wasn't there?

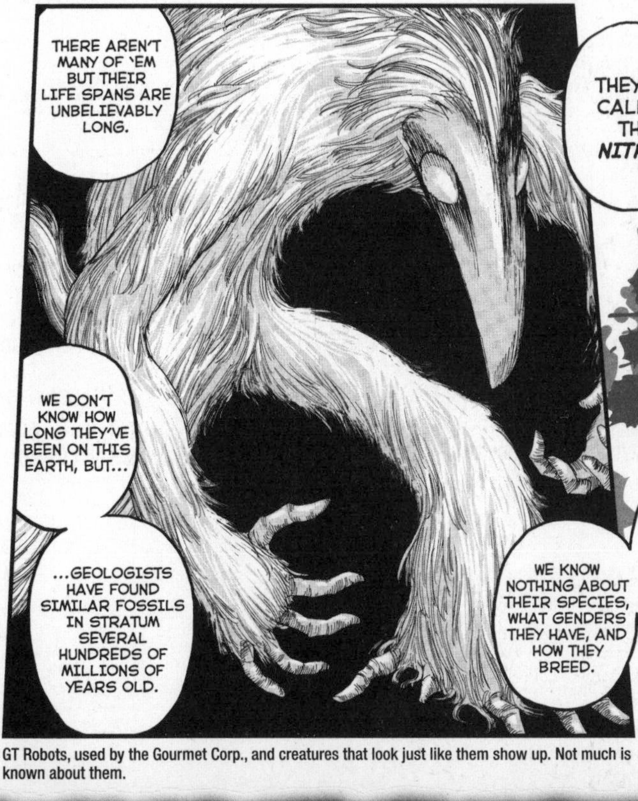

THEY'RE CALLED THE NITRO.
THERE AREN'T MANY OF 'EM BUT THEIR LIFE SPANS ARE UNBELIEVABLY LONG.
GOURMET GOD ACACIA DISCOVERED 'EM 600 YEARS AGO GIVE OR TAKE.
WE KNOW NOTHING ABOUT THEIR SPECIES, WHAT GENDERS THEY HAVE, AND HOW THEY BREED.
WE DON'T KNOW HOW LONG THEY'VE BEEN ON THIS EARTH, BUT...
...GEOLOGISTS HAVE FOUND SIMILAR FOSSILS IN STRATUM SEVERAL HUNDREDS OF MILLIONS OF YEARS OLD.

GT Robots, used by the Gourmet Corp., and creatures that look just like them show up. Not much is known about them.

ADVICE FOR ASPIRING MANGA ARTISTS

Is there anything that people aspiring to become manga artists should do?

Kishimoto: Let's see… Get plenty of sleep, eat right and stay healthy.

Shimabukuro: You're serious?! (*laugh*)

Shimabukuro: That's right. I had to make it the very last chapter (*laugh*). The truth is, I hadn't expected *Takeshi* to continue on for that long. *Takeshi* ran for five years, and even though *Toriko*'s entering its fifth year, *Takeshi* felt like it went on forever, and *Toriko* feels like it's gone by in the blink of an eye.

Kishimoto: Probably because *Takeshi* was a gag manga, right? You have to think up a completely new scenario each week, so it's tough to continue a gag for that long.

Shimabukuro: It's hard to have a gag manga run for even a year.

Kishimoto: I'm shocked it lasted five years.

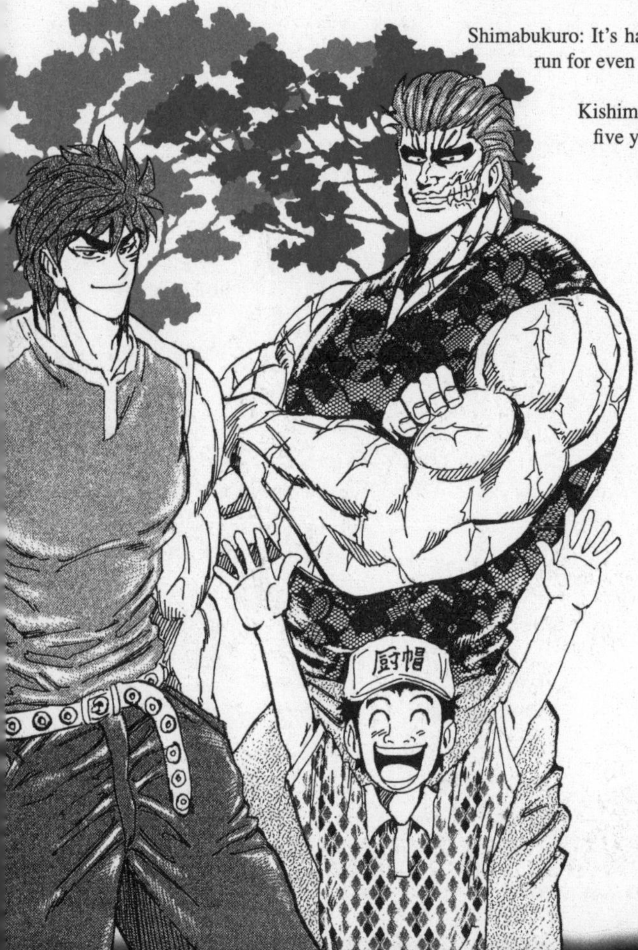
厨帽

A WORD TO THE FANS

Do you have any messages for your fans?

Kishimoto: *Naruto* is going to start heading toward its climax and get even more action-packed. I hope all you readers stick with it to the very end.

Shimabukuro: Same here. I have a lot of exciting things in store for what comes after the fight with Gourmet Corp. Keep reading!

Kishimoto: But really it's important to be healthy. Since my body's not that sound, it's always been a concern for me.

Shimabukuro: When I was young, pulling all nighters for several days in a row was no big deal. But now three days is my limit.

Kishimoto: I can't even do three days. I'd say two is my limit. But my level of activity when I started serialization was off the charts. I thought to myself, "Is this what it means to publish weekly?!" I thought I was going to die, for sure.

Shimabukuro: Same for me. Nearly all 24 hours in the day were used for manga.

Kishimoto: I couldn't think about anything else. Besides eating, bathing and going to the bathroom, I devoted all my time to manga.

So you're saying that when you're publishing weekly chapters, you need to have preparedness and willpower.

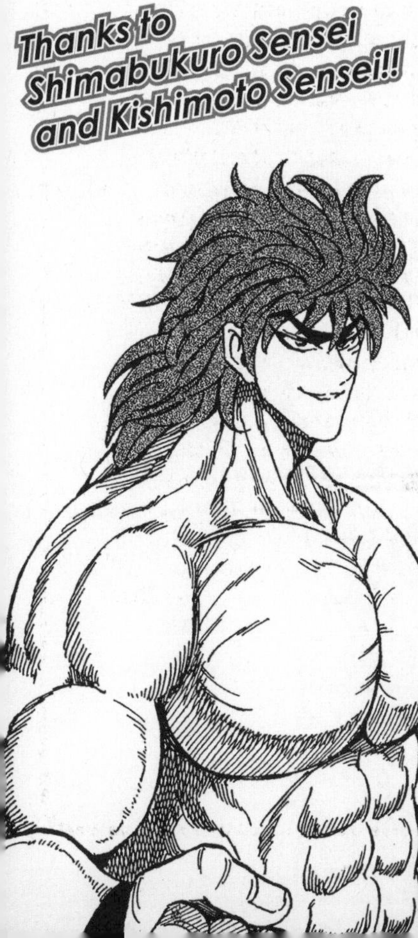
Thanks to
Shimabukuro Sensei
and Kishimoto Sensei!!

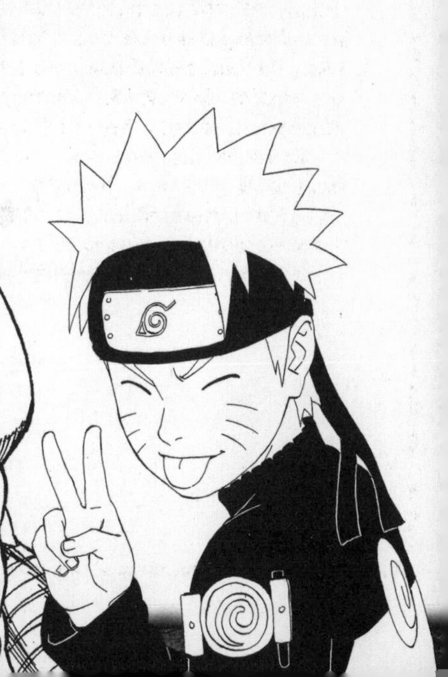

SHIMABU SPEAKS

(A follow-up to the interview with Masashi Kishimoto)

I think this is the first time I've ever been interviewed. The interview ran in this year's (2013) special spring issue of *Jump VS*. The topic was "Leaders of Manga." If you've read it, I'm sure you'll pick up on the fact that it was really casual and stress free. It was less like an interview and more like discussing manga with a fellow manga lover over drinks (*laugh*). It helped that Kishimoto was already an acquaintance of mine, but even so it was remarkably relaxed from start to finish. But I'll say that when the conversation is about manga, we can both get pretty passionate. During our conversation there were a lot of times when I would marvel at how much Kishimoto really thinks about manga. Since I'm originally a creator of gag manga, I've never given proper thought to how to make a story manga. I learned a lot during the interview. I felt like a complete newb! I think I'd like to do it again some time, should I ever have the chance. Best of all, it reminded me how fun it is to talk about manga and how much I love the medium. It was a whole ton of fun. Also, the drinks were good (though that has nothing to do with manga). Well, see you again soon, same time, same place. This is Shimabu, signing off and thinking daily how small the sticky pads that you can get from gum bottles are! See you again soon!

END

COMING NEXT VOLUME

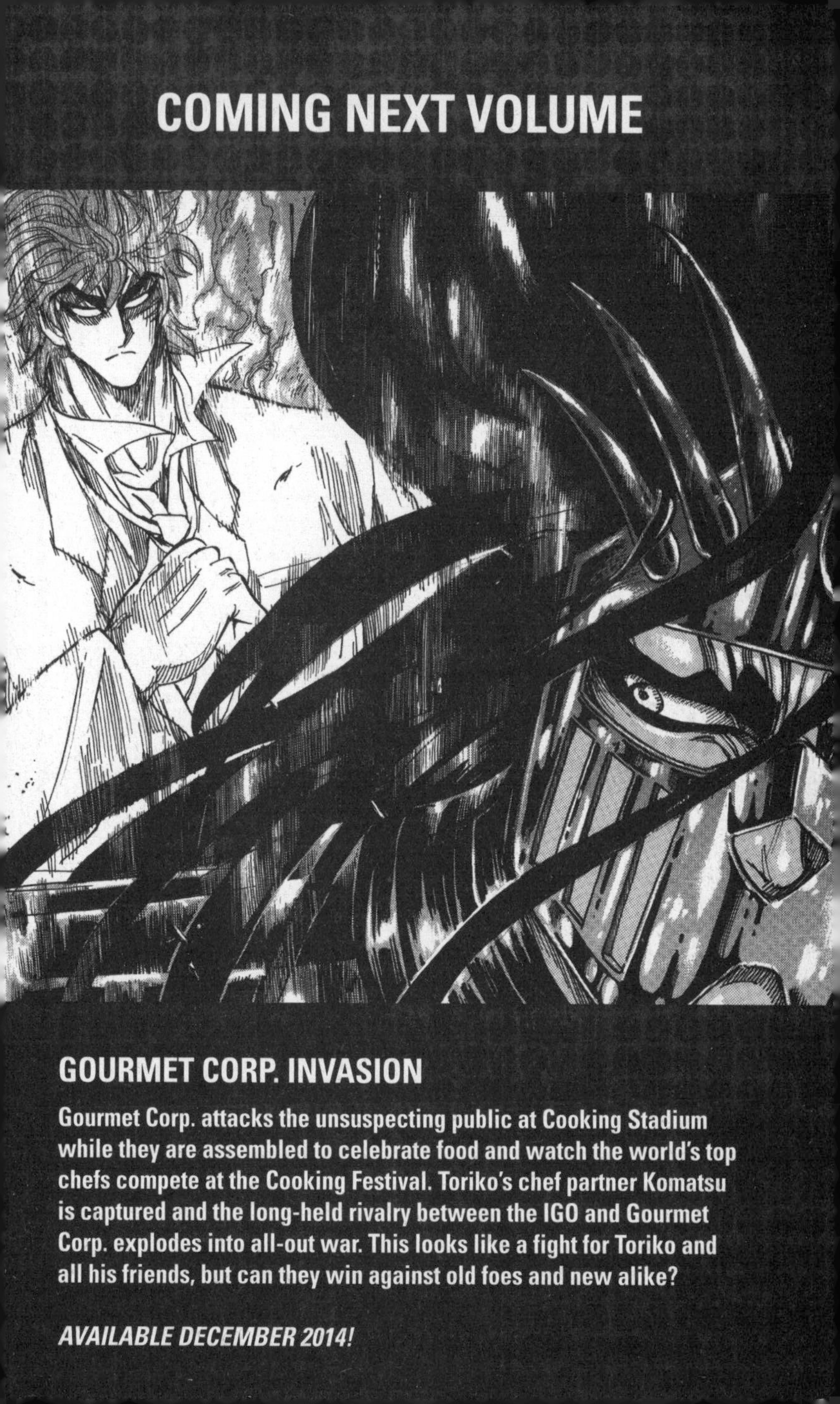

GOURMET CORP. INVASION

Gourmet Corp. attacks the unsuspecting public at Cooking Stadium while they are assembled to celebrate food and watch the world's top chefs compete at the Cooking Festival. Toriko's chef partner Komatsu is captured and the long-held rivalry between the IGO and Gourmet Corp. explodes into all-out war. This looks like a fight for Toriko and all his friends, but can they win against old foes and new alike?

AVAILABLE DECEMBER 2014!

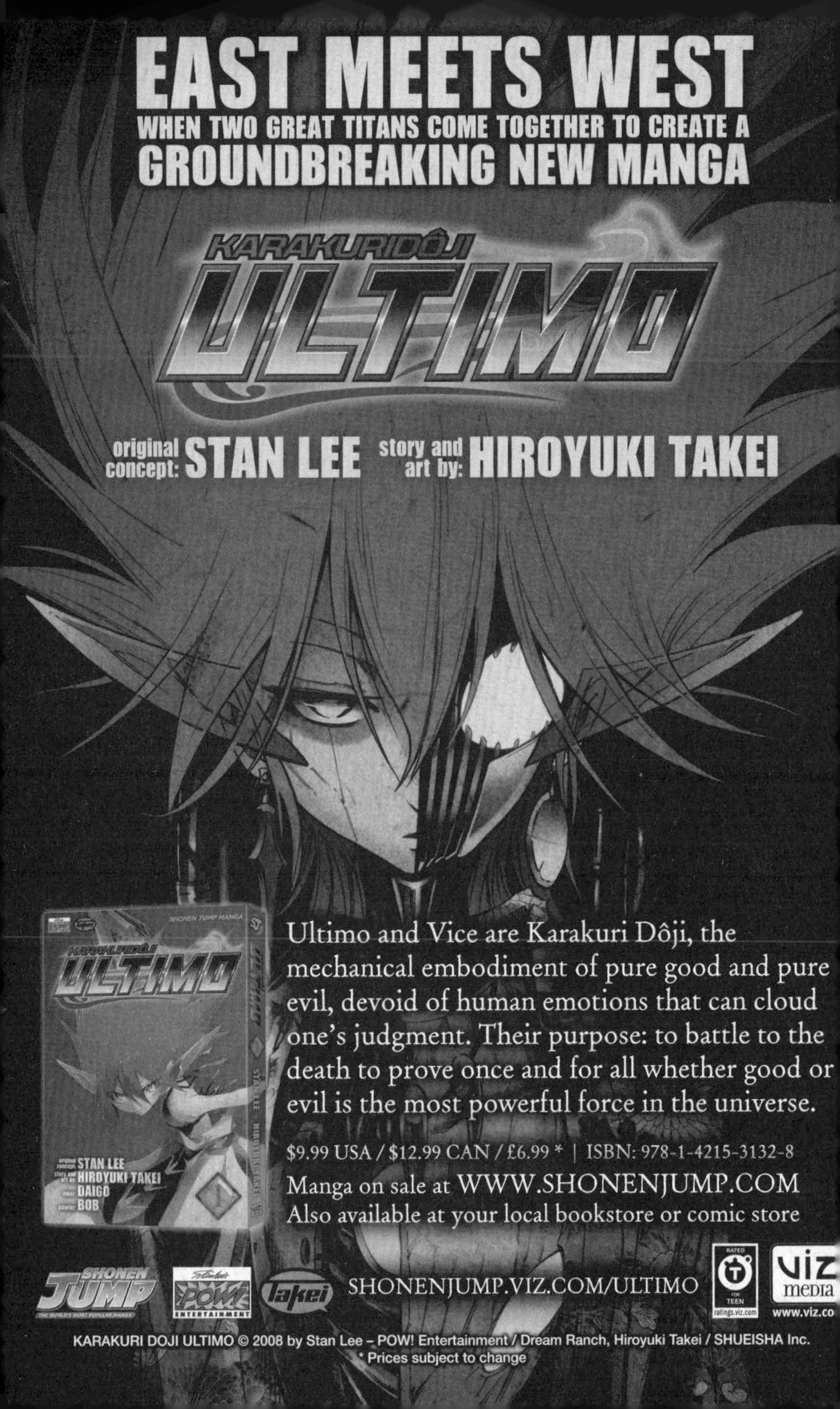
EAST MEETS WEST
WHEN TWO GREAT TITANS COME TOGETHER TO CREATE A
GROUNDBREAKING NEW MANGA
KARAKURIDÔJI ULTIMO
original concept: STAN LEE story and art by: HIROYUKI TAKEI
Ultimo and Vice are Karakuri Dôji, the mechanical embodiment of pure good and pure evil, devoid of human emotions that can cloud one's judgment. Their purpose: to battle to the death to prove once and for all whether good or evil is the most powerful force in the universe.
$9.99 USA / $12.99 CAN / £6.99 * | ISBN: 978-1-4215-3132-8
Manga on sale at WWW.SHONENJUMP.COM
Also available at your local bookstore or comic store
SHONEN JUMP MANGA
original concept: STAN LEE
story and art by: HIROYUKI TAKEI
DAIGO
BOB
SHONENJUMP.VIZ.COM/ULTIMO
RATED T FOR TEEN
ratings.viz.com
viz media
www.viz.co
KARAKURI DOJI ULTIMO © 2008 by Stan Lee – POW! Entertainment / Dream Ranch, Hiroyuki Takei / SHUEISHA Inc.
* Prices subject to change

You're Reading in the Wrong Direction!!

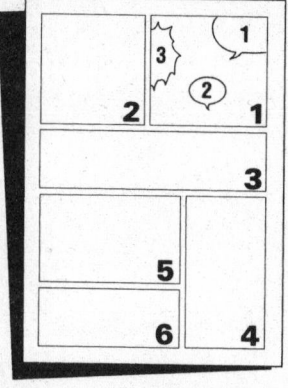

Whoops! Guess what? You're starting at the wrong end of the comic!

...It's true! In keeping with the original Japanese format, **Toriko** is meant to be read from right to left, starting in the upper-right corner.

Unlike English, which is read from left to right, Japanese is read from right to left, meaning that action, sound effects and word-balloon order are completely reversed... something which can make readers unfamiliar with Japanese feel pretty backwards themselves. For this reason, manga or Japanese comics published in the U.S. in English have sometimes been published "flopped"— that is, printed in exact reverse order, as though seen from the other side of a mirror.

By flopping pages, U.S. publishers can avoid confusing readers, but the compromise is not without its downside. For one thing, a character in a flopped manga series who once wore in the original Japanese version a T-shirt emblazoned with "M A Y" (as in "the merry month of") now wears one which reads "Y A M"! Additionally, many manga creators in Japan are themselves unhappy with the process, as some feel the mirror-imaging of their art skews their original intentions.

We are proud to bring you Mitsutoshi Shimabukuro's **Toriko** in the original unflopped format. For now, though, turn to the other side of the book and let the adventure begin...!

—Editor

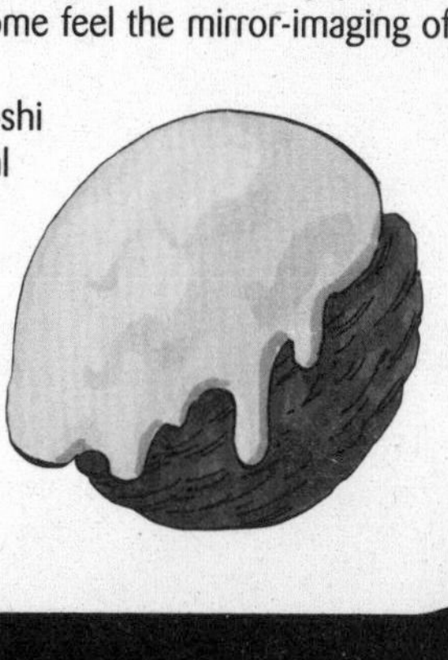